EUL VERLAG

WIRTSCHAFTSINFORMATIK

Herausgegeben von Prof. Dr. Dietrich Seibt, Köln, Prof. Dr. Hans-Georg Kemper, Stuttgart, Prof. Dr. Georg Herzwurm, Stuttgart, Prof. Dr. Dirk Stelzer, Ilmenau, und Prof. Dr. Detlef Schoder, Köln

Band 63
Ulrike Dowie
Testaufwandsschätzung in der Softwareentwicklung – Modell der Einflussfaktoren und Methode zur organisationsspezifischen Aufwandsschätzung
Lohmar – Köln 2009 ♦ 320 S. ♦ € 62,- (D) ♦ ISBN 978-3-89936-789-8

Band 64
Volker Lanninger
Prozessmodell zur Auswahl Betrieblicher Standardanwendungssoftware für KMU
Lohmar – Köln 2009 ♦ 564 S. ♦ € 76,- (D) ♦ ISBN 978-3-89936-870-3

Band 65
Stefan Winkler
Monitoring kritischer Prozess- und Projektaktivitäten mithilfe persönlicher Assistenten
Lohmar – Köln 2010 ♦ 296 S. ♦ € 59,- (D) ♦ ISBN 978-3-89936-881-9

Band 66
Stefan Scholz
Geschäftsmodelle für Grid Computing in der Medizin und der Biomedizin
Lohmar – Köln 2010 ♦ 352 S. ♦ € 64,- (D) ♦ ISBN 978-3-89936-894-9

Band 67
Sven-Carsten Hanssen
Bestimmung und Bewertung der Wirkungen von Informationssystemen
Lohmar – Köln 2010 ♦ 352 S. ♦ € 64,- (D) ♦ ISBN 978-3-89936-912-0

Band 68
Michael Röthlin
Management of Data Quality in Enterprise Resource Planning Systems
Lohmar – Köln 2010 ♦ 332 S. ♦ € 63,- (D) ♦ ISBN 978-3-89936-963-2

JOSEF EUL VERLAG

Reihe: Wirtschaftsinformatik · Band 68

Herausgegeben von Prof. Dr. Dietrich Seibt, Köln, Prof. Dr. Hans-Georg Kemper, Stuttgart, Prof. Dr. Georg Herzwurm, Stuttgart, Prof. Dr. Dirk Stelzer, Ilmenau, und Prof. Dr. Detlef Schoder, Köln

Dr. Michael Röthlin

Management of Data Quality in Enterprise Resource Planning Systems

With a Foreword by Prof. Dr. Gerhard F. Knolmayer, University of Bern

EUL VERLAG

Bibliografische Information der Deutschen Nationalbibliothek

Die Deutsche Nationalbibliothek verzeichnet diese Publikation in der Deutschen Nationalbibliografie; detaillierte bibliografische Daten sind im Internet über <http://dnb.d-nb.de> abrufbar.

Dissertation, Universität Bern, 2010

Inauguraldissertation zur Erlangung der Würde eines Doctor rerum oeconomicarum der Wirtschafts- und Sozialwissenschaftlichen Fakultät der Universität Bern

Die Fakultät hat diese Arbeit am 10. Dezember 2009 auf Antrag der beiden Gutachter Prof. Dr. Gerhard Knolmayer und Prof. Dr. Reinhard Jung als Dissertation angenommen, ohne damit zu den darin ausgesprochenen Auffassungen Stellung nehmen zu wollen.

ISBN 978-3-89936-963-2
1. Auflage September 2010

© JOSEF EUL VERLAG GmbH, Lohmar – Köln, 2010
Alle Rechte vorbehalten

JOSEF EUL VERLAG GmbH
Brandsberg 6
53797 Lohmar
Tel.: 0 22 05 / 90 10 6-6
Fax: 0 22 05 / 90 10 6-88
E-Mail: info@eul-verlag.de
http://www.eul-verlag.de

Bei der Herstellung unserer Bücher möchten wir die Umwelt schonen. Dieses Buch ist daher auf säurefreiem, 100% chlorfrei gebleichtem, alterungsbeständigem Papier nach DIN 6738 gedruckt.

Foreword

The use of business information and the often inadequate quality of data have challenged organizations long before the advent of computers. However, stupendous advances in information technology (IT) have revolutionized the way information is collected, transformed, and distributed in organizations. Most notably, Enterprise Resource Planning (ERP) systems became the backbone of corporate IT infrastructures by standardizing and integrating a broad range of applications and organizational data. Since the end of the 1990s, ERP systems provided new opportunities for handling information on an organization-wide basis but also introduced new risks resulting from the rapid diffusion of poor quality data entered by some system users to other application areas.

Despite an unceasing interest, an increasing number of publications, and many solutions prepared by software vendors, assuring data quality in business applications remains a difficult endeavor. The concept of quality incorporates subjective and context-dependent aspects, many organizational and technical interfaces in organizations put data quality at risk, and data care activities are typically costly and may not always result in tangible benefits. These problems pertain especially to the case of ERP systems, as their standardized base design is aligned to a multitude of application domains, inhomogeneous IT landscapes, and organizational idiosyncrasies.

Over the past 20 years, information engineering in the context of ERP systems has been an area of focus for the Institute of Information Systems at the University of Bern. Continuing in this tradition, Michael Röthlin bases his research on professional experience in the domain of ERP systems, on findings obtained from the literature, and his own highly valuable field research.

As the study points out, successful ERP system implementation and maintenance projects clearly require attentive information engineering activities. By providing a practice-oriented, structured approach for integrating both quality and data management concerns, along with a balanced review of data quality instruments, the author puts ERP professionals in a better position to successfully manage data quality in their ERP environments. Thus, reading and following the recommendations given by Michael Röthlin could remarkably improve the benefits of applying ERP systems. That is why I hope that the present book will find a broad audience in practice as well as in academia.

Bern, 2010-06-16   Prof. Dr. Gerhard F. Knolmayer, University of Bern

Acknowledgements

This study was carried out at the Institute of Information Systems of the University of Bern from 2000–2009. First of all, I would like to thank Prof. Dr. Gerhard Knolmayer for his excellent mentoring throughout the entire thesis, his constant encouragement and support, and the opportunity to apply some of the "recipes" presented here in real-world projects. Next, I owe thanks to Prof. Dr. Reinhard Jung, who acted as second advisor. Then I wish to express my gratitude to all the people and organizations who have contributed in various ways, with responses in the surveys, expert interviews, comments, and other kinds of support for my work. Finally, I am deeply indebted to my family – this project would not have been completed without their love and understanding.

Contents

List of Figures

List of Tables

Abbreviations

4

4GL   Fourth Generation Language.

A

ABC   Activity Based Costing.

ACID   Atomicity, Consistency, Isolation, and Durability.

AIS   Accounting Information System.

ALE   Application Link Enabling.

ARTS   Association for Retail Technology Standards.

ASAP   Accelerated SAP.

B

B2B   Business-to-Business.

B2C   Business-to-Consumer.

BAPI   Business Application Programming Interface.

BC   Business Consultant (ASAP Role).

BI   Business Intelligence.

BOM   Bill of Materials.

BOR   Business Object Repository.

BPM   Business Process Modeling.

BPO   Business Process Owner (customer side) (ASAP Role).

BPR   Business Process Reengineering.

BRMS   Business Rules Management Systems.

BSC   Balanced Scorecard.

C

CAD   Computer Aided Design.

CC   Cutover Coordinator (ASAP Role).

CDI   Customer Data Integration.

CIO   Chief Information Officer.

COBIT   Control Objectives for Information and related Technology.

COQ   Cost of Quality.

CRM   Customer Relationship Management.

CSF   Critical Success Factor.

CTP   Critical-to-Process Characteristics.

CTQ   Critical-to-Quality Characteristics.

D

DBMS   Data Base Management System.

DEC   Development Consultant (ASAP Role).

DEM   Development Manager (ASAP Role).

DEV   Developer (customer side) (ASAP Role).

DFSS   Design for Six Sigma.

DLL   Dynamic Link Library.

DMADV   "Define–Measure–Analyze–Design–Verify".

DMAIC   "Define–Measure–Analyze–Improve–Control".

DMM   Data Migration Manager (ASAP Role).

DMQM   Data Migration Quality Assurance Manager (ASAP Role).

DQ   Data Quality.

DQA   Data Quality Act.

DQM   Data Quality Management.

DWH   Data Warehouse.

E

EC   European Community.

EDC   Education Consultant (ASAP Role).

EPC   Event driven Process Chain.

ER   Entity-Relationship.

ERP   Enterprise Resource Planning.

ETL   Extraction, Transformation and Load.

F

FMEA   Failure Mode and Effects Analysis.

FTE   Full Time Equivalent.

G

GDP   Gross Domestic Product.

GIS   Geographical Information System.

GRC   Governance, Risk, and Compliance.

GUI   Graphical User Interface.

H

HDM   Help Desk Manager (customer side) (ASAP Role).

HOQ   House of Quality.

HTTP   Hypertext Transfer Protocol.

I

IAU   Internal Auditor (customer side) (ASAP Role).

ICOFR   Internal Control over Financial Reporting.

IDoc   Intermediate Documents (SAP).

IMF   International Monetary Fund.

IMR   Integration Manager (ASAP Role).

IP-MAP   Information Production Map.

IQR   Interquartile range.

IRR   Internal Rate of Return.

IT   Information Technology.

ITIL   Information Technology Infrastructure Library.

J

JIT   Just in Time.

K

KPI   Key Performance Indicator.

L

LUW   Logical Units of Work.

M

MAPI   Messaging Application Programming Interface.

MDM   Master Data Management.

MIS   Management Information System.

MMCS   Material Master Coordination System.

MRP   Material Requirements Planning.

MRP II   Manufacturing Resource Planning.

MTC   SAP Methods and Tools Consultant (ASAP Role).

N

NOGA   Nomenclature Générale des Activités économiques.

NPV   Net Present Value.

O

OCA   Organizational Change Manager (ASAP Role).

OCE   Organizational Change Member (ASAP Role).

OLE   Object Linking and Embedding.

P

PDCA   "Plan–Do–Check–Act".

PM   Project Manager/Senior Project Manager (ASAP Role).

PMO   Project Management Office Team Member (ASAP Role).

PPC   Production Planning and Control.

PR   Project Reviewer (ASAP Role).

PS   Project Sponsor (ASAP Role).

PTM   Business Process Team Member (customer side) (ASAP Role).

Q

QC   Quality Control.

QFD   Quality Function Deployment.

R

RACI   Responsibility – Accountability – Consulting – Information.

RAM   Role and Authorization Manager (ASAP Role).

RFC   Remote Function Call.

RFID   Radio Frequency IDentification.

ROI   Return on Investment.

RPN   Risk Priority Number.

S

SA   System Administrator (ASAP Role).

SaaS   Software as a Service.

SCM   Supply Chain Management.

SERM   Structured Entity Relationship Model.

SFSO   Swiss Federal Statistical Office.

SIPOC   Supplier, Input, Process, Output, Customer.

SISP   Strategic Information Systems Planning.

SMB   Small and Midsize Businesses.

SOA   Service-Oriented Architecture.

SOC   Solution Consultant (ASAP Role).

SOX   Sarbanes-Oxley Act.

SQL   Structured Query Language.

SSA   SAP Solution Architect (ASAP Role).

STCM   Steering Committee Member (ASAP Role).

STM   Support Team Member (customer side) (ASAP Role).

T

TAQM   Test and Quality Manager (ASAP Role).

TC   Technology Consultant (ASAP Role).

TCO   Total Cost of Ownership.

TDM   Training and Documentation Manager (ASAP Role).

TDQM   Total Data Quality Management.

TDTM   Training and Documentation Team Member (ASAP Role).

TPM   Technical Project Manager (ASAP Role).

TQdM   Total Quality data Management.

TQM   Total Quality Management.

TR   Trainer (ASAP Role).

U

UML   Unified Modeling Language.

V

VoC   Voice of the Customer.

VoP   Voice of the Process.

X

XML   Extensible Markup Language.

Chapter 1

Introduction

1.1 Relevance of Data Quality

Organizations[1] create and use data, images of real world facts in their environment,[2] for recording the history of actions, driving processes, and taking decisions based on information extracted from the data.[3] Information has become an important driver for today's economy, as a typical enterprise senses a "continuously increasing, constantly changing need for current, accurate, integrated information, often on short notice or very short notice, to support its business activities."[4] High-quality data is also important in many domains of government, to cover information needs for tax, social security, or military purposes.[5]

The effectiveness of all kinds of information systems used by organizations depends on the quality of the data processed. In their "information systems success model," DeLone and McLean identified data quality as a pivotal driver for the use of and the satisfaction of users with an information system, and finally as a precondition for information system success.[6] Data quality issues concern both manufacturing industries (in which data is a by-product of operations) and professional or governmental services (where data typically is a principal outcome of a process).[7] As Information Technology (IT) is an important object of corporate spending (already by the end of the 1990's, IT was found to consume nearly 50% of capital expenditures in the U.S.),[8] data quality is of economic interest, as it influences the effectiveness of an IT system and, hence, its economic impact.

---

[1] If not specified otherwise, this research focuses on the use of data in software applications in a business organization (i.e., enterprise) context. In order to not exclude non-profit or governmental organizations, the general term "organization" will be preferred where possible.
[2] Redman (1996), p. 230; Watson (2002), pp. 13–14.
[3] Alter (2002), p. 69; Olson (2003), p. 4.
[4] Brackett (2000), p. 3.
[5] Herzog et al. (2007), p. 10.
[6] DeLone and McLean (1992), pp. 83–88.
[7] Redman (1996), p. 7; Alter (2002), p. 61.
[8] Carr (2003), p. 41.

All types (and combinations) of IT systems in the context of an organization require quality data. Firstly, internal corporate initiatives need quality data, as successful operations of a new IT system are only possible when data is correct and useful to all concerned parties in an organization.[9] Secondly, external business partners can get directly in touch with enterprise data if, for example, applications such as Customer Relationship Management (CRM) systems or Web shops are used. Here, the negative impact of poor data quality is immediate, and organizations are forced to use high quality data in managing their relationship with their customers in order not to disappoint (and lose) them. Following an industry study carried out by The Data Warehousing Institute (TDWI), the activities for maintaining data quality appear amongst the most important challenges in CRM projects.[10] Thirdly, insufficient data quality in advanced purchasing and Supply Chain Management (SCM) systems, which are operated by several business partners, can hinder electronic collaboration and lower its effectiveness. Finally, approaches involving a combination of IT systems in an organizational context (architectures composed of software components from different vendors), exhibit problems at the component interfaces: although systems can be integrated on a technical level, a semantic data integration and integrated presentation of the information needed at a business user workplace level often proves to be very costly, if not impossible.[11] Organizations can at the same time be "data rich" and "information poor," overloaded with large quantities of data contained in several IT systems, but facing enormous problems when trying to retrieve useful information from these systems.[12]

Despite the many possible definitions, the quality of data can be tentatively characterized as the degree it conforms to a specification (e.g., respecting the constraints of a data model) or the extent it meets data users' expectations (e.g., by being "useful"), in analogy to other quality management contexts.[13] In a positive view, data has to possess certain properties that describe its conformity or usability, in order to fulfill consumers' expectations; frequently mentioned attributes of data quality are *accuracy, completeness, consistency*, or *timeliness*.[14] Negative definitions often refer to the costs of non-performance, stemming from the prevention, detection, and correction of errors. As it will be shown, the concept of data quality can include highly subjective aspects, depending on the use a person makes of some data item, and is hence hard to define, since "the user is the one ultimately deciding whether the data is of quality."[15]

---

[9]   Beuthner (2005).

[10] Eckerson and Watson (2000).

[11] Thole (2007).

[12] Königer and Reithmayer (1998), p. 13.

[13] Redman (1996), p. 19.

[14] Wand and Wang (1996), p. 87.

[15] Bosavage (2005).

The academic literature and articles from magazines, journals, and newspapers provide numerous anecdotes of high-stake data quality problems.[16] Data errors can cost lives, as the bombing of the embassy of a non-involved nation in a military conflict shows,[17] or can ruin lives and careers, as errors in criminal records may send people to jail or cause them to lose their jobs.[18] Closer to the domain of interest of this study, numerous cases of data quality issues have been reported from the business world; as an example, during its "Global Business Excellence" program, Nestle – the world's largest packaged food company – discovered that about 56% of the data in their IT systems was "garbage," causing anomalies in operations.[19]

Interest in data quality issues is regularly stimulated by catastrophic events and the subsequent reaction of legislators. The Mexican financial crisis of 1994–95 has led to an enforcement of the surveillance of the International Monetary Fund (IMF) members' economic policies and the adoption of international standards in financial reporting and the related quality of data.[20] The ENRON disaster, triggering a sudden loss of confidence in corporate accounting and reporting practices, gave way to new legislation on internal controls, such as the Sarbanes-Oxley Act (SOX).[21] As another source of legislation, data protection regulations, such as the OECD Guidelines on the Protection of Privacy and Transborder Flows of Personal Data, the Convention 108 of the European Council, or the Directive 95/46/EC of the European Community, seek to protect personal data.

Many authors have proposed methods to analyze the causes of data quality problems, in various information systems application contexts. As an example, according to Wang and Strong, data quality problems can be categorized into intrinsic weaknesses (data values do not correspond to the actual or true values), representational weaknesses (data is not intelligible or clear), contextual weaknesses (data is not pertinent to the task of the data user), and accessibility weaknesses (data is not available or obtainable).[22] Other authors differentiate irrelevance, unsoundness, suboptimal process of delivery, and insufficient data processing infrastructure as principal categories of data quality problems.[23]

---

[16] Cf., e.g., Redman (1996), p. 5, English (1999b), pp. 7–10, or Wang et al. (2001), p. 1, for a list of examples.

[17] U.S. Department of Defense (1999); Redman (2001), p. 39. It has to be questioned whether the case described here relates to an application (or process) failure, rather to than a "mere" data quality problem. Cf. Fisher and Kingma (2001) for another case of fatal data quality problems in the military-political context.

[18] Ballou and Tayi (1989), p. 320; Bobrowski et al. (1998), p. 4.

[19] Shpilberg et al. (2007).

[20] Carson (2001), p. 5.

[21] Lagace (2004).

[22] Wang and Strong (1996), pp. 18–20.

[23] Eppler (2003), p. 60.

1.2 Characteristics of ERP Systems

In the last decade of the 20th century, many organizations have replaced their "legacy" IT infrastructure (applications using older technologies, often containing home-grown code, which must be maintained because they manage important data and control business critical transactions[24]) by packaged applications, so-called Enterprise Resource Planning (ERP) systems. Most large organizations world-wide have at least one ERP system in operation; many Small and Medium-sized Businesses (SMBs) have been attracted by the advantages of ERP systems as well, or have been forced to integrate with the ERP platform of large customers or suppliers.[25] Pushed by the forced modernization of IT landscapes before Year 2000 – ERP was often commonly considered a "quick fix" to the related "Year 2000 problem"[26] – ERP systems are still widely used today, in all kinds of industries, and will remain a building block of IT infrastructures for years to come.

ERP systems can be characterized as follows: as standardized application software packages, suitable for virtually any type of organization, they offer a large functionality (more than a specific organization will ever need) and are expected to cover almost every computing need for managing organizations. From a technical viewpoint, the basis of ERP systems consists of powerful database back-ends with a predefined enterprise data model, which provides data structures for describing the business environment and reliably processing complex business transactions. ERP systems are semi-finished "mass products," in the sense that organizations do not develop such application systems in-house, but rather have system specialists tailor the standard system to their specific needs. Consequently, in an implementation project, the business functionality as needed by an organization has to be identified and configured in the software package, organizational structures have to be designed according to the possibilities of the ERP system, and add-on modules and third-party applications have to be integrated, in order to support the diverse processes of an organization.

An interesting economic aspect of ERP systems is their market diffusion, as the same ERP system "products" from leading vendors such as ORACLE or SAP can be found in many organizations world-wide, creating a community of knowledge for ERP professionals, and enabling information system researchers to carry out general assessments of ERP systems. In order to illustrate the properties and the behavior of a typical ERP system, the SAP ERP system (successor of the SAP R/3 system introduced in the 1990's) developed by German vendor SAP will be used several times as a showcase.

---

[24] Watson (2002), p. 579.

[25] Klaus et al. (2000), p. 141.

[26] Davenport (1999a), p. 181.

1.3 Data Quality and ERP Systems

After citing many positive properties of ERP systems described in the previous section, why relate data quality problems to ERP systems? Evidence collected from the information systems literature justifies an in-depth analysis of this field.

Firstly, prominent authors have raised a number of criticisms of the design principles of ERP systems: most ERP packages tend to be overly "generic" in their data structures and they lack precise data integrity rules, which must be added as "bolt-ons."[27] As ERP systems most often cannot hold the promise of covering the entire computing needs of an organization, ERP applications must be treated and integrated just like another software component in an existing IT landscape, and their specific data model and application structure can increase the overall complexity of data processing.

Secondly, the theme of data quality is addressed in ERP vendor documentation. SAP's "Continuous Business Improvement" guidelines, as an example, address possible ERP data issues after system implementation by advising consultants to challenge the quality of existing ERP data. Data quality in this context appears, however, only as a sub-issue of legacy data conversion: common vendor methods do not cover activities to design organizational structures for assuring data quality or do not recommend data quality instruments for the production phase of a newly implemented ERP system.[28]

Thirdly, many data quality problems have been documented in the literature on business applications such as accounting, production, or inventory planning systems.[29] As these application domains are today most often covered by ERP systems, it seems likely that ERP systems suffer from the same data quality problems.

Finally, data quality problems are also one of the main causes for Data Warehouse (DWH) implementation failures, as data warehousing is particularly exposed to data quality problems when integrating data from heterogeneous sources.[30] DWHs typically import data from transaction systems, such as ERP packages; if the quality of the ERP data passed on to data aggregation and analytic tools is insufficient, the result of such post-processing may be heavily affected, resulting in a "garbage-in-garbage-out" cycle.[31] Consequently, DWH project failures can also be seen as an indicator for ERP data quality problems.

As these statements show, data quality problems may potentially occur in an ERP environment, and some of them are ERP-specific. The question of adequate data quality management in the ERP system domain clearly deserves closer attention.

---

[27] Cf., e.g., Brackett (2000), p. 317.
[28] Umar et al. (1999), p. 279.
[29] Cf., e.g., Kaplan et al. (1998), Wermers (2000), Piasecki (2003), or Sheldon (2004).
[30] English (1999b), p. xxiv.
[31] Levitin and Redman (1998), p. 97.

1.4   Purpose and Coverage of Research

In contrast to the evidence that data quality in ERP systems may be an important issue, specific academic or press reports, data quality models, or system implementation guidelines are very rare. Consequently, a general focus research question can be formulated as follows:

> How does information systems research consider data quality in an ERP context, how do organizations handle data quality in ERP systems, and what should be done to improve or maintain ERP data quality?

This thesis aims to contribute to the research in this field by presenting findings obtained in three stages. Firstly, the applicability of data quality management concepts to the ERP world was examined. Then evidence for the existence of data quality problems was collected and existing data quality management methods were documented, in a field study covering both ERP vendor and user views on data quality. Finally, based on these findings, an ERP specific data quality management model was developed, suitable for the implementation and improvement of ERP systems.

In order to increase the specificity of the research, some limitations on the research topic and geographic focus have been introduced. In contrast to other works addressing the overall information needs of business organizations,[32] this thesis focuses on structured data in business processes supported by ERP systems. Further, as justified later in Chapter 4, the author has limited the coverage of the field study (ERP surveys) to the situation in Swiss enterprises.

1.5   Research Questions

Table 1.1 presents the 9 research questions treated in this study: while the relevance of data quality (Q1), the level of data quality in ERP systems (Q2), and the factors determining data quality (Q3) stand on their own, the next five questions (Q4–Q8) are directly based on the "Define, Measure, Analyze, Improve, and Control" (DMAIC) quality method used several times throughout this research.[33] The last question Q9 refers to the development of an ERP system implementation model that addresses data quality concerns with specific activities, roles, and tools.

---

[32] Cf., e.g., Königer and Reithmayer (1998), Eppler (2003), or Batini and Scannapieco (2006).
[33] Cf. Section 2.1.5.4.

#	Research Question
Q1	How relevant is data quality in the context of ERP systems?
Q2	What is the level of data quality in ERP systems?
Q3	What are the factors influencing data quality?
Q4	How do ERP practitioners define and quantify data quality?
Q5	How can data quality be measured in an ERP environment?
Q6	What are the methods available and used to analyze data quality issues in an ERP system?
Q7	How can data quality be improved?
Q8	By which means can ERP data processing be controlled to ensure permanent data quality?
Q9	What are the implications of data quality concerns for ERP software implementation and organizational design?

Table 1.1: Research Questions.

1.6   Research Method

In this project, descriptive and inductive research methods were used: "why" and "how" research questions were treated with case studies (and examples drawn from the literature), while the "who," "how many," and "where" questions were analyzed in structured surveys.[34] Starting with the data quality literature, the applicability of generic information systems guidelines to the ERP system context was reviewed, and the author checked whether the advice given in the literature, such as Redman's "Field tips for data quality,"[35] are of practical value in the ERP field. Common strategies and tools for ensuring sufficient data quality were documented and classified. Based on these findings, two surveys – one for enterprises and another one for ERP vendors – were carried out. The results of the two surveys were used, together with other findings from the literature review and case studies, to formulate recommendations for effective data quality management in the ERP context. Figure 1.1 graphically shows the sequence of research activities in an overview.

The following principal sources of information have been used during this research project:

- *Source L1: Information Systems and Data Management.* General data management methods and tools may also be relevant for the ERP system context, in particular relational database theory and applications.
- *Source L2: Quality Management.* Research in the domain of quality has provided the foundations and instruments for quality management. Moreover, quality standards such as ISO9000 or frameworks such as Six Sigma are used today by many organizations using ERP systems worldwide and are, hence, candidates for supporting ERP data quality management principles as well.

---

[34] Yin (1994), pp. 4–9.
[35] Redman (2001), pp. 209–216.

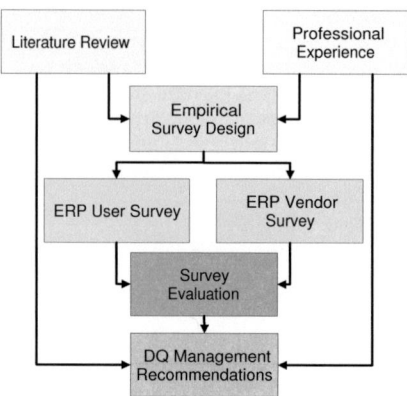

Figure 1.1: Research Method.

- *Source L3: Data Quality.* Data quality issues and the ways to manage data quality have been a research topic for years.[36] In the past, main areas of interest for data quality research and application have been data-intensive applications such as Geographical Information Systems (GIS), environmental and health data programs, or the use of data warehouses in business organizations.

- *Source L4: ERP Literature.* Since ERP systems can be considered as a mature category of IT applications (SAP's R/3 ERP package, as an example, was released more than 15 years ago), publications on the topic are plentiful. Loos and Theling have found that SAP ERP systems are the ones best covered by the ERP literature; in their selection of 144 ERP-related works published from 1996 to 2003 (in German language), 111 refer to the SAP product family.[37]

- *Source ES: ERP Systems and Implementation Models.* SAP ERP is a leading ERP system worldwide, with a very large customer base in Swiss industries, which have been amongst the early adopters of ERP technology. Relatively easy access to SAP ERP implementations and ERP specialists was a strong argument for focusing on this ERP system, including its technologies and the design of data structures and applications. Access to an SAP ERP installation, provided by SAP's University Alliance program in Switzerland, and implementation tools such as SAP's AcceleratedSAP (ASAP) have helped to imagine "clean-room" situations of quality defects and to develop a data quality-oriented ERP implementation model.

---

[36] Cf., e.g., the Total Data Quality Management (TDQM) program (http://web.mit.edu/tdqm/) of the MIT or the yearly International Conference on Information Quality (ICIQ) (http://mitiq.mit.edu/iciq/).

[37] Loos and Theling (2003), p. 17.

- *Source C1: Case Study 1 (Heterogeneous ERP Systems).* This comprehensive case study provides findings from the analysis of a complex, heterogeneous ERP application landscape and explores the influence of large organizational structures and multiple ERP system instances on data quality.

- *Source C2: Case Study 2 (Data Quality Management).* Guidelines issued by the Federal Bureau of Prisons at the U.S. Department of Justice show how data quality in a productive ERP system can be controlled and improved.

- *Source C3: Case Study 3 (ERP System Implementation).* This case study shows some typical challenges organizations can encounter during ERP implementation projects, and describes ERP practices, data quality problems, and their root causes.

- *Source S1: ERP User Enterprise Survey.* Data quality problems and management practices in the ERP system domain were explored using a questionnaire targeting IT managers in large Swiss enterprises.

- *Source S2: ERP Vendor Survey.* A second survey dedicated to ERP system vendors examined design principles of ERP systems, features implemented to address possible data quality problems, and the role of data quality in the marketing of ERP systems.

- *Source EI: ERP Expert Interviews.* In a last step, the validity of the findings and the suitability of the ERP specific data quality management model proposed by the author were assessed during reviews with recognized ERP experts.

Findings from the two surveys S1 and S2 (in which identical questions were posed to different audiences) were compared, in order to obtain a multi-perspective view and to build explanations based on the different perspectives of ERP users and vendors.

Table 1.2 shows how the sources of information map to the research questions formulated earlier in Section 1.5.

Research Question	Theory				Practice						
	L1	L2	L3	L4	ES	C1	C2	C3	S1	S2	EI
Q1 Relevance	•		•	•	•			•	•	•	•
Q2 State						•		•	•		•
Q3 Influence factors						•		•	•	•	•
Q4 Definition	•	•	•		•		•		•		•
Q5 Measurement	•	•	•		•		•		•	•	•
Q6 Analysis	•	•			•		•		•	•	•
Q7 Improvement	•	•	•	•	•		•		•	•	•
Q8 Control	•	•	•	•	•		•		•	•	•
Q9 Design	•	•	•	•	•		•		•	•	•

Table 1.2: Research Questions and Related Research Methods.

1.7   Structure of Thesis

The thesis is structured in six chapters plus appendices:

- *Chapter 1* puts the importance of data quality in a business context, describes the coverage of research, the sources of information, and presents the research methods applied by the author.

- *Chapter 2* introduces elements from quality and data quality research literature qualified as relevant for the domain of discourse and as useful for later integration in an ERP data quality management model.

- *Chapter 3* describes the characteristics of ERP software systems: their range of application, the basic technologies employed, and the methods for implementing ERP systems in organizations. This chapter further presents strengths and weaknesses of ERP systems with regard to data quality and shows, by conceptual considerations, in which way ERP systems are exposed to data errors and how far general data quality recommendations apply to the ERP system context.

- *Chapter 4* presents results from the two surveys carried out to explore the opinions and experiences of ERP system users and vendors with respect to data quality. Besides addressing the question of the relevance of data quality, the facts presented cover the perceived state of data quality, factors for data quality, the usage of data quality control methods and instruments in practice, and responsibilities for data quality.

- *Chapter 5* presents a method for embedding data quality concerns in an ERP project context, based on the findings of the preceding chapters. The framework describes relevant roles, activities, and tools, and incorporates them into a time line view of an ERP implementation or improvement project.

- *Chapter 6* recapitulates the main findings of this research. The relevance of a model-driven data quality approach in the ERP field is discussed and domains for future research are defined.

- *Appendices* document the diverse questionnaires, provide summary data collected in the field surveys and expert interviews, and list the references.

Chapter 2

Quality Concepts for Business Data

Data Quality (DQ) management encompasses activities from both IT and quality management domains, which can be framed by a data "governance" environment that defines the relevant roles and responsibilities.[1] This chapter presents the main characteristics and applications of data quality management by departing from a quality management perspective.

2.1 Quality Management Overview

2.1.1 Role and Definition of Quality

To deliver "high quality," "superior," or "excellent" products and services to a market is a strong and frequently used objective in the business world, as the importance of satisfied and (consequently) loyal customers has been widely recognized. As an example, companies with a 98% customer retention rate have been found to be twice as profitable as those operating at 94%.[2] Moreover, research results obtained back in the 1980's have established a link between improved product quality (design and conformance), increased revenue, and lower manufacturing and service costs; higher product quality was found to lead to higher overall profitability.[3]

Quality as a factor for economic success in business has always been deeply rooted in producer–consumer relationships, associated with the manufacturer of a product. In the Middle Ages, a craftsman was at the same time designer, manufacturer, salesman, and quality inspector.[4] With the Industrial revolution, this bundling of economic interest and informal quality assurance disappeared, and quality inspection became a formal part of manufacturing. In the beginning of the twentieth century, Taylor's philosophy of manufacturing introduced a theoretical foundation for the segmentation of job activities

---

[1] Otto et al. (2007), pp. 916–918; Otto and Wende (2008), p. 267.
[2] Evans and Lindsay (2002), p. 157.
[3] Evans and Lindsay (2002), pp. 24–25.
[4] Evans and Lindsay (2002), p. 4.

into planning and execution tasks; product defects were now detected by inspectors and removed from production. After World War II, publications and consulting activities of quality authors such as Juran or Deming contributed to the ascent of Japan's economy, its gain in competitive power, and finally an increasing awareness of the importance of quality world-wide.[5]

Over time, the initial concept of quality as "conformance" or "reliability" was expanded, to include aspects such as "performance," "features," "durability," "serviceability," or "aesthetics" as well.[6] As focus shifted away from finding and removing production defects towards customer orientation and manufacturing quality, quality and management concepts were combined in an initiative known as Total Quality Management (TQM), in which quality was related with overall performance ("excellence") of an organization and no longer a purely engineering-related science.[7] The trend to customer focus is also visible in the evolution of quality standards. In 1978, the American National Standards Institute (ANSI) and the American Society for Quality (ASQ) defined quality as "the totality of features and characteristics of a product or service that bears on its ability to satisfy given needs." In the late 1980's, the definition changed to "quality is meeting or exceeding customer expectations,"[8] where a "customer" could stand for a person within the organization (internal customer) or an external customer ("consumer").

After having focused on the product itself and isolated services, today's quality initiatives mainly target the *business processes* used to define, produce, and distribute the products and services customers require.[9] A business process can be defined as an "end-to-end set of activities," started by a request from an internal or external customer, and resulting in some benefit delivered to this customer.[10] Processes are subject to variation, which can be reduced by implementing feedback loops;[11] important feedback concepts used in this context are the "Voice of the Process" (VoP), consisting of information on how a process is performing, and the "Voice of the Customer" (VoC), represented by specification limits acceptable to customers.[12]

Many awards are dedicated every year to quality-thriving organizations. As an example, the "Malcolm Baldridge Award"[13] defines six "balanced" areas of organizational performance: product and service outcomes, customer-focused results, financial and mar-

---

[5] Evans and Lindsay (2002), p. 6.
[6] Garvin (1987), pp. 104–107.
[7] Evans and Lindsay (2002), p. 9.
[8] Evans and Lindsay (2002), p. 15.
[9] El-Haik and Roy (2005), p. 20.
[10] English (1999b), p. 40.
[11] Juran (1992), p. 275; Gitlow et al. (2006), pp. 9–11.
[12] Gitlow et al. (2006), p. 11.
[13] http://www.quality.nist.gov/.

ket results, human resource results, organizational effectiveness results (including internal operational performance measures), and leadership and social responsibility results.[14]

In order to follow a systematic approach to frequently used definitions of quality, Garvin conceived a scheme including five classes of quality criteria:[15]

1. The concept of *transcendent quality*, first introduced by Shewhart, understands quality as an abstract excellence or "superiority" of a product or service.[16] In a forward-looking context, the concept of transcendent quality is of little use, as it can be grasped only by experience.

2. In a *product-based view*, quality stands for the presence or absence of certain (measurable) attributes. Quality can therefore be "measured" by simply counting the number of attributes; increasing the quality of a given product means adding more attributes, which leads to increased costs.

3. A next approach is the *user-based* view, which defines quality as the fulfillment of customer expectations or the ability of a product to satisfy customers' needs, in other words, the quality of a product or service is defined by its "fitness for (intended) use."[17] Typically very subject-specific views on "usability" make this concept more difficult to operationalize compared to the product-based view.

4. The *process-based* (or *manufacturing-based*[18]) philosophy defines quality as an objective freedom from errors, which is the result of a manufacturing process operating according to specifications. A quality test hence assesses conformity of a product to the underlying specifications.[19] In this conception, high quality manufacturing processes help to reduce production costs, since they help to avoid "scrap and rework;" conversely, low quality stands for high costs.[20]

5. A *value-based approach* focuses on the tradeoff between usefulness (or customer satisfaction[21]) on one side and price on the other: if the price of a product is too high – however good it may serve customer's needs – the quality of the product will not be considered adequate.[22]

Garvin stresses the fact that organizations often use different competing quality definitions concurrently: marketing staff will prefer product or customer-oriented quality concepts, while in the domain of product design and manufacturing, technical specifications

---

[14] National Institute of Standards and Technology (2005), p. 6.
[15] Garvin (1984), pp. 25–28.
[16] Evans and Lindsay (2002), p. 11.
[17] Garvin (1984), p. 27; Strong et al. (1997b); Evans and Lindsay (2002), p. 12.
[18] Evans and Lindsay (2002), p. 13.
[19] Crosby (1980), p. 15.
[20] Deming (2000), p. 11.
[21] Evans and Lindsay (2002), p. 12.
[22] Garvin (1984), p. 28.

are used to guarantee the promised level of quality of a final product.[23] Evans and Lindsay show how these different views of quality can be consolidated in the case of an industrial production–distribution cycle (Figure 2.1).[24] Firstly, customer needs are captured by marketing specialists and translated into product specifications, targeting user-based quality requirements. Designers will be forced to trade off conformity to specifications against cost constraints (value-based definition). Next, manufacturing processes are designed to meet production tolerances as prescribed by the design department in their specifications (process- or manufacturing-based view). Finally, a customer will perceive the quality of a manufactured product when holding it in his or her hand (transcendent view), and judge its "fitness for use" when actually using it (product- or value-based quality).

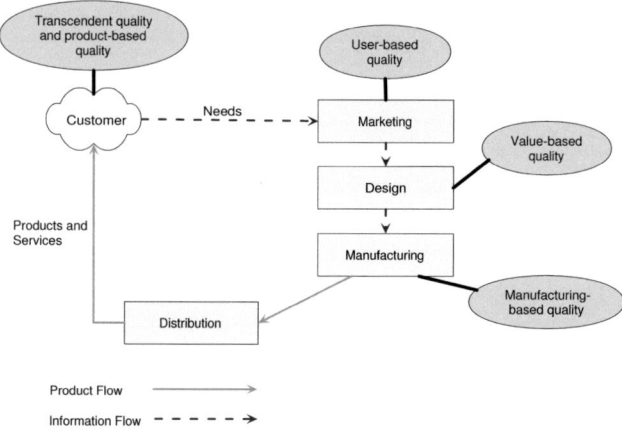

Figure 2.1: Quality Perspectives in a Production-Distribution Cycle [Evans and Lindsay (2002)].

2.1.2 Taxonomies of Quality Problems

The quality of a product or service can often only be defined by contrast with the opposite, non-quality, as "there is no quality in this world that is not what it is merely by contrast."[25] For quality control and quality improvement, the analysis of quality problems is hence an important activity. A first step for classifying recognized quality problems consists in gathering contextual information. Once sufficient information about a problem has been collected, errors can be classified, and problems can be tackled using repair,

---

[23] Garvin (1984), p. 29.

[24] Evans and Lindsay (2002), p. 14.

[25] Melville (1851), p. 53.

improvement, and engineering activities. Smith proposed the following classification of
quality problems (cf. also Figure 2.2):[26]

1. *Conformance problems:* The production system as such is well defined and apparently under control, but its output is unsatisfactory;
2. *Unstructured performance problems:* The system is poorly structured and, as a
   consequence, production results are unforeseeable;
3. *Efficiency problems:* In this case, a problem is perceived by stakeholders of the
   organization because, e.g., organizational objectives such as productivity goals are
   not met;
4. *Product design problems:* The outcome of a production process does not correspond
   to customer expectations;
5. *Process design problems:* The capabilities of production processes do not match
   customer requirements.

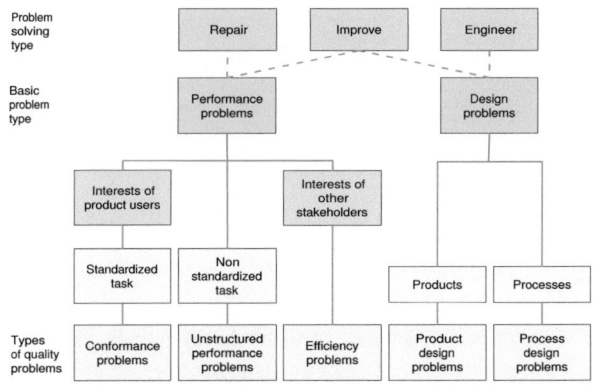

Figure 2.2: Classification of Quality Problems [Smith (2000)].

2.1.3   Cost of Quality and Non-Quality

The fundamental concept of Cost of Quality (COQ) appeared in the 1950's, mirroring the
financial impact of quality problems on organizations, and using four main categories of
quality costs, detailed in Table 2.1:[27]

---

[26] Smith (2000), pp. 44–48.
[27] Evans and Lindsay (2002), p. 468.

1. *Prevention costs* are the result of defect and damage prevention;

2. *Appraisal costs* are caused by the activities for error detection (measurement, analysis);

3. *Internal failure costs* are caused by defects observed before a product is shipped to a customer;

4. *External failure costs* are incurred after a product containing defects has been received by the customer.

Category	Cost Elements
Prevention	• *Quality planning costs* are caused by activities for quality planning and problem-solving, or process improvement • *Process control costs* describe process management costs • *Information systems costs* are related to setting up quality measurement systems • *Training and general management costs*
Appraisal	• *Test and inspection costs* are determined by quality treatment of physical goods and services • *Instrument maintenance costs* cover the use of measurement instruments • *Process measurement and control costs* contain, e.g., salaries of quality inspectors
Internal failure	• *Scrap and rework costs* include material, work, and administrative work needed to correct errors • *Costs of corrective action* are incurred for the root cause analysis of problems • *Downgrading costs* are the reduction in sales price granted to customers as a consequence of insufficient quality • *Process failures* include excess production equipment downtime or extraordinary maintenance
External failure	• *Costs due to customer complaints and returns* include the effects of order cancellations or extra freight expenses • *Product recall costs and warranty claims* occur when a defective item has to be repaired or replaced • *Product liability costs* result from legal action taken by product and service consumers.

Table 2.1: Cost of Quality: Categories and Cost Elements [Evans and Lindsay (2002)].

The overall cost of quality equals to the sum of the four cost components, i.e., prevention, appraisal, internal and external failure costs. This broad definition shows that the COQ concept is resistant against "manipulations" as, for example, an attempt to directly reduce visible internal and external costs by increasing inspection will result in higher appraisal costs and therefore not reduce overall quality cost. A typical mix of resources spent on the first three cost types tends to be 10% for prevention, 30% for appraisal, and 60% for repair.[28]

Ideally, through improved and constant preventive management activities, the structure of quality cost can be altered and the part of internal and external failures can be reduced, in order to increase the operational benefit.[29] Evans and Lindsay show that the conventional economic model of quality of conformance, having a total "optimum" cost somewhere between 0 and 100% of quality of conformance, presents at least two weaknesses: firstly, it ignores the effect of bad quality on sales (customers who are victims of

---

[28] Herzog et al. (2007) p. 12; conversely, the authors recommend a mix of 45% of resources for prevention, 30% for detection, and only 25% for repair activities.

[29] Lorente et al. (1998), p. 732.

a bad quality product or service will restrain from repeat business with that supplier), and secondly, modern technology can help organizations to reach "perfect" quality at a finite cost.[30]

2.1.4 Quality Tools

In the following sections, the use of well-known tools in quality management will be illustrated using the example of the seven classic quality control instruments and a selection of other frequently used tools.[31]

2.1.4.1 Seven Classic Quality Control Instruments

Quality control is "the activity of ensuring conformance to requirements and taking corrective action when necessary to correct problems."[32] The set of most often used Quality Control (QC) instruments – cause and effect diagram, check sheet, control chart, flow chart, histogram, pareto chart, and scatter diagram – is called the "Seven QC Tools" in the literature:

- *Cause and effect (also Ishikawa or fishbone) diagram:* Shows in a rational way the relationship between causes and effects;
- *Check sheet:* Used to condense information in an efficient format; often a simple listing of observations;
- *Control chart:* Traces the results of a process over time; shows the variability inherent to a process (common cause variation) and the outliers (data points lying outside a zone defined by lower and upper control limits);
- *Flow chart:* Represents a process in graphical form; allows location of errors by analyzing the process step by step;
- *Histogram:* Provides a graphical view of the dispersion of the results of a process and can help to identify a malfunction in a process;
- *Pareto chart:* Plots the cumulative frequency of defects per defect type, in descending order; helps to focus on the "vital few" factors, out of a multitude of potential causes of a problem;
- *Scatter diagram:* A graphical tool showing the relationship between two variables in an X-Y diagram; useful in identifying outliers.

---

[30] Evans and Lindsay (2002), p. 583.

[31] For a comprehensive description of quality instruments and their applicability, the reader is referred to textbooks such as Evans and Lindsay (2002) or John et al. (2006).

[32] Evans and Lindsay (2002), p. 644.

2.1.4.2   Business Processes and Business Process Modeling

Process orientation is a pivotal element of any modern quality management system, as collaboration of often many enterprise functions is needed to fulfill customer expectations through a complex sequence of activities. The elements defining a process are a process definition ("what should be done?"), process objectives ("why should something be done, what are the goals to be accomplished?"), a location ("where must the activities take place, the results be delivered?"), roles ("who has to do it"), triggers or dependencies ("when, under which conditions should it be done?"), procedures ("how must it be done?"), and quality measures ("how to measure the success of the process").[33] Responsibility for a process may be given to a "process owner," a senior middle-level manager responsible for resolving operational issues between business strategy and operations,[34] able to oversee all activities in a process.

Service processes have characteristics that differentiate them from physical manufacturing processes: the output of service processes is seldom as well defined as in the case of physical products; service processes demand a higher level of interaction with customers; finally, the possibility of "scrap and rework" is very limited, forcing the organization to provide a first class service the first time.[35] Quality standards for service processes, however, are in many cases as easy to define as in manufacturing contexts (e.g., "customers receive a confirmation at the latest two work days after order placement").

Business Process Modeling (BPM) is about describing business processes, using formal and informal, often graphical techniques; applications of BPM are process improvement, process re-engineering, or technology transfer. Business process modeling is itself a business process that involves naming business processes and subdividing them into their basic elements so that they can be understood and improved by an organization.[36] The value of business process modeling resides in making process knowledge explicit; BPM is therefore highly recommended in environments where knowledge of a process is critical to a business.[37]

2.1.4.3   Variance and Process Control

Process control describes all the activities needed to evaluate process performance and to make corrections to the process when needed.[38] Control is needed because all real-world processes are subject to variation, which is either due to "special causes," trigger-

---

[33] English (1999b), p. 40.
[34] Shang and Seddon (2003), p. 75.
[35] Evans and Lindsay (2002), p. 399.
[36] Alter (2002), p. 87.
[37] Succi et al. (2000), p. 49.
[38] Evans and Lindsay (2002), p. 401.

ing uncontrolled variation during normal operations (e.g., due to breakages), or "common causes" (due to the process itself).[39] A system is considered to be in "statistical control" if both process averages and variances are constant over time;[40] if special causes intervene, the process can get out of control. The design of a production system and the management of the inherent common causes of variation are under process management's responsibility, while long-term action is normally the responsibility of line management.[41]

2.1.4.4 SIPOC Models

When supplier and customer roles need to be added to a description of activities in a process, the SIPOC (Supplier, Inputs, Process, Outputs, and Customers) formalism can be used to describe processes in detail.[42] The outcome of a process and the degree of agreement with customer requirements can be measured and presented in a summarized way, e.g., using key figures.

2.1.4.5 Quality Function Deployment

In an attempt to bridge the gap between the languages of customers and engineers, Japanese quality engineers developed the Quality Function Deployment (QFD) tool in the 1960's, as an instrument to meet customer requirements in product and production process design.[43] This method helps organizations to evaluate the impact of new products, to analyze causes of customer dissatisfaction, and to accelerate the product launch process. QFD uses a series of matrices to match customer needs, process capabilities, and operations; these steps are tied to a graphical construct known as the "House of Quality" (HOQ), shown in Figure 2.3.[44] Activities for designing a HOQ include:[45]

1. *Identify customer requirements:* The VoC is the main input channel for the QFD process; market research can provide insights into the expectations of customers.
2. *Identify technical requirements:* The technical requirements for the product and service design are formalized; at the roof of the HOQ, interrelationships between pairs of technical requirements can be qualified.
3. *Relate the customer requirements to the technical requirements:* By involving expert experience or customer intelligence, it can be checked whether customer requirements are adequately addressed by technical requirements.

---

[39] Bank (2000), p. 87.
[40] Evans and Lindsay (2002), p. 686.
[41] Evans and Lindsay (2002), p. 101.
[42] Redman (2001), p. 96; El-Haik and Roy (2005), p. 142.
[43] English (1999b), p. 47; Evans and Lindsay (2002), p. 387; El-Haik and Roy (2005), p. 111; Gitlow et al. (2006), pp. 112–132.
[44] Gitlow et al. (2006), pp. 112–132.
[45] Evans and Lindsay (2002), p. 388.

4. *Conduct an evaluation of competing products or services:* Managers have to evaluate the importance of customer requirements and the organization's competitive situation, highlighting strengths and weaknesses of main competitors, and exhibiting selling points.

5. *Evaluate technical requirements and develop targets:* On the basis of customer requirements and an analysis of strengths and weaknesses of competitors, targets for technical characteristics are set.

6. *Determine which technical requirements to deploy in the remainder of the production/delivery process:* Technical characteristics with high impact on customer relationship are selected first for inclusion in the product and process design.

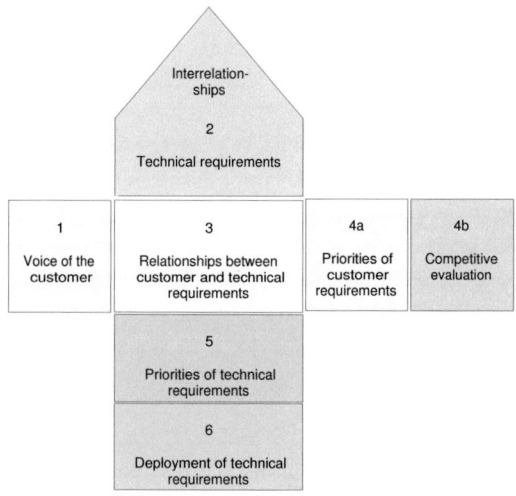

Figure 2.3: Structure of the "House of Quality" [Gitlow et al. (2006)].

Overall, the "House of Quality" is a practical tool to convert relevant customer requirements into adequate design features, in a wide range of application cases.[46]

2.1.4.6 Poka-Yoke

As humans cannot be expected to work like a programmed machine, mistakes are a "natural" phenomenon, as they "just happen," due to inadvertence, bias, and lack of technique.[47] Japanese engineer Shigeo Shingo developed the concept of Poka-yoke in the

---

[46] El-Haik and Roy (2005), p. 140.

[47] Juran (1988), p. 128.

1960's.[48] Using tools, techniques, and processes, humans can be assisted to avoid mistakes; to achieve this, Poka-yoke consists of the two approaches "prediction" (that a defect is about to occur) and "detection" (that a defect has occurred, leading to a halt of the process).

Errors and their impact can be reduced by an elimination of technical risks (switching to a different technology), replacing human intervention with automation (e.g., by installing a robot), facilitation (providing means to avoid errors), detection (finding an error as quickly as possible, in order to minimize the damage done), and mitigation (errors are still possible, but the related damages are avoided).[49]

2.1.4.7   FMEA

Another popular tool for designing quality into processes and products is the Failure Mode and Effects Analysis (FMEA). FMEA basically poses the questions "what can go wrong?" and "where can variation come from?", and can be used as concept FMEA (to analyze systems in the early concept and design stages), project FMEA (to track real or possible failures during a project), or software FMEA (to address failures in software).[50] FMEA helps to identify potential "failure modes" (the loss of at least one functional requirement) of a design and the potential failure effects; a risk can then be defined using the following parameters:

- Severity of the problem (S, with a rating ranging from 1 ["small"] to 10 ["huge"]);
- Probability or likelihood of occurrence (O, 1 ["rare"] to 10 ["frequent"]);
- Ease of detection (D, 1 ["in early design stage"] to 10 ["only after being put into operation"]).

Based on this assessment, a Risk Priority Number (RPN) quantifying the risk of failure can be computed as follows: $RPN = S \cdot O \cdot D$. A potential failure having $RPN = 1$ would hence get the smallest priority, a situation with $RPN = 1,000$ the highest attention. Interpretation problems can arise when a very high component factor is paralleled by a very low one, resulting in an "acceptable" RPN;[51] Goebbels and Jakob consequently recommend to sort risks first by their RPN, then by factor S, then D, and finally by O.[52] A sample of typical parameter values for using FMEA in software development is provided in Table C.1 in Appendix C.1.[53]

---

[48] Juran (1992), p. 233; Evans and Lindsay (2002), pp. 617–618.
[49] Juran (1992), p. 234.
[50] El-Haik and Roy (2005), pp. 241–243.
[51] Wermers (2000), p. 115.
[52] Goebbels and Jakob (2004), p. 15.
[53] El-Haik and Roy (2005), p. 250.

2.1.4.8 Quality Tools and Product or Service Life Cycle

The applicability of specific quality tools depends on the life cycle phase of a product or service. As an example, El-Haik and Roy structure the life cycle of a service in 10 phases and propose the usage of the following quality methods and tools per phase (Table 2.2).[54]

#	Stage	Quality Methods/Tool
1	Idea Creation	• Market and customer research • Technology road maps • Growth strategy
2	Voice of the Customer & Business	• QFD • Customer engagement (surveys etc.)
3	Concept Development	• QFD • FMEA • Simulation
4	Preliminary Design	• Creativity tools • FMEA • Design reviews • Process management
5	Design Optimization	• Reliability engineering • Simulation • Change management • Hypothesis testing
6	Verification	• Prototyping • Simulation • Testing of hypotheses
7	Launch Readiness	• Training plans
8	Production	• Inspection
9	Service/Product Consumption	• Service/product quality management.
10	Phase Out	

Table 2.2: Use of Quality Methods/Tools in Service Life Cycle [El-Haik and Roy (2005)].

2.1.5 Traditional Quality Management Concepts

In the next sections, fundamental quality management approaches formulated by Deming, Juran, and Crosby will be presented, followed by a brief description of Total Quality Management (TQM), ISO 900x, Six Sigma, and the Balanced Scorecard (BSC) approach. With this selection, the most relevant classic quality authors and current "mainstream" quality management approaches will be covered, in view of their application to data management practices in an ERP system context.

2.1.5.1 Fundamental Ideas of Deming, Juran, and Crosby

The starting point of W. Edward Deming's ideas was that variation in processes is the main driver for poor quality.[55] If an organization can reduce variability in manufacturing and service delivery, its costs decrease, productivity improves, market share increases,

---

[54] El-Haik and Roy (2005), pp. 5–10 (simplified and adapted).

[55] Evans and Lindsay (2002), p. 91.

the enterprise stays in business, and finally creates more jobs.[56] In Deming's philosophy, system thinking, understanding of the sources and effects of variation, theory of knowledge, and psychology are the most important concepts.[57] These interests shine through in Deming's famous 14 points, formulated and first used in the 1950's for management training in Japan, containing famous slogans such as "Create constancy of purpose toward improvement," "Cease dependence on inspection to achieve quality," or "Drive out fear, so that everyone may work effectively for the company."[58] Deming's intent was to provide a "basis for transformation of American industry," inviting the management of companies "to stay in business and aim to protect investors and jobs."[59] (With regard to data quality, the application of Deming's quality objectives and activities to data appears quite natural, as the variations of Deming's 14 points proposed by Redman[60] and English[61] show.)

Deming also proposed a simple four-step quality improvement sequence, known as PDCA, Shewhart, or Deming cycle (Figure 2.4).[62] It consists of the four steps *Plan* (the quality objectives and activities), *Do* (perform trial actions to improve quality), *Check* (if the improvement targets have already been achieved or are within the reach of the intended method), and *Act* (to implement improvements on a broad base and institutionalize the change). After acting, the process restarts with planning for new quality objectives, thus closing the circle. Deming replaced the term "check" by "study" in 1990;[63] nevertheless, PDCA remains the more common form and will be retained in the following discussion.

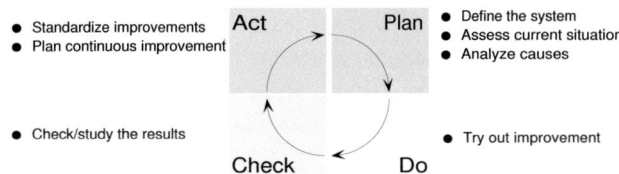

Figure 2.4: Deming's (PDCA) Cycle [Deming (2000)].

Joseph M. Juran diagnoses the same causes of quality defects as Deming: namely variation in manufacturing and service provision. An important aspect of his recommendations for quality management is the wide focus of quality improvement projects: besides the purely statistical "control" of quality, project activities such as a careful design of the

---

[56] Deming (2000), p. 3.
[57] Evans and Lindsay (2002), p. 92.
[58] Cf. Table C.2 in Appendix C.2 for a complete list.
[59] Deming (2000), pp. 23–24.
[60] Redman (1996), pp. 65–66 and 276.
[61] English (1999b), pp. 337–399.
[62] Deming (2000), p. 88.
[63] Evans and Lindsay (2002), p. 587; Gitlow et al. (2006), p. 43.

support organization are recommended.[64] Juran's quality management recommendations are ordered in the form of a "trilogy," containing the three phases of *quality planning, quality control,* and *quality improvement* (Table 2.3).[65]

Quality Planning	Quality Control	Quality Improvement

• Establish quality goals
• Identify who are the customers
• Determine the needs of the customers
• Develop product features which respond to customers' needs
• Develop processes able to produce the product features
• Establish process controls; transfer the plans to the operating forces
	• Evaluate actual performance
	• Compare actual performance to quality goals
	• Act on the difference
		• Prove the need
		• Establish the infrastructure
		• Identify improvement projects
		• Establish project teams
		• Provide the teams with resources, training, and motivation to
		  – Diagnose the causes
		  – Stimulate remedies
		• Establish controls to hold the gains.

Table 2.3: Juran's Three Quality Management Processes (Trilogy) [Juran (1992)].

In Juran's thinking, constant efforts for quality improvement and quality cost reductions have to be undertaken, and chronic losses (due to common causes of variation) have to be tackled by "quality breakthroughs."[66] Firstly, to accomplish a quality breakthrough, managers have to justify the need for improvement, looking at the economic impact of quality problems. Secondly, an improvement project has to be set up, with participation of the relevant stakeholders. Next, the environment for breakthrough has to be built; clear responsibilities, project managers with sufficient authority to perform a diagnosis and to apply remedies. Then the problem has to be solved by performing a diagnosis on management/operator levels and then by starting a "remedial journey" to implement corrective actions.[67] Finally, the new procedures have to be integrated into the organizational standards and controls have to be put in place to guarantee a permanent effect of the breakthrough.

Philipp B. Crosby emphasizes, in his famous work "Quality is Free,"[68] that management and organizational processes – rather than statistical techniques – are likely to help a company to progress in the direction of quality,[69] and that traditional quality control programs can have a "negative and narrow" impact.[70] He also denies the existence of an economic trade-off in the domain of quality, as it is "always cheaper to do things right the first time."[71] Crosby's "quality management maturity grid" further helps to gauge the quality system of an organization, by measuring organizational behavior (such as man-

---

[64] Juran (1988), pp. 61–62; Evans and Lindsay (2002), p. 105.
[65] Juran (1992), pp. 14–16.
[66] Evans and Lindsay (2002), p. 588.
[67] Juran (1988), pp. 61–62.
[68] Crosby (1980).
[69] Evans and Lindsay (2002), p. 107.
[70] Crosby (1980), p. 9.
[71] Crosby (1980), p. 16.

agement's attitude to quality) in five stages ("uncertainty," "awakening," "enlightenment," "wisdom," and "certainty").[72] In Crosby's view, motivation and adequate behavior are key concepts for successful improvement projects. His "14-step program for quality improvement" summarizes these ideas and is reported in Table C.3 in Appendix C.3.[73]

2.1.5.2 ISO 900x Family

The European Norm ISO 9000 cites eight quality management principles helping managers to "lead an organization towards improved performance,"[74] describing the core quality activities of customer focus, leadership, involvement of people, process approach, system approach to management, continual improvement, factual approach to decision-making, and mutually beneficial supplier relationships.[75] A child of the 1980's, the ISO 9000 initiative addresses all types of industries and service enterprises, and represents a platform to build a quality system for organizations.[76] In the sense of continuous improvement, and in analogy to other quality approaches such as the PDCA cycle presented before, ISO 9000 connects the four major phases of management responsibility, resource management, product realization, and measurement/analysis/improvement in the form of a wheel (Figure 2.5).[77]

The ISO 9000 standards family encompasses the following core standards:

- ISO 9000: Quality Management Systems – Fundamentals and Vocabulary;
- ISO 9001: Quality Management Systems – Requirements;
- ISO 9004: Quality Management Systems – Guidance for Performance Improvements;
- ISO 19011: Guidelines on Quality and Environmental Auditing.

Despite its wide acceptance in practice and its nature as a *de facto* standard, many criticisms have been raised, and are still voiced against ISO 9000. Critics highlight that the standard does not represent a comprehensive business framework: meeting the ISO 9000 standard does not ensure high product or service quality, but is only a good starting point for businesses having no quality system at all.[78] As English puts it, an ISO 9000 certification should be seen merely as an intermediate step to excellence and not as a business objective in itself.[79]

---

[72] Crosby (1980), pp. 32–33.
[73] Crosby (1980), pp. 112–119.
[74] European Committee for Standardization (2000), p. 6.
[75] European Committee for Standardization (2000), p. 7.
[76] Evans and Lindsay (2002), p. 137.
[77] European Committee for Standardization (2000), p. 11.
[78] Evans and Lindsay (2002), p. 137.
[79] English (1999b), p. 50.

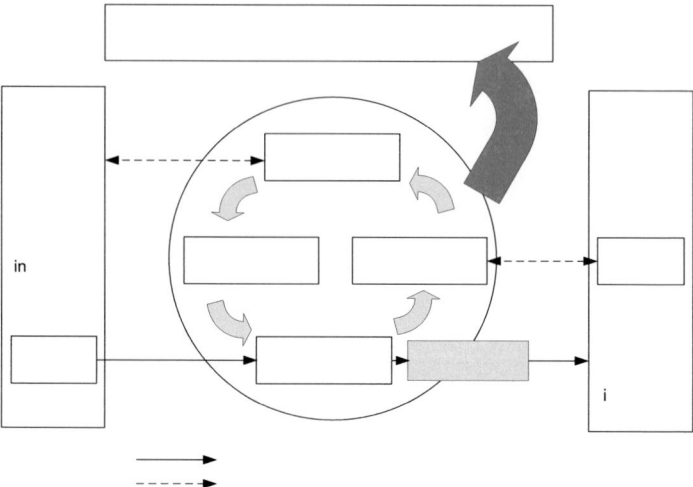

Figure 2.5: ISO 900x Component and Process Model [European Committee for Standardization (2000)].

2.1.5.3 TQM

The origins of Total Quality Management (TQM) lie in the Japan of the 1970's, from where the movement came to the U.S. in the 1980's, as a second "quality main stream" together with ISO 9000.[80] Benefits targeted by TQM include quality enhancement, customer satisfaction, zero defects, culture change, better communications, cost reduction, and flexible working practices.[81] TQM is based on the three fundamental principles of focus on customers and stakeholders, participation/teamwork by everyone in the organization, and focus on processes (supported by continuous improvement and learning).[82]

As Evans and Lindsay show, these principles were not addressed by traditional Taylorist-inspired management concepts, in which companies focused on the optimization of production, but mostly neglected customer requirements, did not use teamwork, considered "quality" as synonym for inspection, or were overstrained with removing the waste and error from production – improvements in such an environment could only be achieved through technological innovation, and not through learning and improvement of the whole organization.[83] Any support system for TQM has to include specific management practices, a set of tools and techniques, and an infrastructure containing five elements:[84]

---

[80] Sun (2000), p. 168.
[81] Currie and Hlupic (2000), pp. 15 and 27.
[82] Evans and Lindsay (2002), p. 17
[83] Evans and Lindsay (2002), p. 17.
[84] Evans and Lindsay (2002), pp. 21–23.

1. *Customer relationship management:* customer needs and customer segmentation must be the starting point of any business strategy; satisfaction and dissatisfaction signals received from customers are particularly important;

2. *Leadership and strategic planning:* for delivering quality to customers, management has to enter into (mutually beneficial) long-term relationships with customers and stakeholders;

3. *Human resources management:* for achieving quality goals, the workforce has to be committed, skilled, and attentive to customer signals;

4. *Process management:* processes have to be designed in a way that they produce quality products; they must focus on organizational learning, and must continually be improved;

5. *Data and information management:* performance has to be measured and analyzed in order to improve the operational efficiency and product conformance; information received from customers has to be analyzed and used to improve product and service design.

2.1.5.4 Six Sigma

The term "Six Sigma" relates to the normal distribution used in statistics, and carries the idea that the output of a process should be designed and controlled in a way that customer specifications are met, even if the variation of a process increases over time.[85] In a less technical language, Six Sigma management stands for "the relentless and rigorous pursuit of the reduction of variation in all critical processes to achieve continuous and breakthrough improvements that impact the bottom line and/or top line of the organization and increase customer satisfaction."[86]

Most methods and tools used in the context of Six Sigma have been adopted from earlier quality concepts; it can, however, be argued that the method is novel in the sense that it focuses on structured improvement processes, provides strong metrics for quality discussions, considers the bottom-line impact of quality, targets quick improvements, has been promoted by business managers (and not by academics or quality consultants), and uses a unique expert organization.[87]

In Six Sigma, breakthrough improvements of existing processes are using a process model containing the five steps *Define, Measure, Analyze, Improve,* and *Control* (DMAIC):[88]

---

[85] Gitlow et al. (2006), p. 16.
[86] Gitlow et al. (2006), p. 15.
[87] Gitlow et al. (2006), p. 28.
[88] Evans and Lindsay (2002), p. 600; El-Haik and Roy (2005), pp. 29–30; Gitlow et al. (2006), p. 22.

1. *Define (D):* customers and their requirements are analyzed; improvement projects are selected by considering their strategic and operational business impact; customer relevant, so-called "Critical-to-Quality" (CTQ) characteristics are identified;

2. *Measure (M):* the way to measure the performance of a process is defined, performance is measured with regard to CTQs;

3. *Analyze (A):* the most likely causes of defects are detected and the drivers of variability of the process are identified;

4. *Improve (I):* the causes of the defects are removed, the acceptable range for process variation is identified, and changes for improving a process are carried out;

5. *Control (C):* process improvements have to be integrated permanently in the business system; procedures and tools have to be put in place to ensure that quality limits are not exceeded.

While the DMAIC approach targets the improvement of *existing* processes and designs, "Design for Six Sigma" (DFSS) seeks to create *new* processes and products that are consistently of high quality,[89] are based on customer needs, resource efficient, minimal in complexity, robust to process variation, capable of generating high yields, and "quick to generate a profit."[90] The five-phase DMADV model is a very popular "flavor" of DFSS,[91] standing for *Define, Measure, Analyze, Design,* and *Verify:*[92]

1. *Define (D):* the objectives of the new product, process, or service are defined, and a business case of the project is established, showing the expected benefits of the design (e.g., reduced or avoided costs), the resources needed, and the related risks;[93]

2. *Measure (M):* customer needs are identified in terms of CTQ (e.g., using QFD design considerations), prioritized, and measured;[94]

3. *Analyze (A):* CTQ are broken down into "Critical-to-Process" (CTP) parts; high-level design concepts and process options likely to meet CTP requirements are analyzed and selected;[95]

4. *Design (D):* the product, process, or service is designed according to requirements, measurement systems are integrated;[96]

5. *Verify (V):* (also called "Validate" phase) the performance and the ability to meet the requirements are verified, e.g., using a prototype which is built and pilot tested.[97]

---

[89] El-Haik and Roy (2005), p. 33.
[90] Gitlow et al. (2006), p. 26.
[91] Gitlow et al. (2006), p. xxiv.
[92] El-Haik and Roy (2005), p. 43; Gitlow et al. (2006), pp. xxv–xxvi and 27–28.
[93] Gitlow et al. (2006), p. 78.
[94] Gitlow et al. (2006), p. 108.
[95] Gitlow et al. (2006), pp. 158 and 161.
[96] Gitlow et al. (2006), p. 208.
[97] Gitlow et al. (2006), p. 250.

Figure 2.6 summarizes the steps proposed by both Six Sigma project patterns, DMAIC and DMADV.[98]

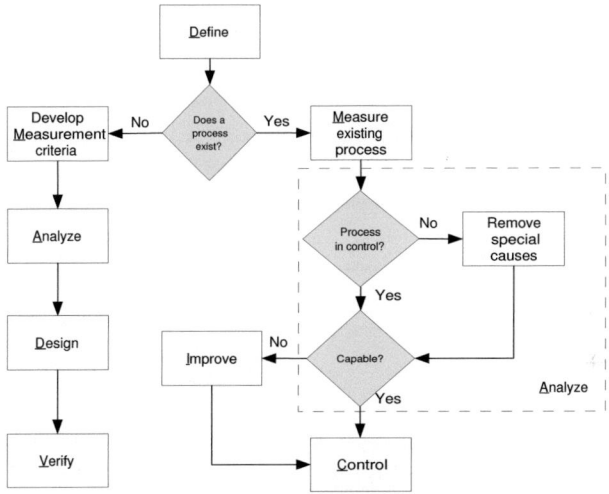

Figure 2.6: Six Sigma DMAIC and DMADV Pattern Overview [Pyzdek (2003)].

2.1.5.5   Balanced Scorecard

Many of the early performance measurement systems in organizations lacked coordination, showed a tendency to reward the wrong behavior, focused on business functions rather than processes, and only measured quantities, not qualities.[99] In attempt to better link strategies and performance measurement, Kaplan and Norton have developed the BSC, a tool to transparently communicate corporate vision and strategy, which uses both lagging (concerning the outcome) and leading (driving) measures.[100] Four perspectives describe a BSC in its most common form (cf. also Figure 2.7):[101]

1. *Financial perspective:* Traditionally, financial data has been the primary object of enterprise performance evaluation. Profitability or growth of revenue are typical measurements in this domain. In the light of financial regulatory requirements such as SOX, financial risk assessments also have to be considered.

---

[98] Pyzdek (2003).

[99] Evans and Lindsay (2002), p. 455.

[100] Evans and Lindsay (2002), p. 455.

[101] Kaplan and Norton (1996), p. 9.

2. *Customer perspective:* Any organization needs to find ways to successfully interact with customers. Indicators for the success of a customer strategy are, e.g., the level of service or customer satisfaction indices.

3. *Internal perspective:* Internal processes are responsible for business results, such as productivity or cycle time. Any organization has to develop its processes in order to improve productivity or to respond faster to customer requirements.

4. *Innovation and learning perspective:* The people and the infrastructure in an enterprise are the base of its success or failure; learning how to adopt new processes or to develop new skills is a prerequisite for the survival of any business organization.

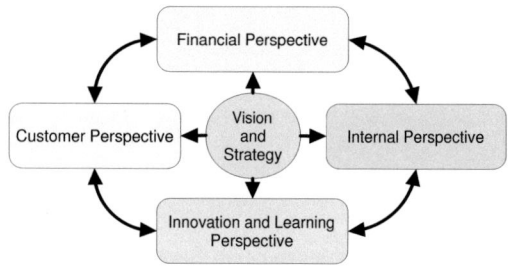

Figure 2.7: Balanced Scorecard [Kaplan and Norton (1996)].

2.2 Data, Information, and Related Concepts

On the way to a discussion of data quality, the terminology used in this area must briefly be reviewed, as most authors see a hierarchy between data, information, and related concepts. As an example, Alter presents the relationship between data, information, and knowledge, as shown in Figure 2.8: data forms the base for distilling information, the use of information in actions leads to results and, as a consequence, to an accumulation of knowledge, which in turn influences all other transformations.[102]

2.2.1 Data

2.2.1.1 Definitions of Data

Following a classification proposed by Redman, six different views on "data" can be distinguished:[103]

---

[102] Alter (2002), p. 69.
[103] Redman (1996), p. 228.

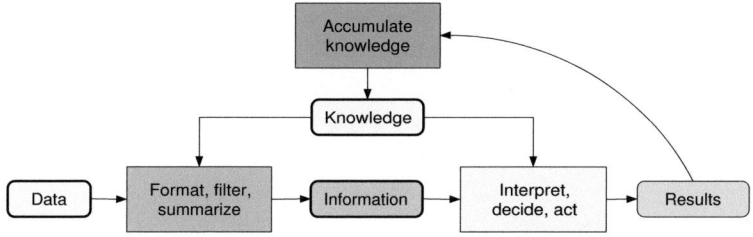

Figure 2.8: Relationship between Data, Information, and Knowledge [Alter (2002)].

1. *Data as a set of facts:* Data can be considered as a synonym for facts,[104] or as "streams of raw facts representing events occurring in organizations or the physical environment before [being] organized and arranged into a form that people can understand and use."[105] In addition, Alter distinguishes "soft" and "hard" data: hard data is related to "hard" facts, whereas soft data is intuitive or subjective, and collected by informal means such as talking to people.[106] The fact-centered concept can also be broadened by defining data as the "representation of facts, concepts, or instructions in a formalized manner suitable for communication, interpretation, or processing by humans or by automatic means."[107]

2. *Data as a result of measurements:* Data can be the result of measurement processes;[108] nevertheless, many types of data do not stem from observation, as the example of the social security number shows.[109]

3. *Data as raw material for information:* Data represents the individual facts and the raw material for producing information.[110] "Raw" data is a relative term as data processing commonly occurs in stages, and the data processed in one stage may be the raw data of the next.

4. *Data as symbols:* Data can be defined as symbols, images, sounds, and ideas that can be coded, stored, and transmitted.[111]

5. *Data as surrogates for real-world objects and concepts:* Data can represent portions of the real world in information systems;[112] the term "real world," however, should be broadened to "external world," since many things have no counterpart in the

---

[104] Brackett (2000), p. 2.
[105] Laudon and Laudon (2000), p. 7.
[106] Alter (2002), p. 71.
[107] U.S. Department of Defense (2007), p. 142.
[108] Evans and Lindsay (2002), p. 510.
[109] Redman (1996), p. 228.
[110] Brackett (1994), p. 7; English (1999b), p. 52.
[111] Lawrence (1999), p. 3.
[112] Wand and Wang (1996), p. 88.

"real" world. Historical information is no longer (or has never been, in the case of falsifications) "real," and plans will never reflect any "reality" in a database.[113]

6. *Data as representable triple (entity, attribute, value):* This definition, derived from database research, considers a data item as a representable triple `<entity,attribute,value>`, containing a representation allowing it to be stored as a (physical) record.[114]

2.2.1.2 Data Management and Databases

Data management covers the activities of planning, procuring, administrating, and using data resources in an enterprise, as well as the management of the organizational units responsible for executing those processes.[115] The objective of data management is to ensure the high quality of enterprise data, over their entire life-cycle, and to obtain a maximum "return on data."[116] Depending on its nature, data can be managed in structured form, e.g., in a relational database system, or in non-structured form, such as non-text storage media for voice and image data.[117]

A database is a structured collection of electronically stored data that is controlled and accessed through computers, based on predefined relationships between predefined types of data items, related to a specific business, situation, or problem.[118] To effectively store and access data, a data model is used to describe the structures of a database in which data is stored or accessed.[119] Data models can be checked for well-formedness and the degree of fidelity of the image they carry; in order to be well-formed, a data model has to exclude any ambiguity, all entities and relationships must be clearly identified, and it has to "faithfully describe the world it is supposed to represent."[120] Standardized data models have also been created by industry groups to facilitate software interoperability; an example is the Retail Data Model created by the Association for Retail Technology Standards (ARTS).[121]

Hornberger and Schneider provide a concise definition stating which kind of data has to be included in an organizational data model, in order to promote a fair, legitimate, explicit, adequate, relevant, not excessive, and accurate use of data:[122]

---

[113] Kent (1987), pp. 16–18.
[114] Redman (1996), p. 230.
[115] Schwinn et al. (1999), p. 36.
[116] Schwinn et al. (1999), p. 149.
[117] Huang et al. (1999), p. 146.
[118] Alter (2002), p. 137.
[119] Alter (2002), p. 140; Geiger (2007).
[120] Watson (2002), pp. 160–161.
[121] ARTS (1997).
[122] Hornberger and Schneider (2000), p. 238.

1. Only capture data which is really needed;

2. Use data only for its intended use;

3. Inform all partners about the purpose and intent of its use;

4. Forward data only if it is in the sense of partnership;

5. Communicate openly about the status and the location of data;

6. Keep data current, update outdated (and otherwise incorrect) data;

7. Leave partner organizations the ownership over their data;

8. While collecting data, avoid anything that could harm the partner.

A Database Management System (DBMS) is an integrated set of programs used to define, update, and control databases.[123] DBMS are today most often based on the relational model;[124] relational DBMS have encountered enormous success and the Structured Query Language (SQL)[125] is today considered as the "lingua franca of data access."[126]

2.2.1.3   Use of Data in Organizations

Even if data is "inert" and does not directly confer any particular benefit to an organization,[127] it is the "fuel" to make (business) decisions, as the history of all activities in a business organization is reflected by data. Important industries such as insurance or banking companies can even be considered as "data processing engines."[128] Several categories of data may be relevant in a business context:

- Master data (containing attributes for describing core business objects such as customers, products, or suppliers),

- Transaction data (created perpetually by business processes, resulting from the combination of master and event-related data for describing business events),[129] and

- Meta-data ("data about data," e.g., the description of the data structure or source).[130]

Business data is often created as a by-product of business transactions which, "like waste material from manufacturing processes, is disposed of at the end of the process."[131] This view may lead to a wrong perception of data: managing data as a mere by-product of business processes will lead to a situation in which data fails to meet many users' needs, when they expect data to be as a product on its own.[132]

---

[123] Alter (2002), p. 138.
[124] Codd (1970); Astrahan et al. (1976).
[125] Chamberlin and Boyce (1974).
[126] Seltzer (2008), p. 52.
[127] Kelly (1997), p. 4.
[128] Olson (2003), p. 3.
[129] Wermers (2000), p. 64.
[130] Brackett (1994), p. 14.
[131] Kelly (1997), p. 5.
[132] Huang et al. (1999), pp. 9–10 and 21.

2.2.2 Information

2.2.2.1 Definitions of Information

Information has been touted as an economic driver of the "information age," and as an important input (and output) of knowledge-intensive business processes.[133] Information can be used for planning, executing, and controlling; planning is about the future, execution is about the present, and control is about the past – in all three situations, information is needed for supporting business activities and is exposed to specific threats.[134] Information is also (when used in context) the base for knowledge, which in turn is required to control a system.[135]

Most authors agree that information is based on data, needs some form of context or interpretation,[136] and has to be relevant and useful to the recipient at a specific time, for a specific purpose.[137] The purpose of information may consist of simple descriptions of statements about customers, products, or market situations, or may be requests for action that demand a certain behavior.[138] Depending on the focus, information can be regarded by looking at the creation process, as a series of activities during which information is generated or absorbed, but it can also be considered as the result of the creation process.[139] Information has the highest likelihood of being useful if it is integrated into structured business processes and is used by people with the knowledge and training needed to interpret and apply it correctly;[140] English consequently uses the term "knowledge worker" to designate the persons who are using information, via an information system.[141]

A piece of information may be absolutely unusable for some knowledge worker, but may be indispensable for another; also, an information object can be of no interest today, but may become vital the next day.[142] Lesca and Lesca show that the concept of a user's "information needs" often does not exist: many people cannot state which kind of information they need, in order to be able to perform a given task.[143]

Some authors use the term "information" as a synonym for "data,"[144] a terminology Redman qualifies as "unacceptable."[145] Data and information are, in reality, often difficult

---

[133] Eppler (2003), p. 19.

[134] Alter (2002), p. 107.

[135] Ackoff (1989), p. 4.

[136] Kelly (1997), p. 4; Davenport (1999b), p. 25; English (1999b), p. 18; Huang et al. (1999), p. 146; Laudon and Laudon (2000), p. 7; Alter (2002), p. 70; Eppler (2003), p. 19.

[137] Brackett (1994), p. 8; Brackett (2000), p. 11.

[138] Königer and Reithmayer (1998), p. 73.

[139] Lesca and Lesca (1995), pp. 29–30.

[140] Alter (2002), p. 69.

[141] English (1999b), pp. 19 and 55.

[142] Lesca and Lesca (1995), p. 79.

[143] Lesca and Lesca (1995), p. 80.

[144] Cf., e.g., Huang et al. (1999), p. 146, Wang et al. (2001), p. 2, or Pipino et al. (2002), p. 212.

[145] Redman (1996), p. 227.

to differentiate: the same piece of information for one person can be a data item for another. The natural ambiguity of the concepts of "data" and "information" is resolved in the context of a situation; this capability is, however, lost when the same facts are used in multiple contexts, when data "gets integrated into a database serving multiple applications" and "assumptions appropriate to the context of one application may not fit the contexts of other applications."[146]

In the remainder of this thesis, the concepts of "data" and "information" will be distinguished as follows: data corresponds to the sum of individual facts, represents the raw material for producing information,[147] and is typically machine-readable.[148] Information, on the other hand, is data that has been adapted to a particular context,[149] is meaningful and useful to human beings,[150] and allows users to ask questions and make statements about situations.[151]

2.2.2.2 Information Management

Schwinn et al. define information management as the set of conceptual, technical, methodical, and organizational measures used to obtain high quality in information production processes in an organization.[152] From an information logistics viewpoint, the general intent of information management is to "provide the right information, in the right format and quantity, at the right time, to the right person, at reasonable costs."[153] Good information management helps an organization to make sure that customers are receiving the requested level of service, that workers get feedback to verify their progress, that reward and recognition systems are provided with accurate information about individual and group performance, and that the costs of operations can be reduced through better planning and improvement actions.[154] Information ownership should be attached to persons, in order to define responsibility for information products or classes of data records; even if data is shared or referenced in different contexts, this responsibility should not change.[155] As data in organizations is usually distributed over several IT systems, data management and enforcement of responsibility for information often has to be centralized.[156]

---

[146] Kent (1987), p. 3.
[147] Brackett (1994), p. 7.
[148] Huang et al. (1999), p. 146.
[149] Alter (2002), p. 70.
[150] Laudon and Laudon (2000), p. 7.
[151] Eppler (2003), p. 19.
[152] Schwinn et al. (1999), p. 224.
[153] Schwinn et al. (1999), p. 225; Eppler (2003), p. 10.
[154] Evans and Lindsay (2002), p. 450.
[155] Königer and Reithmayer (1998), pp. 74–75 and 175.
[156] Lesca and Lesca (1995), p. 154.

2.2.2.3   Analogy between Physical Products and Information Products

When the creation, management, and usage processes of data in organizations are analyzed, it is quite evident that information (products) can be considered as a result of a manufacturing process.[157] Consequently, many authors have proposed manufacturing management approaches to the treatment of data and its conversion to information; English further extends the concept of information manufacturing to an entire "information supply chain," describing the roles of information producers and information intermediaries, who "transcribe data from one form into another."[158]

Information products also differ from physical products in several ways: they are not consumable, depend on the context, are copyable at will, their value does not diminish with use, they are fragile but not fungible (unlike money), suffer from time lags (affecting currency), can be used by several applications or persons nearly simultaneously, and are of almost unlimited supply (e.g., as by-products of business processes).[159]

2.2.3   Knowledge

Information can be transformed into knowledge when it is correctly interpreted and connected with prior knowledge, for guiding actions and decisions;[160] conversely, information can be defined as any stimulus that has changed a recipient's knowledge.[161] With regard to the IT system domain, Lee and Strong identify three types of knowledge needed: "knowing-what" is factual knowledge about activities and relationships, "knowing-how" refers to procedures, and "knowing-why" is characterized as contextual knowledge that "enables inquirers to direct questions based on understanding relevant purposes and underlying principles."[162]

2.2.4   Information Systems

In a very broad definition, an organization's information system consists of the entire collection of data sources and related information service capabilities, both internal and external to the organization, from which the users of the system can obtain messages about the internal operations (e.g., business transactions) and the evolution of the environment.[163] In another broad approach, an information system is composed of three inter-

---

[157]Lesca and Lesca (1995), p. 124; Wang et al. (1998); Schwinn et al. (1999), p. 229.

[158]English (1999b), pp. 53 and 57.

[159]Redman (1996), pp. 13, 42, and 233–234.

[160]Huang et al. (1999), p. 146; Alter (2002), p. 70; Eppler (2003), p. 19.

[161]Lawrence (1999), p. 2.

[162]Lee and Strong (2004), p. 14.

[163]Lesca and Lesca (1995), p. 51; English (1999b), p. 52; Lawrence (1999), p. 7; Brady et al. (2001), p. 13; Batini and Scannapieco (2006), p. 9.

related concepts: people, organization, and technologies,[164] where "organization" stands for a social system deserving as much attention as the technological and the business environments.[165] As the purpose of an information system is to show a selection of aspects of an external reality, "the lawful states of [a good] information system should reflect the lawful states of the real-world system."[166]

Two fundamentally different views on information systems are possible: an external view (considering the system as a "black box," addressing its purpose, justification, and deployment in an organization) and an internal view (addressing the software design and operation needed to obtain a required functionality).[167] As to the users of IT systems, Strong et al. identified the types of data producers (generating data), data custodians (who provide and manage data resources), and data consumers (who use data); to each of the three roles, specific tasks or processes can be attached.[168]

Information systems may help users to analyze problems, visualize complex subjects, and create new products,[169] serving as a backbone for information logistics.[170] A Management Information System (MIS) provides managers with information for managing their organization, supporting decision-making, coordination, and control.[171] The usage of the latest IT system technology in this domain is, however, no guarantee for better business performance: better information systems may have no effect on the performance of a business process if the limiting factors are the characteristics of the business process or the participants.[172]

2.2.5   Definition of Data Quality and Data Quality Management

2.2.5.1   Applicability of Quality Management Practices to Data

In the field of manufacturing, an extensive body of literature on quality management, with principles, guidelines, and techniques for managing product quality exists.[173] In view of this, several authors have discussed whether findings of quality management research and practice can be transferred to the domain of data quality. An interesting historical note in this context is the fact that, before W. Edward Deming went to Japan for his studies and teaching, he applied statistical control principles to data and the "production

---

[164] Lesca and Lesca (1995), p. 53.
[165] Pasmore (1988), p. 49.
[166] Wand and Wang (1996), p. 89.
[167] Huang et al. (1999), pp. 34–35.
[168] Strong et al. (1997b), p. 104; Lee and Strong (2004), p. 17.
[169] Laudon and Laudon (2000), p. 7.
[170] Evans and Lindsay (2002), p. 450.
[171] Alter (2002), p. 200.
[172] Alter (2002), p. 47.
[173] Wang et al. (2001), p. 3.

of information," when he was working for the 1940 U.S. census.[174] Likewise, when analyzing supplier and customer interactions, Joseph M. Juran was deeply interested in "data manufacturing" in collaborative processes.[175]

The application of quality management methods to data quality can be justified with the arguments that an information product (such as a report(can be seen as a result of a production process and that the concept of "conformance to specifications" in the design and manufacturing of data appears natural.[176] Moreover, customer orientation in information product design and manufacturing, focusing on end customers, internal knowledge workers, and external stakeholders is a common approach in the data quality literature.[177] As much as quality management, data quality management is an "applied" and cross-functional discipline, targeting technology, organizational processes, and technical issues.[178] On the other side, the very distinct nature of data[179] may require a special approach to quality management:[180] limitations of the analogy between physical and information products must be considered, e.g., when it comes to quality attributes such as "timeliness" or "believability" of facts, which have no counterpart in the physical properties domain,[181] due to the abstract character of data.[182]

In the economic context considered in this study, data quality is always embedded in an organizational setting in which quality programs have been implemented for many years. For this reason, data quality management programs will have to build, to the extent possible, on the existing organizational quality management infrastructure. Also, data is often an intermediary product of quality management, as the measurement of quality generates data; quality management includes comprehensive data management activities, which can be supported by the usage of specific software packages.[183] In the case of *data* quality management, the same types of quality measurement data are created and the same data-oriented software tools can be used; there are, however, also methods and tools which are specific to IT systems, which will be addressed later in Section 2.5.

---

[174] English (1999b), p. 43.
[175] Juran (1988), p. 12; English (1999b), p. 44.
[176] Veregin (1998); Wang et al. (2001), p. 3.
[177] Cf., e.g., English (1999b), p. 52; Huang et al. (1999), p. 17.
[178] Ballou et al. (2004), p. 10.
[179] Cf. Section 2.2.2.3.
[180] Eppler (2003), pp. 8 and 17–18.
[181] Wang et al. (2001), p. 3.
[182] Schwinn et al. (1999), p. 229.
[183] Such as the "Quality Companion" from Minitab, http://www.minitab.com/products/qualitycompanion/.

2.2.5.2 Data Quality from a Quality Management Perspective

Only if the quality of the data contained in and retrieved from an IT system is adequate, data users can find, trust, access, and share data.[184] In analogy to physical products, the quality of data or information products such as reports can be defined and measured by using the quality concepts presented in Section 2.1.1. Firstly, objective attributes such as granularity, completeness, validity, or consistency of an information product determine the "conformance to specifications" of the underlying data.[185] Secondly, starting from a data consumer view, data quality can be defined as a situation in which knowledge worker and consumer expectations are consistently met.[186] With the concept of the transcendent quality in mind,[187] Ballou et al. state that "if users of the data feel that its quality (...) is sufficient for their needs, then, from their perspective, at least, the quality of the information available to them is fine."[188] Data consumers typically expect that data is relevant to the context of their job, correct and consistent, up-to-date, formatted in a way that suits intended usage, accessible, secure, and private; visibly, these expectations are organization and job context specific, and may vary among individuals.[189]

2.2.5.3 Data and Information Quality Management

Some authors distinguish between data and information quality management, when discussing objectives, methods, and tools. Eppler argues that data quality problems can be resolved using data cleansing, data profiling, or statistical process control, while information quality problems require an in-depth analysis of the business context, changes in work practices, and instruments such as design guidelines, publishing policies, validation rules, or new authoring processes.[190]

Price and Shanks interpret data quality from a product-based perspective, as being characterized by quality criteria such as completeness and accuracy, characteristics that are accessible to objective measures; information quality includes an additional "service-based perspective," taking into account the user-related components of a quality description, with descriptors such as "timeliness," "relevancy," or "accessibility."[191] While the data itself stemming from an IT system is important, the delivery processes are also vital for successful usage of an information system by data consumers.

---

[184]Brackett (2000), p. 20.
[185]SAP (2004a).
[186]English (1999b), p. 24; Price and Shanks (2004), p. 659.
[187]Cf. Section 2.1.1.
[188]Ballou et al. (2004), p. 10.
[189]Wand and Wang (1996), p. 88.
[190]Eppler (2003), p. 25.
[191]Price and Shanks (2004), p. 659.

Brackett agrees that information quality is determined by the quality of the data used to create information;[192] in the context of MIS, data quality determines the perception of decision-related risks and the degree of uncertainty perceived by decision makers.[193] On the other hand, not all data elements in an organization need to be complete or accurate, in order for managers to make good decisions. In the case of data warehousing, correct decisions can still be made even when working with erroneous data, if data warehouse users are aware of the presence of low quality data and know how to deal with it.[194]

Finally, data quality must clearly be separated from software quality: even a perfectly designed software application cannot detect and insulate all kinds of entry and process-ing errors, and will give wrong results when fed with wrong data. Conversely, a poorly designed application will likely become an important source of data errors.

2.2.6 Classification of Data Quality Attributes

Data quality is – as much as quality – a subjective and multi-faceted concept encompass-ing multiple dimensions.[195] Data quality that is sufficient for "operational processes" in one context may be insufficient in other contexts, such as analytic applications;[196] data quality finally resides "in the eye of the beholder."[197] Besides "objective" data quality characteristics such as the accuracy of data values, dozens of external factors influence a customer's perception of the quality of data or an information product;[198] the follow-ing sections will briefly explain the elements of data quality, their relationships, and their association to information systems.

2.2.6.1 Attribute Hierarchies and Classification

Data quality attributes often overlap in their meaning, or are composed of other attributes: as an example, the usefulness of a given data element will be determined by its accuracy, timeliness, completeness, and consistency. In such a case, one attribute is used to define the other, a means that is insufficient for defining either.[199] In the same line, Eppler proposes a list of sixteen basic quality criteria, of which twelve have to be traded off with

---

[192] Brackett (2000), p. 11.
[193] Ritchie and Brindley (2001), p. 32.
[194] English (1999b), p. 25.
[195] Wang et al. (1995a), p. 369; Wand and Wang (1996), p. 87; Huang et al. (1999), p. 33; Wang et al. (2001), p. 4.
[196] English (1999b), p. 5; Schwinn et al. (1999), p. 209.
[197] Wang et al. (1993), p. 672.
[198] Arnold (1992), p. 36.
[199] Wand and Wang (1996), p. 87.

other criteria.[200] Finally, data quality criteria may contradict each other, as easy access to data may conflict, e.g., with requirements for security, privacy, and confidentiality.[201]

Depending on the role of IT users (who might be, e.g., data collectors, custodians, or consumers),[202] some attributes may be more important than others. As an example, data collectors are anxious to get relevant, accurate, and complete data; data custodians primarily focus on complete, accurate, and timely data; data consumers finally may be interested first in relevant data.[203]

Quality attributes of data can be categorized by many dimensions, e.g., by making the following distinctions:

- Quality of the data model, the data values, the presentation of data, or the information technology used;[204]
- A conceptual view (addressing content, scope, level of detail, composition, consistency, and reaction to change), the data values (characterized by accuracy, consistency, completeness, or currency), and the representation of data (including questions of format and physical instances);[205]
- Content-related criteria (describing intrinsic properties of data), technical criteria (related to the data processing system), intellectual criteria (containing the more subjective aspects), and instantiation-related criteria (describing the presentation of the data to the user);[206]
- Aspects related to the user (providing subject-criteria scores), the data processing stage (providing process-criteria scores), and the data source (providing object-criteria scores);[207]
- Intrinsic quality of data (e.g., accuracy of values, conformance to business rules), data definition (e.g., relevance), and data presentation (e.g., accessibility, timeliness, or interpretability);[208]
- Time, form, and content considerations.[209]

Several authors have attempted to analyze the many facets of data quality in a "divide-and-conquer" manner, using grouping criteria ("dimensions").[210]

---

[200] Eppler (2003), p. 75.
[201] Strong et al. (1997a), p. 44.
[202] Cf. Section 2.2.4.
[203] Lee and Strong (2004), p. 31.
[204] Redman (1996), p. 20.
[205] Redman (1996), p. 267.
[206] Naumann (2002), p. 30.
[207] Naumann (2002), p. 41.
[208] English (1999b), pp. 27–30.
[209] Aiken (1996), p. 36.
[210] Wang et al. (1995a), p. 351; Wang and Strong (1996) – a discussion of and numerous examples for the dimensions presented by Wang and Strong can be found in Rohweder et al. (2008), pp. 32–43; Wang et al. (2001), p. 5.

Firstly, Wand and Wang propose a matrix with internal (design, operation) vs. external (use, value), and data-related vs. system-related data quality dimensions (Table 2.4).[211] Visibly, the classification of data quality attributes is not always unique: as an example, timeliness can be understood, on the one hand, as the situation in which data values are up-to-date (internal view, data-related); on the other hand, timeliness can be the state of availability of output on time (external view, system-related).[212]

View	Dimensions	
	Data-Related	System-Related
Internal	Accuracy, reliability, timeliness, completeness, currency, consistency, precision	Reliability
External	Timeliness, relevance, content, importance, sufficiency, usableness, usefulness, clarity, conciseness, freedom from bias, informativeness, level of detail, quantitativeness, scope, interpretability, understandability	Timeliness, flexibility, format, efficiency.

Table 2.4: Internal and External Data Quality Dimensions [Wand and Wang (1996)].

Then Wang et al. present a four-level classification scheme of data quality dimensions, which exhibits the fact that some of the attributes are composed of others and a hierarchy among the "dimensions" of the attributes exists (Figure 2.9).[213]

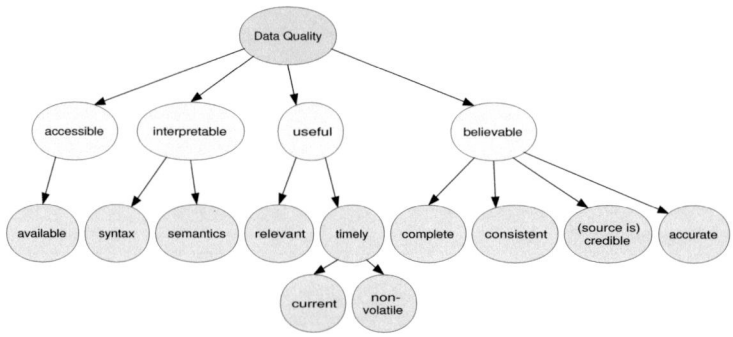

Figure 2.9: Decomposition of Data Quality Dimensions [Wang et al. (1995a)].

As a last example, Liu and Chi propose a data quality life cycle comprising the phases of data collection, data organization, data presentation, and data application, during which data quality problems can appear.[214] For each of the four phases, Liu and Chi define a set of five or six quality attributes that can be influenced at that stage (Figure 2.10).[215]

---

[211] Wand and Wang (1996), p. 92.
[212] Wand and Wang (1996), p. 93.
[213] Wang et al. (1995a), p. 350.
[214] Liu and Chi (2002), p. 259.
[215] Liu and Chi (2002), p. 302.

Figure 2.10: Evolutional Data Quality [Liu and Chi (2002)].

2.2.6.2 Data Quality Attribute Overview

As no general consensus on the relative importance of quality attributes exists, only a selection of the most often cited quality attributes will be discussed in this section, using the "top-ten" attributes from the ranking established by Wand and Wang.[216] For all attributes, a dimensional classification,[217] an overview of definitions found in the literature, and examples for problems with regard to the data quality attribute will be provided.

Accuracy (Internal View, Data-Related)

Data elements are accurate if they are sufficiently precise for a given purpose,[218] correct, and free of error.[219] A further differentiation can be made between semantic accuracy (the correct data value) and syntactic accuracy (the membership of a value to a reference domain).[220] Redman shows that finding "the true" data value, reflecting exactly a state in an external world, can be very difficult, as more than one correct value may exist, or a correct value may not exist at all, e.g., when regarding the employee number of a person who has not yet been assigned an identification number).[221] To specify the type of accuracy, English separates "accuracy to surrogate source" (equality with another authoritative source) from "accuracy to reality," which describes the representation of real-world facts by the data.[222] Moreover, as data is accurate if an observed value is close enough to an accepted reference value or standard,[223] increasing the frequency of measurement is a typical way to increase time-related accuracy.[224]

Threats to accuracy include the inherent variability or volatility of the external world facts being measured, the way they are measured, and inadequate data entry controls

---

[216] Wand and Wang (1996), pp. 92–94.
[217] As proposed by Wand and Wang, cf. Table 2.4.
[218] Brackett (1994), p. 145; Schwinn et al. (1999), p. 211.
[219] Lee and Strong (2004), p. 18.
[220] Batini and Scannapieco (2006), pp. 20–21.
[221] Redman (1996), p. 255.
[222] English (1999b), p. 142.
[223] Alter (2002), p. 163; Evans and Lindsay (2002), p. 658; Batini and Scannapieco (2006), p. 20.
[224] Brackett (1994), p. 146; Batini and Scannapieco (2006), p. 29.

and procedures for correcting mistakes.[225] Syntactic accuracy can typically be enforced through "edit checks" (predetermined constraints[226]) or data cleansing ("scrubbing"[227]) procedures; semantic accuracy may be much more difficult to ensure, as the example provided by Aiken shows: is a numerical value of 289.34 accurate, or simply rounded up from 289.336, or must a markup of 10% be added if a "robust" image of an external world situation has to be reported?[228]

Reliability (Internal View, Data-Related)

In a general quality context, reliability describes the ability of a product to perform as specified or expected.[229] From a data usage perspective, reliability refers to the trust (credibility) users have in their data and the data sources.[230] Often, the sources of data or the various processes applied to produce an information product remain, however, unclear. Most end-users wish to know the source of the data they access, as this source knowledge may help them to apply their judgment to the credibility of the data.[231] A data source tagging approach, which consists of attaching source information to a data item at the cell level, may be a solution to increasing credibility;[232] as an example, Wang et al. propose data source tagging using an attribute-based model, by introducing a specific quality indicator algebra.[233]

Timeliness (Internal View, Data-Related; External View, System-Related)

Timeliness can be expressed in terms of the amount of time that has passed since the data was produced, or the extent to which the age of the data is appropriate for a specific task and user,[234] i.e., is up-to-date or sufficiently "fresh."[235] Related to the timely availability, the existence and accessibility of data to consumers are also relevant.[236]

Relevance (External View, Data-Related)

In a decision-making context, cost-effective decisions can only be achieved by using rel-

---

[225] Alter (2002), p. 165.
[226] Winkler (2004), p. 531.
[227] Watson (2002), p. 371.
[228] Aiken (1996), p. 35.
[229] Evans and Lindsay (2002), p. 763.
[230] Schwinn et al. (1999), p. 211.
[231] Wang et al. (2001), p. 20.
[232] Wang et al. (1993), p. 673; Redman (2001), p. 132.
[233] Wang et al. (1995a), p. 354.
[234] Alter (2002), p. 163.
[235] Bouzeghoub and Peralta (2004), p. 59; Lee and Strong (2004), p. 18; Batini and Scannapieco (2006), p. 29.
[236] English (1999b), p. 143; Schwinn et al. (1999), p. 211; Alter (2002), p. 163.

evant data.[237] Data items have to be significant for the context they are assigned to,[238] i.e., they have to be either explicitly required by end users or applications[239] or otherwise useful for a task.[240] Relevance may often be connected with availability, completeness, or the source of data: depending on who or what produced the data, it may be more or less relevant.[241] Redman argues that explicit requirements for data relevance can be very difficult to state, and recommends that any organization should only collect and store data which is (or will very soon be) required, applying a criterion of "essentialness."[242]

Completeness (Internal View, Data-Related)

Completeness of data can be described as the extent to which data is available (not missing)[243] and adequate for a given task.[244] In a more technical approach, completeness can integrate three distinct characteristics, namely schema completeness (concepts and properties are not missing in a database schema), column completeness (as a measure of the existence of values in a column or property), and population completeness (all values exist, with regard to a reference population).[245]

Completeness should just cover the needs of all applications – but not more, as too much irrelevant data can slow down the performance of any IT system. Not only current but also future demand for data has to be included in the design of an information system, even if it is difficult and often almost impossible to include *every* relevant data item, and managers are typically forced to act and to take decisions in a state of incomplete information.[246]

Currency (Internal View, Data-Related)

In a dynamic environment, facts in some external worlds are constantly changing, a situation which leads to a "downward spiral" of data quality, if no corrective action is taken.[247] Currency expresses the extent of the delay between a change in the external world and the update of the related data in the database.[248] Currency can also be considered as the promptness of updates, often directly measurable by analyzing the "last update" entry in a data table.[249]

---

[237] Al-Najjar and Kans (2006), p. 619.
[238] Schwinn et al. (1999), p. 211.
[239] Redman (1996), p. 248.
[240] Lee and Strong (2004), p. 18.
[241] Alter (2002), p. 163.
[242] Redman (1996), p. 249.
[243] English (1999b), p. 142; Lee and Strong (2004), p. 18.
[244] Brackett (1994), p. 148; Redman (1996), p. 256; Alter (2002), p. 163.
[245] Batini and Scannapieco (2006), p. 24.
[246] Redman (1996), p. 249.
[247] Brackett (2000), p. 10.
[248] Redman (1996), p. 258.
[249] Batini and Scannapieco (2006), p. 29.

Consistency (Internal View, Data-Related)

In the database literature, consistency is often seen as a related but slightly opposed concept to data integrity. As an example, Sinha sees consistency constraints as specifying a relationship between two or more data items, while integrity constraints describe the (absolute) "to be" characteristics of data.[250] Consistency is an important concept in database technology, as a part of the four transaction quality characteristics known as the "Atomicity, Consistency, Isolation, Durability" (ACID) properties: atomicity (all elements exist either at the same time or not at all), consistency (respect of protocols, correctness of transformation, or conformance to rules), isolation (operations are independent from each other), and durability (effects survive failures) should guarantee that transactions in a database are processed as expected.[251] Eswaran et al. describe consistency as a dynamic concept, in which consistency constraints cannot be enforced immediately at any (insert or update) operation, but only at the end of transactions.[252] Consistency problems most often arise due to overlaps among data collections which are, e.g., caused by uncontrolled redundancy.[253] As Redman notes, "consistent" data, having successfully passed data edits and database constraints, is not necessarily correct – it simply fulfills predefined structural requirements, and may not correspond to any real external world "fact."[254]

Integrity can be seen as a set of rules that must not be violated when entering or manipulating data; if a database is in a state of integrity, no known integrity rule is violated.[255] Brackett describes four levels of data integrity: integrity of values (describing the allowable values), structures (integrity of relations, qualified by attributes such as "required" or "optional"), derivation (specifying how data has to be derived from other data), and retention (preventing the loss of critical business data through updates or deletions).[256] Tasker also proposes four levels of integrity, however with a different focus: validation of individual characters (e.g., test if a string contains non-numeric characters), value limit checking (quantities are within expected ranges, in the right precision), instance or "list" checking (analyzing the extension of a domain), and value restrictions involving the current state of other values in the database (Table 2.5).[257] Finally, in a broader, non-technical view, the aspects of human objectivity in handling data and the "institutional foundations that are in place to ensure professionalism in policies and practices, transparency, and ethical standards" have also been included in the concept of integrity.[258]

---

[250] Sinha (1983), p. 60.
[251] Gray (1981); Frank (2004), p. 420; Batini and Scannapieco (2006), p. 30.
[252] Eswaran et al. (1976), p. 624.
[253] Redman (1996), p. 259.
[254] Redman (1996), p. 266.
[255] Date (1995), pp. 440–442.
[256] Brackett (1994), pp. 130–139.
[257] Tasker (1989), pp. 67 and 80.
[258] Carson (2001), p. 8.

Level	Type of validation	Concept involved	Typical error message
I	Individual characters of a value	Data type (e.g., alphanumeric, numeric, etc.)	"Invalid character(s)," "Not numeric"
II	Quantity within defined limits and precision / labels within size limits	Intention of data item	"Amount exceeds limit," "Name too long"
III	New instance of label is unique / referenced label exists	Extension of data item / referential integrity	"Code already in use," "Part number not on file"
IV	Multi-data item dependency	Complex business rules	"Employee not eligible for benefits."

Table 2.5: Four Levels of Data Item Validation [Tasker (1989)].

Flexibility (External View, System-Related)

Flexibility describes the extent to which data is "expandable, adaptable, and easily applied to other needs,"[259] a concept used by Wang and Strong as a sub-category to the relevance of data.[260] Khalil et al. argue that flexibility, together with ease of aggregating and manipulating data, is a principal IT system-related factor influencing data quality.[261]

Precision (Internal View, Data-Related)

In a statistical view on data quality, precision relates to the variance of repeated measurements.[262] Under the angle of data quality, data values have to be present in the right level of granularity, in order to represent precise values.[263] Precision and accuracy are not exactly synonyms; a measurement can be accurate but not precise (when the variance is too high), or precise but not accurate (low variance, but too distant from the true value).[264]

Format (External View, System-Related)

A format is the form in which data is displayed to the user.[265] The data needs to be presented in understandable form, adapted to the purpose and the intended audience;[266] a good format should hence help a data consumer to interpret values correctly and to prevent misinterpretations.[267] In order for data to be understood in the context of a task, the meaning of data values must be intelligible and correspond to their original definition.[268] Software developers and users need assistance in using data, which can be provided by adding meta-data, such as data descriptions.[269] When required, data can also be encrypted, i.e., converted to a coded form that unauthorized users cannot decode.[270]

---

[259] Wang and Strong (1996), p. 32.
[260] Wang and Strong (1996), p. 16.
[261] Khalil et al. (1999), p. 53.
[262] Evans and Lindsay (2002), p. 658.
[263] Redman (1996), p. 249; English (1999b), p. 142.
[264] Alter (2002), p. 163; Evans and Lindsay (2002), p. 659.
[265] Alter (2002), p. 163.
[266] Schwinn et al. (1999), p. 211.
[267] Redman (1996), p. 261.
[268] English (1999b), p. 142.
[269] Redman (1996), p. 248; Carson (2001), p. 9.
[270] Alter (2002), p. 163.

2.2.7   Data Quality Indicators

In order to measure the quality of data, indicators have to be defined to assess the quality on a task-specific level;[271] high-quality indicators have to be comprehensible, unambiguous, and trustworthy, even if they are based on generic indicators such as consistency, completeness, currency, or accuracy.[272] Pipino et al. distinguish simple ratios (e.g., measuring the relation of desired outcomes and total outcomes), minimum/maximum aggregation operations (if several data quality indicators have to be combined), or a weighted average approach (if several variables with known relative importance have to be combined).[273] As a quality assessment of a full database is often not feasible, due to access restrictions or cost/performance reasons, samples have to be designed that mirror the state of the entire data population, by using techniques such as random, stratified, or cluster sampling.[274] It may also be necessary to use surrogate databases, when data reflecting the "reality" is not available; for this situation English proposes a choice of data validations sources for typical enterprise contexts.[275]

A quantitative assessment and description of data quality may often be difficult.[276] When counting errors and calculating, e.g., the proportion of data fields free from inadmissible null values (which is an important data quality criterion[277]), several levels of granularity have to be distinguished: the field level, the record level, and the data domain level.[278] Würthele provides an example of a data quality assessment in which a field-level inaccuracy of 8% corresponds to a record-level inaccuracy of 50%.[279]

2.2.8   Aggregation of Indicators

In order to obtain a concise picture of the many dimensions and indicators of data quality in a given context, an aggregated view is needed. As an example, individual data quality dimensions and measurements can be combined in the form of a "data quality radar," a high-level management tool tracking several indicators for a given data item, at some time.[280] Figure 2.11 shows a possible arrangement of dimensions in the form of a radar chart;[281] the proximity of two segments denotes the degree of proximity of data quality attributes, while several cells are deliberately left blank to show non-existing influence.

---

[271] Pipino et al. (2002), p. 211.
[272] Würthele (2003), pp. 115–116.
[273] Pipino et al. (2002), pp. 213–215.
[274] English (1999b), pp. 170–172.
[275] English (1999b), pp. 166–167.
[276] Galway and Hanks (1996), p. 9.
[277] Loshin (2001), pp. 171–174.
[278] Redman (1996), pp. 5–6; Loshin (2001), pp. 217–220; Würthele (2003), p. 114.
[279] Würthele (2003), p. 114.
[280] Würthele (2003), p. 30.
[281] Würthele (2003), p. 31.

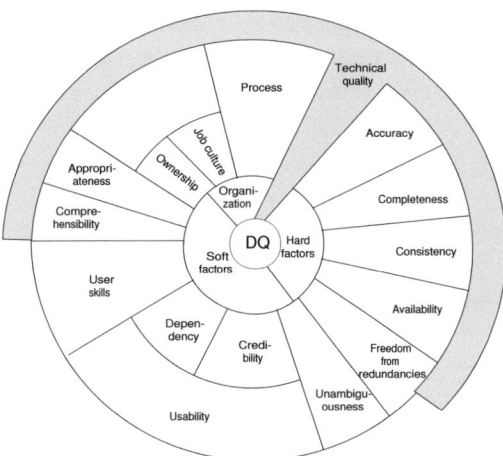

Figure 2.11: Data Quality Radar [Würthele (2003)].

As the dimensionality of the radar illustrates, the quality of some data at a given time typically consists of several dimensions. In this situation, aggregation matrices can be used to consolidate detailed quality attributes into high-level dimensions such as "hard," "soft," "organizational," and "technical" aspects.[282] Data quality scorecards can provide dashboard views on the state of data quality, its evolution over time, and detailed ("drill-down") information about selected data quality indicators.[283] However, such scorecards also have to show the impact of (record-level) data quality indicators on process and decision support provided by ERP systems, as business managers most often have no meaningful interpretation of purely technical data quality indicators and cannot evaluate the impact of the "accuracy" or "currency" of a given category of data.[284]

2.2.9   Data Quality Problems

Regarding the definition of what "bad data" is, it is generally easy to find anecdotes about poor data and its impact, but much harder to deliver a generally applicable and precise definition.[285] Generally speaking, a data quality problem or a data deficiency is a difference between an observable fact and its representation in an information system context.[286] In a customer-oriented definition of data quality, an error has occurred when "data as

---

[282] Würthele (2003), pp. 120–124.

[283] Loshin (2006), pp. 13–16.

[284] Sarsfield (2009).

[285] Galway and Hanks (1996), p. 11.

[286] Wand and Wang (1996), p. 88; Huang et al. (1999), p. 36.

supplied by the information producers does not meet the expectations of the knowledge workers."[287] Brackett defines a data error as a "data value that provides incorrect or false knowledge about the business, or about business objects and events that are important to the business."[288] Often, data may initially be correct, but due to changes in the environment, suffers from "data accuracy decay" and, after some time, is no longer correct.[289] Then moving or restructuring data can create data problems, mainly due to a change of context, such as a conversion from a legacy application to an ERP system infrastructure, or the integration of several data sources in a DWH.[290] Finally, during the use of data in the form of information products, problems can occur due to insufficient access to data or an insufficient data presentation.[291]

Brackett explains the creation of low-quality data situations by a self-perpetuating circle ("disparate data cycle"):[292]

1. People cannot find (or do not trust, or cannot access) data, so
2. People are uncertain about the data, so
3. People create their own data, which is not integrated and not documented, so
4. People cannot find data (and so on).

This cycle is not being stopped by the advent of new IT instruments; on the contrary, low quality data is pushed into new platforms and suffers from a "natural drift" towards a state of low quality, if not kept under strict control.[293]

Lesca and Lesca describe ways in which information manufacturing processes can suffer from a lack of reliability, traceability, credibility, or from distortion, as the meaning of a piece of information changes when several persons interpret given data differently.[294] Table 2.6 shows product and process related problems, means for detection, and causes described by Lesca and Lesca.

In the following sections, explanations for data quality problems will be presented in the dimensions of "people," "process," and "technology," a popular way of thinking in the quality domain.[295] As it will quickly become clear, the three components are most often interrelated, and two or three factors have to be considered simultaneously when discussing data quality problems and their causes.

---

[287] English (1999b), p. xxiv.
[288] Brackett (2000), p. 112.
[289] Olson (2003), p. 50.
[290] Olson (2003), p. 52.
[291] Olson (2003), p. 62.
[292] Brackett (2000), p. 8.
[293] Brackett (2000), p. 10.
[294] Lesca and Lesca (1995), pp. 136–162.
[295] E.g., used by Piasecki (2003), Hawking et al. (2004), or Weigel (2008).

Problem	Detection	Causes
Information over-load (product aspect)	Ask for usability of information provided	No adequate information dispatching; no adequate information tools; insufficient targeting of information
Ambiguity (product aspect)	Difficult – a person might not be aware that information is interpreted differently by another person	Task may require ambivalent information, especially if not formalized
Incomplete information (product aspect)	Difficult, would require comprehensive, formal description of information	Often a result of an "intuitive way of management;" excessive division of work (too small units of work); poor information sharing; insufficient coordination amongst organizational units; low integration of IT systems; IT systems not aligned with organizational strategy
Incoherent information (product aspect)	Identify suspicious information objects; if possible, automated search for incoherencies	Fragmentation of information; organizational fragmentation; lack of coordination; no information governance; multiple information sources
Presentation weaknesses (product aspect)	Difficult – only few organizations measure the cost of non-quality information	Lack of coordination amongst information providing and consuming organizational units; style of work differs, and uses different forms of presentation
Information distortion (process aspect)	Identify information for which distortion or ambiguity is possible	Involuntary distortion: different understanding of the same concept; voluntary distortion: modification of information object, delays or interruptions of the data flow.

Table 2.6: Classification of Information Problems [Lesca and Lesca (1995)].

2.2.9.1 Problem Factor People

When regarding the human factors influencing data quality, several aspects such as the work environment, the skills of users, or their personal motivation have to be considered. Data can first be incorrect because of a wrong perception of reality by users when entering data into an information system, be it by error or due to malicious intent.[296] Then accurate or "true" data may not be disclosed by data providers (e.g., customers answering the telephone) due to concerns of protecting one's privacy or to gain an advantage with regard to competitors.[297] In order to accomplish an effective sharing of data amongst several people in an organization, processes and IT systems must be designed in a way that caring for data and data sharing are natural elements of regular business tasks.[298]

Königer and Reithmayer have observed a sort of fatalism, as IT users simply accept that databases in their organization contain redundant and variant copies of the same fact.[299] In the same line, Olson complains of a "high tolerance for errors in primary systems,"[300] while English concedes that IT users (especially in data warehousing) can "live with some degree of omission and error" – if they are able to cope with the problems.[301]

Finally, the fact that IT system users are often confronted by heterogeneous data semantics is an important source of data quality problems. Due to representational and ontological heterogeneity of the data models, misinterpretations of intrinsically correct data can occur at the receiver side; in combination with a temporal factor representing the

---

[296] Wand and Wang (1996), p. 92.
[297] Bleiholder and Schmid (2008), p. 131.
[298] Brackett (2000), p. 14.
[299] Königer and Reithmayer (1998), p. 98.
[300] Olson (2003), p. 12.
[301] English (1999a).

evolution of semantics, Madnick and Zhu define four cases of potential data errors due to misinterpretation:[302]

1. Representational heterogeneity (the same concept can have different representations at the sender and receiver sides, possibly due to a lack of unambiguous identifiers),

2. Temporal representational heterogeneity (the representation of a concept undergoes changes, as the ticker symbol "C" shows: it first stood for Chrysler, after the merger of this company with Daimler-Benz, the same "C" then stood for Citygroup),

3. Ontological heterogeneities (the same term denotes different concepts), temporal ontological heterogeneities (the meaning of a term can shift over time), and

4. Aggregational ontological heterogeneity (inclusion or aggregation rules are not the same at source and receiving side, e.g., when specifying the "total number of employees" in the case of a consolidation of partially owned subsidiaries).

2.2.9.2   Problem Factor Process

IT systems and their users have to be embedded in a meaningful operations concept. If business processes are not designed in a way that is supported by an IT system, the system's impact on the processes will be poor or negative, and data quality will suffer. Employees participating in a business process must be informed of the role they play and have to master the required interactions with business process and IT system partners, besides possessing the access rights to retrieve data from IT systems.[303] Data quality literature also recommends that organizations handle data forwarded to external stakeholders, such as customers or suppliers, with special care, in order to remain a trustworthy business partner.[304] If data producers and consumers belong to different organizational units which suffer from grave inter-organizational communication and cooperation problems, data quality in a transversal business process will most likely be affected.[305] Finally, data that has been useful at a given time in the past may no longer be useful, due to ageing or changes in the process or the surrounding organization.[306]

2.2.9.3   Problem Factor Technology

Design problems in IT systems basically appear in the form of incomplete representation, ambiguous representation, and meaningless states.[307] The deficiencies result in data structures and values that are not suited for use in an application context. Typical errors caused

---

[302] Madnick and Zhu (2006), pp. 461–465.

[303] Strong et al. (1997a), p. 44.

[304] Evans and Lindsay (2002), p. 168; Atkins (2003); Maydanchik (2007), p. 22.

[305] Galway and Hanks (1996), p. xii.

[306] Strong et al. (1997a), pp. 40 and 44; Maydanchik (2007), pp. 18–19.

[307] Wand and Wang (1996), p. 91.

by IT systems during processing of data are transaction breakdowns, checks that do not stop data errors, or data edits checks that refuse correct data.[308] Also, data structures defined in and used by IT systems may be designed in a way that creates data problems; data format problems leading to process failures – typically, insufficient storage allocated for data structures, too limited range of possible data values, or arithmetic or string operations that are hit by data overflow – have been described, e.g., by Herzog et al.[309] Well known in this domain is the Year 2000 problem (also known as the "millennium" or "Y2K" bug), created by insufficient space left for storage of temporal data.[310] Moreover, the complexity of multi-user, multi-channel IT system designs and the almost ubiquitous need for system integration may lead to architectures and user interfaces that promote data errors.[311] In the context of standardized software packages, the design problem is exacerbated as the use of data is outside of IT system designers' control.[312]

During the operation phase of an IT infrastructure, processing errors (e.g., interruptions in communications or an unplanned server re-boot) lead to the appearance of data quality errors.[313] Wand and Wang call the reason for this kind of operational data problems "garbling:" a perceived state of the external world is mapped into a "wrong" or incomplete state in the IT systems, which leads to a lack of realism of the description contained in the database.[314] Finally, the high rate of new data arriving in databases ("data deluge") is an issue for many organizations and their IT users, aggravated by the fact that users capture or create additional – redundant – data, as they are unaware of existing data or cannot easily access it.[315]

2.2.10 Organizational Models for Data Quality

In the case of business data, it is often difficult to attach responsibility for data to a specific business entity, as data in already moderately complex organizations crosses organizational borders and many stakeholders (such as business process managers, operational IT users, or IT staff) are using the same data elements.[316]English recommends to structure organizations that produce and use data in a form that:[317]

- Formal processes in the treatment of data are established, independently of existing business processes;

---

[308] Strong et al. (1997a), p. 41.
[309] Herzog et al. (2007), p. 22.
[310] Knolmayer and Myrach (2000).
[311] Naumann (2002), p. 6.
[312] Huang et al. (1999), p. 17.
[313] Naumann (2002), p. 6.
[314] Wand and Wang (1996), p. 91.
[315] Brackett (1994), pp. 2–3; Strong et al. (1997a), p. 41.
[316] Brackett (1994), p. 39.
[317] English (1999b), pp. 303–309.

- Business and "data manufacturing" process owners can be held accountable for data quality (a superior must be accountable for decisions made and executed on his or her behalf[318]);
- Data producers and data consumers undergo formal training, which shows the role and the interconnections of processes and data (quality);
- Producers receive immediate feedback from data users (feedback loops);
- Reasonability tests for data can be conducted and producers are capable of correcting data errors themselves;
- Data user satisfaction surveys are carried out;
- "Steward" functions for critical data elements are installed.

2.2.10.1   Data Management Policy and Data Strategy

As a starting point to data management or data quality management initiatives, Seiner recommends to create a "data management policy" along the following principles:[319]

- Business data is the property of an organization as a whole, and is not "owned" by an individual or business unit;
- All strategically important data elements must be modeled, named, and defined according to corporate standards;
- Enterprise data must be maintained close to source, be secured and accessible;
- All data structures and standards applicable in an organization have to be documented by meta-data;
- Data stewards are accountable for enterprise data;
- Job descriptions incorporate data quality accountabilities.

Adelman et al. see a "data strategy" as a master concept for explaining how a state of data quality can be reached, combining elements such as data integration, data quality, meta-data, data modeling, organizational roles and responsibilities, performance and measurement, security and privacy, business intelligence, the treatment of unstructured data, and an assessment of the business value of data.[320]

2.2.10.2   Data Governance

Once a strategy for data management has been set out, data governance has to be installed, for defining ownership, policies, and decision-making authority around data.[321] Often,

---

[318] Dressler (2004), p. 180.
[319] Seiner (2005).
[320] Adelman et al. (2005), p. 6.
[321] Seiner (2006a); Dyché (2007), p. 2.

several organizational levels are needed to implement data governance, which can be cross-referenced with existing organizational units or role models.[322] Otto and Wende and Weber et al. have found a "common denominator" for organizing data governance, requiring the levels executive sponsorship, data quality board, group-wide ("chief") data steward, and business and IT data steward.[323]

2.2.10.3   Data Stewardship

The function of a "data steward" or other specialized "data governance" staff has been described and postulated by many authors.[324] In general terms, data stewardship has been described as "the formalization of accountability for the management of data resources" and is often assumed by persons that already exert similar accountabilities.[325] Formal data steward positions are not always necessary, depending on the situation; nevertheless, organizations most likely need a data steward function when: [326]

- No one has the responsibility to determine data quality criteria;
- No one has the responsibility to monitor data quality;
- No business rules have been formally defined (resulting in corrupted data);
- Data is often misinterpreted because its definition is not available;
- Sensitive data risks to be exposed to unauthorized persons;
- Little coordination among organizational units exists, leading to extensive interfaces;
- Relationships between IT systems are difficult to establish and IT systems hard to integrate;
- Labor-intensive reconciliation of inconsistent data between systems is needed;
- No standards for the treatment of data exist, resulting in a waste of resources.

Effective stewards have to be familiar with business values and practices, but also data models and other IT topics, in order to "champion high-quality data" on its way from repositories to reports.[327] Typical tasks of data stewards are the definition of data elements and the related business rules, the establishment of quality and security levels for data, or the specification of reference data sources.[328] Moreover, stewards have to ensure the consistency and accuracy of data between applications, define data quality metrics in their domain, foster data sharing and master data management, identify issues with

---

[322] Seiner (2006b); Smalltree (2006a); Weber et al. (2008).
[323] Otto and Wende (2008), p. 272; Weber et al. (2008), p. 351.
[324] Cf., e.g., Adelman et al. (2005), p. 151, Kimball et al. (1998), p. 70, or Brackett (2000).
[325] Seiner (2006a).
[326] Adelman et al. (2005), pp. 152–153.
[327] Laurent (2005).
[328] Kelley (2003); Seiner (2005).

source systems, create or update document taxonomies, and participate in the semantic reconciliation of data models.[329] Finally, a permanent data quality stewardship has to manage the removal of unused data elements ("data purging"[330]), to supervise the actual use of data (compared to the intended use), and to address the problem of data accuracy decay by scheduling periodic events to update data in a database.[331]

2.2.11 Economic Value of Data Quality

Lately, with the globalization of trade and the rapid progress of the Internet in Business-to-Consumer (B2C) and Business-to-Business (B2B) relationships, the ability to use enterprise data is broadly considered to be an important factor of success in today's business world.[332] Enterprises are facing an increasing demand to not only deliver (physical) products or services, but also information products to potential and existing customers and suppliers. Referring to the debate on the economic impact of IT,[333] Tallon and Scannell hold the view that "a consensus has emerged that if corporate IT assets such as hardware, software, and networks are susceptible to replication by competitors, a competitive advantage can only come from the information created by such assets."[334] The value of information does not come from the ability to merely have access to a piece of information, but rather from its use in decision-making.[335]

In order to make sound decisions, data of adequate quality is needed, and any organization that has not successfully implemented data management processes will not be able to successfully manage information.[336] Information produces value for an organization by improving the input for decision-making,[337] when decision makers have to choose one from two or more alternative courses of action. As information helps to reduce uncertainty about a particular decision, the value of a given piece of information can be estimated by comparing the expected monetary value of the outcome of two decisions, one made using this piece of information and the other one without it.[338] The availability of consistent, accurate, and timely information across all levels of an organization provides it with the instruments needed for evaluating, controlling, and improving processes, products, and services to meet business objectives and fulfill customer expectations.[339]

---

[329] Gartner Group (2008).
[330] Maydanchik (2007), pp. 17–18.
[331] Olson (2003), p. 51.
[332] Laudon and Laudon (2000), p. xix.
[333] Cf., e.g., Brynjolfsson (1993) or Carr (2003).
[334] Tallon and Scannell (2007), p. 65.
[335] Wand and Wang (1996), p. 87; Alter (2002), p. 69.
[336] Schwinn et al. (1999), p. 2.
[337] Lawrence (1999), p. 1.
[338] Alter (2002), p. 162.
[339] Evans and Lindsay (2002), p. 448

Data that supports business activities of an organization is most often not available for free, and an economic tradeoff between quality and costs to obtain (or create) it has to be found.[340] On the one hand, the costs to collect data and to ensure its quality are most often clearly visible to an organization, e.g., in terms of time or resources consumed; on the other hand, the benefits of high quality data may be unclear, especially in large organizations, where responsibilities for data are distributed.[341] Business companies also have to keep their data safe for many years, due to regulatory compliance requirements or for product maintenance purposes;[342] as the data has to provide an invariant representation of some state in the past, regardless of the constant changes in IT systems and their databases, this situation creates significant potential for friction and costs.

Poor data quality impacts a typical enterprise in many ways: at the operational level, poor data leads directly to customer dissatisfaction, increased cost, and lowered employee job satisfaction.[343] Employee job satisfaction suffers when friction at the interfaces of organizational units occurs.[344] Overlapping databases in organizations, or managers refusing to promote the quality of data used by other departments can cause work overload and lower job satisfaction of employees. Then, at a tactical level, poor data quality compromises decision-making and re-engineering projects. Finally, at a strategic level, insufficient data quality may complicate the definition and execution of business strategies.

Examples illustrating the economic effects of insufficient data quality in IT systems and the subsequent human and economic damage abound. As an example, English reports six pages full of examples illustrating the high cost of low data quality.[345] Wang et al. claim losses of billions of dollars of U.S. federal loan money because of poor data quality at a single agency.[346] In a case study on a customer service center system, Campbell reports that due to a lack of consistent data definition, poor data edit checks, and an inappropriate performance measurement of employees, an Australian service company lost AUD 80,000 *per day* in revenue.[347] Overall, according to the Data Warehousing Institute, data quality problems cost U.S. businesses more than USD 600 billion per year.[348]

Nonquality costs of data appear in the form of process failure costs (business processes fail, or perform ineffectively because of poor-quality data), "scrap and rework" (data is defective, must be cleaned or re-engineered), and lost and missed opportunity

---

[340] Brackett (1994), p. 128.
[341] Galway and Hanks (1996), p. 3.
[342] Markus et al. (2003a), p. 50.
[343] Redman (1996), pp. 6–12; Redman (1998), p. 80; Strassmann (2006b).
[344] Redman (1996), p. 8.
[345] English (1999b), pp. 7–12.
[346] Wang et al. (1995b), p. 629.
[347] Campbell (2000), p. 34.
[348] Lais (2003).

costs (lost business opportunities, unhappy customers or shareholders).[349] Assessment and inspection costs include the costs for consultancy services, software, and work time for performing audits. Data quality problems are hidden consumers of resources: IT system production is wasted or missed, time is spent on the diagnosis and fixing of problems, system developments fail, and business systems become inefficient.[350]

In contrast to the costs, the *benefits of improved* data quality can only indirectly be perceived in an organization's ability to successfully manage operational systems or the knowledge generated in Business Intelligence (BI) processes:[351]

- *Higher throughput in processing:* since delays caused by data errors (i.e., their detection and correction) are reduced, the overall output of an organization increases and the cost per transaction decreases;
- *Better customer visibility:* better knowledge of the customer profile leads to higher sales, better service, and improved customer retention;
- *Better use of resources:* as less personal and technical resources are used to track down and correct errors, resource allocation and utilization is improved;
- *Better predictability in IT projects:* projects in the domains of CRM, DWH, or BI are no longer delayed (or do no longer fail) because of poor data quality.

2.3 Data Quality Publications Overview

2.3.1 Academic and Professionals Initiatives

Many national and international conferences on data quality are being held on a regular basis. Well established are the International Conference on Information Quality (ICIQ),[352] organized by the Massachusetts Institute of Technology (MIT) for the first time in 1996, the International Workshop on Information Quality in Information Systems (IQIS)[353] (conjointly held with the SIGMOD conference, since 2004), the International Workshop on Data and Information Quality (DIQ)[354] (conjointly held with the CAiSE conference, since 2004), or the International Workshop on Quality of Information Systems (QoIS),[355] (conjointly held with the ER conference, since 2005).[356]

---

[349] English (1999b), pp. 209–210.
[350] Aiken (1996), p. 44.
[351] Brown and Kros (2003); Loshin (2003); Pfeiffer (2009).
[352] http://mitiq.mit.edu/iciq/.
[353] http://iqis.irisa.fr/.
[354] http://www.computing.dcu.ie/research/dataquality/diq/.
[355] http://deptinfo.cnam.fr/qois2006/.
[356] Batini and Scannapieco (2006), p. IX.

Moreover, several professional associations for data quality exist, such as the "International Association for Information and Data Quality" (IAIDQ)[357] or the "Deutsche Gesellschaft für Informations- und Datenqualität e.V."[358] These associations regularly publish guidelines for data quality practitioners, besides providing specific services to their members.[359]

2.3.2 Data Quality Project Methods

In the following sections, a selection of data quality project management concepts relevant for this research will be presented in temporal order of their publication: a generic data quality project and infrastructure model (presented by English), a 17-step data quality "practice" program (Loshin), and the "complete data quality methodology" (Batini and Scannapieco).

2.3.2.1 English

In his "practical book about using information quality as a business management tool," English provides a comprehensive framework for quality initiatives, called "Total Quality data Management" (TQdM), which includes definitions of (data) quality, quality concepts, economic considerations, and action plans (Figure 2.12).[360]

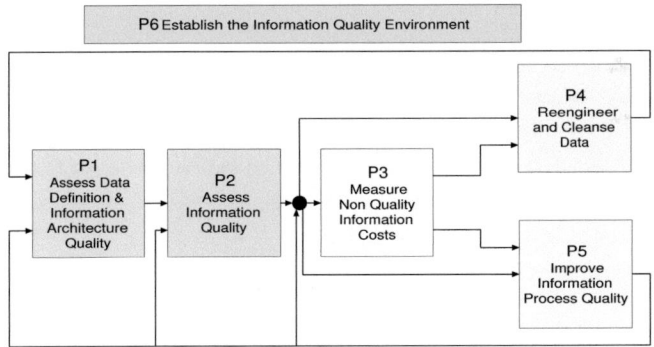

Figure 2.12: English's Total Quality Data Framework [English (1999b)].

---

[357] http://www.iaidq.org/.
[358] http://www.dgiq.de/index.html/.
[359] Deutsche Gesellschaft für Informations- und Datenqualität (2007).
[360] English (1999b), pp. 22 and 144. English generally uses the term "information quality" instead of "data quality."

Process P1: Assess Data Definition and Information Architecture Quality

Before measuring the quality of data values, the processes and IT system architectures involved in data processing have to be critically reviewed; objects of this analysis are, e.g., the quality of data standards or the definition of data.[361] Firstly, data quality standards describe the availability of norms regulating the use of data in an organization; the clarity of business terms, the consistency of domain types, or the understandability of entity type names are elements that must be addressed whenever a new IT system enters the organization. Secondly, data definition quality has to be controlled: business terms have to be described in a complete, accurate, and clear manner, before any data record is inserted in a corporate database. Data names have to be designed consistently, abbreviations and acronyms must be used coherently. An organization-wide glossary of business terms is recommended, in order to obtain an organization-wide consensus on terms and to avoid synonym and homonym issues. Business rules (policies), often implemented as database constraints, are exposed to changes, and need special attention if inconsistencies are to be avoided. Lastly, the data architecture must correctly reflect business needs: data models must cover the entire scope of the organization, must be consistent, descriptions of entities and relationships must match reality, and redundancy of distributed databases has to be controlled.

English proposes six steps to assess data definition and architecture quality:[362]

1. Identify data definition quality measures (planning, root cause analysis, and prioritization of measures);
2. Identify groups of data records to assess;
3. Identify data stakeholders (producers, intermediaries, knowledge workers/data consumers, process owners, external customers, etc.);
4. Assess technical quality of data definition (e.g., conformance to standards);
5. Assess information architecture and database design quality (completeness, correctness, and redundancy of data structures);
6. Assess data user satisfaction.

Process P2: Assess Data Quality

In this process step, the objectives for the measurement of data quality are set, and guidelines on how to perform a quality assessment on critical data records are established, before samples are extracted and analyzed.[363] The critical design decisions in a data quality assessment consist of choosing the right objects of measurement, the right instruments

---

[361] English (1999b), pp. 90–136.
[362] English (1999b), pp. 118–136.
[363] English (1999b), pp. 137–197.

to gauge data quality, and the right timeframe, with the intent to avoid any bias. The activities in this phase – which has been described as "data profiling" by other authors[364] – are in detail:[365]

1. Select data to analyze, set priorities for the analysis of the – usually very large quantities of – data used in an organization;
2. Identify data quality objectives and measures;
3. Identify the information product value and cost chain (a map of all databases or files, the business processes and IT systems creating or transforming data, interfaces, and data producers and consumers);
4. Determine files or processes to assess;
5. Identify data validation sources (if needed, find surrogate sources);
6. Extract random sample of data for detailed analyses;
7. Measure data quality (e.g., completeness of values, conformance to business rules, accuracy with respect to validation sources, timeliness);
8. Interpret and report data quality.

Process P3: Measure Costs of Non-Quality Data

An important requirement during quality assessment is the knowledge about the (ex ante) state of quality costs and the possible cost savings realized with a data quality project. All activities in a data item's life cycle, related with its acquisition ("create"), application ("retrieve"), maintenance ("update"), and disposal ("delete"), incur costs to an organization; the steps for measuring the quality costs of data recommended by English are:[366]

1. Identify business performance measures (derived from organizational objectives, focus on the ones that are most hardly hit by poor data quality);
2. Calculate data costs;
3. Calculate the proportion of non-quality data costs;
4. Identify customer segments hit by processes suffering from low data quality;
5. Calculate the lifetime value of affected customers;
6. Calculate data value by replacement or market valuation.

Process P4: Re-Engineer and Cleanse Data

After having identified the defects in an organization's database, steps must be undertaken to re-engineer and cleanse the data. Information products can be improved by a cleansing

---

[364] Olson (2003), pp. 121–122; Maydanchik (2007), pp. 49–50.
[365] English (1999b), pp. 155–197.
[366] English (1999b), pp. 199–235.

of source data (mostly in operational IT systems) or by cleansing during conversion (e.g., when moving data from a legacy system to a new transactional system or a DWH). All kinds of data definition or content defects are to be removed during cleansing. English recommends the following activities:[367]

1. Identify data sources (make a list of "authoritative" and "redundant" data sources);
2. Extract and analyze source data: Are there attributes needed but not present in the database? Have published business rules been violated? Have new rules been created by daily business practice? Are there cases of domain "schizophrenia" (the value of a given data field can be interpreted only after considering the value of other fields)?
3. Standardize data (remove inconsistencies of format, non-atomic field types, or embedded meaning in data);
4. Correct and complete data (perform the actual cleansing);
5. Match and consolidate data (consolidate databases, tag duplicate entries);
6. Analyze data defect types;
7. Transform and enhance data;
8. Calculate derivations and summary data;
9. Audit and control the usage of data, manage the ETL process (if available).

Process P5: Improve Information Process Quality – Data Defect Prevention

The processes P1–P4 described above have shown how quality problems can be identified and removed, on a project basis. On the other hand, process improvements in the way organizations use information are required to bring costs down permanently. Avoiding errors at an early stage, eliminating proactively the causes of errors is better than recurring quality improvement projects; fixing a process that produces defective data should have priority over fixing existing data errors. English proposes a five-step scheme for quality projects, based on the PDCA[368] cycle:[369]

1. Select processes for data quality improvement (from a list of candidates);
2. Develop a plan for data quality improvement (e.g., by using cause-and-effect diagrams to study the influence of applications, data sources, business processes, and people on a specific data defect);
3. Implement data quality improvements;
4. Check impact of data quality improvements on business processes;
5. Act to standardize information quality improvements.

---

[367]English (1999b), pp. 238–283.
[368]Cf. Section 2.1.5.1.
[369]English (1999b), pp. 289–310.

Process P6: Establish the Information Quality Environment

Executed in parallel to the processes P1–P5, process P6 encompasses the systemic man-agement and the cultural activities for a high-quality environment, leading from an atti-tude of "data as by-product" to a situation in which data is managed as an asset.[370] As a result of a data quality improvement project, organizations may have to modify business process definitions, adopt data management procedures, modify application programs and database schemata, and launch specific (user) education programs.

2.3.2.2 Loshin

Loshin presents an economic quality framework which highlights the impact of data flows and information chains in enterprises, describing the processing stages of data supply, data acquisition, data creation, data processing, data packaging, decision-making, decision im-plementation, data delivery, and data consumption.[371] Loshin explores the dimensions of data quality and shows how business rules can be used to enforce data quality. To summarize the results of his analysis, Loshin proposes a data quality "practice" program comprising 17 elements, ranging from problem recognition to making improvements per-manent:[372]

1. *Recognize the problem:* look for evidence, find problems;

2. *Management support and data ownership policy:* get senior-level management sup-port, define and assign roles for data quality;

3. *Spread the word:* educate, organize a training program;

4. *Mapping the information chain:* identify processing stages and communication channels, build the information chain;

5. *Data quality scorecard:* establish the cost of low data quality and a business case for the data quality program;

6. *Current state assessment:* choose measurement points, choose appropriate data quality dimensions, measure data quality;

7. *Requirements assessment:* analyze costs and impact of data quality in the organiza-tion, assign responsibilities for data and data quality;

8. *Choose a project:* decompose the (usually large) entire enterprise data problem into smaller parts and choose a first sub-project which has impact, management support, and a reasonable chance to be solved;

9. *Build the team:* engage project managers, system architects, and domain and busi-ness rule experts;

---

[370]English (1999b), p. 71.
[371]Loshin (2001), pp. 76–77.
[372]Loshin (2001), pp. 463–484.

10. *Build the arsenal:* evaluate, purchase, and design data quality tools;

11. *Meta-data model:* define a model of meta-data, if it does not already exist, e.g., in the form of a data dictionary;

12. *Define data quality rules:* identify data domains, mappings, and rules;

13. *Data archaeology/data mining:* explore and discover hidden structures in the database;

14. *Manage data suppliers:* put in place a supplier management process for external data;

15. *Execute the improvement:* define the IT system's architecture, perform cleansing, integrate and test rules, build a nonconformance resolution system, integrate rules in production system;

16. *Measure improvement:* integrate measurements and compare with current state assessment;

17. *Build on each success:* make the improvement permanent and address the next issue.

2.3.2.3   Batini and Scannapieco

Batini and Scannapieco propose a "complete data quality methodology," encompassing ten steps and structured in three phases:[373]

Phase 1: State reconstruction

1. Reconstruct the state and meaning of most relevant databases and data flows exchanged between organizations, and build the database and data flow/organization matrices.

2. Reconstruct most relevant business processes performed by organizations, and build the processes/organizations matrix.

3. For each process or group of processes related in a macroprocess, reconstruct the norms and organizational rules that discipline the macroprocess and the service provided.

Phase 2: Assessment

4. Check the major problems related to the services provided with the internal and final users. Fix these drawbacks in terms of process and service qualities, and identify the causes of the drawbacks due to low data quality.

5. Identify relevant data quality dimensions and metrics, measure data quality of databases and data flows, and identify their critical areas.

---

[373] Batini and Scannapieco (2006), p. 181.

Phase 3: Choice of the optimal improvement process

6. For each database and data flow, fix the new data quality levels that improve process quality and reduce costs under a required threshold.

7. Conceive process re-engineering activities and choose data quality activities that may lead to data quality improvement targets set in step 6, relating them in the data/activity matrix to clusters of databases and data flows involved in data quality improvement targets.

8. Choose optimal techniques for the data quality activities.

9. Connect crossings in the data/activity matrix to obtain reasonable candidate improvement processes.

10. For each improvement process defined in the previous step, compute approximate costs and benefits, and choose the optimal one, checking that the overall cost-benefit balance meets the targets of step 6.

Data quality management activities in an improvement process (Phase 3) encompass the acquisition of new data, standardization/normalization (modification of data in order to make it comply with standard or reference formats), object identification (record linkage, record matching, entity resolution, in order to identify records in two or more tables representing the same external world object),[374] data integration (to present a unified view of data), source trustworthiness evaluation (rating a data source on the base of data quality), quality composition (defining an algebra for composing data quality dimension values), error localization or detection, error correction, and cost optimization (to achieve a given data quality objective in a cost-effective way).[375]

2.3.3   Data Quality in a Business IT System Context

The history of data quality literature in a business context can be traced back at least to the late 1980's, when business organizations were increasingly forced, by strong competitive pressure, to re-engineer and improve their processes, and data began to be seen as a valuable corporate asset.[376] Many sources describe data quality problems which are specific to organizational functions, such as accounting or materials management. Typical elements of such publications are factual reports on how data errors occur (in the context of other "operational" problems), economic reasoning (cost and benefit aspects), and measures to counter these problems. The findings presented in the following sections will be relevant for data management in ERP systems, as the application functionality needed, e.g., in accounting or materials management is today mostly provided by ERP systems.

---

[374] Herzog et al. (2007), p. 81.
[375] Batini and Scannapieco (2006), p. 70.
[376] Galway and Hanks (1996), p. 5.

2.3.3.1   Materials Management

Inventory keeping is an important activity in many businesses, in manufacturing, distribution, and retail trade contexts. Inventory data quality is a crucial concept to successful management of inventories: financial planning, marketing and sales planning, procurement planning, and many corporate initiatives such as Manufacturing Resource Planning (MRP) and Just-In-Time (JIT) programs cannot be carried out without reliable inventory records.[377] Costs incurred by inaccurate inventory figures include unnecessary replenishment costs, opportunity costs (due to capital tied up in excess inventory), the risk of having obsolete and orphaned inventory, stockout costs (related to misalignment between available and required inventory), and control system costs.[378] Many textbooks, written mainly by practitioners, treat the question of quality in inventory data. In the next sections, important publications by Brooks and Wilson, Piasecki, and Sheldon will be discussed.

Definition of Inventory Data Quality
Accuracy (and data quality in general) is a context-dependent concept: perfection is often not achievable or not necessary; for this practical reason, tolerances have to be defined, which limit the degree of acceptable deviations.[379] Tolerances necessarily depend on the importance or criticality of an item: it is clear that planning systems suffer from inaccurate data, but it is often almost impossible to specify a limit beyond which a planning system will fail.[380] A general trend exists to fix a general 5% tolerance on data values: respecting a "95% of inventory items accuracy, with a ± 5% tolerance" should bring an organization "into the top 10 or 20% of all manufacturing and distributions companies in the world," with regard to inventory record accuracy.[381]

The setting of tolerances for "acceptable" quantities may be highly controversial, taking days and weeks for project teams to debate. Factors such as usage patterns, monetary value, lead time (the longer the lead time, the smaller the admissible tolerance), level in the assembly hierarchy (the higher in the hierarchy a part is, the lower the tolerance), criticality, and method of handling have to be considered.[382] By combining several of these factors and applying ABC classification (ranking inventory items by their value, in order to classify them according to their criticality), organizations can define levels of tolerance to quantities of physical items. Rather than wasting time on debating relative tolerances, organizations are recommended to establish threshold levels in monetary value.[383]

---

[377] Brooks and Wilson (1995), pp. xi and 4–8.
[378] Sheldon (2004), pp. 8–9.
[379] Brooks and Wilson (1995), p. 13.
[380] Piasecki (2003), p. 173.
[381] Brooks and Wilson (1995), p. 22.
[382] Brooks and Wilson (1995), pp. 17–20.
[383] Piasecki (2003), p. 153.

Measurement of Inventory Data Quality

Results of quality measurements can generally be expressed in the form of "Good Count Bad Count,"[384] e.g., as the ratio of total accurate records divided by total records. Such measurements are, however, unsatisfactory with respect to the information they carry and their sensibility against manipulations: "tricks" such as counting only items with a low probability for error can strongly affect results gained from accuracy measurements.[385] Using a scorecard to combine several measurements will provide a more complete and accurate picture of the actual situation.[386]

Various types of accuracy measurements can be carried out in the domain of materials management, in process contexts such as shipping, receiving, replenishment, or manufacturing. Many ways exist to measure inventory data accuracy; the methods of individual checks, systematic (physical) inventories, and cycle counting will briefly be compared.

Firstly, a natural way to measure accuracy consists in individual "fact-finding" missions, e.g., when production managers make sure the proposals generated by an IT system are in line with reality, the actual material requirements. Piasecki warns, however, against admitting individual, unapproved inventory checks: a situation in which employees enter the warehouse, personally check the on-hand stock, and then decide themselves on what to produce next, can severely disturb purchasing and production operations.[387]

Secondly, physical ("wall-to-wall") inventories are often requested by the accounting department, in order to state the monetary value of materials on stock – a practice that is criticized by Sheldon and Piasecki: besides the fact that physical inventories are a time-consuming and non-value-added activity, it is very difficult to count a usually large number of items in many storage locations, without disturbing normal operations, and with perfect accuracy.[388] Accuracy in counting is of tremendous importance, as feeding inaccurate results from a physical inventory back into an inventory IT system can corrupt any well-managed inventory record.[389] Typical causes of the problems related with physical inventories lie in the challenge to properly identify parts or units of measurement, or in employee-related factors such as poor training of counters, lack of morale, or confusion over open orders and allocations.[390] As many physical inventory counts result in financial asset value, errors in quantities from different parts (workers counted too much in one category, too little in another) may be counterbalanced, since monetary values are "fungible;"[391] in such a situation, financial regulatory requirements may be fulfilled, even if

---

[384] Piasecki (2003), p. 152; Maydanchik (2007), pp. 255–256.
[385] Piasecki (2003), pp. 158–159.
[386] Piasecki (2003), pp. 159–161.
[387] Piasecki (2003), p. 79.
[388] Piasecki (2003), p. 133.
[389] Sheldon (2004), p. 60.
[390] Brooks and Wilson (1995), p. 97; Piasecki (2003), p. 135.
[391] Brooks and Wilson (1995), p. 16.

quantities are not accurate at all.[392] Nevertheless, it is normally much easier for managers to track monetary values "down to the cent" than to account for quantities in materials, parts, or products.[393]

If physical inventories are inevitable, Piasecki recommends conducting test counts, worker training, and well-designed count plans, paperwork, forms, and other supplies needed for the inventory.[394] Also, materials to be counted have to be organized prior to counting, and special handling techniques such as counting in multiples can make counting easier and better.[395]

Lastly, a better alternative to physical inventory processing is "cycle counting," i.e., performing periodic checks for process control of inventory accuracy. The advantages of cycle counting compared to periodic physical inventory checks are, among others, a timely understanding of root causes of errors, the reduction of part identification errors, lower production losses, and a more accurate statement of financial assets.[396]

Analyzing Inventory Data Quality Issues

Variation is a normal phenomenon hitting any inventory processing activity, stemming from demand forecast inaccuracies, scrap reporting errors, or machine downtime. The driver for inventory accuracy may be hidden in the inventory process itself, the receiving of parts, their storage, withdrawal, issue, and movement through work-in-progress, or the recording of the related events.[397] Measurements help to track the frequency and distribution of certain error types such as "replenishment error wrong location" or "location consolidation error."[398]

Typically, the following questions concerning the root cause of the variance have then to be answered:[399] "is it a known source of error?," "is it a new source of error?," or "is it variance or not?". The impact of data inaccuracies can be measured by looking at missed shipments, production interruptions, schedule changes caused by inaccuracies, labor hours spent on searching for "lost" items, or safety stock intended to compensate for inventory data inaccuracy.[400]

Improving Inventory Data Quality

Several authors have described ways to improve inventory data quality. As an example of

---

[392] Sheldon (2004), p. 125.
[393] Brooks and Wilson (1995), p. 4.
[394] Brooks and Wilson (1995), pp. 97–98; Piasecki (2003), p. 138.
[395] Piasecki (2003), p. 249.
[396] Sheldon (2004), p. 125.
[397] Brooks and Wilson (1995), p. 34; Piasecki (2003), p. 299.
[398] Piasecki (2003), p. 158.
[399] Piasecki (2003), pp. 110–116.
[400] Piasecki (2003), p. 171.

an improvement method, Sheldon provides a "guide to sustainable (...) excellence in 120 days," promising to achieve 95% inventory balance accuracy; as every (inventory) quality improvement program starts with attitude, the project kickoff could include a message such as "inventory accuracy is fun, so have fun with it."[401] As another example, Brooks and Wilson propose a three-phase model to developing inventory record accuracy.[402] Even if accuracy problems will possibly never be eliminated and many savings associated with better quality cannot be captured with traditional ROI models,[403] data problems can and should be significantly reduced through process changes, documentation, training, and application of technology.

For humans, it is difficult to consistently execute a task thousands of times right *every time*, in contrast to doing it right just once.[404] Consequently, the human-machine interface is a prime target for improving accuracy, as most problem data are finally entered or caused by humans.[405] Input devices, such as bar code readers, Radio Frequency Identification (RFID) technology, or voice recognition systems can help to facilitate and stabilize data entry processes, and to meet traceability requirements.[406]

With regard to process improvement, procedures have to be documented in a simple, user-centered language, using terminology at the education level of the employees, and have to be task specific;[407] together with the procedural documentation, a glossary – especially for new or non-standard terms – should be made available. As an example, Web site design programs can help to design documentation which is both current and easy to browse, accessible online via intranet.[408] Procedures must be designed to make accuracy easy (in the sense of Poka-Yoke[409]); providing sales managers with a straightforward way to withdraw stock items both makes their life easy and maintains inventory accuracy.[410]

Documenting a "to be" process does not mean it is *implemented*; education and training of the stakeholders of a process are needed.[411] "Education" is the process of dealing with the "why" a new procedure is needed,[412] including a transfer of facts (factual knowledge) and a behavior change.[413] Education should include the principles of how business processes are implemented, the importance of data accuracy in the context of an orga-

---

[401] Sheldon (2004), p. 16.
[402] Brooks and Wilson (1995), p. 28.
[403] Piasecki (2003), p. 69.
[404] Piasecki (2003), p. 6.
[405] Piasecki (2003), p. 29.
[406] Kelepouris et al. (2007), p. 183.
[407] Piasecki (2003), p. 47.
[408] Piasecki (2003), p. 51.
[409] Cf. Section 2.1.4.6.
[410] Piasecki (2003), p. 68.
[411] Piasecki (2003), p. 53.
[412] Sheldon (2004), p. 114.
[413] Brooks and Wilson (1995), p. 89.

nization's success in the marketplace, and examples of how high-performers implement process controls for improving data quality.[414] "Training" on the other hand is an act of transferring process and procedural knowledge.[415] Education of process owners and a task force (level 1), other employees and managers involved with inventory transactions (level 2), and all employees (level 3) is particularly important. Brooks and Wilson recommend to start training sessions with a flowchart showing the high-level "to be" process, followed by a thoughtful selection of transactions needed to handle inventory management.[416] As a means to ensure that the objectives of the training sessions have been achieved, test questions can be submitted at the end to trainees, and employees failing the test must then be given additional training.[417] At the minimum, employees must understand, and be held accountable for, working according to policies and procedures,[418] even if some employees seem to be "specifically more accurate" than others.[419]

Sheldon shows how an excessive choice of options with regard to materials movement transactions offered by inventory support systems (today typically ERP systems) may lead to mistakes. As each of these transactions requires specific skills and knowledge, the risk of committing mistakes is high, and a good practice is to limit the number of such options to a minimum. Transactions for managing inventory items should not be complicated or confusing[420] and each of the fields in the materials master records must have a defined ownership, even if these records do not belong to a given group or department, but to all groups.[421] Finally, despite widespread use of IT in organizations (especially, digital displays), paper documents often remain an important information carrier in any organization, and need to be considered and improved, e.g., using alternate line shading to make it easy to remain on a line when reading a report, or adding formats to highlight important data elements.[422]

Controlling Inventory Data Quality

The result of inventory accuracy measurements and the progress of improvement projects should be tracked, per controlled inventory domain, and displayed in high-traffic areas.[423] Besides giving training sessions, responsibilities for actions and results have to be permanently assigned; as a rule, responsibility should be assigned at the lowest possible

---

[414] Sheldon (2004), p. 23.
[415] Brooks and Wilson (1995), p. 90; Sheldon (2004), p. 114.
[416] Piasecki (2003). p. 54.
[417] Piasecki (2003), p. 59.
[418] Piasecki (2003), p. 69.
[419] Piasecki (2003), p. 21.
[420] Broeckelmann (1999), p. 49.
[421] Sheldon (2004), p. 180.
[422] Piasecki (2003), p. 33.
[423] Sheldon (2004), p. 138.

organizational level.[424] With regard to user skills, it is further essential that, after an initial education and training effort, new employees joining an organization are given the same training, as otherwise process degradation will occur over time.[425]

2.3.3.2 Production Planning and Control

Production Planning and Control (PPC) systems are often very complex software systems, with a multitude of configuration options. As an example, the production planning module of SAP ERP offers a range of 150–200 parameters, of which 40 are bound to individual material master datasets; applied to the case of a company using 25,000 active parts, it will have to manage about 1,000,000 individual parameter settings.[426] The complexity of and pressure in software implementation projects often lead to sub-optimal parameter settings (e.g., implementers just retaining default values) and, in the worst case, to economic damage.[427] Moreover, due to the complexity of the data model used by PPC applications, data errors may propagate through the many functional modules of the system.[428]

Wermers gives examples of the impact of low data quality on applications in production planning, such as a need for increased efforts to find, maintain, and effectively use data, or the fact that users create their "own" (duplicate) database.[429] As the accuracy of scheduling of production and sales orders heavily depends on the data used, customer satisfaction can also be affected and additional costs can arise (e.g., due to "scrap and rework") if data quality is insufficient.[430] In order to cope with data problems in material master and other critical data, correction strategies aimed at both the field and dataset levels are recommended, and need to be embedded in a control loop oriented data quality management system.[431]

2.3.3.3 Accounting Information Systems

Accounting Information Systems (AIS) manage financial transaction data generated by purchasing, production, and selling processes. Besides applications of accounting data for operational purposes and for decision-making, information products created with AIS are also relevant for external stakeholders, such as shareholders or government agencies. Information products such as income statements or balance sheets have to be certifiably error-free: auditors can use "black box" tests (considering only the inputs and outputs of

---

[424] Brooks and Wilson (1995), p. 91.
[425] Sheldon (2004), p. 116.
[426] Dittrich et al. (2000), p. 1.
[427] Dittrich et al. (2000), pp. 10–13.
[428] Wermers (2000), p. 114.
[429] Wermers (2000), p. 63
[430] Wermers (2000), p. 64.
[431] Wermers (2000), pp. 96–116.

an IT system) or "white box" tests (identifying and examining the data quality controls put in place) to assess the quality of accounting data.[432] Among the factors influencing data quality in AIS, Xu cites the role of top management, data quality polices and standards, user education, organizational structures, process management, and supplier involvement.[433]

2.3.3.4   Supply Chain Planning

In the domain of B2B collaboration, involving several business partners, supply chain processes can be planned and executed using dedicated Supply Chain Management (SCM) software. SCM systems can help to improve planning quality in a supply chain, but they must be fed with accurate data from all partners' systems, in order to operate according to specifications.[434] Often SCM systems are built on top of ERP systems; in the case of SAP software environments, SAP ERP data can be imported into SAP SCM systems, a fact that helps to avoid redundancies between SAP transaction and planning systems.[435]

Even if retailers normally use technologies such as bar code scanners in order to achieve high data accuracy, Raman et al. found in a study that data used for SCM in retail was "often wildly inaccurate," leading to a reduction of a company's profits by 10%, because of excess inventory costs and lost sales due to stockouts.[436] Reasons for the errors are, however, not only data entry problems, but also misplaced items or poor practices in internal logistics. Operational optimization initiatives in retail, aimed at "speedy checkouts" or "reducing paperwork" pursue respectable objectives, but must be well designed to not compromise the quality of supply chain data.[437]

2.3.3.5   Customer Relationship Management

The success of Customer Relationship Management (CRM) applications depends on the quality of customer data, a fact that is also recognized by many specialized data quality software vendors.[438] Corporate management is rarely aware of operational problems due to a lack of data quality in CRM systems until the financial impact becomes evident.[439] Typical forms of data quality flaws hitting CRM systems are typographic errors (wrong representation or spelling of an entry, blank values, or the use of nicknames)[440] occurring when call center agents capture details about customers, the unwillingness of Web users

---

[432] Kaplan et al. (1998), p. 72.
[433] Xu (2000), p. 630.
[434] Müller and Seuring (2007), p. 491.
[435] Wood (2007), p. 15.
[436] Raman et al. (2001), p. 2.
[437] Raman et al. (2001), p. 3.
[438] Swoyer (2007).
[439] Betts (2002).
[440] Herzog et al. (2007), p. 88.

to disclose personal data, or duplicate records created by mistake when several communication channels to customers are used.[441] Results of insufficient data quality include
the financial losses caused by sending expensive product catalogs in duplicate, increased
credit risk incurred due to several identities used by a same customer when shopping, or
the loss of customer goodwill.[442] On the other hand, incorrect customer data can frustrate
customers and drive them away, leading to reduced revenues and increased costs.[443]

2.3.3.6 Data Warehousing and Business Intelligence

A very large part of the data quality literature focuses on DWHs and the related design
and usage processes.[444] DWHs are software applications characterized as "subject oriented, integrated, nonvolatile, and time variant collections of data in support of management's decisions."[445] "Subject orientation" stands for the grouping of data around subjects
such as customers or suppliers, by aggregating data from a large number of transactions;
"integrated" means that input data can come from many sources, including transaction
systems or external market intelligence providers;[446] "nonvolatile and time variant" stand
for the requirements of long-term availability of data. In most DWH environments, tool-
supported Extraction, Transformation, and Loading (ETL) processes are implemented to
ensure that data from various sources fulfills the quality requirements imposed by analytic applications.[447] The principal reason for data quality issues in DWHs is the fact
that they integrate data from heterogeneous sources and have implemented views which
source systems generating the imported data could not anticipate.[448]

Built mostly on top of DWHs, Business Intelligence (BI) applications also suffer heavily from insufficient data quality, especially from a lack of clear definitions of source data
and application specifications: visually designing a "pretty pie chart" may be straightforward, but in order to implement an application useful for business users, a BI project team
has to focus on the quality of data that will be displayed.[449] An effective management of
data during an ETL process typically means addressing data quality aspects such as multiple meanings for the same data elements, multiple sources of data elements, differing
levels of history, or data cleanliness and accuracy.[450]

[441] Treiblmaier (2005); Maydanchik (2007), p. 11; Naumann (2007), p. 27.
[442] Sarsfield (2007).
[443] Klier (2008), p. 235.
[444] Cf., e.g., Jarke and Vassiliou (1997); Gebhardt et al. (1998); Ballou and Tayi (1999); English (1999b);
    Taylor (1999); Ma et al. (2000); Scherz (2000); Leitheiser (2001); English (2002); Kim (2002); Dijcks
    (2004); Agosta (2005); Imhoff (2005); Payton and Zahay (2005); Ferengul (2006); Russom (2006b).
[445] Inmon (1996), p. 33.
[446] Ballou and Tayi (1999), p. 73.
[447] Kimball et al. (1998), p. 23.
[448] Strong et al. (1997a), p. 42.
[449] Gonzales (2005), p. 3.
[450] Gonzales (2005), p. 5.

2.3.3.7 Internal Audit

During corporate Governance, Risk, and Compliance (GRC) activities, internal auditors are called upon to provide management with analyses, consulting for process improvement, and risk management services.[451] Business IT applications – such as ERP systems – are most often an important source of information for internal audits, as transaction data is assessed using individualized procedures, statistical sampling, or mass data audits.[452]

Software vendors address this domain with specific applications: SAP, as an example, offers an "SAP GRC Process Control solution," providing control documentation, evaluation, certification, and reporting and analysis tools, to enable internal audit teams to gain better visibility into business processes and to ensure the reliability of financial statement reporting.[453] But even when using dedicated software tools in combination with ERP systems, finding and accessing relevant business data in large organizations can be challenging: besides ERP packages, legacy systems and their data have to be considered, and merger and acquisition activities may further increase complexity.[454]

The points of contact between internal audit and data quality are twofold: internal auditors firstly have to rely on the quality of business data needed to assess an organization's internal operations; secondly, data quality itself is often an indirect indicator of the smoothness of operations and a partial result of internal audit activities.

2.3.4 Other Application Domains

2.3.4.1 Governmental Agencies

In the U.S., the Congress has promoted the Federal "Data Quality Act" (DQA)[455] as a means of putting pressure on the administration to use and disseminate accurate information.[456] Additionally, guidelines have been issued to provide policy and procedural guidance for ensuring and maximizing the quality, objectivity, utility, and integrity of information disseminated by Federal agencies, including statistical information.[457] Both initiatives can be seen as a response to increased use of IT systems in administrations.[458] However, many government agencies face problems in implementing the necessary procedures and coping with the high costs and the other negative impacts of such regulations.[459]

---

[451] Institute of Internal Auditors (2004).
[452] Boenner et al. (2006), p. 257.
[453] Kennedy (2007); Schöler et al. (2007), p. 175; SAP (2008d).
[454] Boenner et al. (2007), p. 120.
[455] U.S. Office of Management and Budget (2002).
[456] Bisong (2003); Gasser (2003).
[457] U.S. Office of Management and Budget (2002), p. 8452; U.S. Office of Special Counsel (2002); Todd Stevens (2007).
[458] Gasser (2003), p. 24.
[459] English and Perez (2003).

2.3.4.2   Banking: Basel II

The "Basel Accords," especially the second agreement ("Basel II"), constitute a framework for initiatives requiring a minimum amount of capital to guarantee the financial stability of banking institutions.[460] "Basel II" increases the pressure on financial institutions to document and permanently evaluate risks and, hence, also addresses data management policies and practices.

2.3.4.3   Healthcare

In the increasingly information-intensive healthcare sector, data quality aspects are gaining importance in the eyes of legislators, consumers, and service providers. Lorence and Jameson provide an overview of the legislation and the implementation of data quality management procedures in the U.S., observing that a consistent adoption of data management practices is still lacking, due to poor usage of data error checking and editing functions in IT systems, and a lack of adoption of standardized language dictionaries.[461] Belshé and Shewry present a comprehensive data quality framework for improving the data collection processes related with an AIDS drug assistance program.[462] Finally, the U.S. Joint Commission has issued detailed specifications on how to collect and validate clinical data, and how to measure and report its quality.[463]

2.3.4.4   Defense

As in the domain of healthcare, data quality can save lives and/or cause death in the area of defense, as the cases of the bombing of the Chinese embassy[464] or the downing of the Iranian Airbus 655[465] show. The large size and the complexity of military organizations and their operations may expose them to data quality problems. In this context, Galway and Hanks describe severe data quality problems existing between "retail" and "wholesale" logistics units of the U.S. Army in the product identification domain, such as a lack of consensus on definitions and data management practices, leading to operational problems and a lack of decision support in military logistics.[466]

---

[460] Bank for International Settlements (2004).
[461] Lorence and Jameson (2002), p. 751.
[462] Belshé and Shewry (2004).
[463] Joint Commission (2004).
[464] Redman (2001), p. 39.
[465] Fisher and Kingma (2001).
[466] Galway and Hanks (1996), p. 2.

2.3.4.5   Geographical Information Systems

Geographical Information Systems (GIS) manage objects such as points or lines, serving spatial applications for planning and administration in civil engineering; the effort to create and maintain data is by far the largest cost item in a GIS project and the life span of data is the longest of any system component (hardware, software, data).[467] Data quality is hence both a factor affecting decisions involving real world costs and a long-term IT issue. The ISO/TS 19138 standard defines a typical set of data quality measures for the applications of GIS.[468]

2.4   Legislation in the Area of Data Quality

2.4.1   Corporate Finance

As a reaction to a series of large enterprise failures – Enron's collapse in 2001 was considered as a "trigger for increased scrutiny of corporate reporting and governance procedures"[469] – the U.S. Congress legislated the Sarbanes-Oxley Act (SOX) in 2002.[470] This Act contains prescriptions about corporate governance and, in particular, corporate financial risk assessment and reporting in Section 404 (SOX 404). Any company listed in the U.S. has to carry out several mandatory activities in relation with SOX 404:[471] management has to assess the effectiveness of an organization's Internal Controls over Financial Reporting (ICOFR) and an independent auditor has to report on the management's assessment and to comment on the effectiveness of the ICOFR.

Even though SOX appears as a "gold mine" for academic research,[472] the first evidence collected on the impact of SOX on information quality in financial reporting is mixed. Begley et al. found that overall information quality had increased immediately after the enactment of SOX, but declined in the years after: management reduced voluntary public disclosures after litigation concerns, thus reducing the availability of relevant information.[473]

2.4.2   Privacy

Council of Europe Convention 108 ("for the Protection of Individuals with regard to Automatic Processing of Personal Data"), ratified by 32 European countries, aims for a rec-

---

[467] Stanek et al. (1995).
[468] International Organization for Standardization (2006).
[469] Begley et al. (2007), p. 6.
[470] Bibawi and Nicoletti (2005).
[471] Bibawi and Nicoletti (2005); Agami (2006); Public Company Accounting Oversight Board (2007), p. 1.
[472] Boyle and Grace-Webb (2007), p. 2.
[473] Begley et al. (2007), pp. 26–27.

onciliation between the fundamental values of the respect for privacy of individuals and the free flow of information between peoples.[474] In particular, Article 5 declares that automatic processing of personal data ("any information relating to an identified or identifiable individual") is to be "(a) obtained and processed fairly and lawfully; (b) stored for specified and legitimate purposes and not used in a way incompatible with those purposes; (c) adequate, relevant and not excessive in relation to the purposes for which they are stored; (d) accurate and, where necessary, kept up to date; (e) preserved in a form which permits identification of the data subjects for no longer than is required for the purpose for which those data are stored."[475] The Convention further defines categories of data (about racial origin, political opinions, religious and other beliefs, health, sexual orientation, or criminal convictions) which must not be processed automatically, "unless domestic law provides appropriate safeguards." European Community (EC) Directive 95/46/EC ("on the protection of individuals with regard to the processing of personal data and on the free movement of such data") targets the same objectives in the EC countries and requires member states to enact specific data protection legislation.[476]

As a consequence, at least personal data processed by business IT systems is protected by law, in European countries. Means have to be provided to inhibit unwanted or illegal modification of data values, endangering the integrity of personal data; voluntary modification of such data is subject to lawful pursuit.[477] Consequently, most business IT systems contain functions aimed at protecting data against illicit or accidental modification, such as user authentication or cryptographic procedures; these functions must, however, be well understood by implementers and configured correctly.

2.5 Tools and Techniques for Data Quality Management

When discussing instruments for data quality management, it must first be noted that quality instruments such as the Seven QC tools[478] can very often be used for data quality improvement projects. Additionally, a specific software market and modeling techniques for data quality exist, which will be described in this section.

2.5.1 Software Market for Data Quality

The market for data quality software has evolved from a neglected domain to a competitive "battlefield" of the IT industry; in the most recent years, major data quality software

---

[474] Council of Europe (1981).
[475] Council of Europe (1981), Art. 5.
[476] European Parliament and Council (1995).
[477] Hornberger and Schneider (2000), p. 65.
[478] Cf. Section 2.1.4.1.

suppliers have been taken over by larger software vendors.[479] At the same time, the market for data quality software has grown from its traditional focus on Customer Data Integration (CDI) to product and financial data quality oriented software tools, including typical functions for data profiling, matching of datasets, parsing of documents, standardization of data values, and functions to normalize and integrate international data.[480]

English distinguishes five categories of data quality software products, namely analysis/assessment, rule discovery, cleansing, data defect prevention, and meta-data quality tools:[481]

- *Analysis products* typically measure data quality characteristics such as the completeness of values or the precision of data values. These tools are, however, often not capable of measuring data accuracy, and only check conformance to rules.
- *Rule discovery* tools identify business rules in databases, typically by using data mining techniques. A major limitation of rule discovery tools is their inability to identify the totality of relevant rules.
- *Cleansing tools* are used to improve data quality, by standardizing, enhancing, and consolidating data. Cleansing tools are limited by the fact that they are not able to correct the entirety of lacking or imprecise data.
- *Defect prevention products* try to eliminate the creation of data errors at the source, by providing data edit or validation rules. They are able to enforce validity of data values, i.e., their conformance to rules; on the other hand, they cannot guarantee correctness of data values.
- *Meta-data tools* enforce the conformity of data to naming standards, the normalization of data models, or foreign key integrity. Again, tools of this category cannot guarantee that managed data is complete, relevant, or correctly defined.

Many data quality problems are more than a "simple violation of declared database integrity constraints"[482] and the rules describing "good" data can be very complex and subject to frequent changes.[483] Business Rule Management Systems (BRMS)[484] can help organizations to address a large proportion of data quality issues (such as consistency or completeness problems) through enforcement of complex rules at the data capture, exchange, or integration stages.[485] BRMS have emerged in the information systems context

---

[479] Swoyer (2007).

[480] Smalltree (2006b).

[481] English (1999b), pp. 314–325. InfoImpact also maintains a database with an updated catalog of data quality products, cf. InfoImpact (2007).

[482] Maydanchik (1999).

[483] Chanana and Koronios (2007), p. 262.

[484] Cf., e.g., Herbst and Knolmayer (1994), Herbst (1997), Schlesinger (1999), Von Halle (2002), Ross (2003), Endl (2004), or Klaus (2005).

[485] Chanana and Koronios (2007), p. 263.

as tools for separating business logic from their implementation in software applications, allowing business professionals – and not only IT staff – to describe the "should be" behavior of organizational processes.[486] Rules recommended for data quality management applications of BRMS include null value and domain membership rules for assuring quality of references, domain and enumeration rules for assuring quality in mappings, value constraints and attribute value restrictions, and rules to enforce relationships.[487]

2.5.2   Data Quality Modeling Techniques

Data quality modeling techniques have been touted as a tool to specify data quality problems, to carry out root cause analyses, and to configure software packages:

- Schwinn described a procedure for defining information requirements of an organization using "data maps," drafting the complexity of reports against the retention period of the data.[488]

- Shankaranarayanan et al. proposed a modeling notation called "Information Production Map" (IP-MAP) using elements of data flow and process modeling, in order to represent the production and consumption of information.[489] The eight constructs contained in the formalism include well-known elements such as data sources, processes, or data storage, but also specific ones such as a "data quality filter," which implements data quality checks and allows branching in the case of correct or incorrect data.[490]

- IP-MAP has also been used to extend other modeling approaches, such as Event-driven Process Chains (EPC)[491] or the Unified Modeling Language (UML).[492]

- Wang et al. described a variant of the Entity-Relationship model consisting of an extension to existing data structures, adding quality characteristics, quality indicators, inspection tags, and credibility information (e.g., the name of the producer or the source of a data item).[493]

- Buneman et al. developed an algorithm for computing the provenance of data generated by a database query, adding information on where and why data has been created.[494] The method applies to any annotation information for data, such as a

---

[486] Chanana and Koronios (2007), p. 262.
[487] Chanana and Koronios (2007), p. 264.
[488] Schwinn (2008), p. 256.
[489] Shankaranarayanan et al. (2000).
[490] Shankaranarayanan et al. (2000), p. 6.
[491] Cf., e.g., Keller et al. (1992); IP-MAP extension for EPC described in Pierce (2002).
[492] Cf., e.g., the UML resource pages of the Object Management Group http://www.uml.org/; IP-UML extension described in Scannapieco et al. (2002).
[493] Wang et al. (2001), pp. 7–10; Batini and Scannapieco (2006), pp. 52–54.
[494] Buneman et al. (2001), p. 1.

source relation or a comment on the data.[495] As Groth et al. found, the determination of the set of data sources used to produce a given data item is difficult in the context of database systems,[496] even if tools for performing a "data lineage" have been developed that allow analysts to track information objects to the source items they were derived from, through a series of transformations.[497]

- In an attempt to assess data quality and to optimize the effectiveness of data quality controls under cost constraints, Bagchi et al. demonstrated how process models can be linked to data quality estimates. The authors proposed to augment existing business process models with data quality controls, for detecting and mitigating errors; in case of errors, a transaction can be sent back for rework, resuming at an earlier point in the process.[498]

2.6 Guidelines for Improving Data Quality

The beginning of a data quality initiative may be planned or may be the consequence of a "disparate data shock" opening managers' eyes.[499] It must always be held in mind that correcting low-quality data is always a costly and non-value-added project activity;[500] on the other hand, English points out that the business case should not be made for data quality improvement projects, but rather for the costs of maintaining a state of "scrap and rework" caused by *not* having quality data.[501] In this area, Arnold gives a summary of reasons why organizations are not willing to correct data quality: changing a software environment in operation is a costly and difficult experiment, the priority of a change may be too low to warrant the investment, the software is too constraining for modifications, the Return on Investment (ROI) of the project does not meet an organization's targets, or copyright or legal issues impede a possible modification of the software.[502]

Data quality can basically be improved using reactive or proactive methods.[503] Reactive approaches used for addressing data quality issues can consist of waiting until a customer or member of staff signals a data error, checking data regularly against external world facts or a reference database ("database bashing"), or enforcing data integrity

---

[495] Batini and Scannapieco (2006), p. 59.
[496] Groth et al. (2006), p. 141.
[497] Cui and Widom (2001), p. 471.
[498] Bagchi et al. (2006), p. 401.
[499] Brackett (2000), p. 12.
[500] Brackett (2000), p. 288.
[501] English (1999b), p. xvii.
[502] Arnold (1992), p. 36.
[503] Brackett (1994), p. 144.

and conformance by data edit checks; all reactive "methods" have, however, substantial disadvantages, as it will be shown in the next paragraph.[504]

The first approach – to passively wait for data quality problems to "surface on their own" – is considered the worst method,[505] as it is obvious that expecting customers to find and report data errors is unthinkable in any quality-driven customer philosophy. Waiting for employees to find errors, possibly while they are experiencing severe problems during the execution of business processes, is not an acceptable alternative either. Secondly, comparing existing data with an external "reality" quickly poses questions in terms of coverage, time, and resources spent; if the procedure has to be repeated, checking errors may occur. Moreover, comparing data to external world facts, even on a regular basis, does not help to avoid future errors. As an alternative to checking data against reality, it may sometimes be possible to compare data against a second database (database bashing); when data items from both sources agree, they are considered to be correct. Such checks pose several problems:[506] when a discrepancy is found, which data source will be the correct one? And what if both values are equal, but wrong? Thirdly, data edits (edit checks) are application components testing whether a given data record fulfills certain rules,[507] e.g., before inserting a record entered in an entry screen into a database table, "currency" attribute values could be checked against a table containing the list of ISO 4217 3-letter codes. Such checks, however, may affect software performance, to the extent that database-backed integrity checks are often disabled in business applications. Moreover, full integrity of data as enforced by rules does not automatically imply data accuracy, as also data having no counterpart in the external world may be perfectly respecting constraints.[508]

When looking at data quality management models, many similarities between quality initiatives in production/process and data management exist:[509]

1. *Strategic positioning:* Any (data) quality initiative must be embedded in a strategic framework, ensuring that improvements are targeting real economic benefits and that financial funding is assured. Also, for larger projects which go beyond relatively simple efficiency considerations, board-level support has to be secured.

2. *Never automate a poor process:* As Hammer advocates, organizations should "obliterate," rather than "automate" processes: in particular, low quality processes should never be automated.[510] Also, it is almost always less costly to design and

---

[504] Redman (1996), pp. 22–24.

[505] Herzog et al. (2007), p. 12.

[506] Maydanchik (2007), p. 10.

[507] Batini and Scannapieco (2006), p. 31.

[508] Maydanchik (2007), p. 8.

[509] Redman (1996), p. 18; Schwinn et al. (1999), p. 229.

[510] Hammer (1990), p. 2; Redman (1996), p. 10.

produce a product or service correctly the first time, in order to avoid at least the direct costs of insufficient (data) quality such as the efforts for rework or warranty.[511]

3. *Project environment:* (Data) quality initiatives have to be managed as projects, with clear objectives, planning, and resources, as "all quality improvement takes place project by project."[512]

4. *Customer orientation:* (Data) quality requirements formulated by (data) customers have to be collected in a systematic way and must be broken down to an application level.[513] Here, it has to be considered that data is not only used for the immediate purpose of the persons in operational business processes, but also for monitoring or analytic purposes.[514]

5. *Chain of responsibilities:* A data quality project must lead to a situation in which data processing is under control. As responsibility is always an important prerequisite for quality, data management or information product management must be explicitly attached to critical domains.[515]

6. *Integration with existing quality and process frameworks:* The description of (data) production and application can borrow heavily from quality frameworks such as ISO 9000 or TQM. Any major (data) quality initiative must therefore integrate with existing quality and process management procedures.

7. *Life cycle view:* Data quality has to be managed over the entire life cycle of data items.[516] Loops are essential for the stability of control and quality systems and, using a life cycle perspective, quality feedback loops can be used for data quality improvement.[517]

8. *Modeling and documentation:* (Data) quality processes have to be modeled, in order to correctly define "as is" and "to be" processes and to realize improvements.[518] Besides incorporating real-world processes, organizational structures, applications, and data structures, the models must also cover restrictions and rules.[519] To efficiently treat data, many authors recommend using special meta-data repositories, for documenting applicable formats and constraints.[520]

---

[511] Redman (1996), p. 8.
[512] Juran (1988), p. 35.
[513] Wang et al. (1993), p. 674.
[514] Schwinn et al. (1999), p. 230.
[515] E.g., by imposing requirements such as "the responsibility for compiling balance of payments statistics is clearly specified" by Carson (2001).
[516] Schwinn et al. (1999), p. 230.
[517] Lesca and Lesca (1995), p. 170; Orr (1998), p. 67; Schwinn et al. (1999), p. 229.
[518] Wang et al. (1993), pp. 673–675.
[519] Schwinn et al. (1999), p. 230.
[520] Cf., e.g., Schwinn et al. (1999), p. 230; Todd Stevens (2007).

9. *Focus:* A focus on the most critical (data) objects is essential, as any IT system contains large quantities of data structures and values, and not all of them are equally important. The amount of data under consideration has to be limited, as an organization collecting data that no one uses or requires simply wastes time and other resources.[521] Factors for criticality are, e.g., risk and economic damage of low quality, or the frequency of usage of some data item.[522] For business companies seeking to minimize the economic impact of errors, Redman recommends to focus first on customer data, then on billing and pricing relevant records.[523]

Data quality can be managed in two fundamental ways. Firstly, data quality can be built into process design, avoiding (or quickly eliminating) entry errors by organizational responsibility and feedback, and usage of technologies such as bar-code readers or data edits. Secondly, in an "inspection and rework" oriented improvement approach, information products are inspected for conformance to standards, e.g., using "data quality firewalls;"[524] rejected items are reworked or disposed of until successful inspection.[525]

To put the findings of this chapter in an order usable for their later application to ERP systems, the essential steps for designing data quality into an information system context and for setting up data quality improvement projects will be briefly summarized, using the DMADV and DMAIC patterns.

2.6.1 Data Quality and the DMADV Model

The early consideration of data quality aspects in the design of an IT system architecture or the implementation of an IT system in an organization can help to avoid many of the problems arising during operations. With a focus on data quality, the DMADV approach[526] can be interpreted as follows:

Define: As in other contexts of quality management, the mapping of customer (i.e., data user) requirements to design features (i.e., the design of enterprise applications and of the organization in which IT systems and users are embedded) is essential, and can be supported by quality methods such as QFD.[527] Moreover, modeling can help information system professionals to plan and identify data quality problems before they occur, e.g., using IP-MAP,[528] FMEA,[529] or SIPOC[530] models. Also, a possi-

---

[521] Evans and Lindsay (2002), p. 451.
[522] Schwinn et al. (1999), p. 231.
[523] Redman (1996), p. 28.
[524] Imhoff (2005).
[525] Redman (1996), p. 22.
[526] Cf. Section 2.1.5.4.
[527] Cf. Section 2.1.4.5.
[528] Cf. Section 2.5.2.
[529] Cf. Section 2.1.4.7.
[530] Cf. Section 2.1.4.4.

bility to formally model data quality is to extend existing data models by "tagging" data records with characteristics such as source, creation time, or collection method of data.[531] Customer requirements have to be captured in business or end user language (e.g., in the form of a specific data dictionary), project staff have to develop a consistent set of data quality requirements, customer requirements have to be translated into technical requirements, performance specifications for each process have to be established by "budgeting" requirements to the relevant processes of the information chain, and overall specifications for each process have to be compiled.[532] The impact of low quality data in all relevant application domains of an IT system has to be assessed and the possible benefits of special data quality extensions ("add-ons") must be quantified.[533]

Measure: Based on the information gathered in the previous step, possible partial system design choices are generated, assessed for use in the situation described above, and prioritized.

Analyze: High-level information system design concepts which prevent certain categories of errors such as organization-wide numbering schemes, a "master" database with controlled redundancy, or a business rule management system are set up.

Design: During the Design Phase, the retained candidate elements of an overall solution are designed in detail, and additional software components are purchased and integrated. As an example, Redman suggests the following preventive actions for improving the handling of data: unnecessary interfaces should be avoided; data capture must be as automatic as possible (e.g., using sensor technologies such as RFID) and placed close to the point of origin; entry screens and forms should be simple and intuitive, providing definitions and explanations; intermediary steps in the handling of the Graphical User Interface (GUI) must be automated; redundant data entries have to be eliminated.[534] Besides software and data management aspects, the design of organizational structures and workplace-level job descriptions may have to be reviewed.

Verify: In this final phase, the IT solution as designed is implemented in a prototype stage and tested in a testbed, before being rolled out to the entire organization.

Table 2.7 summarizes the relevant steps in the design of data quality using the DMADV pattern, juxtaposing activities, methods, and tools suitable for Data Quality Management (DQM).

---

[531] Cf. Section 2.2.6.2.
[532] Redman (1996), p. 149.
[533] Cf. Section 2.5.1.
[534] English (1999b), pp. 305–306.

Phase	DQM Activities	DQM Methods	DQM Tools
D	• Collect data user quality requirements • Classify data • Set objectives for data quality • Establish business case for data quality	• Information product modeling • Project management	• SIPOC, IP-MAP • FMEA • Fishbone diagram
M	• CTQ factor analysis, measure importance of data quality dimensions • Consider factors for data quality: data model, values, formats, etc. • Quality measurement of existing data	• Estimation of quality costs (COQ)	• QFD • FMEA
A	• Identify CTP factors • Analyze and select design options, aiming at CTQ as found above • Optimize life cycle cost	• Creativity methods • Process modeling	• Ontologies (e.g., Zachman framework) • SIPOC, IP-MAP • QFD • FMEA • Fishbone diagram
D	• Design the detailed CTP, the details of the information system support, including software settings and usage processes	• IT architecture planning and implementation • Organizational design • User education and training • User documentation • Simulation	• Ontologies • SIPOC, IP-MAP • QFD • FMEA
V	• Build a prototype of the information system, including organizational and human components • Run pilot tests • Document solution and anchor in process framework	• Measurement, observation	• Statistical methods • QFD.

Table 2.7: Data Quality Aware Information System Design (DMADV Pattern).

2.6.2 Data Quality and the DMAIC Model

In this section, data quality specific methods and tools for quality *improvement* will be presented. The DMAIC model[535] can be applied as follows to data quality improvement:

Define: Business-oriented data quality improvement projects must specify the need for and the level of data quality expected for successful use by data users;[536] this activity is identical to the "Define" phase in the application of the DMADV model.[537]

Measure: In this second step, characteristics of the data (e.g., the occurrence or frequencies of data patterns, on a database, record, or field level[538]) are extracted, possibly by using configurable data adapters for extracting data from transaction systems

---

[535]Cf. Section 2.1.5.4.
[536]English (1999b), p. 143; Huang et al. (1999), p. 42.
[537]Cf. Section 2.6.1.
[538]Naumann (2007), pp. 28–29.

(such as Xtract for SAP[539]) or sampling techniques, if full measurements are not possible, e.g., due to the large number of data items involved or the complexity of their relationships.[540] To effectively measure data quality, a multi-dimensional data quality assessment scheme is recommended, based on several criteria,[541] business rules to specify conformance, and acceptability thresholds.[542] Specific data analysis tools (e.g., from Arrah,[543] Datras,[544] or Talend[545]) can be used for profiling data and finding errors. With regard to measurements of the impact of data quality problems, the true costs of low quality may be hidden: finding and correcting wrong data is usually not charged to an account named "data quality," but will be included (and hidden) in normal operating costs. Visible damage caused by insufficient data quality can be observed at the customer and supplier interfaces of the enterprise, e.g., when financial transactions are affected.

Analyze: Once the quality of the data has been measured, classification schemata for data quality problems have to be used to frame the errors,[546] to detect the "diseases" affecting the data.[547] Data quality ranking methods can be used to consolidate data quality scores stemming from different contexts.[548] Classes of quality metrics serving to gauge the current status of data quality have to be defined, metrics must be linked to the organization's goals and objectives, and cost-benefit analyses allowing informed decision-making about initiatives to improve the quality of information have to be carried out.[549] Once a list of differences between the required and the current quality of data has been established and the activities needed to close the gap have been defined, it will be straightforward to quantify the costs of the data quality improvement project and to estimate the impact of improved quality in the processes considered. The "economic optimum level of quality"[550] will ultimately depend on factors such as the expected savings due to improved data quality.

Improve: Data errors have to be removed and the creation of future errors has to be prevented by adequate means. As a first step, the "to be" data flow (the creation process of information products) has to be modeled, together with the information about or-

---

[539] http://www.theobald-software.com/.

[540] Cf., e.g., Wang (1998), p. 61, Bobrowski et al. (1999), p. 7, or Wermers (2000), p. 77.

[541] Wang et al. (1995a), p. 352; Huang et al. (1999), p. 60; Naumann (2002), p. 42; Loshin (2005).

[542] Loshin (2008).

[543] http://www.arrah.in/.

[544] http://www.datras.de/.

[545] http://www.talend.com/.

[546] Cf., e.g., Lesca and Lesca (1995), pp. 136–162; Rahm and Do (2000), p. 3; Smith (2000).

[547] Lesca and Lesca (1995), pp. 15–20.

[548] Naumann (2002), pp. 51–66.

[549] Wang et al. (1995a), p. 349; Huang et al. (1999), p. 61.

[550] Burgess (1996), p. 9.

ganizational units to be traversed.[551] As to the sequence of activities, Redman recommends that the source and the creation of data errors have to be stopped, before extensive cleansing projects are initiated.[552] Actions focusing people, processes, and technology have to be taken:[553]

- Firstly, with regard to *people*, instruments focusing on IT users are management directives and/or incentives for employees, motivating them to correctly enter and periodically update "their" data.[554]

- Then *process* improvements can target (data) management procedures with external data suppliers, the establishment of formal data management processes (in parallel or in addition to existing business processes), and the assignment of responsibility for data quality.[555] Organizational problems created by the need for sharing data amongst separated organizational units can be settled by systems in which a unit A using data created by another unit B will have to pay unit B for providing high-quality data ("pay-for-quality").[556]

- Finally, on the *technology* side, the enforcement of integrity rules, a reduction of data redundancy,[557] or the integration of data quality "add-ons" can be envisaged.[558] Address data quality is particularly critical for successful customer-oriented marketing, as a continuous shift away from mass marketing to tailored (one-to-one) approaches can be observed[559] and permanent interfaces to services provided by specialized vendors (such as CDYNE[560] or Direct Mail Company[561]) are often inevitable: experts estimate that even in high-quality address databases (such as the 1990 U.S. Census data), 30% of the first names and 25% of the last names of individuals contain errors.[562] Integrity rules which can be measured and enforced by a database management system should be implemented, addressing domain, column, entity, referential, and user-defined integrity.[563] User front-ends should be designed in a way that keystrokes are minimized, values can be selected from a list where possible (instead of using free-form entries), and plausibility checks must be

---

[551] Cf. Section 2.5.2.
[552] Redman (2001), p. 33.
[553] Weigel (2008), p. 82.
[554] Alter (2002), p. 75.
[555] English (1999b), pp. 303–309.
[556] Galway and Hanks (1996), p. xiii.
[557] English (1999b), p. 305.
[558] Time Link International Corp. (2003).
[559] Stevens (2006), p. 228.
[560] http://www.cdyne.com/.
[561] http://www.direct-mail-company.com/.
[562] Herzog et al. (2007), p. 131.
[563] Codd (1990), pp. 243–258.

available (however, with the possibility of overriding the constraints).[564] Once data production is re-designed in a way to avoid data errors and relevant metadata objects (in particular database schemata) have been normalized, matched, and cleansed,[565] existing dirty data can be cleansed using specialized instruments such as ETL tools in a DWH environment.[566] However impressing data quality cleansing tools are, cleansing by eliminating "wrong" or "outdated" values may also carry a potential risk, as the "overwritten" values may have contained other (unexpected but valuable) data.[567]

Control: The final step of a DMAIC project, the control phase, standardizes (successful) process changes to maintain improved quality levels, develops and documents control instruments, and hands the controls over to process owners.[568] Feedback schemes have to be implemented, in order to ensure that data quality management becomes part of an organization's permanent quality environment.[569] To ensure long-term quality of data, a formal data quality assurance program is required,[570] which will typically include components such as business direction, management infrastructure, program administration, and an operational plan for improvement projects.[571] The objectives in the domain of data quality have to be agreed upon and communicated, responsibilities have to be allocated, and a measurement system has to be installed, tracking the implementation of a data quality strategy.[572]

Table 2.8 summarizes the application of selected methods and tools from quality management in data quality improvement activities, using the DMAIC project pattern.

2.6.3 Findings from the Literature: Quality of Business Data

Finding 2.1. As this chapter has shown, concepts developed in production and process oriented quality management literature can be applied to data quality by analogy.

Finding 2.2. Methods, formalisms, and tools used for data modeling can be extended to include data quality characteristics.

Finding 2.3. In an information systems setting, data quality improvement requires an interdisciplinary approach; elements addressing people, processes, and technology are needed.

---

[564] English (1999b), p. 305.
[565] Batini and Scannapieco (2006), p. 71.
[566] Cf. Section 2.3.3.6.
[567] Weigel and Schmid (2004), p. 2.
[568] Gitlow et al. (2006), p. 71.
[569] English (1999b), Section 2.3.2.1.
[570] Olson (2003), p. 3.
[571] Redman (1996), pp. 18–19.
[572] Evans and Lindsay (2002), p. 108.

Phase	DQM Activities	DQM Methods	DQM Tools
D	• Collect requirements for data quality improvement, at management and data user levels • Set and agree on objectives for the improvement project	• Information product modeling • Project management	• SIPOC, IP-MAP
M	• Define metrics for monitoring achievement of improvement goals • Measure the existing data processing system and the quality of data with regard to objectives	• Data profiling	• Data adapters for extracting data • Result databases
A	• Establish business case for data quality • Analyze and select options for improvements, aiming at CTQ • Optimize life cycle cost	• Statistical analyses • COQ	• SIPOC, IP-MAP • FMEA • Pareto chart analysis • Fishbone diagram
I	• Improve current capturing and processing methods • Improve data management and assign responsibility	• Organizational design • User education/training • User documentation • Simulation	• Metadata management • Data "tagging" • Fishbone diagram • *People:* directives, incentives, education/training, support • *Process:* specific information system processes, "pay-for-data" • *Technology:* adaptation of GUI, rule-based data edits, database bashing, data cleansing
C	• Establish data stewardship • Install data quality monitoring • Include data quality aspects in performance objectives • Adapt process landscape to (potentially) new procedures	• Management by objectives • Performance management	• Data quality monitoring.

Table 2.8: Data Quality Aware Information System Improvement (DMAIC Pattern).

2.7   Summary

Data is a critical resource in an organizational context, since most of today's activities
in enterprises generate and use electronic data. Poor data quality can affect an organization in many ways; adverse impacts on organizations with regard to operational, tactical,
and strategic levels have been documented. The causes of data quality problems are to
be found in an IT system itself (technology, architecture, application design) or in the
operational practices (system implementation, operations).

Data quality literature typically defines high quality data as data which is "fit" for
being used by data consumers, i.e., can be transformed into information products that
fulfill users' expectations. As seen in other domains of quality management, data quality
is hence a subjective and multidimensional concept, as expectations and the evaluation
of "fitness for use" may vary among individuals. To cope with multidimensionality, data
quality literature typically proposes the use of several data quality dimensions (e.g., describing the quality of a data model, of the data values contained in a database, or of the
way of presenting the data), which in turn include one or several data quality attributes,
such as "completeness," "accuracy," or "consistency." A data quality problem can then be
defined as a difficulty in one or more quality dimensions that makes data unfit for use or
violates relevant specifications. Because organizations often produce and use large quantities of data of various nature, origin, and quality, selection and classification of data to
be treated is crucial.

Successful data quality management has to be seen as a top-down initiative, which
includes management involvement, the design of chains of responsibility, and means to
plan, measure, and improve data quality in all organizational levels. The usage of widely
used quality methods such as DMADV or DMAIC in data quality design and improvement projects appears straightforward, and helps to integrate data quality projects in other
business improvement initiatives or quality management infrastructures.

The findings presented in Chapter 2 will now be used to critically analyze data quality in the context of ERP systems in Chapter 3, and will also serve as groundwork to
formulate a data quality management model suitable for the ERP context in Chapter 5.

Chapter 3

Critical Review of ERP Systems

Since the mid-1990's a large number of organizations, companies of all sizes or governmental agencies have decided to replace older, mostly home-grown IT systems by packaged ERP applications, in a decision to buy an organization-wide information infrastructure supporting their processes, rather than building (or continuing to maintain) it themselves.[1] In the context of this "package transition"[2] of the 1990's, the success of ERP systems can mainly be explained by the following factors:[3]

- Legacy systems – older, highly modified software applications with considerable internal development and maintenance costs – could be replaced by standard packages, incurring smaller and predictable maintenance fees;
- Rising concerns regarding the capability of the legacy IT infrastructure to work after Year 2000;
- Globalization of markets and businesses, requiring data availability and distributed data processing on a global scale;
- Increasing national and international regulatory environment, calling for more and more accurate product and business process documentation;
- A trend towards Business Process Re-engineering (BPR) and a focus on process standardization, fostered by standardization and quality initiatives such as ISO 9000;
- Emerging scalable and flexible client/server IT infrastructures;
- The "old managerial dream" of unifying and centralizing all IT systems needed by an organization into one single system.

---

[1] Markus et al. (2003b), p. 419; Swanson (2003), p. 56.
[2] Swanson (2003), p. 57.
[3] Austin (2001); Skok and Legge (2001), p. 189; Watson (2002), pp. 362–365; Adam and O'Doherty (2003), p. 277; Lightfoot and Salaway (2003), p. 2; Swanson (2003), p. 57; Songini (2004).

3.1 Important Concepts of ERP Systems

Until the end of the 1990's, ERP research was rare, and focused mostly on ERP implementation projects and success-and-failure research.[4] Since then, ERP systems have become prominent in research and practitioner papers: as an example, Moon counted 313 articles in 79 journals, published from January 2000 to May 2006.[5] The topics addressed by these publications can be divided into the following categories:[6]

- ERP system implementation (case studies, analysis of critical success factors, organizational change management, or cultural issues);
- Use of ERP systems (transaction and decision support, maintenance);
- Extension, e.g., in an inter-organizational integration perspective;
- Economic value, including productivity impact issues;
- Trends and perspectives;
- User education.

In the following section, the terminology used in the ERP system domain, the technical specifics, and the economic benefits will be explored, before narrowing the view on the processing of data and the related data quality problems in ERP environments.

3.1.1 Terminology

Finding a broadly agreed definition of what ERP exactly represents is difficult.[7] The American Association for Operations Management (APICS) has used several definitions of what ERP is, definitions which highlight the dual aspects of software system and embedded business process[8] and which document the shift of focus away from a software to a business and operations concept:[9] the APICS Dictionary (8th edition) defined an ERP system in 1995 as an "accounting-oriented information system for identifying and planning the enterprise-wide resources to take, make, ship and account for customer orders," while the APICS Dictionary (10th edition) in 2001 considered ERP to be "a method for the effective planning and controlling of all the resources needed to take, make, ship and account for customer orders in a manufacturing, distribution or service company."

In the production oriented information systems literature, ERP systems are often considered as a logical refinement of former Material Requirements Planning (MRP) and Manufacturing Resource Planning (MRP II) systems.[10] In this view, ERP answered pri-

---

[4] Parr and Shanks (2000); Rosemann (2003), p. 319; Møller (2005), p. 483.
[5] Moon (2007), p. 235.
[6] Moon (2007), p. 239.
[7] Klaus et al. (2000), p. 141.
[8] Sheldon (2004), p. 10.
[9] Deis (2006).
[10] Hayman (2000); Langenwalter (2000); Kennerley and Neely (2001), p. 103; Umble et al. (2003), p. 242.

marily the needs of manufacturing companies for better materials and logistics planning and management, then "made rapid inroads into other industries as companies saw improved information flow, productivity, and efficiency."[11] This (controversial) interpretation of ERP systems as descendants of manufacturing support systems has also motivated several authors to use a different terminology for this kind of IT system, in order to avoid the term "ERP."[12] As a matter of fact, ERP systems have "other legacies" in domains such as accounting or human resources administration:[13] from a historical perspective, major ERP vendors first implemented financial (SAP) or human resource (PeopleSoft) management components, before adding MRP functionality. When the development of SAP RF, SAP's first packaged software – a predecessor of today's SAP ERP – was completed in 1973, the first component made available was the financial module,[14] followed by materials management functionality.[15] The grouping of ERP system functionality around a financial base module appears natural, because most business activities have to be documented at least for fiscal or legal purposes.

In this study, the term "ERP system" will be used as an information system concept *per se*, drawing on the broader definition proposed by Shang and Seddon who define ERP systems as "large-scale organizational systems, i.e., systems composed of people, processes, and information technology, built around packaged enterprise application software."[16] The term "large-scale" takes a concrete form when considering the number of users of ERP systems, which can go up to hundreds or thousands of users; in one of the world's largest human resource management system applications, SAP has delivered an ERP system intended to provide self-service applications to nearly 700,000 U.S. postal workers.[17]

Three principal characteristics of ERP systems, namely data and process integration, business process orientation, and standardization of application functionality will be presented in the next sections.

3.1.1.1 Data and Process Integration

Many authors define ERP systems by their role as integration devices in the domains of transaction-oriented business processes in an organization.[18] Business-wide data integration is an important challenge in enterprise computing and is, as ERP systems promise to

---

[11] Hayman (2000), p. 137.

[12] Cf., e.g., Davenport (2000), p. 2, Grabski et al. (2003), p. 136, or Shang and Seddon (2003), p. 75.

[13] Møller (2005), p. 484.

[14] Meissner (1997), p. 35.

[15] Brady et al. (2001), p. 22.

[16] Shang and Seddon (2003), p. 75.

[17] SAP (2007d).

[18] Cf., e.g., Davenport (1999a), p. 160, Kennerley and Neely (2001), p. 103, Markus et al. (2003a), p. 23, or Holsapple and Sena (2005), p. 575.

address this issue, one of the major decision factors in favor of ERP systems.[19] Fragmentation of information in large business organizations leads to an inability of management to make decisions based on facts; in this situation, ERP systems provide the means for a consistent picture of the environment.[20] ERP systems such as SAP ERP enforce a tight coupling between information about the material flow and cost/financial accounting, as any transfer of materials (such as a goods entry movement or the passage of an item from one plant to the next) is instantly mirrored by an increase or decrease of the monetary value in the balance sheet. Such a strict coupling enforces the visibility in the supply chain and can help logistics to better comply with internal and external regulations.

Traditionally, enterprises have been organized into business functions (providing an orientation on the content of the work) or divisions (focused on product lines or customers); business functions correspond typically to departments such as production, sales, and marketing, and operate processes that may be commonly used throughout the enterprise, leading to a situation in which centralized IT support is possible and economically reasonable.[21] In contrast to "stovepipe" (or "silo") applications[22] designed to exclusively support a specific functional area,[23] ERP systems aim to replace distributed, interfaced applications and databases by a pool of applications and data, in order to avoid the waste of time and risk of errors related with interfaces.

ERP systems typically rely on a single database, in which data entered by any system user in the organization is stored and from which data is forwarded on demand to a multitude of applications; this "enter once, use many times" design extremely centralizes and streamlines the information flow, addressing the problem of fragmented information in large organizations cited above.[24] The resulting reduction of data errors in ERP systems should eventually lead to better decisions and better efficiency in processes, compared to stovepipe infrastructures.[25]

The integration of data and the sharing of application functionality help to automate data flows and business processes: in the example of a goods entry process, purchasing statistics (e.g., purchased quantity per item group, supplier, or purchasing manager) and supplier assessment records (e.g., the percentage of on time deliveries) are updated, storage locations are found and internal transport orders dispatched, the orderer of the goods is notified, and the costs incurred by the purchasing order are charged automatically on the issuing cost center – by the ERP system, without any manual intervention.[26] Besides

---

[19] AFOS (1996), p. 55.
[20] Davenport (1999a), p. 164.
[21] Alter (2002), pp. 10–11.
[22] Bancroft et al. (1998), p. 15.
[23] Schwinn et al. (1999), p. 65; Brown (2004), p. 6.
[24] Davenport (1999a), pp. 164–166; Brady et al. (2001), p. 13.
[25] Rizzi and Zamboni (1999), p. 368; Schwinn et al. (1999), p. 67; Poston and Grabski (2001), p. 273.
[26] AFOS (1996), p. 24.

automation, the data integration promised by ERP systems has several other beneficial effects. As an example, the way a customer pays off outstanding debts may influence the conditions used in the ensuing calculation of a quote to this same customer: if he or she is known to be a "bad payer" (information produced by the accounting department), the risk premium to be included in quotes (by the sales department) will be high; moreover, deliveries to "bad customers" can automatically be stopped (in the shipping department). The enforcement of this kind of business rule would not be possible without comprehensive data and process integration. Conversely, missing or inaccurate data can strongly affect data processing and even stall the execution of the physical process in ERP systems.[27]

3.1.1.2 Business Process Orientation

In a business environment, ERP systems are software packages designed to support the entire internal value chain of an enterprise, as a single piece of software that provides functionality to organize, manage, and supervise many business processes.[28] Their integrated database provides a consistent, readily accessible repository of data used in business processes such as purchasing, inventory control, manufacturing, sales, delivery, billing, accounts receivable, and human resources,[29] enabling integration of process fragments into consistent end-to-end, e.g., account-to-report, procure-to-pay, order-to-cash, or hire-to-retire processes.[30] The high degree of integration promises to assist organizations in the efficient management of their business processes and to exploit the potential of automation in information management. Better insight into the nature and sources of costs in business processes can be gained, serving as a starting point for business improvement. Management and accounting concepts, such as Activity Based Costing (ABC), need an integrated view of corporate processes and data, something ERP systems can offer.

3.1.1.3 Standardization of Application Functionality

In contrast to custom-designed software, ERP systems are "unlikely to be a perfect fit with every client's needs." They represent generic semi-finished software products which organizations must complete and shape to their needs before they can serve their purpose.[31] According to the terminology used by SAP, the term "customization" will be used in this study to describe the entire range of activities of adapting, tailoring, adding non-standard features, writing special reports, or changing the code of ERP packages.[32] The use of standardized packages that can be customized to the specific needs of an organization has

---

[27] Cf. case study 3 in Section 3.5.3.

[28] Rizzi and Zamboni (1999), p. 368; Kennerley and Neely (2001), p. 104; Alter (2002), p. 51.

[29] Alter (2002), p. 215.

[30] Galoppin and Caems (2007), p. 34.

[31] Shanks et al. (2003b), p. 3.

[32] Brand (1999), pp. 87–88; Buck-Emden (1999), p. 290.

many benefits, which will be explored later in Section 3.2.2. On the other hand, as the
functionality of a standard system must cover the most complex application case, the considerable functionality of the application software cannot just be "reduced to the needs"
of a given organization, a typical ERP system therefore contains a plethora of application
code that many organizations may decide they will never need.

SAP's first-generation SAP R/3 system, a typical ERP system representative of the
1990's and still in use today, bundled application functionality in modules as shown below:[33]

- *The Sales and Distribution (SD)* module contains all master and operational data
  for managing transactions with customers, especially sales orders;
- *Materials Management (MM)* facilitates purchasing and warehousing processes,
  supporting the handling of goods throughout the enterprise;
- The *Production Planning (PP)* module contains PPC functionality;
- *Quality Management (QM)* assists users in controlling quality parameters through-
  out the various business processes (e.g., goods entry or production testing);
- The *Plant Maintenance (PM)* module allows planning of preventive maintenance or
  handling customer inquiries;
- The *Human Resources (HR)* module supports employee recruiting, hiring, training,
  payroll, and compensation management;
- *Financial accounting (FI)* collects data from financial transactions and is the key
  information base for external reporting;
- The *Controlling (CO)* module collects data from business processes, covering the
  information needs for costs of profit centers, product management, and financial
  controlling;
- *Asset Management (AM)* supports the management of fixed assets, including the
  handling of depreciation;
- The *Project System (PS)* contains controlling instruments for time, cost, and revenue
  management in all kind of projects;
- The *Workflow (WF)* module facilitates the controlled execution of formalized business processes;
- *Industry "Solutions" (IS)* deliver predefined, industry-specific configuration settings and introduce extensions to the ERP standard which are not needed for other
  application cases.

---

[33] Brady et al. (2001), p. 22.

3.1.2 Technological Outline – From Client/Server to SOA

SAP's first-generation ERP system SAP R/3 was designed using a traditional three-tier client/server architecture, using database, application, and presentation layers;[34] in this setting, client programs operated by system users send requests for services such as transactions or data reports, using middleware protocols, to application servers that will perform the requested processing.[35] In the early 1990's, SAP R/3's market success was driven by the perception that client/server technology was in general much more flexible and cost efficient than host-based applications.[36] Other advantages attributed to client/server technology included user convenience ("local" servers providing higher performance on users' desktops), technical scalability (additional application servers could be added to increase processing power), and higher ability to accommodate and maintain hardware and software from different vendors.[37]

Service orientation is a major trend in both IT and business worlds of the last few years, even if many business organizations still rely on client/server architectures.[38] On a technical level, as a means to design distributed software systems across wide-area networks, service orientation considers any object as a service provider, accessible via a standardized interface.[39] Even though every software vendor uses a proprietary jargon, Service-Oriented Architectures (SOA) describe loosely coupled systems, which share a formal contract, include abstract underlying logic, are composable, reusable, autonomous, stateless, and discoverable.[40] Providing the capabilities to connect applications to the ERP core system – using Web interfaces – promises to provide benefits in terms of an accelerated adaptation of business processes to changing needs, easing software release management and making disruptive system updates unnecessary. Further, the ability to call in external service providers to perform specific tasks in a fully integrated way, the extension and automation of business partner value networks, or the implementation of new, innovative processes without changing the base infrastructure are objectives of SOA-enabled ERP systems.[41]

Most major ERP vendors such as Oracle or SAP are on the way to transform their ERP offerings into service-oriented redesigns of their ERP product range.[42] Winter describes, using the example of the transition from SAP R/3 to SAP ERP, the change of a traditional

---

[34] Bancroft et al. (1998), p. 17.
[35] Alter (2002), p. 319.
[36] Jaccottet (1997), p. 84.
[37] Alter (2002), p. 320.
[38] Cherbakov et al. (2005).
[39] Burner (2004).
[40] Crawford et al. (2005); Erl (2005).
[41] SAP (2007c).
[42] Zhao et al. (2007).

client/server to a service-oriented architecture.[43] In late 1999, SAP announced a substantial change in their product strategy, away from the first-generation SAP R/3 software towards Web-enabled applications, introducing a new enterprise application platform called "mySAP.com," later renamed "mySAP."[44] The building blocks of the mySAP technology are a portal infrastructure for user-centric collaboration, an application server called "NetWeaver" for providing services, also over the web, and an exchange infrastructure for process-centric collaboration.[45] The integration of a portal infrastructure was, in particular, expected to increase business velocity and to extend the "reach of a business" over the Web.[46] In 2004, SAP formulated their vision of an "Enterprise Service-Oriented Architecture" (Enterprise SOA) and began to release enterprise Web services, which should eventually become the new web-based application interface to their ERP functionality.[47]

The conversion of an existing ERP landscape to a service-oriented architecture creates flexibility and versatility, as "composite applications" can be designed in a short time, combining existing, loosely coupled components and services together with existing data.[48] Service-oriented wrappers can be a flexible and straightforward way to integrate legacy applications,[49] or to deploy data error detection and cleansing services in several IT systems enterprise-wide.[50] On the other hand, enterprise SOA initiatives require a solid IT architecture planning, as a simple linking of formerly unrelated organizational databases and applications is dangerous or even impossible.[51] In SOA environments, complex interactions involving heterogeneous and distributed IT systems call for sophisticated mechanisms to track data processing, in order to ensure, amongst others, regulatory compliance.[52] In particular, SOA approaches have to carefully address data quality issues: service decomposition and process orchestration are interesting technical features, but care has to be taken to manage the data used and produced by the transaction, in order to reach the same level of business process transaction integrity as offered by monolithic, closed ERP systems. SOA *technology* alone will solve only a part of any integration problem (typically enabling communications between systems or application components), while the semantic data integration risks to be left to the implementers.

---

[43] Winter (2007).

[44] SAP (2007e).

[45] Fuchs (2007), p. 432.

[46] Agassi (2001), p. 41.

[47] SAP (2007e).

[48] Hack and Lindemann (2007), p. 25; SAP (2009b).

[49] Sneed (2006), p. 10.

[50] Arlt (2007).

[51] Marinos (2004); Dubois (2005); McKendrick (2005); Smalltree (2005); Strassmann (2006a).

[52] Moreau et al. (2008), p. 54; Pfeiffer (2009).

3.1.3 Data Quality Add-Ons for ERP Systems

ERP vendors and specialized software partners today are selling a large range of add-on components for data quality management in the ERP system domain, for example:

- SAP offers specific add-ons for inspecting, transforming, cleansing, and enriching data, for applications such as address checks in the public security domain.[53]
- BusinessObjects, taken over by SAP in 2007, offers data quality functionality for various ERP systems with its "Data Quality XI" software family;[54] this product integrates, e.g., with the SAP ERP GUI to validate in real-time customer addresses.[55]
- In the same area, FUZZY! Informatik AG (acquired by BusinessObjects in 2007, now a part of SAP) markets SAP-compatible add-on tools for interactive duplicate search and postal address check.[56]
- Products and services offered by DataFlux address common data quality problems due to typographical errors appearing in the various components of a complete SAP installation (including CRM, SRM, and ERP system components), and include adapters for integrating its application server with an SAP SOA architecture.[57]
- Finally, Trillium Software markets data quality products dedicated to, amongst others, postal address validation and correction purposes in ERP environments.[58]

3.1.4 Implementation Models

ERP systems bring along their own understanding of how business processes should work and force organizations to adapt their structures and processes according to the specifications of the software.[59] Such ERP adoption projects can be very costly, can take years,[60] and may have a tremendous impact on the workforce, as the replacement of an existing IT infrastructure – which had been tailored to an organization's needs – by a poorly configured ERP package may lead to user frustration and loss of expertise.[61] Despite the impression that ERP technology and ERP implementation was a topic of the 1990's, large consulting firms are very active in ERP implementation projects; as an example, Accenture was involved in over 1,000 ERP projects (employing 21,700 SAP consultants) and IBM Global Services in over 450 projects (with 16,350 consultants) worldwide, in 2007.[62]

---

[53] SAP (2008a).
[54] Business Objects (2008).
[55] Business Objects (2007).
[56] FUZZY! Informatik AG (2004).
[57] Ferguson (2007).
[58] http://www.trilliumsoftware.com/.
[59] Wieder et al. (2006), p. 13.
[60] Brady et al. (2001), p. 26.
[61] Eppler (2003), p. 33.
[62] Moore and Herbert (2007), p. 8.

Many ERP vendors and service providers have developed tools and methods to facilitate the implementation and maintenance of their ERP software products.[63] The use of an implementation project method reduces both project risks and costs, and is considered one of the most important factors for implementation success.[64] As an example, SAP's implementation methods and tools will be briefly reviewed. The product names used by SAP to label their implementation methods and tools have changed over the years. The "AcceleratedSAP" (ASAP) method[65] was developed after the launch of SAP R/3 in the mid-1990's, with the intention of speeding up the implementation of SAP R/3 systems.[66] SAP's "Implementation Assistant" was the first PC-based implementation tool designed for the SAP R/3 product, used in many implementation projects. In 1999, SAP announced "ValueSAP," which integrated various components to offer a consistent set of methods for the life cycle phases "discovery & evaluation" (basically for the selection of an SAP ERP system), "implementation" (of the ERP software), and "operations & continuous improvement."[67] Today, the SAP "Solution Manager" serves as a central project administration and component management tool for the products sold by SAP.[68]

Depending on the complexity, a number of project roles are needed to carry out the various activities and to reach the goals of an ERP implementation. As an example, SAP refers to 32 role profiles in its ASAP implementation method; for each one, SAP specifies the required skills with respect to business/functional knowledge (in the domains of tools and methods, SAP experience, industry experience, and additional business knowledge), personal competency (core, function, and managerial competency), and technical knowledge (technology, SAP integration, testing, SAP configuration, and programming knowledge).[69] Table 3.1 gives an overview of the role profiles used by ASAP.[70]

Most often, organizations have to make a trade-off between an unmodified implementation of an ERP package – typically preferred by IT management – and specific application functionality and customization, requested by system users.[71] In any case, gaps identified in the software functionality must be documented as early as possible in an implementation project.[72] To close the gaps, several ways exist. For example, an immediate measure against insufficient coverage of the specific needs of a business is an extension of the ERP system, resulting in purchasing (or custom programming) add-ons,

---

[63] Somers and Nelson (2004).
[64] Cf. Section 3.4.1.
[65] http://service.sap.com/asap.
[66] SAP (1997).
[67] SAP (1999).
[68] SAP (2003).
[69] SAP (2004a).
[70] SAP (2004a); the abbreviations (codes) have been assigned by the author for reference purposes, as this role concept will be used again in Chapter 5.
[71] Sumner (2003), p. 165.
[72] O'Donnell (2001).

Code	Role	Description
BC	Business Consultant	Forms a "trusted advisor relationship" with customers on ERP strategy issues, carries out strategy studies or establishes business cases
BPO	Business Process Owner (customer side)	Owns the business process from a strategic point of view, decides on changes to the process and the approval of the ERP settings
PTM	Business Process Team Member (customer side)	One person per process area (e.g., marketing), responsible for the execution of the detailed design and configuration of business processes
CC	Cutover Coordinator	Key person in the planning of all aspects of the cutover
DMM	Data Migration Manager	Defines a migration strategy and is responsible for the delivery of the data conversion from legacy systems
DMQM	Data Migration Quality Assurance Manager	Responsible for the validation of the data converted from legacy systems
DEV	Developer (customer side)	Develops add-on and (portal) interface software components
DEC	Development Consultant	Provides expertise in the application of customizing and development tools
DEM	Development Manager	Coordinates a team of developers for add-on and (portal) interface programming
EDC	Education Consultant	Responsible for creating the curriculum and assembling site specific training schedules
HDM	Help Desk Manager (customer side)	Defines Help Desk procedures
IMR	Integration Manager	Works as intermediary between the project teams, looking for convergence of the solution building
IAU	Internal Auditor (customer side)	Responsible for the review/audit of a project implementation and its adherence to company policies and procedures
OCE	Organizational Change Member	Carries out various activities in organizational change management
OCA	Organizational Change Manager	Identifies potential project risks in the organizations and manages the resolution processes
PMO	Project Management Office Team Member	Advises project management, maintains project handbooks or project databases
PM	Project Manager, Senior Project Manager	Coordinates day-to-day activities of the project
PR	Project Reviewer	Responsible for investigating the applications to ensure business process objectives are being met, caring for "good implementation practices"
PS	Project Sponsor	The ultimate owner of the project (with budget authority), has the authority to set priorities, define project scope, and to settle company-wide issues
RAM	Role and Authorization Manager	Responsible for the definition of the authorization system (user roles and authorization design)
MTC	SAP Methods and Tools Consultant	Supports the project with detailed knowledge of SAP standard methods and tools
SSA	SAP Solution Architect	Creates a suitable ERP system landscape, including (possibly) legacy systems
SOC	Solution Consultant	Responsible for delivering the SAP solution as specified in the Business Blueprint
STCM	Steering Committee Member	Responsible for understanding important issues of the project and keeping the SAP project on track
STM	Support Team Member (customer side)	Responsible for the Help Desk operation as defined by the Help Desk Manager
SA	System Administrator	Responsible for the delivery of the SAP solution on a technical level, respecting business requirements identified in the Business Blueprint
TPM	Technical Project Manager	Manages IT concerns in the project, together with the main project manager, defines parts of the operating and technical architecture
TC	Technology Consultant	Facilitates the definition of aspects of the operating and technical architecture of the system and carries out feasibility studies and training courses
TAQM	Test and Quality Manager	Responsible for the identification of business processes to test/test cases
TR	Trainer	Performs training
TDM	Training and Documentation Manager	Responsible for the ERP user training and documentation, on both strategic and implementation levels
TDTM	Training and Documentation Team Member	Develops end user training and documentation material, participates in integration/acceptance testing, populates training database with data.

Table 3.1: Project Roles in ASAP ERP Implementation Projects [SAP (2004a)].

user screens, and reports. Altering the core code of ERP systems, however, can be difficult and risky:[73] by modifying the standard code, the ability to upgrade the software in

---

[73] Markus et al. (2003a), pp. 45–46; Holsapple and Sena (2005), p. 584.

future releases could be compromised, vendor guarantee may be broken, or certificates for acceptance by fiscal authorities risk being cancelled.[74] Such "hard" modifications of the ERP software are in general considered very dangerous and most organizations try to avoid them; on the other hand, "soft" modifications – adding specific application code, without touching the standard – are less critical. A soft and often used way to modify and extend the functionality of the base system without changing the core in the SAP ERP domain is the usage of "user exits," application hooks by which SAP customers can link their own software functionality to the standard application, for adding specific validation routines or inserting their own data structures.[75]

3.2 Economic Value of ERP Systems

3.2.1 Overall Impact of ERP Investments on Productivity

Business organizations are exposed to environmental trends such as globalization (management and control in a global marketplace, global work groups, and global sourcing and delivery systems), transformation of industrial economies (towards information- and knowledge-based economies), and transformation of the enterprise (e.g., organizational "flattening," decentralization, flexibility, or collaborative work).[76] In this setting, high hopes are pinned on IT systems, and ERP systems in particular, to improve the competitive situation of an enterprise.

Since the 1990's, organizations have massively implemented ERP systems for various reasons, even if the marketing of software vendors mostly focused on the increased ability of an organization to obtain business benefits from using their products. As an example, SAP uses slogans such as "business transformation made simple" or "enhance productivity and insight for your enterprise."[77] The real economic benefits of ERP are, however, still a matter of considerable debate. Purely financial indicators of the impact of ERP systems in organizations typically ignore a large part of their very complex inner-organizational and business effects,[78] even if methods of financial analysis such as Net Present Value (NPV), Internal Rate of Return (IRR), or payback calculation may all be applicable.[79]

The assessment of the financial return of IT spending is generally difficult, also in the context of ERP systems; most studies focus on short and medium term financial factors, while the dimensions of strategic improvement, such as higher productivity or improved

---

[74] AFOS (1996), p. 182.
[75] Kessler (1999), pp. 192–194.
[76] Laudon and Laudon (2000), p. 5
[77] SAP (2007f).
[78] Wieder et al. (2006), p. 13.
[79] Nucleus Research (2007).

customer service, are neglected.[80] The measurable success of the use of ERP systems in an organization may depend on the time frame of observation: early ERP successes can be combined with later failures and vice-versa. Markus et al. have proposed to measure the success of ERP systems in terms of indicators classified by life cycle phase:[81]

- *Project phase:* project cost relative to budget; project completion time relative to schedule; completed and installed system functionality in relation to original project scope;
- *Shakedown phase (after system go-live):* short-term changes in key business performance indicators such as operating labor costs; the time performance indicators need to return to "normal" or to attain expected levels; short-term impacts on suppliers and customers, such as average time on hold when placing a telephone order;
- *Onward and upward phase:* achievement of the business results expected of an ERP project, such as reduced IT operating costs or reduced inventory carrying costs; ongoing improvements in business results, after the initially targeted objectives have been achieved; ease in adopting new ERP releases, integrating new information technologies, improved business practices; improved decision-making once the ERP system has reached stable operation.

Hunton et al. found, in a comparison of 63 ERP adopters and 63 nonadopters, that financial performance of adopters did not change during a transition to ERP; in the mean time, however, performance of nonadopters *declined*.[82] The authors warn ERP adopters that the potential for performance improvement seems to be a function of enterprise size and health: large and "unhealthy" businesses are likely to reach higher performance levels with the help of ERP systems than large and healthy ones; conversely, small firms may be unable to sufficiently invest in IT to reap the full benefits of ERP-driven business process innovation.[83] On the other hand, another study observed that purchasing ERP software *without* further internal business transformations does not have a discernable positive impact on productivity or financial performance.[84]

Wieder et al. observed, in a study amongst 2,170 (Australian) companies, that organizations using ERP systems "failed to achieve higher supply chain performance, both in the short and long-term, and (...) failed to achieve higher overall firm performance, although the latter improved with time since the adoption (learning curve)."[85] They also found that the learning curve of an organization, from go-live until the moment ERP performance

---

[80] Kennerley and Neely (2001), p. 104.
[81] Markus et al. (2003a), pp. 25 and 38.
[82] Hunton et al. (2003), p. 181.
[83] Hunton et al. (2003), p. 182.
[84] Aral et al. (2005), p. 4.
[85] Wieder et al. (2006), p. 26.

outmatches the state before ERP implementation, is much longer than often suggested: instead of a commonly supposed two-year drop in performance after switching to an ERP system ("performance dip") they found a four- to five-year learning period.[86]

Poston and Grabski noticed, in a survey of a sample of 50 companies who had implemented ERP systems from 1993 to 1997, that financial results saw "no significant change in costs as a percentage of revenue until 3 years after the implementation of the ERP system, and then a significant decrease in costs only for cost of goods sold as a percentage of sales (...) However, there was a significant decrease in the number of employees as a percentage of revenue 3 years after ERP implementation."[87] The authors explained this paradox by emphasizing the complex impact of ERP systems in organizations and the assumption that gains in productivity had to be passed on to consumers.[88]

As these examples show, the financial bottom-line impact of ERP adoption deserves to be questioned. In the following sections, some economic aspects of ERP projects in terms of costs, benefits, and risks will be discussed in more detail.

3.2.2 Benefits

Following Holsapple and Sena, the most often cited reasons to adopt ERP systems are (by decreasing importance) the integration of data or operations, an increase in productivity, standardization of company processes, and increased business flexibility.[89] Poston and Grabski add the possible objectives of a reduction of assets, obtaining better bases for decisions (through more accurate and timely data), reduced financial closing cycles, increased procurement leverage, increased customer satisfaction (through availability of accurate customer information), pressure from partners in the supply chain who already have implemented ERP systems, integration in a global supply chain, E-business readiness, and explicit process knowledge (which should allow the swift implementation of business processes in a competitive context).[90] Finally, Shang and Seddon propose a framework encompassing 5 dimensions (operational, managerial, strategic, IT infrastructure, and organizational benefits) with 21 sub-dimensions (cf. Table 3.2); this pattern will be used for structuring the discussion of the benefits of ERP systems in the next sections.[91]

---

[86] Wieder et al. (2006), p. 24.
[87] Poston and Grabski (2001), p. 286.
[88] Poston and Grabski (2001), p. 288.
[89] Holsapple and Sena (2005), p. 580.
[90] Poston and Grabski (2001), p. 273.
[91] Shang and Seddon (2003), p. 79.

Dimensions	Sub-Dimensions
Operational	1.1 Cost reduction 1.2 Cycle time reduction 1.3 Productivity improvement 1.4 Quality improvement 1.5 Customer services improvement
Managerial	2.1 Better resource management 2.2 Improved decision-making and planning 2.3 Performance improvement
Strategic	3.1 Support business growth 3.2 Support business alliance 3.3 Build business innovations 3.4 Build cost leadership 3.5 Generate product differentiation (including customization) 3.6 Build external linkages (customers and suppliers)
IT Infrastructure	4.1 Build business flexibility for current and future changes 4.2 IT costs reduction 4.3 Increased IT infrastructure capability
Organizational	5.1 Support organizational changes 5.2 Facilitate business learning 5.3 Empowerment 5.4 Build common visions.

Table 3.2: Benefits of ERP Systems [Shang and Seddon (2003)].

3.2.2.1 Operational Benefits

Cost reduction: ERP systems are built to support and automate business transactions, thereby lowering operating costs;[92] transaction handling is improved through standardization of processes and integration of operations and data.[93] The reduction of excess inventories (in pre-ERP times caused by ineffective logistics processes and a lack of IT support) releases capital, lowering costs of capital. Financial costs of overdue or lost accounts receivable, caused by incorrect invoicing or poor management of the customer relationship, can be reduced by better visibility and automation of office and logistics processes. A reliable, well-planned parts ordering process is a precondition for obtaining favorable purchasing conditions; allowing a supplier to base production planning on long term sales contracts creates win-win situations, giving room for cost reductions.

Cycle time reduction: ERP success stories report results such as "quotation cycle down by 90%, from 20 days to two days," "on time deliveries increased from 60% to 80%," "financial closing took place in just five days, rather than the ten days required prior to installation of the ERP system."[94]

Productivity improvement: Better scheduling of in-house production allows production staff to focus on process improvements instead of running after late or missing parts. The automation of office processes (e.g., electronic submission of time sheets or approval

---

[92] Kelly (1997), p. 7; Shang and Seddon (2003), pp. 79 and 98.
[93] Holsapple and Sena (2005), p. 575.
[94] Hayman (2000), p. 137.

of travel expenses) enables every member of an organization using an ERP system to individually access cost-effective on-demand services.

Quality improvement: Consistent design, production, and sales order handling processes improve the quality of products and services. Reporting of costs incurred by errors in business processes increases the visibility of overall quality costs and helps to identify the potential for improvement.

Customer services improvement: As a consequence of faster access to inventory and customer information, improved stock availability through better inventory management, and shorter delivery time due to better process transparency, customer service and, consequently, customer loyalty can be increased.[95]

3.2.2.2   Managerial Benefits

Better resource management: The costs to supervise employees can be reduced due to better "insight:" ERP systems promise to improve process visibility, more performance data than ever is immediately available, and this data can be "drilled down" from an aggregated enterprise level to a view on a specific functional unit.[96] Davenport argues in this context that executives could be tempted to adopt ERP systems with the intent to "inject more discipline" into their organizations.[97] Moreover, ERP systems can provide means to establish flat forms of internal organization and grant employees access to vital business information, reducing the need for middle management.[98]

Improved decision-making and planning: The single view on enterprise data and the possibilities for access to decision-relevant information provided by ERP systems can lead to better decisions, are hence beneficial to managers[99] – even if most managers do not exclusively rely on computer-based information to make decisions.[100] Certain decisions can be automated to minimize process downtime (e.g., by using automated forwarding of workflow tasks in case of absence of the first person in charge).[101]

Performance improvement: Increased volume of sales due to customer satisfaction and lower costs result in higher profit margins, which can be passed on to shareholders.

---

[95] Fryer (1999); Robinson and Dilts (1999); Ross et al. (2003), p. 104.
[96] AFOS (1996), p. 26.
[97] Davenport (1999a), p. 172.
[98] Shang and Seddon (2003), p. 81.
[99] Shang and Seddon (2003), p. 80.
[100] Davenport (1999b), p. 7.
[101] Alter (2002), p. 118; Holsapple and Sena (2005), p. 576.

3.2.2.3 Strategic Benefits

Support business growth: Customer-specific products or services can be produced at lower costs and data-driven links with customers and suppliers, facilitating differentiation of products and services can be installed.[102]

Support business alliance: In some industries, ERP systems have gained the status of an "industry standard," and it would be hard for an enterprise to survive without a compatible ERP infrastructure.[103]

Build business innovations: ERP systems are considered to be instruments for business innovation, as they are expected to improve business processes, implement best practices, and, for this sake, can integrate systems within and outside the borders of an enterprise.[104]

Build cost leadership: ERP systems can help both to lower product costs and to increase sales volume,[105] i.e., to reinforce the principal elements of cost leadership.[106]

Generate product differentiation (including customization): ERP-supported product configuration in sales order handling (e.g., by customizing a product to the particular needs of a customer in an SAP CRM/ERP environment[107]), together with a flexible mass production, allows a company to differentiate itself from competitors.[108]

Build external linkages (customers and suppliers): Through the use of ERP systems, organizations can create an "E-enabled" business environment, ready to participate in customer and supplier partner networks.[109] ERP systems are built on "best practice" models, as vendors have integrated experience from other ERP projects in their designs, helping organizations to import "best of class" processes and to close the gap to industry leaders;[110] this approach of both improving and standardizing processes should also lead to better collaboration between organizations and their business environment.

---

[102] Fryer (1999); Shang and Seddon (2003), p. 80.
[103] Davenport (1999a), p. 171.
[104] Hunton et al. (2003), p. 166.
[105] Cf. Section 3.2.2.1.
[106] Witzel (2004), p. 16.
[107] SAP (2004f).
[108] Witzel (2004), p. 143.
[109] Dressler (2004), p. 191.
[110] Schwarz (2000), p. 37; Wagner et al. (2006).

3.2.2.4   IT Infrastructure Benefits

Build business flexibility for current and future changes: After the apparition of commercial relational database technology and application development tools using so-called Fourth Generation Languages (4GL) in the 1980's, many business organizations were able to develop business applications on their own.[111] Even if this (often first) entry of IT into organizations was improving productivity of operations, "islands" of software and data were created, which were unconnected or only loosely coupled by batch interfaces. Besides the fact that many systems had been designed by departments to cover primarily their own specific needs, the inability of "business people" to describe the relevant objects of their work (the attributes of and relationships between data) led to redundancies in data models even within a single organization and a need to repeatedly enter the same fact in several IT systems. As a consequence, decentralized growth of IT systems resulted in increasing data disparity and low data quality.[112] Initiatives to design applications for the *entire* organization were welcomed, but building a consistent and accurate IT model of a business is not a trivial exercise and the budgets required to launch a lengthy data modeling exercise have always been rare.[113] Many enterprise data modeling programs were therefore abandoned and the "lofty goal of the enterprise-wide data model" remained unrealized in most organizations.[114]

The core competence of a typical business organization is *not* (or should not be) business software development, but governing its principal manufacturing or marketing processes; reducing internal IT system development – after having implemented an ERP system – has allowed companies to invest their capital, time and energy into their core competencies. With ERP systems, the focus of information systems has shifted from an IT issue to a business system challenge, from software engineering and programming aspects to configuration activities carried out by non-technical staff, departing from a business process perspective.[115] Adopters of ERP system technology have also reached the goal of a single data model, almost inadvertently and at no (additional) cost: redundancy, inconsistency, reentry errors, and omissions in enterprise data are all reduced through the use of a single database.[116] Moreover, ERP systems are a cure against the "natural mess" of multiple meanings in information, since concepts such as "customer" or "order" are now both embedded in a consistent business language and formally documented in the metadata of the system.[117]

---

[111] Schwinn et al. (1999), p. 14.
[112] Brackett (1994), p. 5.
[113] Taylor (1999).
[114] Taylor (1999); Koll (2007).
[115] Wieder et al. (2006), p. 13.
[116] Rizzi and Zamboni (1999), p. 368; Poston and Grabski (2001), p. 272.
[117] Davenport (1999b), p. 8.

IT costs reduction: ERP systems can be regarded as a means to overcome internal software management problems: instead of executing risky, complex in-house application development projects, organizations simply purchase a ripe, fully functional, well-documented, and widely proven software product. Even if the costs of implementing – selecting, adapting, deploying, and training – ERP software packages are high, they are in general lower than those incurred by developing custom made software.

Increased IT infrastructure capability: In the late 1990's, many experts expressed the fear that software applications could produce errors or even could come to a stand-still because they stored the year information in a two-digit format (e.g., "10" denoting "1910" or "2010"); the background of this phenomenon is to be found in the early days of software engineering, when programmers had to save space by storing dates into as little memory as possible, rather than providing applications with the capability to function after Year 2000.[118] Instead of re-engineering all possibly affected applications, many organizations decided, with the Year 2000 approaching, to replace their applications by new systems. The introduction of the Euro currency by January 1, 2002 had a different background but a comparable impact on IT systems in Europe as the Year 2000 problem, and forced many enterprises to update their financial transaction and reporting systems. Finally, the pressure to ensure the traceability of production and logistics operations motivated companies to re-engineer their processes and to implement new IT systems, e.g., in order to fulfill the requirements of passing ISO 9000 quality certification.[119] In all three situations, the implementation of new ERP systems has helped organizations to cope with the challenges and to ensure business continuity and infrastructure capability, at reasonable costs.

3.2.2.5 Organizational Benefits

Support organizational changes: As a direct consequence of ERP adoption, standardized and streamlined business processes promised to better support organizational changes,[120] with ERP systems taking the role of a tool to implement a "business change infrastructure."[121] In addition, when considering the job market, the standardization of applications helps organizations to find trained ERP professionals, e.g., using a job profile such as "SAP SD professional" (describing persons having knowledge on how to use the SAP ERP Sales and Distribution module functionality[122]), on both IT and business sides.

---

[118] Knolmayer and Myrach (2000).
[119] Rizzi and Zamboni (1999), p. 367; Kennerley and Neely (2001), p. 103.
[120] Robinson and Dilts (1999).
[121] Davenport et al. (2004), p. 24.
[122] Cf. Section 3.1.1.2.

Facilitate business learning: The most important organizational effects of an ERP implementation are improved visibility across organizational units and transactional process integration between corporate functions.[123] Together with horizontal re-arrangement of activities and more computer-oriented jobs, ERP systems require a profound re-thinking of business activities, and foster constant mutual learning processes of all persons involved.

Empowerment: Better internal information – through data and process integration – and a stronger usage of IT-supported processes in ERP environments can confer ERP users more power to get involved in the business, to become a visible part in processes, to take correct, fact-based decisions in their job context, or to participate in organizational improvement processes; also, much of the clerical work related with documenting business activities can be left to the ERP system. On the other hand, middle managers who merely collect and forward business-relevant information to employees are no longer needed in this model.

Build common visions: An organization adopting an ERP system can promote a common understanding of its business system, as the system imposes a standardized business vocabulary and forces implementers to design a process landscape based on defined and documented process variants. Based on this common understanding of terms and rich process (data) feedback, ERP systems can lay a common base for discussing and defining future business directions.

3.2.3   Costs

Generally, the implementation of an ERP system consumes important resources, ERP projects are risky, retain valuable human resources, and tend to tie manager's hands.[124] Often, an ERP project represents a company's largest ever investment in IT,[125] the overall project cost reaching USD 200,000 for small companies, 600,000 to 800,000 for mid-size companies (40 to 80 million USD annual sales), and up to many million USD for large companies.[126] The duration of an ERP project can be important, ranging typically from a couple of months to several years. When considering the usual "performance dip" after the go-live,[127] ERP implementation projects are quickly an endeavor of financial "life and death" for an organization, demanding huge investments in terms of financial

---

[123] AFOS (1996), p. 58; Schuster (1999), p. 286.
[124] Davenport (1999a), p. 159; Hanscome (2003), p. 2.
[125] Sumner (2003), p. 157.
[126] Ragowsky and Gefen (2008), p. 35.
[127] Cf. Section 3.2.1.

and human resources, before a positive payback can be expected.[128] Typical cost items in ERP implementation projects are:[129]

- *Hardware:* server and desktop stations; often computing hardware has to be upgraded when first installing or upgrading an ERP package;
- *Software licenses and maintenance fees*;
- *Education:* training of the project team and (later) of all ERP users;
- *Customization/configuration:* typically, two man years of one-time customizing are required during an implementation project, plus one person on a continuous basis for the time after;[130]
- *System optimization:* for hardware and software adjustments;
- *Add-on software:* additional software for, e.g., interfacing various non-ERP software components such as legacy applications;
- *Implementation project management:* for a company with up to 300 persons, a project team should encompass at least three persons, plus one more team member for every 200 employees;
- *Miscellaneous:* some 10% of the funds should be reserved for unexpected events.

Organizations typically overestimate the cost of ERP software licenses during an implementation project, while underestimating internal staffing cost.[131] But ERP software maintenance (major vendors such as ORACLE and SAP typically charge up to 22% of initial software licenses in their maintenance plans) may consume an important part of the annual IT budget of an organization.[132] Standard software packages promise to cope with technological progress through software upgrades, even if license fees and upgrades may be very costly.[133] Since the client/server concept used by ERP installations traditionally requires a "fat" client software for providing the user interface, the cost of keeping user frontend computers up-to-date (with respect to hardware and software) can also be considerable.[134] Portal-based GUIs, requiring only an Internet browser running on a user's desktop, may be a cost-effective solution for non-frequent users, but have drawbacks as not all business transactions may be supported and system performance is likely to be lower, compared to a "fat" client.[135] Finally, user training costs may often be understated, as every upgrade or change in the customization of the software potentially creates a demand for additional user training.

---

[128] Hunton et al. (2003), p. 170.
[129] Robinson (2006a).
[130] Robinson.
[131] Silberberger (2003), p. 7.
[132] Richardson (2008).
[133] Markus et al. (2000), p. 183.
[134] Bancroft et al. (1998), p. 17; Watson (2002), pp. 363–364.
[135] Jay (2008), p. 39.

The costs caused by ERP system implementation and operation over years may be very high, and most organizations using ERP systems are hence looking for cost savings, increased IT productivity, and system optimizations. One natural approach to reduce ERP system costs consists of measuring an existing installation using a set of specific criteria, comparing the results to some benchmark, and proposing recommendations for improving the use of the system. As an example, West Trax[136] has developed a system for measuring the efficiency of SAP ERP installations, using Key Performance Indicators (KPIs) such as "unused relevant standard potential," "share of custom developments," or "share of unused custom developments." Based on an assessment with respect to these KPIs, West Trax customers can obtain a certificate (gold, silver, or bronze "Awards"), attesting to the "economic efficiency" of their SAP installation.[137] The aspects considered in such an audit relate to the IT aspects of an ERP system and can help to improve ERP system maintenance and upgrade projects; on the other hand, this type of analysis can hardly assess the business process impact of an ERP system, will not be able to issue recommendations on how to improve its use, and cannot uncover the potential of future ERP system upgrades.

Advanced costing concepts such as Total Cost of Ownership (TCO) calculation models[138] may turn out to be too complex for many organizations (most ERP project managers have been found to be unable to provide measurements of the major cost drivers[139]) and the fact that TCO does not consider revenue aspects of a project hinders its use for calculating the bottom line impact.[140] And even if the revenue impact is known, the result of NPV calculations may depend on the timeframe, as many ERP adopters incur a negative NPV in their ERP project over a period of five to six years, while a majority of adopters eventually will have realized positive cash flows.[141]

3.2.4 Risks

Sufficient evidence shows that ERP projects often fail in practice, that implementations are delayed, planned costs are exceeded, and promised functionality is not delivered.[142] Skok and Legge summarized the idiosyncrasies of ERP systems which induce specific risks in an implementation project as follows: the number and variety of stakeholders in any implementation project, the high costs of implementation and consultancy, the integration of business functions, the configuration of software representing core processes,

---

[136]http://www.westtrax.com/.
[137]West Trax (2008).
[138]Silberberger (2003); West and Daigle (2004); Gartner Group (2005).
[139]Silberberger (2003), pp. 5 and 8.
[140]Nucleus Research (2007).
[141]Fryer (1999).
[142]Aiken (2002).

the management of change and political issues associated with BPR projects, and the enhanced training and familiarization requirements.[143] Bancroft et al. emphasize, in their presentation of implementation practices in the context of SAP ERP systems, that the technical, business process, and behavioral changes necessary to implement an ERP system create a very complex project situation.[144]

Table 3.3 recapitulates the types of risk IT implementation projects inevitably face, namely organizational fit, skill mix, management structure and strategy, software system design, user involvement and training, and technology planning and integration, as described by Sumner;[145] in addition, the table highlights risk factors which are specific to ERP systems.

Category	Risk Factors [* = ERP Specific Factors]
Organizational fit	• Failure to re-design business processes* • Failure to follow an enterprise-wide design which supports data integration*
Skill mix	• Insufficient training and re-skilling* • Insufficient internal expertise* • Lack of business analysts with business and technology knowledge* • Failure to effectively mix internal and external expertise • Lack of ability to recruit/retain qualified ERP system developers*
Management structure and strategy	• Lack of senior management support • Lack of proper management control structure • Lack of a champion • Ineffective communications
Software system design	• Failure to adhere to standardized specifications which the software supports* • Lack of integration*
User involvement and training	• Insufficient training of end-users • Ineffective communications • Lack of full-time commitment of customers to project management and project activities • Lack of sensitivity to user resistance • Failure to emphasize reporting
Technology planning/integration	• Inability to avoid technological bottlenecks* • Attempting to build bridges to legacy applications.

Table 3.3: Risk Factors in ERP Implementation Projects [Sumner (2003)].

3.3   Data Processing in ERP Systems

3.3.1   Classification of ERP Data

For the context of this study, the following three categories of data in relation to ERP systems are considered relevant:[146]

- *System configuration data:* describes the way the ERP system operates; in the case of SAP ERP, customizing data is entered using the (standard) SAP GUI and stored in database tables;

---

[143] Skok and Legge (2001), pp. 189–190.
[144] Bancroft et al. (1998), p. 9.
[145] Sumner (2003), p. 174.
[146] Bancroft et al. (1998), pp. 28–29.

- *Master (or reference) data:* facilitates business transactions and changes very rarely, is used to derive other data;
- *Transaction (or operational) data:* entered by an ERP system user or generated by the system during business transactions.

All three types of data are needed when an ERP system carries out a business transaction or gathers data for a report. With regard to potential problems hitting the three categories of data, configuration and master data is particularly exposed, as these two types of data can directly influence the operation of the system, are intended for use in a broader context (large quantities of transactional data can potentially be derived from a single master data record), and will be actively used for a longer span of time, in contrast to transaction data. 80% of data problems in enterprise IT systems are reportedly caused by insufficiently managed configuration and master data.[147]

Address data is particularly affected by frequently changing facts in the external world: analysts in the U.S. estimate that 2% of a company's customer data gets corrupted *every month.*[148] Besides the fact that address data is often inaccurate (e.g., due to typographical errors or the unwillingness of customers to disclose personal data), duplicate master data records are a well-known phenomenon: Betts reports 20% duplicate entries in supplier master data in many organizations, created by IT system users who are unable to find existing data or who are deterred from thoroughly searching the system.[149] Another problem in this context relates to the identification and the accurate mapping of customer and supplier hierarchies (e.g., the relation between parent companies and their subsidiaries), a domain addressed by professional services and software products from providers such as Dun & Bradstreet.[150]

The consequences of inaccurate master data in an ERP system context may be severe:[151] a spelling error in a contact address causes ineffective marketing response and lowers trust in the company's competences, while a wrong shipping address leads to additional logistics costs, tampered customer satisfaction, and unpaid invoices. Redundancies in master data increase the cost to enter and maintain data and lead to reporting difficulties: the turnover of a given product will be incorrect if the same product is handled under two different product codes. Also, in supplier performance reporting, a wrong picture of a relationship is reported if the revenue is split up under two or more supplier codes, all representing the same real-world business partner.

---

[147]Rademacher (2004).
[148]Mello (2002).
[149]Betts (2001b).
[150]http://www.dnb.com/.
[151]Cf. Section 2.3.3.5.

Once an ERP system has successfully gone into operation, changes in the external world, such as the introduction of a new local currency, can lead to structural changes in the ERP system configuration and may endanger the stability of the software and the quality of data. ERP software vendors are also challenged by the fact that changes in software concepts often occur before the existing technology is fully mastered.[152]

3.3.2 Data "Producers" and "Consumers" in ERP Systems

An IT system generally represents a model of a small, finite subset of an external world, consisting basically of three basic components: a repository or database (data layer), a user interface (presentation layer), and a processor (application layer).[153] Figure 3.1 shows how human and non-human users interact with an ERP system, how they create, store, and use data;[154] this model will be used in this section to describe the data flow in ERP systems.

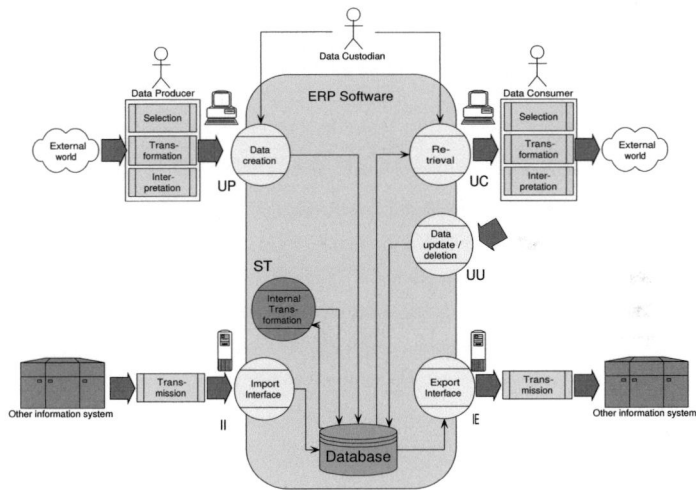

Figure 3.1: Interactions with ERP System Data.

When reading Figure 3.1 from left to right and from top to bottom, the roles of data "producers" (or "collectors"), "consumers" (or "users"), and "custodians" can be distinguished:[155] at the "input" interface UP, a data producer acquires or collects data from

---

[152]Olson (2003), pp. 5–6.

[153]Kent (1987), pp. 1 et 21.

[154]Inspired by Redman (1996), pp. 42–43 (who adds the activity of modeling data structures), English (1999b), p. 203, and Laudon and Laudon (2000), p. 8.

[155]Lee and Strong (2004), p. 33.

the external world, mentally adapts or translates it, and enters it into the system via the GUI. This is usually done by referring to existing master or configuration data. Typical data producers are ERP system users in the "front-end" departments such as sales or purchasing; however, when designing an ERP user organization, it must be observed that "clerical" data management activities do not divert front-end staff from doing their business efficiently.[156] Moreover, E-commerce initiatives or self-service applications have increasingly brought customers and employees to enter data via Web interfaces. Data may also enter the system via import interfaces (II) or is generated by internal system (transformation) processes (ST). Importing data from external systems always poses specific risks, as the quality of data exported from a third-party system may suffer from intrinsic quality problems or handling errors. Internal transformation processes may also cause data problems, when new data is automatically derived from incorrect existing data, or when software changes or hardware problems disrupt regular data processing.[157]

Once the data has entered the system, the processing steps embedded in a transaction convert the raw inputs into a different form, apply business rules, possibly update other business objects and aggregated customer or consumption statistics, besides storing the data submitted with the transaction.[158] ERP systems implement protection for such transactions, including commit and rollback operations (even on an application/business logic level, in the case of SAP ERP), in order to guarantee consistency in the database.[159]

During data retrieval and consumption processes (UC), data consumers transfer data to an application context or forward it to the activities in which it will be used, possibly involving data aggregation and integration.[160] Data maintenance leads to updates or deletions in the database (UU), e.g., for mirroring changes in the external world.[161] Moreover, data can leave the system on demand or regularly via export interfaces (IE). Finally, data custodians have to supervise operations, import and export interfaces, and the internal processing of data.

The following sections demonstrate the processing of data in a three-tier system architecture[162] – database, application, and presentation layers – using SAP ERP as a landmark case. On all three levels, the IT system perspective, a view on data handling, and ERP-specific challenges to data quality will be presented.

---

[156] AFOS (1996), p. 57.
[157] Maydanchik (2007), pp. 14–15.
[158] Laudon and Laudon (2000), p. 8.
[159] Buck-Emden (1999), pp. 136–139.
[160] Strong et al. (1997a), p. 39.
[161] English (1999b), p. 204.
[162] Watson (2002), pp. 363–364.

3.3.3 Database Layer: Data Definition, Storage, and Exchange

3.3.3.1 IT System Perspective

ERP systems store data about many facts in the environment of an organization ideally in a single database. In the case of SAP ERP, besides master and transaction data, information about the customizing of the system, the application source code, and metadata in the form of a data dictionary are stored in the same database.[163] The data dictionary serves as a glossary of business terms: the formal definition of a "sales order" (in textual and technical terms) can be found here and its metadata can be accessed, e.g., by application developers.

ERP systems typically provide comprehensive data structures: as an example, SAP's first-generation ERP system R/3 contains about 20,000 data fields, arranged in about 10,000 data tables.[164] SAP's ERP data model exhibits a high level of stability: relevant parameters of SAP ERP, such as data table or attribute names, have not changed for many years.[165] From a database viewpoint, the SAP system uses a single database user (called SAPR3), which has full access to all SAP ERP tables.[166] As most other ERP systems, SAP ERP uses SQL statements understood by database management systems. Two flavors of SQL are supported by SAP: an abstraction layer called "Open SQL," which enables ABAP applications to directly access most database platforms (full portability), and "Native SQL," which allows application programs to make use of the full SQL functionality of the DBMS.[167] SAP ERP divides transactions internally into Logical Units of Work (LUW), which guarantee that transactions are processed consistently with regard to atomicity, consistency, insulation, and durability.[168]

The SAP middleware is built on top of the (operating) system software and ensures secure communication amongst the different function modules. SAP's Application Link Enabling (ALE) is an important middleware technology for opening the SAP ERP world to automated machine-to-machine communication. ALE covers two main tasks: exchange of application data based on the (asynchronous) exchange of standardized Intermediate Documents (IDocs)[169] and the controlled replication of data.[170] IDocs are generated and processed by SAP's application server; IDoc adapters are offered for many middleware systems such as IBM MQSeries/Websphere MQ[171] or TIBCO.[172] ALE is capable of rout-

---

[163] SAP (1994), p. 8-4; Bancroft et al. (1998), pp. 16, 21, and 71; Alter (2002), p. 157.
[164] AFOS (1996), p. 19.
[165] Boenner et al. (2006), p. 257.
[166] Brand (1999), p. 345.
[167] SAP (1994), p. 2-23; Brand (1999), p. 75.
[168] Gray (1981); Brand (1999), p. 80; Hornberger and Schneider (2000), pp. 65–66.
[169] SAP (1994), p. 3-7.
[170] Brand (1999), p. 83.
[171] International Business Machines Corp. (2009).
[172] TIBCO (2009).

ing data, maintaining security, and buffering the data on both sender and receiver sides: when a receiver is down, ALE stores the message temporarily and retries automatically to send after reestablishment of the connection. ALE is further able to automatically detect changes in one SAP ERP database and to securely distribute the changes to other SAP and non-SAP systems. In SAP's current NetWeaver product offering, the SAP NetWeaver Process Integration (PI) component serves as a central integration engine, using open standards such as the eXtensible Markup Language (XML) and the Hypertext Transfer Protocol (HTTP), but also supporting IDocs and other protocols.[173]

3.3.3.2   Data Perspective

To design and document the data structures of its ERP systems on a high level of abstraction, SAP used a proprietary semantic modeling formalism which is based on the Structured Entity Relationship Model (SERM) introduced by Sinz.[174] SERM is an extension to the Entity Relationship (ER) model described by Chen, intended to facilitate the design of complex ER diagrams, to visualize dependencies, and to avoid inconsistencies and unnecessary relationship types.[175] SERM also includes layout prescriptions – the independent entity is always placed at the left, to facilitate navigation – and a mixed entity-relationship type.[176] Using the data management tools integrated with the SAP GUI, the data modeler, the data dictionary, and the data browser, developers can navigate through data structures, browse table records, or extend the existing SAP data model.[177]

Configurable ERP systems such as SAP ERP implement complex conceptual foreign key mechanisms, but cannot enforce them on a database level, because rules defined on a business transaction level are technically so complex that checks have to be carried out by the application layer.[178]

3.3.3.3   Challenges to Data Quality

Organizations adopting ERP systems often want to benefit from "best business practices" promised by the system, which requires the usage of standard data attributes for the description of the business objects and processes. The data structures provided by the ERP system are predefined and cannot be modified at will, whereas customer-specific data fields can be added in some situations.[179] Despite vendor promises, typical ERP systems

---

[173] SAP (2009a).
[174] Sinz (1988).
[175] Ferstl and Sinz (2005), pp. 146–147.
[176] Staud (2005), p. 221.
[177] SAP (1994), pp. 8-8–8-9; Bancroft et al. (1998), pp. 70–74; Staud (2005), p. 205.
[178] van de Riet et al. (1998), p. 275; Kessler (1999), pp. 218–219; Hornberger and Schneider (2000), pp. 122–123.
[179] E.g. in SAP ERP, as described in SAP (2005a).

contain data structures that are not compatible with the needs of a specific organization and, conversely, some needs may not be covered by the ERP software.[180] It seems therefore to be quite common to intentionally store data in the "wrong" fields in ERP systems, due to the limitations of the (ERP) software.[181]

Cultural differences in the design of ERP packages may also be a reason for implementers to intentionally "abuse" some of the standard data structures, as the business models adopted by ERP packages typically have a bias towards "Western" business contexts. Soh et al. provide an example of unusable data structures in an ERP software package implemented in a health care institution in Singapore.[182] The new ERP system used by this customer required names to be entered in the Western format, as first, middle, and last name. Asian staff had, however, a difficult time understanding which part of an Indian, Malay, or Chinese name should be considered as first_name and which as last_name. A first attempt to cope with the situation was to simply use the first_name field to capture the entire name. Both first and last name fields were, however, restricted to a maximum of 30 characters by the ERP data model, and changing the field length would have touched the core, which was considered unacceptable. The convention to circumvent the problem was finally found in entering the Asian name as last_name field, and then to continue in the first_name field if the name was longer than 30 characters. Clearly, such an approach is likely to raise problems when the "abused" fields are needed by the business application functionality or for analytic purposes.

Besides the ERP production software environment, an organization typically needs additional work environments (called "clients" by SAP) of the ERP software, e.g., for development and testing purposes. SAP recommends a two-system landscape (one system for production and one for development) including several development areas for customizing, integration tests, and training. SAP also ships predefined environments: client 000 contains the SAP software in a non-modified version (for reference purposes), client 001 (a copy of client 000) is intended for customization purposes, and client 066 is used for technical monitoring by SAP and accessed by services such as "Early Watch."[183]

Even if the original ERP system concept includes a centralized, unique enterprise database and a single application pool, a typical large organization will have to operate several ERP system instances (installations) in parallel; reasons can be of historical nature (when an organization is the result of a merger of formerly separated units each having their own ERP system) or be the result of technical constraints (e.g., when a manufacturing division needs a special release of an ERP system, while a wholesale unit finds better

---

[180] Brackett (2000), p. 316.
[181] Weigel and Schmid (2004), p. 2; Maydanchik (2007), p. 10.
[182] Soh et al. (2000).
[183] Brand (1999), p. 85; SAP (2000); SAP (2008c).

support with a "mainstream" variant of the same ERP software).[184] In this situation, de-centralization of master data to several "partial" ERP systems must be controlled through well-defined data management processes.[185]

Master Data Management (MDM) tools, ensuring data synchronization amongst several ERP instances, can be used to enforce consistency of master data between several IT systems.[186] MDM systems are not a "silver bullet:" as most enterprises have a subdivision along process or functional lines, global responsibility for data is still hard to establish. Most MDM products specialize in one domain (e.g., integration of customer or product master data); "one-fits-all" MDM products, integrating several kinds of data types used in organizations, are not on the market today.[187] An example of an independent vendor MDM product is the "Master Data Management Cockpit for SAP" marketed by OR Soft Jaenicke GmbH;[188] SAP's own MDM offering, SAP MDM, is based on SAP's NetWeaver platform, supports different database systems,[189] and includes master data storage and for-warding across different systems and locations.[190] The scenarios supported by SAP MDM include master data consolidation (for cross-referencing identical copies of the same data or finding duplicate records in order to remove them), master data harmonization (for importing, consolidating, and distributing records back to connected client systems), and central master data maintenance (for centrally creating new data records and distributing them).[191] From a technically point of view, master data records are extracted from client (e.g., other ERP) systems and sent in IDoc format to SAP MDM, where they are con-verted and processed by the MDM engine.[192] Alternatively, vendor, customer, material, or employee master data records can be created on the SAP MDM server and submitted to validation tests, before they are forwarded to the target systems.[193]

Simply removing duplicate entries or correcting errors in databases often proves to be very difficult in closely integrated ERP systems, due to technical or regulatory constraints. The usage of MDM system, on the other hand, allows a company to control data quality without adjusting the original applications: an MDM system may, e.g., help to discover the fact that supplier #123 in one system is identical to supplier #987 in a second system, map this fact in its database, and automatically synchronize the updates between the two systems.

---

[184]Cf. case study 1 in Section 3.5.1; Gulledge et al. (2002); Gulledge et al. (2004); David (2006).
[185]SAP (2004b).
[186]Duff (2005); Smalltree (2005); Hildenbrand (2006); Hack and Lindemann (2007), p. 337; for the related "hype" cf., e.g., Wailgum (2007).
[187]Koll (2007).
[188]OR Soft Jänike (2008).
[189]David (2006), p. 99.
[190]Wittebrock (2003).
[191]David (2006), p. 98.
[192]David (2006), p. 102.
[193]David (2006), p. 104.

3.3.4 Application Layer: Implementation of Business Logic

3.3.4.1 IT System Perspective

Even if ERP systems promise to manage the entirety of data of an organization, they typically cannot provide the functionality required by specific applications such as Computer Aided Design (CAD) systems. For this reason, all major ERP packages offer interfacing technologies that help to integrate third-party applications with the ERP systems; in the case of SAP ERP, many application integration technologies rely on SAP's Remote Function Call concept (RFC).[194] When looking at distributed computing, the RFC protocol facilitates communication between computers within an SAP system environment and allows integration with IT systems from other vendors.

An application can use the RFC protocol to call a function of the SAP system which will be executed on another computer, or SAP applications can call external functions available on remote computers. On the Microsoft Windows platform, the RFC functionality is implemented as a Dynamic Link Library (DLL) and distributed together with the SAP GUI. Using this DLL, any Microsoft Windows application can issue RFC calls and access SAP applications. As an example, Lotus Notes based applications can be integrated with SAP ERP using RFC,[195] or a CAD application can make calls to an ERP system using interfaces such as Porta-X from SolidLine, for requesting a unique drawing identification number from the ERP system – an operation that is completely transparent to CAD system users.[196]

3.3.4.2 Data Perspective

The business logic of a typical ERP system such as SAP ERP is implemented in the application layer, which exchanges data with the underlying database layer using middleware technologies such as RFC.[197] In order to cope with the paradigm of object-oriented software development, SAP introduced the concept of "business objects types" and "business objects" to break the data of its ERP system down into smaller, better accessible units; business objects can be accessed by methods called Business Application Programming Interfaces (BAPIs).[198] The Business Object Repository (BOR), originally developed for SAP Business Workflow, is used to define the SAP business object types.[199]

---

[194] Brand (1999), p. 80.
[195] Röthlin (2001).
[196] SolidLine AG (2009).
[197] SAP (1994), pp. 3-7–3-9.
[198] SAP (2005b).
[199] SAP (2005b).

3.3.4.3   Challenges to Data Quality

Early ERP packages of the 1990's were intended to administrate the entire resources of a business organization, but not prepared to support organization-specific, advanced buy-side or sell-side processes. Moreover, the activities supported by ERP systems are by nature well-structured, repetitive, and controlled, which leads to the situation that ERP systems are not primarily designed to perform flexible end user-oriented analyses or to provide strategic decision support, as opposed to other IT systems such as DWHs.[200] This was a source of disappointment amongst managers using ERP systems, as they may have believed that ERP systems should provide extensive reporting capabilities.

On the other hand, these functionality "gaps" opened a market for specialized vendors, such as i2 in the SCM domain or Siebel in the CRM area, and made buyers believe these software systems would seamlessly and painlessly integrate with their ERP system.[201] Later on, offerings made by large ERP vendors (which often acquired specialized SCM and CRM vendors) bridged the gap between internal ERP functionality, could provide support for processes involving external stakeholders, and helped to reduce the number of IT systems needed and the related interfacing problems.[202]

3.3.5   Presentation Layer: Desktop Perspective

3.3.5.1   IT System Perspective

To grant users access to business data, ERP systems provide a common application library and a consistent GUI, accessible to all system users in any business area. Integration facilities provided by SAP ERP on the GUI level include support for Microsoft's Messaging Application Programming Interface (MAPI), enabling SAP to communicate with E-mail systems) or Object Linking and Embedding (OLE) for accessing documents. Data gathered and formatted by an SAP report can be downloaded to the workstation in various formats, from where it may then be loaded into text processors, spreadsheet applications, or project management tools.

3.3.5.2   Data Perspective

The presentation layer of the ERP system manages the user interface, which allows users to start transactions or to display data using a high-level GUI, while hiding the application logic of the system.[203] The operations at the interfaces UP, UC, and UU described in Figure 3.1 are typically carried out using an ERP GUI.

---

[200] Kelly (1997), pp. 2 and 5.
[201] Markus et al. (2000), p. 183; Markus et al. (2003a), p. 50.
[202] SAP (2006a), p. 11.
[203] Brand (1999), p. 63.

3.3.5.3 Challenges to Data Quality

Since an ERP package has to cover all kinds of business situations, its GUI has to provide forms for handling the variety of data elements used by transactions, and will therefore mirror the complexity of applications. Especially for master data, which has to incorporate many aspects to cover all application needs, this leads to a situation in which dozens of screens with possibly hundreds of data fields may have to be worked through by users, if the unmodified standard GUI forms are used. As a consequence, daily work may be slowed down and entry errors may occur.

To reduce the quantity of data fields shown to users, several possibilities exist. Firstly, most ERP system GUIs can be configured to hide fields which are not currently needed by an organization. Next, single screen transactions can contribute to reduce the overhead related with data capture, clamping together two or more standard GUI transactions.[204] Easily accessible, portal-based solutions for casual ERP users may reduce both the effort to access the ERP system functionality and the risk of entry errors. Finally, unfiltered user input from the Web (provided by E-commerce or self-service applications) often suffers from inconsistencies and typographical errors in names, addresses, and product numbers; these types of data have to be filtered before they are forwarded to ERP applications.[205]

3.4 Success and Failure in ERP Implementations

3.4.1 Critical Success Factors for ERP Projects

Many research projects have been carried out to identify Critical Success Factors (CSF) for ERP system implementations and to devise recommendations for improving such projects.[206] Attempts have also been made to identify the relative importance of these factors; as an example, Somers and Nelson have established a ranking putting top management support, project team competence, and internal cooperation at the top of the list.[207] In their guidelines, Bancroft et al. focus on the following nine CSF for ERP implementation projects:[208]

---

[204] Mende (1998), pp. 233–246; Kehrli and Thiel (2004).

[205] Atkins (2003).

[206] Cf., e.g., Davenport (1995), Bancroft et al. (1998), Davenport and Prusak (1998), Deutsch (1998), von Arb (1998), Davenport (1999a), Davenport (1999b), Holland and Light (1999), Gupta (2000), Harreld (2000), Ross and Vitale (2000), Trimble (2000), Willcocks and Sykes (2000), Austin (2001), Brehm et al. (2001), Kennerley and Neely (2001), O'Donnell (2001), Romeo (2001), Robinson (2002a), Scott and Vessey (2002), Grabski et al. (2003), Parr and Shanks (2003), Ross et al. (2003), Scott and Vessey (2003), Willcocks and Sykes (2003), Okrent and Vokurka (2004), Strong and Volkoff (2004), Finney and Corbett (2007), or Rettig (2007).

[207] Somers and Nelson (2001), p. 7.

[208] Bancroft et al. (1998), p. 133.

1. *Corporate culture:* understand the corporate culture in terms of readiness and capability for change;

2. *Process re-engineering:* begin business process changes prior to implementation; make the hard decisions early and stick to them;

3. *Communication with users:* communicate continuously with all levels of new users in business, not only in technical terms; set reasonable expectations; then communicate again;

4. *Management involvement:* provide superior executive championship for the project;

5. *Implementation project management:* ensure the project manager is capable of negotiating equally between the technical, business, and change management requirements;

6. *Implementation team composition:* choose a balanced (IT and business) team, and provide it with clear role definitions; expect to shift to non-traditional roles;

7. *Project method:* select a good project method with measurements;

8. *Project team and user training:* train users and provide support for job changes; don't forget to train the project team;

9. *Handling of problems:* expect problems to arise; commit to the change.

These factors will be reconsidered later in Chapter 5, when recommendations for a data quality aware ERP system implementation will be devised.

3.4.2   Spectacular Cases of ERP Failures

The following three cases illustrate spectacular ERP project failures reported in the press, chosen because of the data quality aspects shining through in the discussion of the reasons for the disasters. Even if they must be considered in the context of the U.S. legal system, these well-documented problems deserve closer attention.

1. Once the fourth largest distributor of pharmaceuticals in the U.S., FoxMeyer Drug went into bankruptcy in 1996, after a failed ERP-backed re-engineering attempt of their business system.[209] FoxMeyer had started an SAP implementation project in 1993, with the goal to improve productivity and to increase the volume of shipments. As this goal could not be reached, FoxMeyer alleged that the implementation of the ERP system by Andersen Consulting was poor and that Andersen had been using trainees in lieu of experienced consultants.[210] Under heavy pressure as a consequence of aggressive contract bids, FoxMeyer put its SAP ERP in production

---

[209] Adam and O'Doherty (2003), p. 276.
[210] Scott (1999); Romeo (2001).

three months *sooner* than initially planned; accordingly, tests were slashed, "disastrous data errors" surfaced, causing huge costs, and finally FoxMeyer could not deliver and went bankrupt.[211]

2. In the case of Brother Industries,[212] manufacturer of office products, logistics were seriously disturbed due to a lack of information about the parts replenishment system. Plants did not receive sufficient supplies of parts, since the lead time information had not been entered completely and correctly into the system. Another source of problems found were large quantities of obsolete and inactive part numbers that had been converted during a new (SAP) ERP system implementation. This "dead" data was dramatically slowing down operations and important staffing and management resources were required to avoid duplicate orders of parts.

3. In 2001, Computerworld magazine reported major problems at the Los Angeles city government, leading to false bills: as an example, the Police Department received an invoice over USD 750,000, instead of USD 7,500, due to incorrectly entered data in the procurement and inventory management system, an ERP system delivered by PeopleSoft.[213] Besides the problems in billing, suppliers were paid too late, and inventory shortages occurred. Reasons for this uncomfortable situation were found in inadequate end-user training and poor help desk support. In the eyes of project management, the ERP software was not to blame, but ERP system users: employees overstrained by the complexity of the system were unable to run it correctly.

3.5 Case Studies on Data Quality in ERP Systems

To provide further illustration and discussion of typical data quality problems found in the area of ERP systems, three case studies will be presented in the following section. The first case describes the situation of a large organization, which is supported by a complex ERP landscape consisting of several (divisional) ERP system instances, and which encounters various problems when attempting to consolidate data stemming from its diverse ERP systems. The second case shows how an ERP data quality control system can be set up and used in practice. Case study 3 finally presents the situation of an ERP implementation project, at the end of which several permanent data quality errors persist.

---

[211] Scott and Vessey (2003), p. 260.
[212] Deutsch (1998).
[213] Songini (2001).

3.5.1   Case Study 1: Heterogeneous ERP Systems

This first case study[214] describes the evolution of a complex ERP landscape over the years and the issues encountered in operational and decision-support applications of ERP systems.

3.5.1.1   Situation

The corporate group considered here (referred to as "the group") had a long-standing tradition of industrial excellence. Its operating units (the "divisions") carried out various tasks in the procurement, servicing, and disposal of complex industrial systems. On a group level, a logistics services core unit (referred to as "LSCU") had been installed, which was responsible for efficient logistics and economically sound management of materials handling. LSCU carried out activities in logistics planning and control, the provision of educational programs to employees, or the management of the Logistics Information System (LIS).

Independently of the use of ERP system technology, this unit had also developed a comprehensive process handbook, which defined activities, roles, and responsibilities in logistics. All definitions were based on the specific business language of the group, defining roles independently from the (often changing) group organization. The activities were tied to a high-level reference model, which covered the life cycle from the abstract definition of an industrial system to its withdrawal and disposal. In the domain of materials management, two key figures were especially relevant to management at the group level: the stock availability of products considered critical (which should be as high as possible) and the total monetary value of inventories (which should be as low as possible).

Within the group, many types of IT systems had been implemented over the years to support logistics; for the purpose of this case study, only the role of ERP and DWH systems used in the group will be briefly described. At the time considered, ERP packages had been in use in the group for two decades. By the end of the 1990's, mainly under the pressure of the Year 2000 problem, all remaining legacy applications in logistics had been abandoned in favor of ERP systems, all from the same supplier. The process handbook was taken as a foundation for ERP implementations in the complex group organization. Divisions had been allowed to implement, adapt, and extend the ERP package to their respective business needs, handling implementation projects with their own resources and being assisted by various consultancies.

Beginning at the group's operational level, several ERP systems – typically one instance per division – supported specialists in their daily business. As an example, product managers defined products and assemblies, project managers used functionalities for

---

[214]Cf. Knolmayer and Röthlin (2006) for a comprehensive description of this case.

planning and monitoring project costs, and purchasing managers used the logistics and financial features of their ERP system to order materials or pay suppliers. Product master data for projects, production, and system maintenance was shared amongst divisional ERP systems. To provide strategic and tactical decision support, a DWH was installed, for collecting and consolidating performance data from several ERP systems. LSCU controlling staff produced output based on the content of the DWH, enriched it with context information, and published it in the form of consolidated management reports, for the attention of divisional and group management.

In order to facilitate the sharing of master data used in more than one ERP system instance, LSCU had developed a "Material Master Coordination System" (MMCS), which was used by all divisions in the group, represented by a specific, centralized ERP system instance. Once domain specialists from a division had entered the necessary master data into the MMCS, using standard ERP material master entry transactions, the new master data records were distributed in a unidirectional, "one-to-many" way to the divisional ERP systems requiring the data. This way, new master data had to be entered only once, even if it was used by several ERP system instances. LSCU specialists disseminated a comprehensive documentation on how the MMCS had to be used and which values were acceptable for the entry of master data, on a per-division level.

Manufacturing industries typically use Bills of Materials (BOM) to specify assemblies of parts for sales, production, or maintenance.[215] In the case of the group, such assembly information was, however, traditionally retrieved from manuals and was only partially available in ERP systems. Only in some manufacturing and maintenance divisions was BOM functionality fully used; this lack of information lead to the situation that MRP algorithms could not be used. Instead, future demand was calculated on the basis of the past time series of the consumption of single items, without taking into account future end-system demand or strategic logistics goals (such as inventory reduction targets).

Overall, divisions had found that the data structures provided by the ERP systems did not fully cover their information needs. The few unspecific data fields (intentionally left for customer purposes by the ERP system designers) and also some specific data fields were used with substantial differences in the divisional ERP systems. In some cases, text fields intended for documenting materials properties had also been used to capture coded routing instructions.

Even if the process handbook was a comprehensive document and of high quality, and ERP system support appeared adequate to operational users, several weaknesses in the process and IT landscapes were identified after five years of operations in the configuration described above: IT alignment with the strategic goals of the group was insuffi-

---

[215]Cf. Section 2.3.3.2.

cient, the "to be" processes did not cope with organizational changes, and data quality problems had cropped up that made a consolidated view of group inventory levels or operational performance difficult and inhibited the group to exploit the full potential of its ERP systems. Three problem areas will be the focus of the following sections, namely the mapping of process requirements into the ERP systems, the handling of master data input using the ERP GUI, and the consolidation of inventory data in the DWH.

3.5.1.2   Problem 1: Process Documentation and ERP

In daily practice, the usability of the comprehensive process framework was dampened by the divergent mapping of division-specific business concepts into the configuration of the various ERP systems. The process handbook did not specify how jobs in logistics had to be performed using the ERP system, especially *who* had to enter *which* data *when*, in order for the business process to progress. No "ownership" or "stewardship" for data was specified in the handbook, as the latter exclusively focused on business processes, not data. Material managers, the persons in charge of materials, could not oversee the usage of items they had defined and for which they remained responsible: once a material master dataset had been entered into the MMCS, the related datasets could potentially be distributed to any division and be modified there, without notification to the item manager.

To make things worse, the same business task was supported differently by divisional ERP system instances, which used variants of system transactions to support the same real-world activity: as an example, ERP users could purchase goods using several transactions, all accessible via the same GUI. This meant that an overview of purchasing activities of all divisions could not be gained by simply analyzing the data tracks left by ERP transactions. Moreover, as divisions had been allowed to customize their ERP instances to their needs, the resulting settings of the diverse ERP applications were inconsistent. As an example, one division coded the terms of payment being "within 30 days due net" as ZXB1, another one as ZB30. Consequently, a straightforward, data-based consolidation of inventories kept by several divisions proved to be very difficult.

Besides common data entry problems such as typographical errors, considerable delays between the physical presence of incoming goods and the visibility as "stock" in the ERP system were observed in some departments. Information flow in purchasing was often interrupted, because purchasing managers ordered "one set of spare parts" from some supplier and the details of the content of the order were known only after the physical delivery of goods, when opening the boxes. As a consequence, the notification of the ERP system about the entry of goods had to wait until all material master datasets for the ordered components had been created, a fact that caused delays ranging from days up to weeks. These delays and other inaccuracies related to the goods entry processes led to economic damage, e.g., when purchasing order quantities were calculated based on erroneous net demand or inaccurate inventory levels, it caused excess orders and excess inventory.

Even if the value of having accurate inventory information was intuitively clear to managers, no directives existed for estimating the value of product data. In some cases, important product data was explicitly *not* ordered together with physical equipment purchases, after a superficial "cost-benefit" analysis. Only very few information products (such as inventory reports or supplier evaluation charts) and their data sources were under systematic quality control.

Logistics reporting had been set up within each division, using materials management reports generated by the divisional ERP systems. As a whole, people working on a transactional level with the ERP system were satisfied with the application support provided, even if employees typically had the impression that data in "their local ERP system" was of better quality than the data from other divisions. Local work policies had been established for keeping the data accurate enough for daily routine jobs supported by the ERP system, and divisional controlling staff knew which data sources were the most credible ones. Some data sources were also believed to be of doubtful quality and were thoroughly checked – or simply excluded – from data selection when generating reports.

3.5.1.3   Problem 2: MMCS and its GUI

In daily practice, the MMCS tool suffered from a number of weaknesses, despite the sound underlying concepts: the software could not hide the complexity of the standard ERP GUI, did not assist users to enter data values accordingly to the MMCS documentation, and did not impede the creation of duplicate entries of material master datasets. The reasons for these weaknesses are as follows.

Firstly, the MMCS (ERP) system used for master data entry by the group offered too many screens, which were overloaded with many unneeded data fields and produced a large proportion of useless and incoherent data values. Secondly, the MMCS had been designed as an entry tool destined for frequent, careful, and circumspect ERP users; insufficient precautions had, however, been taken to guide casual users through the GUI and to prevent the entry of duplicate material records. Thirdly, the hasty conversion of data from legacy applications to the current ERP platforms in the late 1990's was identified as a major factor for poor data quality: a large percentage of master data items imported from legacy systems had never been touched since. Many errors in unused data had never been searched for, never been found, and never been corrected.

3.5.1.4 Problem 3: Inventory Consolidation in the DWH

Before LSCU could publish credible group-wide reports on materials inventory levels, data from several ERP systems had to be imported to the DWH and post-processed manually. The downside of such an ex-post data consolidation was that aggregated inventory data could not be accessed by the MRP planning functionality of the underlying ERP systems. As the possible states of material ("On order," "In Stock," "Reserved," "Maintenance," "Retired," etc.) were not clearly defined or used inconsistently amongst divisions, the reports that consolidated such values from several divisions were of doubtful quality. The accuracy of the overall value of inventories was further challenged by the fact that material valuation prices had only been updated for a minority of available products, since their acquisition. This made a consolidation of inventories in monetary terms at least difficult. Overall, credibility of controlling reports in logistics was low, even after manual correction, as the inventory levels shown were not in line with divisions' logistics assessment based on their divisional ERP systems, and did not reflect the business reality as perceived by the different management levels in a consistent way.

3.5.1.5 Lessons Learned

Several conclusions can be drawn with regard to the role of ERP systems as the data processing backbone in the group logistics analyzed in the case study:

- Firstly, ERP systems suffer from the same data quality problems known from other IT systems: processing delays, divisional idiosyncrasies, or operation errors may hit organizations using ERP systems.

- Next, the processes a software system is intended to support must be in line with the form of both customer process orientation and internal (divisional) organization; if there is a lack of organizational alignment, even perfect software will not be able to "fix" this problem. Also, the homogeneous and precisely documented process framework spanning several organizational entities could not ensure a consistent ERP implementation in a distributed ERP landscape, especially as the systems were customized by different persons from various institutions, having divergent interests or work standards. In addition, the case shows that misunderstandings and data quality problems can easily surge, even in the case of an ERP application that ships with an embedded "data dictionary," containing a complete documentation of the data and their meaning, and the presence of a state-of-the-art process framework.

- Finally, ERP systems generate and store a comprehensive range of data, with potential problems appearing in both transactional and master data; it is often difficult to explicitly ignore irrelevant (although clearly visible) errors, while focusing on the ones having potentially dramatic consequences. As material master data can be used in a wide range of transactions and many different organizational contexts, errors in this type of data are particularly bothering, as they can affect the quality of a wide range of transactional data in an ERP database, consolidated management information, and also "real-world" business processes.

Even if, in a distributed ERP environment, a divisional system's process support may be excellent and business functions can perform efficiently, other information concerns may suffer. The focus of a person working with the ERP system is naturally on the transactions he or she performs and (perhaps) on the data created immediately by these transactions. In a typical enterprise setting as described in this case, an ERP system works well, e.g., as a purchasing application in a division, but an enterprise-wide view on inventories is not feasible, as the different ERP instances (and materials management concepts) are not sufficiently coordinated and data stemming from different instances is incommensurable. Also, the larger the organizational distance between data creators and users, the less confidence has been found in data producer–consumer relationships.

Group-level decision-making in logistics in the case described above depended heavily on the quality of the information provided by LSCU reporting; since data quality was low (either due to errors in ERP systems or incorrect consolidation of data stemming from different systems in the DWH), the quality of decisions made on the basis of this information suffered as well. As shown in this case study, multi-instance ERP installations, even when the same type and version of an ERP system are in use, exhibit much of the same problems as heterogeneous pre-ERP IT landscapes. This observation is important, as large organizations today often use many IT systems in parallel, and multiple ERP system instances are rather a norm than an exception.[216]

3.5.2 Case Study 2: Data Quality Management

This second case study illustrates how data quality can be defined and managed in real-world ERP applications. Indirectly, it also gives an impression of the possible data problems occurring in real-world ERP systems.

3.5.2.1 Context and Data Quality Guidelines

Under the title "Customer Order Accuracy," the Federal Bureau of Prisons at the U.S. Department of Justice issued guidelines on how to manage data quality in sales orders handled by an SAP ERP system in one of its service centers. The principal elements of

---

[216]Wyss (2008), p. 2; Bjorlin (2009); Power and Shankar (2009), p. 9.

the procedures specified in the guidelines (a six-page document) are ordered according to the DMAIC approach:[217]

- *Definition:* The declared objective of the program is "to develop and implement a plan to achieve 98% accuracy of sales orders within SAP." As a consequence of higher data accuracy, processes in logistics are expected to improve. The activities of developing and implementing the improvement plan are under the responsibility of the manager of the customer service center.
- *Measurement:* In this step, 11 relevant data elements of a customer order are named (e.g., purchase order number, payment method, or business partner identifiers), the reference sources are prescribed (e.g., a hard copy of a customer order), the size and the collection method of the samples to be analyzed are defined, and the way to determine the level of data quality is specified. As an example, the guidelines describe in detail how 3% of the orders entered in the previous month (or at least 20 different orders) must be analyzed, and how the 11 data fields have to be compared with the surrogate data source (the hard copy of the order).
- *Analysis:* If the accuracy level is below 98%, the service center manager has to review the findings of the measurements in detail and to analyze the causes of the quality problems. Based on the results of this analysis, a corrective action plan has to be developed.
- *Improvement and control:* If the objective of 98% accuracy has been missed, the findings of the root cause analysis and the corrective actions must be submitted to upper management. If the quality of order data is consistently higher than the threshold value of 98%, the tests may be carried out "quarterly instead of monthly," i.e., the frequency of measurements can be reduced.

3.5.2.2   Lessons Learned

The example of this data quality program provides the following findings:

- ERP systems *are* hit by data quality problems, since the program is visibly needed;
- Responsibilities for data quality are clearly linked to the business organization (the manager of the customer service center) – and not to IT staff;
- Data quality management can be implemented using a DMAIC sequence;
- Data quality can be measured in a straightforward way, by using manual procedures.

---

[217] U.S. Department of Justice – Federal Bureau of Prisons (2003).

3.5.3 Case Study 3: ERP System Implementation

This third case describes the findings recorded during the analysis of an ERP implementation project, focusing on the project stage just after the go-live. The case described here will end with open questions; responses will be provided as a proof-of-concept for the ERP-oriented data quality model presented in Chapter 5.[218]

3.5.3.1 Situation

Intended as a replacement of a combination of older legacy applications (which already integrated inventory management with finance), the company in this case study started an initial ERP project a few years ago, focusing on finance and accounting applications. After successful operation in this first stage and an in-depth analysis of the possible support of ERP systems for business processes such as sales, materials management, and production, the company decided to implement an SAP ERP system for all business processes. After a large-scale implementation project, which involved many people on all levels and from all divisions of the company, the configuration of the system, and integration with third-party systems (such as CAD workstations), the ERP system went live as scheduled.

After go-live, several issues emerged in operations that called for management attention; after observing the situation for some time, analyses were undertaken and a number of reasons identified. Due to errors made during the manual conversion of legacy data to the SAP system (ERP users manually entering data from hundreds of inventory items did not fully understand many of the codes used by the ERP system; in addition, the GUI accepted inaccurate but valid entries), data quality in inventories was affected, and reports did not show the "true" figures, with regard to quantities and the value, for several months. Several times shipments were delayed, as the system refused to issue customs invoices, due to user entry errors, misconfiguration, or an allegedly insufficient inventory level. Wrong or incomplete invoices printed by ERP applications caused customer complaints and, subsequently, an increase of accounts receivables in accounting. Also, internal transport orders were ill-routed, and the parts retrieved from stock had to be searched for by "walking the racks."[219]

Confidence into the newly-created material master data in the ERP system was low: logistics clerks preferred the traditional printed catalogs and did not accept the new electronic directory available in the ERP system, as the quality of information provided by the catalogs was perceived as higher. Standard ERP reports proved to be worthless, because not all data fields needed to populate the reports were actively maintained by the organization. Furthermore, correction of data entry errors proved to be cumbersome and

---

[218]Cf. Section 5.5.
[219]Brooks and Wilson (1995), p. 68.

sometimes even impossible, as the ERP system refused modifications of data values due to integrity conditions or locks; errors could not be documented or flagged, as no suitable data fields for error handling were provided by the ERP system. Also, after organizational changes, some electronic documents could not be updated to the new structures, due to integrity constraints of the software.

Admittedly, however, the system worked, and many people in the enterprise were happy to finally have gained more insight into the business environment in which they were operating.

3.5.3.2   Problems

The following core problems still remained after half a year of – otherwise increasingly productive – operations of the ERP system:

1. Due to an excessive number of errors, the material master data creation process as designed – involving sometimes 6 different organizational units for one part – proved to be much too lengthy and error-prone.

2. Creating accounting structures for sales order handling was cumbersome, required the execution of too many screen activities, depended heavily on the type of project and the organizational unit, and produced many errors. As the account items generated were used in many contexts (e.g., purchasing, engineering, or invoicing), errors spread easily and in unforeseeable ways to these application domains.

3. Cost planning on projects was poor: on one hand, the accounting system required a very detailed cost breakdown and on the other, project managers were reluctant to do the "administrative" work associated with constant updates of the fine-tuned cost planning and preferred individual spreadsheet applications for cost controlling. Planning was not timely and the ERP system detected alleged (unreal) "cost over-runs" during financial closing, which resulted in unjustified monthly profit shake-downs.

3.6   Evaluation of Data Quality in ERP Systems

In this section, the specific concerns of data quality management in an ERP system context will be reviewed, drawing on the findings made in this chapter. The analysis will include a review of the impact of ERP system characteristics on data quality and a review of the applicability of data quality recommendations to the ERP system context.

3.6.1 Specific Data Quality Issues in ERP Systems

Referring to the ERP data flow model presented earlier,[220] the data quality problems found at the different user and IT system interfaces are summarized in Table 3.4.

Interface	Data Quality Problem Symptoms	Data Quality Problem Causes
UP	• Inaccuracies when entering data • Incomplete capture of facts • Duplicate entries	• Lack of user motivation and training • Lack of specific data edit checks • Lengthy data entry dialogs
UC	• Wrong data presented to the user • Misinterpretation of data • Late, untimely, or incomplete reports	• Misleading report selection criteria • Reports do not provide links to data dictionary • No currency/completeness checks in reports
UU	• Update or delete operations violate organization-specific business logic	• Specific business logic cannot be embedded in standard ERP system
II	• Data of bad quality enters the system	• No data quality controls at the input interface • Application layer (business) logic is not applied to data • Human or technical (IT system) problems
IE	• Data of bad quality is forwarded to external IT systems	• Requirements of target system are not respected
ST	• Data of low quality spreads out through entire system	• Existing low quality data (especially master data) is used for deriving new data.

Table 3.4: ERP Interface Data Quality Problems.

- At the user interface (UP), data entries suffer from inaccuracies, incomplete mapping of external world facts to the database, or duplicates. Reasons for these problems can be found in user motivation and training, a lack of – possibly business-specific – data edit checks, lengthy data entry dialogs on the GUI level (leading to entry errors and omissions), or insufficient search tools, which can deter users from searching for and referring to existing data records, and entice them to create a new record instead.

- On the data consumer side (UC), the quality of the presentation of data may suffer when wrong data is presented to a user, when data is hard to interpret, or when reports are not timely or incomplete. Causes for these phenomena are to be found in the fact that report selection criteria can mislead an ERP system user, that custom-made reports are not specific enough and do not provide links to a description of the meaning of the values shown, or that (electronic or printed) reports do not show a warning when they are used before data is available in full.

- During data updates or deletions carried out by ERP system users (UU), the organization-specific business logic can be violated, because such rules are seldom formally implemented in ERP systems.

- When importing data from other IT systems through interfaces (II), during ERP system implementation or operations, the quality of the data has to be controlled.

---

[220]Cf. Section 3.3.2.

Data errors occur when no data quality filters are installed, when business rules are not applied at all or inconsistently with regard to manual data entry, and when human or technical problems arise (leading to problems with missing or duplicate data imports). Conversely, and even if the data in the source ERP system is of perfect quality, errors during data exports (interface IE) can be caused by an insufficient transformation of the data to the needs of the target IT system.

- Finally, the internal transformation processes of data in the ERP system (ST), which uses and potentially modifies and creates new data elements, can create dirty data.

For countering the potential problems at the interface of the ERP system, detailed actions to secure the interfaces during the ERP implementation and throughout the entire life cycle will be proposed in Chapter 5.

3.6.2 Applicability of Data Quality Recommendations to ERP Systems

In the following section, ten popular recommendations formulated by Strong et al. (recommendations 1–3), Orr (recommendation 4), and Redman (recommendations 5–10) for improving the quality of data will be presented, together with an assessment of their applicability to the ERP system context.

3.6.2.1 Recommendation 1: "Use only a single way to produce data"

Consistency and believability of data are affected if separate ways to enter data in an IT system exist, typically when using more than a single application.[221] An immediate "patch" to the situation is to declare one application as "reference" or the "master system;" a better solution consists of developing a set of common definitions and procedures.

Appraisal of ERP systems: Through their centralized, organization-wide database and data dictionary, which acts as a "single point of truth," ERP systems both define details of the structure and the meaning of data; moreover, they can reduce redundancy in the storage of data, which in turn can improve data quality.

3.6.2.2 Recommendation 2: "Avoid bias in producing data"

Many data entry processes ask users to make an interpretation of facts and to make a selection from a set of coded values. If this selection is subject to individual consideration of IT system users, bias can occur. With more information, more training, and better rules, users can be instructed on how to correctly enter data into the system.[222]

---

[221] Strong et al. (1997a), p. 40.
[222] Strong et al. (1997a), p. 40.

Appraisal of ERP systems: ERP systems are potentially exposed to the same risks of misinterpretations during data entry as other IT systems, if an interpretation of facts by users is required. To (partially) address this problem, specific guidelines ("interpretation helpers") can be integrated with entry forms.

3.6.2.3 Recommendation 3: "Avoid distributed architectures"

The risk related to distributed, heterogeneous architectures is that the same external world fact may be mapped differently in the various IT systems concerned; as a result, data may be difficult to interpret and aggregate.[223]

Appraisal of ERP systems: Compared to stovepipe architectures, ERP systems preserve consistency of the data they store, as facts are stored only once, in a clearly specified and documented format, and accurate business terminology; this property of ERP systems is a principal means to improve data quality.[224] As interfaces required by older departmental applications are obliterated by strong data integration, data quality issues related to data exchange between systems can be reduced, as fewer systems are involved;[225] if data exchange between an ERP and other IT systems is required, secure middleware components provided by ERP vendors (as an example, ALE in the case of SAP ERP) assist the transfers.[226]

3.6.2.4 Recommendation 4: "Use your data, improve its use"

Orr showed that if an organization is not using the data in its IT systems, the quality of the data will decline, because inconsistencies due to changes in the external world are not discovered and the data is not updated. When considering the common practice of organizations to collect large quantities of unused data in IT systems with the perspective to use them "some day," this clearly creates potential for friction.[227]

Appraisal of ERP systems: In the case of ERP systems, the recommendation to use data as intensely as possible is only partially applicable: on one hand, through frequent uses of master data such as customer or vendor addresses, changes in the external world will be (reactively) detected and data quality can be maintained by correcting the errors found in the database. Because of the fact that no redundancy exists in an ERP environment, a single update is enough to update the entire mapping of the fact to the IT system, to keep the data current. On the other hand, the data structures defined by the ERP system design cannot be altered at will by an organization, therefore many data elements

---

[223] Strong et al. (1997a), p. 42.
[224] Strong and Volkoff (2005), p. 6.
[225] Aiken (1996), p. 41.
[226] Cf. Section 3.3.3.2.
[227] Orr (1998), p. 68.

generated by the system itself and used for its internal operation cannot be "used" by an organization.

3.6.2.5   Recommendation 5: "Assign responsibility for data quality"

Redman sets the question of responsibility at the center of his data quality recommendations: an explicit policy documenting responsibility is formally required, as work that is not assigned is not carried out in most organizations.[228] He also warns against simply attaching responsibility to the IT department: data belong to the business units or the process owners.

Appraisal of ERP systems: Assigning responsibility for data quality in an ERP system environment is complex: the high degree of centralization of data and applications, the claim to be the principal application for the entire organization, and the multiple uses of a data element in the many applications of an ERP system – a typical ERP user loses control over the use of a data record, once he or she has entered it – make it difficult to define responsibility for data.

3.6.2.6   Recommendation 6: "Explicitly manage data flows as information chains"

The typical flow of data in an organization, enabling and documenting business processes, is directed from department to department, not vertically down the line of command. An information chain consists of a series of transformations from inputs (data) to outputs (information); the management of information chains, which run in parallel to business processes, could help to improve collaboration and, eventually, to reduce the cost of poor data quality.[229]

Appraisal of ERP systems: The complexity and probability of inherent contradictions in an IT system context increase in general with the number of persons involved: the chance of achieving a common view of some reality and mapping this reality coherently into an IT system declines when managers try to encompass broader purposes and to involve more people – this is exactly the situation of ERP systems.[230] Besides the number of people involved, cross-border organizational issues or organizational fragmentation in an ERP system environment can be the very source of data quality problems.[231]

---

[228] Redman (2001), p. 181.
[229] Redman (2001), pp. 161–163.
[230] Kent (1987), pp. 202–203.
[231] Galway and Hanks (1996), pp. 2–3; Wand and Wang (1996), pp. 92–93.

3.6.2.7 Recommendation 7: "Develop data structures to meet legitimate business needs"

When confronted by several business units operating under the umbrella of an organization, it may often be impossible to find a common definition for business concepts such as a "customer," mainly due to the fact that the business units run their businesses differently.[232] This lack of agreed convention directly leads to misunderstandings and data inconsistencies.

Appraisal of ERP systems: In such a situation, the implementation of an ERP system in an organization can prove to be very helpful, as ERP systems in their "pure" form (as a single instance, containing a single enterprise database) bring along and impose standardized and documented process and data models, which all business units will have to adopt during an ERP project.

3.6.2.8 Recommendation 8: "Apply supplier management to other departments"

Data supplier management, as described by Redman, includes an analysis of customer needs, quality measurements, quality improvement, and planning; as a result of these management activities aiming at pushing responsibility for data quality back to the producer/supplier, data quality in general should improve, suppliers should be strengthened, and better insight into operations on the supplier's side can be gained.[233]

Appraisal of ERP systems: In inner-organizational producer–consumer relationships, there is no easy way out of the clinch if quality costs occur in one organizational unit and the benefits of using the data in the form of valuable business information are reaped by another. From an economic point of view – if the organizational reward system is not explicitly designed to cope with this kind of situation – it makes no sense for a division creating data to provide "free" data quality services. ERP systems help, by their design, to document and track data entries or updates, with regard to data supplier management (for important types of data), ERP systems therefore appear as an attractive platform to implement formal relationships between producers and consumers of data.

3.6.2.9 Recommendation 9: "Design information chains first, then supporting IT"

In the same line as business processes, information chains have to be designed to meet the needs of the business, before the required IT support can be designed. Likewise, customer focus, responsibility for the information chain, and automation of work processes are important elements of an information chain approach.[234]

---

[232] Redman (2001), p. 25; Gulledge et al. (2002), p. 588; Bjorlin (2009).
[233] Redman (2001), p. 153.
[234] Redman (2001), p. 143.

Appraisal of ERP systems: ERP systems focus on business process support – information management and data processing are clearly subordinate concerns. If specific information needs exist, they have to be integrated during early system evaluation; in an implementation project, an organization has to seek to best "cope" with the internal logic of data processing imposed by the chosen ERP system.

3.6.2.10 Recommendation 10: "Do not apply IT to a poorly defined information chain"

The analogy between business processes and information chains suggests that neither low quality processes nor information chains affected by data errors should ever be automated.[235]

Appraisal of ERP systems: In many organizations, ERP systems have replaced a large number of disparate and often unreliable legacy applications, have eliminated the need for multiple data entries, and, hence, obliterated or automated many internal data transfers between applications, thereby potentially increasing data quality.[236] Easier access to reliable information, predefined information chains, and an elimination of redundant data management activities have been strong arguments for adopting ERP technology.[237] On the other hand, Lynn and Madison argue that "the strength of these new (ERP) systems lies in their ability to access and process more information faster. The quality of the information and processing methods is a different question. This technology, when combined with poor information quality and inappropriate processes, guarantees more wrong answers faster and 'prettier.'"[238] Even if high-quality information chains are provided with the system and used by organizations, the quality of the output will still strongly depend on the data inputs.

Table 3.5 gives a summary of the evaluation of data quality recommendations introduced above and exhibits their applicability to the ERP context.

#	Generic Data Quality Recommendation	Applicable to ERP Systems
1	"Use only a single way to produce data"	Yes, by design
2	"Avoid bias in producing data"	Yes (partially), by design
3	"Avoid distributed architectures"	Yes, by design
4	"Use your data, improve its use"	Partially
5	"Assign responsibility for data quality"	Difficult
6	"Explicitly manage data flows as information chains"	Partially
7	"Develop data structures to meet legitimate business needs"	Difficult
8	"Apply supplier management to other departments"	Yes
9	"Design information chains first, then supporting IT"	Partially
10	"Do not apply IT to a poorly defined information chain"	Yes

Table 3.5: Applicability of Data Quality Recommendations to the ERP Context.

---

[235] Cf. Section 2.6.
[236] Chanana and Koronios (2007), p. 263; Adam and O'Doherty (2003), p. 278.
[237] Robinson and Dilts (1999).
[238] Lynn and Madison (2000).

3.6.3 Findings from the Literature: Data Quality in ERP Systems

Finding 3.1. Data quality in critical domains of the many types of data contained in an ERP system is essential for the success of ERP systems: insufficient data quality increases both implementation project and operation costs, lowers the business benefits of ERP systems, and increases investments and risks.

Finding 3.2. Data quality recommendations formulated for custom-designed software do not directly apply to (semi-finished) ERP systems, as data structures and standard applications of these systems cannot be changed without taking legal and technical risks.

Finding 3.3. Responsibility for data items in an integrated ERP system is difficult to define, and data production is often opaque to users. Data integration appears like a two-edged sword: on one hand, reduced data redundancy increases integrity; on the other hand, once erroneous data has been accepted by the system, errors can spread quickly to compromise many ERP applications.

Finding 3.4. Typical recommendations for data quality assurance issued by ERP software vendors focus on the conversion of legacy data, as a partial activity to be carried out during ERP implementation projects.

Finding 3.5. A complementary software market for data quality exists, addressing mostly specific (and exposed) types of data such as postal addresses or business directories.

3.7 Summary

ERP systems are standardized, integrated software packages, which organizations tailor to their needs, using specialized implementation consultancy services. ERP systems handle recurrent business tasks such as sales order processing, purchasing, inventory management, or accounting, and can help to improve the efficiency of business processes by increasing speed, transparency, and flexibility. The ERP system concept promotes process integration across the diverse units of an organization by providing a common business and IT terminology, a single database, and a common pool of applications. Innovations in ERP systems can help organizations to achieve a competitive advantage in providing them with tools to better serve customers, to increase efficiency of operations, and to facilitate business with their partners. Even if the design of ERP systems has been heavily criticized and its contribution to the productivity of an organization remains questionable, ERP system technology has been embraced by a very high number of organizations world-wide, a fact that makes it an attractive object of information systems research.

The fundamental decisions in an ERP project, regarding the suppliers, the scope, and the sequence of implementation activities, have preoccupied business and IT managers since the 1990's. ERP applications are semi-finished software products that have to be configured to the specific needs of an organization, to a much higher degree than other IT systems such as office applications. ERP system software, organizational structures and processes, add-on tools, and the remaining IT infrastructure must be harmonized to reap the benefits of ERP.

As shown in studies on success factors in ERP adoption, high data quality is absolutely essential for ERP success: users are only willing to use IT systems if they can trust the data in the system. In general, data in ERP systems can be expected to be of higher integrity, as it profits from the "entry once, use many times" property provided by data integration and the single enterprise database. However, the data is also exposed to the same risks known from other IT system contexts: duplicate entries, typographical errors, or ageing of data are well-known problems in ERP systems. ERP-specific data quality problems are due to the forced integration of data and the lack of specificity and flexibility of standard ERP applications. Not all computing needs of an organization can be covered by an ERP system; where data fields required by a business are lacking, interfacing with remaining (third-party) IT systems is needed, and data is increasingly exchanged with business partners in a supply chain. Monolithic, unmodified, "one-fits-all" ERP systems are regrettably an elusive concept.

Clearly, technical, organizational, and user oriented actions are needed to ensure ERP data quality. General recommendations for achieving a high level of data quality, such as a limitation of data to a minimum, the usage of very specific data check rules, clear responsibility for data, or formal cross-organizational data flows often cannot be applied in ERP systems, as implementing such design features would inevitably lead to changes to the standard software system and compromise its ability to be upgraded. Also, vendors and implementation consultants prefer to focus on business process support (the "business value") and the large application functionality provided by an ERP system, eclipsing the need for the permanent availability of high-quality customizing and master data.

Chapter 4

Exploratory Study of ERP Data Quality

Besides a review of the relevant data quality and ERP literature presented in Chapters 2 and 3, this research project aimed to gain insight into the state of data quality in enterprises, best practices in data quality management, and related design principles in ERP systems used by the software industry (research questions Q1 to Q8 as presented in Section 1.5). Firstly, the state of data quality in ERP systems was of interest: is the situation generally as bad as it may be expected when considering reports from other IT domains?[1] Next, when analyzing quality practices in organizations, the presence of elements of quality methods, the existence of agreements on (acceptable) data quality levels, the usage of quality measurements, the process of analyzing data quality problems, methods and instruments employed for improvement projects, and ongoing activities for data quality control were examined. Lastly, as often very cost and resource intensive data quality initiatives have to be justified economically, the decision process for approving and funding projects was reviewed.

As only few, mostly software vendor-initiated and not ERP-focused field studies on data quality management existed, the author conducted two ERP-oriented data quality surveys, with the aim of finding answers to the above formulated questions. To explore concerns from both sides – ERP software vendors and ERP users – and to gain a multi-perspective view on ERP data quality, one survey targeted ERP software vendors, the other IT managers in enterprises. As the two groups could be considered to be more or less homogeneous in themselves, each with a high number of potential respondents, the form of written surveys was chosen.[2] Results of the two surveys presented in this chapter provide inputs which will be used, together with further results from the literature review in Chapter 2 and the analysis of ERP systems made in Chapter 3, for formulating recommendations for effective ERP data quality management in Chapter 5.[3]

---

[1] Cf. Section 1.1.
[2] Bortz and Döring (2003), p. 253.
[3] Preliminary results of the surveys (single-group analyses) have already been published in Röthlin (2003), Röthlin (2004a), and Röthlin (2004b).

4.1   Empirical Study Design

4.1.1   Classes of Questions

Based on the findings of the literature review and the experience gained from other surveys conducted by the Institute of Information Systems of the University of Bern, 17 classes of questions were formulated and included in the two surveys (Table 4.1), each class containing between one and five questionnaire items. Details about the wording of questionnaire items and the meaning of the related variables can be found in Tables A.1– A.17 (pages 245–248), and summary data on responses (answer frequencies) is presented in Tables A.18–A.34 (pages 249–252) in Appendix A.

Class	Class Description	User Survey	Vendor Survey
RR	Relevance of data quality	•	•
RO	Economic considerations around data quality	•	•
IO	Organizational influence on data quality	•	•
IC	Influence of consultancy on data quality	•	•
II	Influence of interfaces on data quality	•	•
IT	Influence of user education on data quality	•	•
ID	Influence of system documentation on data quality	•	•
IS	Influence of user support on data quality	•	•
IU	Influence of user (attitude) on data quality	•	•
IM	Influence of information management on data quality	•	•
IA	Influence of ERP architecture on data quality		•
SD	State of data quality, with regard to selected classes of data	•	
RP	Organizational responsibility for data quality	•	
AE	Implemented actions for enforcing data quality	•	
AP	Priorities when affecting resources for data quality	•	
SA	Data quality in ERP products as a sales argument		•
AV	Data quality instruments implemented in ERP systems		•

Table 4.1:   Classes of Survey Questions and their Usage in Surveys.

4.1.2   Questionnaire Design

The design of survey questions was based on recommendations found in the statistical literature,[4] on which most conceptual and design choices in the surveys could be based. In contrast to other domains of research, however, no publicly available survey standards or examples could be used. To find a trade-off between the power of expressing attitudes on the one hand and the simplicity of the scaling on the other hand, 7-point Likert scaling was chosen as the standard measurement instrument. The larger the number of levels in attitude measurements, the better respondents can differentiate their opinion, but a large number of possible rankings may also cause inconsistencies in responses; Bortz and Döring have shown that a number of levels ranging from 2 to 19 affects neither reliability nor validity of the rating.[5] To guarantee a reliable and simple treatment of the responses, closed items were designed, which provide several advantages over other forms: among

---

[4]   Taylor-Powell (1998); Fink (1995); Fowler (1995); Bortz and Döring (2003).
[5]   Bortz and Döring (2003), p. 179.

others, the objectivity of the survey is increased and no post-hoc categorization or coding is needed.[6] The questions were assembled in concise three-page questionnaires (one per survey), as moderate length of questionnaire was considered to be a factor for improving return rate. Finally, in order to further increase response rate, an accompanying letter was attached to the questionnaire and a reminder was sent to non-respondents after 4 weeks.[7]

Statements were used to explore attitudes of respondents, while numerical and open questions were used to collect quantitative and qualitative information such as frequencies. Question items were structured in the following classes:

- In item classes concerning general aspects of data quality in the ERP system domain, namely relevance (RR), economic aspects (RO), factors (IA, IO, IC, II, IT, ID, IS, IU, IM), and importance for marketing purposes (SA), participants were asked to express their attitude on 7-point Likert scales ranging from -3 ("strongly disagree") to $+3$ ("strongly agree"), with a middle point labeled "neutral." In order to avoid any bias related to the equidistance of verbal coding, numerical rating was chosen for the intermediate steps -2, -1, $+1$, and $+2$.[8]

- For the question items targeting the level of data quality, class SD, a scale going from -3 ("very bad") to $+3$ ("very good") was chosen, with a midpoint called "neutral".

- Looking at enterprise actions against data quality problems (question class AE), respondents were asked to answer "yes" or "no" to whether they had implemented a proposed action or not. Affirmative answers were coded as 1, negative ones as 0.

- In question class AP (priority given when investing funds in data quality programs), participants had to qualify the impact of proposed actions, using values ranging from -3 ("strong deterioration") to $+3$ ("strong improvement"), with a 0 midpoint ("no change").

- The degree of responsibilities for data quality (question class RP) was evaluated using a scale of integers ranging from "no responsibility" to "important responsibility" (coded as 0 to 7).

- To measure the degree of implementation of data quality features in ERP systems, vendors were asked to specify whether they implemented proposed features in their products as "standard," as an "option," or whether they had any plans to do so (question class AV).

Both questionnaires were reviewed and pilot tested with a group of survey specialists and ERP practitioners working at the Institute of Information Systems; as a consequence, initial item wording and coverage in the survey design was modified.

---

[6] Bortz and Döring (2003), p. 254.
[7] Bortz and Döring (2003), pp. 257–259.
[8] Bortz and Döring (2003), p. 178.

4.1.3 Treatment of Responses

Responses have been coded manually, analyzed, and visualized using the statistical software package R[9] and Microsoft Excel XP.

4.1.4 Statistical Method Overview

4.1.4.1 Sampling and Usage of Question Classes

The following three samples were used throughout the surveys:[10]

1. Sample SU contains the 500 addresses provided by the Swiss Federal Statistical Office (SFSO), used to mail the questionnaire to the selected enterprises;
2. Sample RU, a subset of SU, includes the 125 questionnaires returned by respondents;
3. Sample RV contains the 50 questionnaires returned by ERP vendors (out of 111 sent).

Statistical analyses on the survey data were carried out with regard to five directions:

1. In a first analysis, the populations of samples SU and RU were examined for proving the representativity of the enterprise survey;
2. Secondly, the influence of categorical variables "sector" and "size of enterprise" (in terms of number of employees) in sample RU was analyzed;
3. Then the correlation among selected variables in survey RU was tested for dependencies indicating potential causal relationships;
4. Next, the central tendency of responses in both surveys was examined, for testing whether attitudes of IT managers and ERP vendors were consistent;
5. Lastly, the data collected in sample RV was tested for correlations between various response variables.

Figure 4.1 provides an illustration of the samples, question classes, and main categorical variables; Table 4.2 summarizes the analyses and describes the types of hypotheses and statistical methods used.

4.1.4.2 Descriptive Statistics

With the objective of providing an "economical summarization of the raw data," descriptive statistics are used to summarize, describe, and explore data.[11] Typical deliverables of

---

[9] R Development Core Team (2009).

[10] Exact descriptions of the samples will be given later in Sections 4.2.2.1 and 4.2.3.1.

[11] Bartholomew et al. (2002), p. 2.

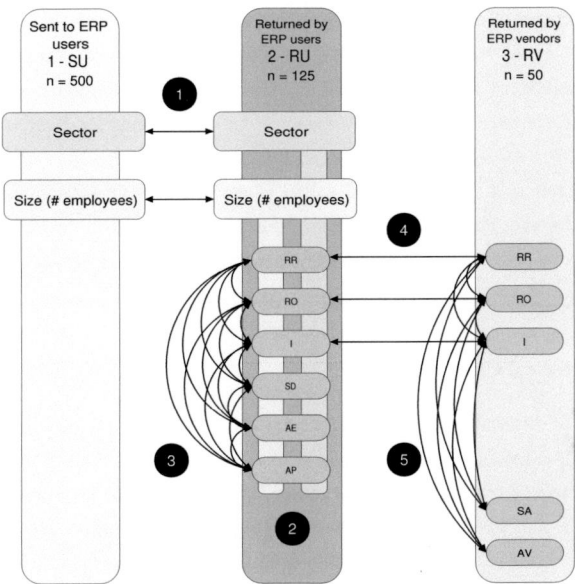

Figure 4.1: Sampling of IT Managers and ERP Vendors.

Domain	Null Hypothesis	Statistical Tests
❶	Sample RU is representative of the population addressed in sample SU	Fisher exact test over categorical variables "sector" and "size of enterprise" in SU and RU
❷	Distribution of responses in RU does not depend on categorical variables "size" or "sector"	Kruskal-Wallis test for > 2 independent samples
❸	No dependencies between variables in RU	Spearman rank correlation test
❹	Central tendency in statements made in RU is not different from responses gathered in RV	Wilcoxon rank sum test for 2 independent samples
❺	No dependencies between variables in RV	Spearman rank correlation test

Table 4.2: Survey Samples, Classes of Hypotheses, and Research Methods.

any descriptive analysis are the distribution characteristics (such as histograms), the central tendency (expressed, e.g., by the mean $[\bar{x}]$ or the median $[\tilde{x}]$ values), and the dispersion (typically the standard deviation SD) of the data.[12] In this research, comprehensive descriptive statistics were computed, and a selection of the most interesting findings per question (or question class) will be presented later in this chapter.

4.1.4.3 Inferential Statistics

Inferential statistics are used to draw conclusions concerning more than just the sample described by the data at hand.[13] Following Tredoux and Durrheim, a hypothesis "is a

---

[12] Trochim (2004).
[13] Trochim (2004).

tentative statement of a relationship" between variables; hypotheses tests are used in inferential statistics to compare characteristics of the entirety or parts of a population.[14]

For the analysis of continuous variables, specific analytic techniques have been developed, such as *t*-tests or ANOVA. However, for the discrete and most often not normally distributed data used in the two surveys of this research, distribution-free methods such as the Wilcoxon rank sum test (also called Mann-Whitney or Mann-Whitney U test), Kruskal-Wallis tests (an extension of the Mann-Whitney U test to the case of more than two groups, a "non-parametric version of one-way ANOVA"[15]), Fisher exact tests, and χ^2 tests were used.[16]

4.1.4.4 Statistical Conventions

Significance of differences of central tendency in the summary tables will be abbreviated by "Sig." and coded as * (when $p < 10\%$), ** ($p < 5\%$), and *** ($p < 1\%$) in this chapter. If not stated otherwise, the significance level for hypothesis testing was fixed at 5% ($\alpha = 0.05$). Being aware of the problem of multiple comparisons when repeatedly performing statistical tests (with a potential risk of unduly rejecting the null hypothesis, i.e., obtaining "false positives"),[17] the author has nevertheless declined to carry out compensatory analyses. Instead, statistical visualizations such as back-to-back histograms (bihistograms) will be provided when appropriate, to graphically explain special characteristics, especially differences in distributions of responses observed between populations.

4.1.4.5 Types of Variables Employed in Survey

As the survey mainly focused on attitudes, most questionnaire items were mapped to *interval variables*. For this type of variable, differences and ranks can be specified, as well as distances between two points on the scale. Characteristics of two interval scaled items can be compared ("equal," "greater than," "less than") or aggregated,[18] properties which were used intensely during the statistical analysis. With regard to the interval scaled coding of responses and the often heavily skewed distributions, the median ($\tilde{x}$ for a sample, MD for the related population) was generally preferred as a "central" characteristic, and attention was paid to unusual distributions of responses. For coding the categorical variables used to classify enterprises, such as "number of employees" or "economic sector" (variables EMP and CAT in the enterprise survey), nominal variables were used.

---

[14] Tredoux and Durrheim (2002), p. 128.
[15] Gardener (2006).
[16] Tredoux and Durrheim (2002), p. 10.
[17] Cf., e.g., Benjamini and Hochberg (1995).
[18] Tredoux and Durrheim (2002), p. 12.

4.1.4.6 Null Hypotheses

The following generic null hypotheses, suitable for the analysis of all groups of questions introduced in Section 4.1.1, were applied to the data collected in the enterprise survey (RU), as all responses in this context could be categorized by the number of employees (EMP) and their sector (SEC):

- H_0^{EMP}: The central tendency of responses does not depend on the size of the organization.
- H_0^{SEC}: The central tendency of responses does not depend on the sector of activity of the organization.

As the ERP vendor survey (sample RV) did not include categorical variables, no generic null hypotheses were used.

4.2 Survey Execution

4.2.1 Survey Profile

Table 4.3 shows the profile of respondent demographics characterizing the two surveys, together with design details of the two surveys.

Indicator	User Survey (Samples SU and RU)	Vendor Survey (Sample RV)
Population	Swiss enterprises employing at least 250 persons (full-time equivalents)	All Swiss ERP vendors listed in *top-soft* database
Population size	869	Presumably several hundred, 136 products listed in database
Population sample	500 (provided by SFSO)	111 (only sent to software vendors, pure service providers excluded)
Excluded from sample	1 (ERP vendor)	0
Questionnaires sent	499	111
Questionnaires returned	125	50
Thereof excluded or unusable	0	0
Return rate	25.1%	45.0%
Number of question classes	14	13
Number of questionnaire items	63	52

Table 4.3: Profile of the Two Surveys.

The number of ERP vendors active in Switzerland can only be estimated to be in the region of several hundred; as an example, Schmid counted "far over 300 vendors" participating at the leading Swiss ERP trade fair *topsoft*.[19]

---

[19] Schmid (2005), p. 16.

4.2.2 Enterprise Survey Demographics

4.2.2.1 Research Population

The principal intent of the enterprise survey was to make assertions about data quality in the field of application of ERP systems. As it is impossible to address all organizations using ERP systems on a global scale, the scope was narrowed with regards to the size of organizations and their geographical location. Swiss enterprises with at least 250 persons employed, expressed in Full-Time Equivalents (FTE), were identified as most probable users of ERP systems, having an organizational complexity calling for adequate IT support and possessing a formal IT organization. This choice also fits the current market strategy of major ERP vendors: SAP, as an example, targets with its "small and medium businesses" (SMB) initiative enterprises having between 100 and 1,000 employees.[20] However, as many ERP systems are designed for SMBs as well, this choice of organizational size must be kept in mind; it will also be critically reviewed at the end of Chapter 6.

The limitation to the Swiss territory can be justified for the prominent position of this country in ERP technology (Swiss firms have been amongst the very early adopters of leading ERP products) and the important level of spending in ICT. In 2005, Switzerland reported the highest spending for ICT world-wide, with 2,724 EUR per inhabitant, followed by Scandinavian countries and Japan; from another perspective, spending for ICT counted for 7.7% of the Gross Domestic Product (GDP), ranking Switzerland in third position, behind Sweden and the United Kingdom.[21] Moreover, Switzerland is an ideal test bed for many ERP vendors: the density of ERP installations is high, ERP as business and software concepts have a long tradition, and Swiss enterprises have been implementing software integration concepts for a long time.[22]

Addresses for the enterprise survey could be obtained at the SFSO, which provided a statistically representative sample of 500 enterprises, out of a population of 869 Swiss enterprises having the required size and being active at the time of the survey. One company – a major ERP software vendor – had to be excluded due to a potential (ERP user vs. ERP vendor) role conflict; the sample also systematically excluded governmental agencies, which are known to be heavy users of ERP systems in Switzerland. The questionnaire described in Section 4.1.2 was mailed to the IT managers[23] of the 499 retained enterprises.

---

[20] Bayer (2006).
[21] Swiss Federal Statistical Office (2006).
[22] Scherer (2006), p. 48.
[23] Exact wording: "Leitung Informatik" in the German and "responsable informatique" in the French version of the questionnaire.

4.2.2.2 Size of Enterprises

Table 4.4 shows the distribution of enterprises present in the response sample (RU): visibly, large organizations are slightly over-represented in this sample, even if no statistically significant differences between the groups SU and RU could be found ($p = 0.29$).[24] Possible explanations for this over-representation could be found in the stronger impact of data quality problems in large organizations, or the availability of experts for ERP and data quality related questions, attracted by the topic of the survey.

Employees	SFSO Code		Sent (SU)	Returned (RU)
[250, 500) FTE	10	Count	314	74
		%	62.9%	59.2%
[500, 1.000) FTE	11	Count	117	27
		%	23.4%	21.6%
[1.000, ∞) FTE	12	Count	68	24
		%	13.6%	19.2%
Total		Count	499	125
		%	100.0%	100.0%

Table 4.4: Distribution of Size of Organizations in Enterprise Survey.

4.2.2.3 Economic Activities of Sample

The data provided by the SFSO was encoded using the NOGA 2002[25] classification scheme, a five-tiered structure used to classify 724 different economic activities.[26] For the purpose of the study, NOGA's 99 level-2 categories were further condensed into 10 classes (Table 4.5).

Category	Code	Description	NOGA Codes
1	1:AM	Agriculture, Mining	1–14
2	2:MA	Manufacturing	15–37
3	3:EL	Electricity, Gas, and Water Supply	40–41
4	4:CO	Construction	45
5	5:TR	Wholesale/Retail Trade, Transportation, Storage, and Communication	50–52; 60–64
6	6:HO	Hotels and Restaurants	55
7	7:FI	Financial Intermediation and Insurance	65–67
8	8:SV	Professional Services	70–74
9	9:PA	Public Administration and Defense, Social Security	75
10	10:OP	Other Public Services	80; 85; 90–93; 95–97

Table 4.5: Classes of Economic Activities and NOGA.

In order to verify that industry sectors of respondents were distributed accordingly to the distribution in the sample SU, a cross tabulation showing the relative frequency

---

[24] Null hypothesis on frequencies (F) H_0: $F_{sent} = F_{returned}$. Fisher exact test for count data, alternative hypothesis: two-sided.

[25] Swiss "Nomenclature Générale des Activités économiques," compatible with the European Union's "Nomenclature of Economic Activities" Rev. 1.1.

[26] Swiss Federal Statistical Office (2005).

of sectors was set up (Table 4.6). Visibly, manufacturing industries are slightly over-represented in sample RU; again, the difference proved not to be significant (p = 0.30).[27]

Sample RU can hence be considered to be a representative description of the selection provided by the SFSO. As the base sample SU used for addressing the questionnaire was also a statistically sound representation of Swiss companies, responses from RU can equally be considered as representative for large Swiss enterprises in general.

Sector	Code		Sent (SU)	Returned (RU)
Agriculture, Mining	1	Count	1	0
		%	0.2%	0.0%
Manufacturing	2	Count	211	66
		%	42.3%	52.8%
Electricity, Gas, and Water Supply	3	Count	2	0
		%	0.4%	0.0%
Construction	4	Count	31	7
		%	6.2%	5.6%
Wholesale/Retail Trade, Transportation, Storage, Communication	5	Count	103	28
		%	20.6%	22.4%
Hotels and Restaurants	6	Count	19	2
		%	3.8%	1.6%
Financial Intermediation and Insurance	7	Count	55	7
		%	11.0%	5.6%
Professional Services	8	Count	33	4
		%	6.6%	3.2%
Public Administration and Defense, Social Security	9	Count	0	0
		%	0.0%	0.0%
Other Public Services	10	Count	44	11
		%	8.8%	8.8%
Total		Count	499	125
		%	100.0%	100.0%

Table 4.6: Distribution of Sectors in Enterprise Survey.

4.2.2.4   Language Represented in Enterprise Survey

The statistical data provided by the SFSO reported the main language of communication reported by businesses, encoded as DE (German), FR (French), and IT (Italian). Table 4.7 shows the proportions of linguistic groups in the address (SU) and response (RU) samples: German-speaking respondents were slightly over-represented, a fact that could be explained by the larger publicity of the Institute of Information Systems of the University of Bern in the German-speaking part of Switzerland.

Language		Sent (SU)	Returned (RU)
DE	Count	373	101
	%	74.7%	80.8%
FR	Count	113	24
	%	22.6%	19.2%
IT	Count	13	0
	%	2.6%	0.0%
Total	Count	499	125
	%	100.0%	100.0%

Table 4.7: Language of Respondents in Enterprise Survey.

---

[27] Null hypothesis on frequencies (F) H_0: $F_{sent} = F_{returned}$. Fisher exact test for count data, alternative hypothesis: two-sided.

No statistically significant differences between the proportions of respondents from the three linguistic regions in the two samples could be found ($p = 0.11$).[28]

4.2.2.5 Function of Respondents

Even if questionnaires were addressed to IT managers, respondents were asked to indicate their job function. Table 4.8 shows the functions as reported; almost 50% of respondents were fulfilling the role of an IT manager. For the sake of simplicity, respondents in the enterprise survey will be referred to as "IT managers" throughout this study, regardless of the actual function reported.

Function	Count	%
IT Manager	60	48%
ERP (Application) Manager	12	10%
Line Manager	9	7%
Project Manager	6	5%
Administration	4	3%
Process Manager	1	1%
Unknown / not specified	*33*	*26%*
Total	125	100%

Table 4.8: Function of Respondents in Organization in Enterprise Survey.

4.2.2.6 Duration of Survey

Questionnaires were mailed to the selected addresses during the first week of September 2003, due September 30, 2003. A reminder was sent on October 6 to enterprises from which no response had been received, with a new due date of October 20, 2003. No responses arrived after November 10, 2003.

4.2.2.7 Response Analysis – Early and Late Respondents

A common first activity in data analysis consists of checking whether late differ from early respondents, and of determining what the reasons for non-responses are.[29] The criterion for a response to be "late" was set to "returned after due date." Out of the 125 responses received, 5 were handed in without a visible postmark (being neither "early" nor "late"), 104 arrived in time ("early"), and 16 arrived after the reminder had been sent ("late"). Question classes RR, RO, IO, IC, II, IT, ID, IS, IU, and IM, all using the same 7-point Likert scale, were used for carrying out the statistical test. Table A.35 on page 253 in Appendix A shows the detailed results of the test of homogeneity of proportions of early and late respondent attitudes, with the null hypothesis that early and late respondents can be considered as a single group.

---

[28] Null hypothesis on frequencies (F) H_0: $F_{sent} = F_{returned}$. Fisher exact test for count data, alternative hypothesis: two-sided.

[29] Bortz and Döring (2003), p. 260.

Overall, no *systematic* evidence on an important proportion of differing variables could be found, a fact that allowed rejection of the null hypothesis. As a consequence, early and late responses will not be distinguished in the remainder of this chapter. Reasons cited by non-respondents for not participating in the study were "refusal to participate in any survey" or "lack of time/work overload" (8 justified non-responses). In another 8 non-response cases, contact persons stated that the activities addressed by the questionnaire were carried out in other divisions. These statements show that non-participants did not have a particular (deviant) opinion that could falsify the results drawn from the evaluation of the returned questionnaires.

4.2.3   ERP Vendor Survey Demographics

4.2.3.1   Research Population

The main idea of the vendor survey was to explore the views of the ERP vendor industry of data quality. As mentioned in Section 4.2.2.1, the scope of possible participants was narrowed to the Swiss ERP industry context. Switzerland is an important ERP software market; as an example, this country was chosen by SAP as bridgehead for its move to the international marketplace in 1984.[30] Even with this geographical limitation, precisely defining the ERP vendor population was difficult, as an agreed upon definition of what an "ERP system" is exactly was lacking, and an official ERP vendor directory did not exist. As a solution, addresses were taken from a professional source, the comprehensive, publicly accessible vendor database *topsoft*.[31] *topsoft* is also the name of a well-established Swiss ERP trade fair, sometimes considered to be "the probably biggest and most focused ERP event world-wide."[32] With regard to representativity, the "convenience sampling" obtained by using the *topsoft* database is clearly not suitable for making statements about the ERP software industry as a whole.

4.2.3.2   Nature of ERP Software Products

With regard to the customers targeted by the ERP systems sold by the vendors, 44% of respondents sold software adapted first and foremost to the needs of large organizations, while 96% had designed their software products also with SMBs in mind.[33] From a technical point of view, 86% of responding software vendors had developed their current ERP product range "from scratch," the rest offered software based on an existing product line.

---

[30] Meissner (1997), p. 284.
[31] http://www.topsoft.ch/.
[32] Scherer (2006), p. 45.
[33] n = 48.

4.2.3.3 Duration of Survey

The questionnaire designed in accordance with the guidelines described in Section 4.1.2 was mailed to the 111 ERP vendors found in the database by the first week of September, 2003, requesting them to hand in their responses by September 30, 2003. A reminder was sent by mail on October 6 to non-responding vendors, asking them to return their copies by October 20, 2003. On November 4, 2003, the last questionnaire was received.

4.2.3.4 Response Analysis – Early and Late Respondents

Again, the first analysis carried out to ensure consistency of responses was to search for possible differences in statements of early and late respondents; in this survey, no non-respondent gave reasons for refusing to participate. Out of the 50 responses, 4 were handed in without a visible post mark, 39 arrived in time ("early"), and 7 after the specified due date ("late"). Table A.36 on page 255 in Appendix A shows the detailed results of the test of homogeneity of proportions of early and late respondent attitudes; one item (IU01) was answered in a significantly different way by these two groups. When considering the graphical description of this situation provided in the appendix (Figure A.10 on page 256), early and late respondents in the vendor survey can nevertheless be considered to belong to the same statistical population.

4.3 Survey Results

In this section, results gained from the two surveys will be presented, per question class, in the following sequence:

1. Firstly, the background of the questions and the variables used in a class of questions are explained; the exact wording of the questions can be found in Section A.2 in Appendix A;

2. Secondly, the class specific hypotheses are explained, together with the results of the tests carried out on the data collected in both surveys;

3. Next, if data from both surveys is available, results from an inter-survey analysis checking for similarities and differences between responses obtained from IT manager (enterprise) and ERP vendor groups are provided;

4. Then results obtained by testing the two null hypotheses formulated in Section 4.1.4.6 (independence of trends from factors size, H_0^{EMP}, and industry sector, H_0^{SEC}) in the enterprise survey (intra-survey analysis) are presented;

5. Lastly, findings are summarized and put into perspective.

4.3.1   Relevance of Data Quality

4.3.1.1   Research Questions and Hypotheses

The importance of high quality data in IT systems has been highlighted in the review of data quality literature in Chapter 2. Several questions were, however, raised at the beginning of the study: Is data quality an issue in an ERP system environment as well? What is the perception of relevance of data quality in the eyes of IT managers and ERP vendors, in the current business context and in the future? Four statement items were used to measure the relevance of data quality in the enterprise and ERP vendor surveys, using a 7-point Likert scale ranging from -3 ("strongly disagree") to $+3$ ("strongly agree").[34]

As the information systems success model introduced by DeLone and McLean argues that data quality is a precondition for IT systems success,[35] the first question (RR01) checked whether data quality carries this role of a precondition also in an ERP system context. Secondly, as data integration across the many IT systems supporting a typical business is another precondition for optimization of business processes,[36] participants were confronted with the idea that the role of data quality in an increasingly integrated use of business information will gain importance (RR02). Integration of the information flow along the supply chains forces businesses to exchange more of their marketing, logistics, or financial data with partners outside their organizational borders.[37] In the context of initiatives engaged to facilitate the flow of physical goods, data management has to be reconciled amongst business partners in the supply chain, and the question of data quality is hence expected to become critical to SCM improvement projects; respondents were asked to comment on this view in RR03. Lastly, the concept of the "Real-Time Enterprise"[38] requires an availability of accurate information in real-time and could impose, e.g., in the context of online Web shops with product availability information, special requirements on the underlying data. The importance of having quality data to fulfill real-time requirements was the object of the last statement (RR04) of question class RR.

4.3.1.2   Specific Hypotheses

Besides the two null hypotheses formulated in Section 4.1.4.6 (independence of trends from factors size, H_0^{EMP}, and industry sector, H_0^{SEC}), the following first specific null hypothesis H_{1-0} with alternative counterpart H_{1-1} was formulated (the symbol MD denotes the median of the population, while $\tilde{x}$ represents the sample median):

---

[34] For statements proposed in question class "Relevance" (RR) cf. Table A.1 on page 245. Summary statistics can be found in Table A.18 on page 249.

[35] Cf. Section 1.1.

[36] Schwinn et al. (1999), p. 96.

[37] Knolmayer et al. (2001).

[38] Gartner Group (2007).

Hypothesis 1.

H_{1-0}: Respondents do not consider data quality as a specific success factor for ERP systems $[MD_{\mathrm{RR0i}} \leq 0; i = 1 \ldots 4]$.

H_{1-1}: Respondents consider data quality as a specific success factor for ERP systems $[MD_{\mathrm{RR0i}} > 0; i = 1 \ldots 4]$.

Table 4.9 shows the results of the Wilcoxon signed rank test with continuity correction for the above hypothesis, computed for all members of item class RR.

Item	Meaning	H_1	H_0 on MD_U			H_0 on MD_V		
			V	p	$Sig.$	V	p	$Sig.$
RR01	Precondition	greater	7875	0.000	***	1275	0.000	***
RR02	Integration	greater	7240	0.000	***	1275	0.000	***
RR03	External data	greater	6781	0.000	***	1222	0.000	***
RR04	Real-time requirements	greater	6752	0.000	***	1081	0.000	***

Table 4.9: Relevance of Data Quality: Test of Hypotheses.[a]

[a] Wilcoxon signed rank test with continuity correction.

Based on this data H_{1-0} was rejected for all of the four items and in both surveys ($p = 0$). The extent of agreement with the propositions can be seen in detail in Table A.1:[39] over 78% of all respondents "strongly agreed" (score $+3$), another 16% "agreed" (score $+2$), and 5% "rather agreed" (score $+1$) with the pretended importance of data quality in the ERP context. Both IT managers and ERP vendors therefore consider data quality to be an important factor of success for ERP systems.

4.3.1.3   Inter-Survey Summary Analysis

The central tendency of responses commenting on the relationship between process support provided by ERP systems and data quality is reported in Tables A.18[40] and 4.10 (below). Over 75% of respondents were fully convinced that data quality is of utmost importance. Interpreting the numbers, the role of data quality is expected to gain importance, together with the increasing number and ongoing integration of IT systems and the need for real-time information. Lastly, IT managers and ERP vendors both saw an increasing interest for data quality criteria and metrics.

Item	Meaning	RU		RV		$MD_U = MD_V$	
		n	$\bar{x}$	n	$\bar{x}$	p	$Sig.$
RR01	Precondition	125	3	50	3	0.261	
RR02	Integration	125	3	50	3	0.464	
RR03	External data	123	2	50	3	0.022	**
RR04	Real-time requirements	122	3	50	3	0.521	

Table 4.10:   Perceived Importance of Relevance of Data Quality.[a,b]

[a] Wilcoxon signed rank test with continuity correction.
[b] Alternative hypothesis: two-sided.

---

[39] Page 245 in Appendix A.
[40] Page 249 in Appendix A.

The only significant difference between responses in the enterprise and ERP vendor surveys (samples RU and RV) is found in the relevance of external data. Figure 4.2 shows the results for this item as a back-to-back histogram (showing the proportions of responses as decimal percentages) and a box plot. The latter is a graphical summary of characteristics in descriptive statistics: firstly, the median is represented by a thick line, which divides the box represented by the Interquartile Range (IQR), delimited by the 1st and 3rd quartile marks; secondly, outliers are observations with values below $1.5 \cdot IQR$ and above $1.5 \cdot IQR$, represented by dots ($\circ$); horizontal tic marks ("whiskers") finally represent the most distant observations excluding outliers.[41] Figure 4.2 supports the numerical results from Table 4.10 in the sense that ERP software vendors value the importance of using external data more than IT managers.

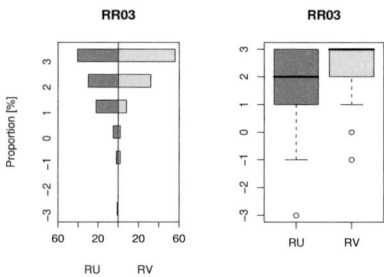

Figure 4.2: Perceived Importance of Relevance of Data Quality – Aspect External Data.

4.3.1.4   Enterprise Survey Detail Analysis

To find divergent opinions amongst respondents from enterprises of different sizes and different industry sectors, the Kruskal-Wallis test for three or more related samples was applied to the data collected in the enterprise survey.[42] As Table 4.11 shows, the perception of the relevance of data quality perceived by IT managers depends only in one case upon the sector.

The rejected null hypothesis (H_0^{SEC}) of variable RR01 concerns the role of data quality as a precondition (Figure 4.3). The "significant difference" found by the statistical test is, however, put into perspective when the small number of responses in some groups (formed by respondents from industry sectors) is considered. Outliers observed in sectors 4 ("Construction," two score $+1$ statements, compared to a total of 7 responses in this group) and 10 ("Financial services," three score $+1$ responses, compared to a total of 11

---

[41] Tukey (1990).
[42] Cf. Section 4.1.4.3.

Item	Meaning	H_0^{EMP}		H_0^{SEC}	
		p	$Sig.$	p	$Sig.$
RR01	Precondition	0.308		0.036	**
RR02	Integration	0.818		0.115	
RR03	External data	0.246		0.120	
RR04	Real-time requirements	0.391		0.220	

Table 4.11: Perception of Relevance of Data Quality.[a,b]

[a] Kruskal-Wallis rank sum test.
[b] Alternative hypotheses: two-sided.

responses in this group), together with the median of respondents from sector 7 (FI) – the result of four score +2 and three score +3 statements – can explain the result of the test. As a whole, it can be concluded from the enterprise survey data that respondents from all sectors strongly agree on the importance of data quality.

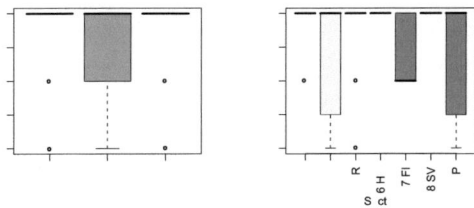

Figure 4.3: Perception of Relevance of Data Quality – Data Quality as Precondition.

4.3.1.5 Summary of Results

Finding 4.1. An overwhelming proportion of respondents (over 80%) in both surveys agreed that data quality is highly relevant for enterprise data processing.

Finding 4.2. Small but significant differences in the perception of relevance of data quality exist between IT managers and ERP vendors with regard to the pressure created by increasing use of external business data: ERP vendors see a higher potential for data problems due to data sharing with external business partners.

Finding 4.3. The role of data quality is gaining importance, as IT systems in organizations have to be integrated, real-time requirements are becoming pervasive, and data is increasingly exchanged over organizational borders. These trends call for careful management of data contained in and exchanged with ERP systems.

4.3.2   Economic Aspects of Data Quality

4.3.2.1   Research Questions and Hypotheses

Economic reasoning appears quickly in almost every (data) quality discussion. Demanding "full accuracy of data" sounds good, but is such a situation technically achievable, at justifiable cost? What about the cost-quality tradeoff perceived by IT managers and ERP vendors? Again, four statement items were designed and used to gauge the economic reasoning behind data quality initiatives.[43]

As the analysis in Chapter 3 has shown, data quality cannot – in a narrow definition – be perfect in ERP systems, even on a theoretical level: a given enterprise may never use many of the data elements provided, or data may be subject to changes in the "real world," which call for constant (and instant) updates, an undertaking no organization could possibly accomplish in real-time and with perfect quality. Item RO01 addressed this challenge, focusing on the specific ERP view of respondents. Next, even if perfect data *could* be created during operations of an ERP system, the costs to do so could be in no reasonable relation to the expected benefit;[44] even if software vendors and industry initiatives are targeting "100% data quality,"[45] traditional quality literature considers the prevention costs to rise asymptotically when approaching a "zero defects" zone.[46] Question RO02 proposed the idea that perfect data quality in ERP systems (even if technically feasible) does not make sense under economic considerations. Then the question of the reasonability of setting a minimum level of data quality was submitted to respondents, with a special focus on data directly accessible to external stakeholders (RO03). Lastly, if the appearance of low quality data in ERP systems cannot be avoided, at least the propagation of errors could be impeded by installing data cleansing routines at the interfaces to analytical applications which rely on ERP data. Negatively worded item RO04 asked respondents whether improving the quality of data in an ERP system itself was absolutely required, rather than improving it if necessary during downstream processing, e.g., using ETL tools in data warehousing.

4.3.2.2   Specific Hypotheses

Besides the two null hypotheses formulated in Section 4.1.4.6 (which also applied to the present question context), several specific hypotheses on economic reasoning of respondents were formulated (Hypotheses 2 to 5):

---

[43] For statements proposed in question class "Economic Aspects" (RO) cf. Table A.2 on page 245. Summary statistics can be found in Table A.19 on page 249.

[44] Ballou et al. (2004), p. 10.

[45] Cf., e.g., Centrale für Coorganisation (2003).

[46] Schneidermann (1986).

Hypothesis 2.
H_{2-0}: Respondents do not consider full (100%) quality of business data as achievable [$MD_{RO01} \leq 0$].
H_{2-1}: Respondents consider full (100%) quality in business data as achievable [$MD_{RO01} > 0$].

Hypothesis 3.
H_{3-0}: Respondents do not consider full (100%) quality of business data a meaningful organizational goal [$MD_{RO02} \leq 0$].
H_{3-1}: Respondents consider full (100%) quality of business data a meaningful organizational goal [$MD_{RO02} > 0$].

Hypothesis 4.
H_{4-0}: Respondents believe that data relevant to external stakeholders of an enterprise does not require special care [$MD_{RO03} \leq 0$].
H_{4-1}: Respondents believe that data relevant to external stakeholders of an enterprise does require special care [$MD_{RO03} > 0$].

Hypothesis 5.
H_{5-0}: Respondents postulate that data cleansing in the ERP system (at the source) does not make sense [$MD_{RO04} \geq 0$].
H_{5-1}: Respondents postulate that data cleansing in the ERP system (at the source) does make sense [$MD_{RO04} < 0$].

Table 4.12 shows the results of the test of above hypotheses: null hypotheses H_{2-0}, H_{4-0}, and H_{5-0} were rejected after analysis of the data received by respondents in both surveys; null hypothesis H_{3-0} was the only one not to be rejected, in one case.

Item	Meaning	H_1	H_0 on MD_U			H_0 on MD_V		
			V	p	Sig.	V	p	Sig.
RO01	100% data quality impossible	greater	6213	0.000	***	857	0.000	***
RO02	100% data quality meaningless	greater	4898	0.000	***	354	0.843	
RO03	External documents	greater	7164	0.000	***	1014	0.000	***
RO04	Correction at source	less	342	0.000	***	118	0.000	***

Table 4.12: Economic Aspects of Data Quality: Test of Hypotheses.[a]

[a] Wilcoxon signed rank test with continuity correction.

The only notable difference between responses from both surveys was observed in question RO02, where IT managers proved to be critical with regard to the 100% data quality target and testified that such an objective makes only little economic sense (MD = 1), while ERP vendor responses were evenly spread across positive and negative values ($MD = 0$).

4.3.2.3 Inter-Survey Summary Analysis

Table 4.13 shows the attitude of respondents towards economic questions behind data quality in ERP systems. As mentioned above, the central tendency (median) of item RO02 differs between IT managers (sample RU) and ERP vendors (RV); Table 4.12 shows that this difference of opinion is significant. IT managers clearly expressed the opinion that 100% quality does not make sense, whereas vendor responses were mixed.

Item	Meaning	RU		RV		$MD_U = MD_V$	
		n	$\bar{x}$	n	$\bar{x}$	p	$Sig.$
RO01	100% data quality impossible	123	2	50	2	0.283	
RO02	100% data quality meaningless	125	1	48	0	0.002	***
RO03	External documents	125	3	50	3	0.458	
RO04	Correction at source	115	-2	50	-2	0.379	

Table 4.13:   Perceived Importance of Economic Aspects of Data Quality.[a,b]

[a] Wilcoxon signed rank test with continuity correction.
[b] Alternative hypothesis: two-sided.

Figure 4.4 illustrates the results of item RO02 in graphical form. It is, however, interesting to note that in both surveys "extreme" opinions prevail, in the sense that respondents either "fully agreed" or "totally disagreed," but rarely expressed a neutral position.

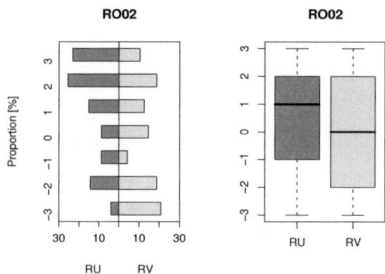

Figure 4.4: Perceived Importance of Meaningfulness of 100% Data Quality.

4.3.2.4   Enterprise Survey Detail Analysis

The Kruskal-Wallis test for three or more related samples was applied again for testing the homogeneity of enterprise survey responses with regard to factors (categorical variables) EMP and SEC. As Table 4.14 shows, perception of data quality economics amongst IT managers shows few significant differences.

Item	Meaning	H_0^{EMP}		H_0^{SEC}	
		p	$Sig.$	p	$Sig.$
RO01	100% data quality impossible	0.458		0.246	
RO02	100% data quality meaningless	0.004	***	0.554	
RO03	External documents	0.388		0.293	
RO04	Correction at source	0.291		0.079	*

Table 4.14: Perception of Economics in Data Quality.[a,b]

[a] Kruskal-Wallis rank sum test.
[b] Alternative hypotheses: two-sided.

The null hypothesis H_0^{EMP} of RO02 in the vendor survey had to be rejected because of the differing attitudes towards the *economic* meaningfulness of 100% data quality, as Figure 4.5 shows (coding see Section 4.2.2.2). Respondents from small and large businesses remained rather skeptical, while their colleagues from medium-sized enterprises adhered much stronger to the idea suggested by RO02, namely to abstain from setting 100% data quality objectives.

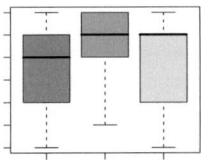

Figure 4.5: Perception of Economics of Data Quality – 100% Data Quality is meaningless.

4.3.2.5 Summary of Results

Finding 4.4. ERP vendors and IT managers strongly doubt that it is possible to reach a state of perfect data quality in ERP systems.

Finding 4.5. IT managers accentuate the cost-quality trade-off when using ERP systems and their data, as it often does not make sense to set too high targets for data quality; on the contrary, the opinion of ERP vendors is mixed on this point. The difference between the viewpoints of both groups is significant.

Finding 4.6. Data exchanged with external business partners has to be managed with special care, as both groups agree.

Finding 4.7. ERP vendors and IT managers expressing their views in the two surveys consistently and strongly believe that data quality has to be controlled already in primary transaction systems (such as ERP systems); cleansing data only for downstream data warehousing or analytical applications is insufficient from an IT management perspective.

4.3.3 Factors Influencing Data Quality

4.3.3.1 Research Questions and Hypotheses

Several factors influencing data quality were considered in the context of this study: organizational parameters, consulting, system interfaces, user training, system documentation, user support, human factors, ERP system management, and architectural aspects.

Organization: Organizational problems can be the cause of data quality issues. Five questionnaire items[47] have been designed to identify the organizational background of enterprises and the attitude of respondents to organizational questions. Data quality awareness should first be in line with a general "quality orientation" of an organization; item IO01 checked this assumption against reality.

Responsibility for data is a principal ingredient of many data management and data quality guides.[48] If nobody is responsible for a data item, nobody will care about its quality; an idea reflected in statement IO02. Next, if responsibility for data is important, it could be difficult to attach responsibilities in an IT environment using a centralized database, as many system users potentially retrieve or modify data records which have been created by many others; item IO03 gauged this difficulty.

With regard to ERP implementation projects, it has been extensively documented that system success depends heavily on successful project management;[49] item IO04 asked respondents to comment on this opinion. Finally, the aspect of sufficient adaptation of an ERP system to the structures, processes, and other attributes of an organization was checked in questionnaire item IO05: as ERP systems are packaged applications, developed for a multitude of contexts, they need careful tailoring to the needs and organizational constraints of the business.[50]

Consulting: Organizations very seldom have the capability to implement an ERP system only with their internal resources. Most often, they depend on external consultants during system evaluation, implementation, and even operations.[51] Together with the quality of the support provided to ERP users, consultant quality is regarded as a factor influencing the success of ERP projects.[52] A critical part of the ERP implementation phase concerns the mapping of business specific rules into the software: as external consultants are by definition outsiders to a company, setting up the system to the exact business needs of an organization is difficult.[53] Four items were designed to gauge the impact of external consultancies on data quality.[54] The first question item IC01 checked whether

---

[47] For statements proposed for factor "Organization" (IO) cf. Table A.3 on page 245. Summary statistics can be found in Table A.20 on page 249.

[48] Cf. Section 2.2.10.

[49] Knolmayer et al. (1997); Bancroft et al. (1998); Holland and Light (1999); Seddon et al. (1999); Gunson and de Blasis (2001); Somers and Nelson (2001).

[50] Cf. Section 3.1.1.3.

[51] Skok and Legge (2001), pp. 192–193; Grabski et al. (2003), p. 142.

[52] Wang and Chen (2006), p. 1036.

[53] Sumner (2003), p. 163.

[54] For statements proposed for factor "Consulting" (IC) cf. Table A.4 on page 245. Summary statistics can be found in Table A.21 on page 250.

business rules[55] are better implemented by external consultants or by internal staff.[56] As an (extreme) alternative, item IC02 aggressively suggested that business rules are not at all implemented by organizations using ERP systems, introducing Brackett's position that "the development of data integrity rules is often left up to the organization implementing the ERP and is seldom accomplished to any degree."[57] The technical capabilities of external consultants were critically reflected in item IC03, while their ability to understand the customer's business problem was the subject of the last question (IC04) in this block.

Interfaces and External Data: Interfaces to ERP systems, allowing data to enter the system, can be either human or machine based;[58] in both cases, a significant risk of introducing incorrect data into ERP systems exists.[59] In order to evaluate the importance of interfaces for data quality, two questionnaire items were used: item II01 for testing respondents' awareness of the risks related to the interfaces between ERP and other IT systems and item II02 focusing on the risks related to the exchange of external data over organizational borders.[60]

Training: The better the training level of employees, the better they will be able to do their jobs. Training in an ERP context includes also knowledge about cross-functional business processes (how does the work of employees affect other users of the ERP system?) and about the ways to recover from erroneous data entries;[61] the surveys focused on these ideas by using four items.[62] Firstly, respondents were asked to state if there is a relationship between data quality and user training at all (IT01). Next, process orientation of training lessons was focused: in contrast to purely functional knowledge about the ERP system's design and operation principles, users should be able to act in the context of a business process with the aid of the system, and training should therefore be both process and task oriented.[63] Item IT03 pretended a general lack of orientation to the business reality in ERP user training, while IT04 suggested that many ERP users are mostly unable to correct faulty data entries made by themselves or others.

---

[55] Cf. Section 2.5.1.

[56] Neither the concept of business rules nor possible applications of business rules in data quality management had been explained to respondents in the context of the survey.

[57] Brackett (2000), p. 317.

[58] Cf. Section 3.3.2.

[59] Brackett (2000), p. 316: "An ERP does not contain data transformation schemes for getting disparate data into the ERP in an efficient and effective manner."

[60] For statements proposed for factor "Interfaces" (II) cf. Table A.5 on page 246. Summary statistics can be found in Table A.22 on page 250.

[61] Markus et al. (2003a), p. 49.

[62] For statements proposed for factor "training" (IT) cf. Table A.6 on page 246. Summary statistics can be found in Table A.23 on page 250.

[63] Piasecki (2003), p. 47.

Documentation: ERP users can only expect adequate training and support if the way the ERP system has to be used is fully and correctly documented. The sound documentation of an ERP system is therefore likely to positively influence the quality of the data entered and processed. Reference models provided by large ERP vendors can be used to evaluate and select process variants and to adapt the software to the actual needs of an organization. But the study of the process model behind an ERP system can be a complex undertaking, as the process documentation shipped, e.g., with SAP R/3 4.6 describes a total of nearly 10,000 objects; also, out of the 604 process models provided with this system over 5% allegedly contain syntax errors or are, at least, exposed to misunderstandings.[64]

Two statements were proposed to investigate the role of adequate documentation. Item ID01 stipulated a dependency between the timeliness and coverage of the system documentation and the quality of the data in an ERP system. Item ID02 suggested that the standard documentation shipped with ERP systems typically ignores important aspects of data handling.[65]

User Support: Most enterprises have installed IT support units or "help desks" in an attempt to help users to successfully interact with IT systems. The only question presented in this domain, IS01, tried to explore the importance of user support for achieving high data quality.[66]

ERP Users/Human Factors: Besides external factors affecting the work environment, the personality of the users, the attitude and interest of users in their jobs, and the influence of work experience are factors expected to influence the quality of data in ERP systems. The following four statements were proposed to respondents:[67] the lack of interest of ERP users with regard to the data flow being a danger to data quality (IU01), experienced users as a positive (IU02, adequate use of ERP system) or negative factor (IU03, due to system or data "abuse") for data quality, and lack of discipline at work as an important threat to data quality (IU04). The background of the idea of possible system abuse addressed in IU03 was that experienced users could have learned how to "trick the system," i.e., could be tempted to change the operation of the ERP system by entering wrong data by intent, in order to "speed up operations" at the expense of an unusable data track and problems in downstream data processing.[68]

---

[64] Mendling et al. (2006), p. 455.

[65] For statements proposed for factor "Documentation" (ID) cf. Table A.7 on page 246. Summary statistics can be found in Table A.24 on page 250.

[66] Statement proposed for factor "Support" (IS) cf. Table A.8 on page 246.

[67] For statements proposed for factor "User" (IU) cf. Table A.9 on page 246. Summary statistics can be found in Table A.26 on page 251.

[68] Olson (2003), pp. 47–48.

ERP System Management: Design choices concerning the functionality and coverage of ERP process support are expected to affect overall data quality. Three items were designed to clarify these matters:[69] enterprises wanting to cover too many business processes could put their data quality at risk (IM01); conversely, the broader the process coverage an ERP system provides, the better the quality of the underlying data could be (IM02). Moreover, a thoughtful classification of data and adequate data management policies could help to assure data quality; this idea was addressed in question IM03.

ERP Architecture (vendor survey only):   Several factors have been identified in Chapter 3 that could make data quality management difficult in an ERP system environment. In the context of the surveys, ERP vendors were asked to express their views about the data quality features in the systems they sold.[70] Firstly, vendors were challenged by pretending that their products, on principle, are unable to exclude data errors due to their semi-finished design and versatility (IA01).[71] Secondly, item IA02 accused the absence of specific business rules to be responsible for data quality issues.[72] Vendors were further confronted with the statement that data integrity could be infringed in their ERP systems even if relational database technology is used (IA03). Lastly, an excessive number of data models present in the diverse IT systems of an enterprise might be a reason for low data quality; this idea was checked with question IA04.

4.3.3.2   Specific Hypotheses

Besides the generic null hypotheses introduced in Section 4.1.4.6, one specific hypothesis comparing several factors was formulated (Hypothesis 6).

Hypothesis 6.
H_{6-0}: There is no difference in perception of the impact of the three principal factors affecting data quality: documentation, support, and training [$MD_{ID01} = MD_{IT01} = MD_{IS01}$].
H_{6-1}: There is a difference in perception of the impact of the three principal factors documentation, support, and training.

The test of Hypothesis 6 above involving items ID01, IT01, and IS01 resulted in a probability of almost zero;[73] H_{6-0} had hence to be rejected as there were significant

---

[69] For statements proposed for factor "Management" (IM) cf. Table A.10 on page 246. Summary statistics can be found in Table A.27 on page 251.

[70] For statements proposed for factor "Architecture" (IA) cf. Table A.11 on page 247. Summary statistics can be found in Table A.28 on page 251.

[71] Cf. Section 3.1.1.3.

[72] The question whether the stated "absence" was due to a lack of functionality in the ERP product or rather caused by a poor implementation project was not addressed here.

[73] Detailed results of statistical tests:
- RU + RV (all answers from both surveys taken together): $\chi^2 = 182, df = 2, p < 2.2 \cdot 10^{-16}$;
- RU: $\chi^2 = 139, df = 2, p < 2.2 \cdot 10^{-16}$;
- RV: $\chi^2 = 45.8, df = 2, p < 1.155 \cdot 10^{-10}$.

differences in the evaluation of the impact of the three factors. Figure 4.6 visualizes the situation for the consolidated statement of "combined IT manager and ERP vendor," "IT manager," and "ERP vendor" perspectives. Groups from both surveys clearly agreed that training is by far the most important factor affecting data quality, followed by user support and documentation.

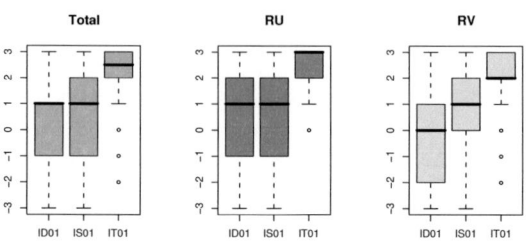

Figure 4.6: Factors Documentation, Support, and Training Compared.

4.3.3.3 Inter-Survey Summary Analysis

Table 4.15 shows the condensed results gained from enterprise and vendor surveys. Clearly, respondents from IT manager and ERP vendor communities disagree on several aspects (variables IO05, IC03, IC04, II01, II02, IT01, IT02, IT03, IT04, ID02, IU03, and IM01).

For detecting the trend of statements (are responses rather affirmative or negative?) in each influence variable, a null hypothesis of "neutrality of statements" (central tendency neither positive nor negative) was formulated, corresponding to a median of zero. Wilcoxon tests were then carried out on all variables concerned, in order to test if this assumption could be invalidated by the survey data. Table 4.16 tabulates the results of the tests, showing that in several cases no unambiguously affirmative or negative trend in responses (resulting in a high p-value) could be found. In the following, further details and explanations for these observations will be provided.

Organization: With respect to the factor "adaptation to organizational needs" (question IO05, details in Figure 4.7), IT managers are significantly more sensitive to the need for and the challenges of adapting an ERP package to the needs of a business than vendors. All other organizational factors (IO01 to IO04) were considered equally by both groups: an organization's overall quality orientation promotes data quality in its ERP systems, assigning responsibility for data is important for its quality, assignment of responsibility for

Item	Meaning	RU		RV		$MD_U = MD_V$	
		n	$\bar{x}$	n	$\bar{x}$	p	$Sig.$
IO01	Quality orientation	124	2	49	2	0.344	
IO02	Data responsibility	124	3	50	3	0.201	
IO03	Data ownership in ERP context	122	1	50	0.5	0.869	
IO04	ERP implementation project quality	124	3	50	2	0.086	*
IO05	Adaptation to organizational needs	123	2	48	2	0.021	**
IC01	Business rules implementation	111	1	47	1	0.240	
IC02	Business rules ignored	109	0	47	-1	0.227	
IC03	Technical know-how of consultants	122	1	50	-1	0.000	***
IC04	Business know-how of consultants	121	2	50	0	0.000	***
II01	Interfaces to other IT systems	122	1	50	-1	0.001	***
II02	External data	121	1	50	1	0.032	**
IT01	Importance of training	124	3	50	2	0.002	***
IT02	Process-oriented training	125	2	50	2	0.012	**
IT03	Reality-based training	121	1	50	0	0.003	***
IT04	Error correction skills	117	1	50	0	0.012	**
ID01	System documentation	124	1	50	0	0.057	*
ID02	ERP standard documentation	115	1	49	0	0.002	***
IS01	Support organization	125	1	49	1	0.892	
IU01	Lack of user interest	122	2	50	2	0.304	
IU02	Experience – capability	124	2	50	2	0.359	
IU03	Experience – system abuse	123	-1	50	-1	0.030	**
IU04	User discipline	124	1	50	1	0.387	
IM01	Functional coverage	120	-1	49	-2	0.003	***
IM02	Actual process coverage	121	2	50	2	0.073	*
IM03	Data classification	113	2	25	2	0.352	

Table 4.15: Influence Factor Overview.[a]

[a] Based on Wilcoxon signed rank test with continuity correction.

data in the ERP systems context is not overly difficult, and a poorly-led implementation project will most likely result in poor data quality.

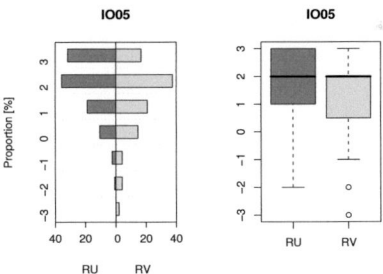

Figure 4.7: Perceived Importance of Adaptation to Organizational Needs.

Consulting: The only point of disagreement between the two respondent groups concerns the business and technical know-how of consultants. While ERP vendors rejected both propositions about a pretended lack of expertise of consultants, IT managers less clearly disapproved of the proposition and expressed a significantly different view than vendors (Figure 4.8). Both groups rated the technical capabilities of consultants higher

Item	Meaning	H_1	H_0 on MD_U			H_0 on MD_V		
			V	p	Sig.	V	p	Sig.
IO01	Quality orientation	two-sided	6361	0.000	***	1085	0.000	***
IO02	Data responsibility	two-sided	7450	0.000	***	1117	0.000	***
IO03	Data ownership in ERP context	two-sided	3410	0.204		581	0.469	
IO04	ERP implementation project quality	two-sided	6997	0.000	***	1123	0.000	***
IO05	Adaptation to organizational needs	two-sided	6016	0.000	***	766	0.000	***
IC01	Business rules implementation	two-sided	2845	0.002	***	632	0.008	***
IC02	Business rules ignored	two-sided	1629	0.597		312	0.117	
IC03	Technical know-how of consultants	two-sided	3580	0.009	***	222	0.002	***
IC04	Business know-how of consultants	two-sided	5447	0.000	***	463	0.390	
II01	Interfaces to other IT systems	two-sided	4381	0.000	***	480	0.676	
II02	External data	two-sided	4050	0.000	***	608	0.640	
IT01	Importance of education	two-sided	7626	0.000	***	1152	0.000	***
IT02	Process-oriented training	two-sided	7370	0.000	***	960	0.000	***
IT03	Reality-based training	two-sided	3948	0.000	***	339	0.470	
IT04	Error correction skills	two-sided	3752	0.000	***	484	0.476	
ID01	System documentation	two-sided	3437	0.003	***	444	0.402	
ID02	ERP standard documentation	two-sided	4348	0.000	***	384	0.007	***
IS01	Support organization	two-sided	4214	0.013	**	682	0.026	**
IU01	Lack of user interest	two-sided	6058	0.000	***	956	0.000	***
IU02	Experience – capability	two-sided	6789	0.000	***	1032	0.000	***
IU03	Experience – system abuse	two-sided	2218	0.016	**	166	0.000	***
IU04	User discipline	two-sided	5849	0.000	***	824	0.000	***
IM01	Functional coverage	two-sided	1468	0.000	***	52	0.000	***
IM02	Actual process coverage	two-sided	4338	0.000	***	968	0.000	***
IM03	Data classification	two-sided	3528	0.000	***	153	0.000	***
IA01	Architecture too open	two-sided	NaN	NaN		858	0.000	***
IA02	Lack of ERP business rules	two-sided	NaN	NaN		953	0.000	***
IA03	Lack of integrity in ERP data	two-sided	NaN	NaN		793	0.000	***
IA04	Too many data models	two-sided	NaN	NaN		788	0.001	***

Table 4.16: Factors for Data Quality: Test of Unambiguousness of Statements.[a,b,c]

[a] Based on Wilcoxon signed rank test with continuity correction.
[b] H_0: $MD = 0$.
[c] NaN: No values available.

than their understanding of specific customer business problems. One respondent in the vendor survey also identified a lack of business know-how in the implementing organization itself.

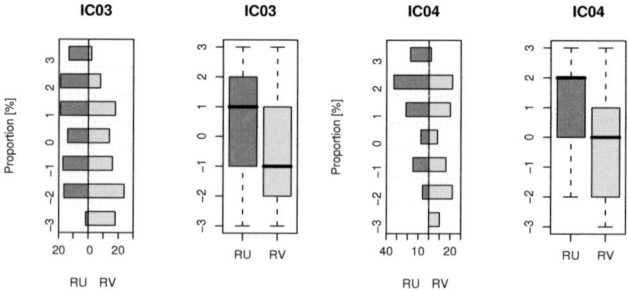

Figure 4.8: Perceived Importance of Know-How of Consultants.

Interfaces and External Data: The results displayed in Table 4.16 show that the software vendors expressed significantly higher trust in the quality of (ERP) system interfaces than IT managers. Also, they rated the risks in the usage of external data clearly lower (Figure 4.9). Overall, vendors showed an undecided attitude – the average "neutrality" of statements being confirmed in Table 4.16 for items II01 and II02 – while IT managers clearly agreed and proved to be more critical with regard to the risks of data integration technology.

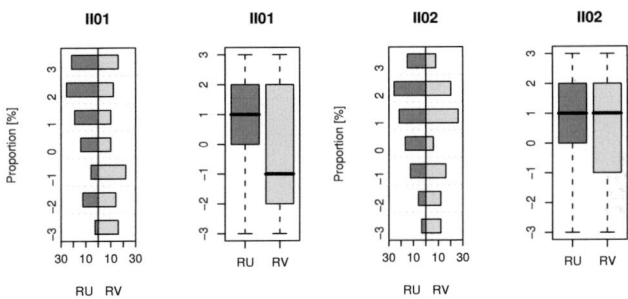

Figure 4.9: Perceived Importance of Interfaces and External Data.

Training: The evaluation of the role of training users proved to be the next difference to be found between both surveyed groups. While IT managers rated the importance of training higher than vendors (one point higher when considering the median of responses), they also showed a significantly stronger belief in the value of process-oriented training sessions, stated a lack of realism in ERP training courses, and confirmed that ERP system users are often insufficiently prepared to correct data errors on their own (Figure 4.10). Overall, vendors showed significantly less skepticism about the degree of skills needed to successfully operate ERP systems.

Documentation: ERP vendors showed higher confidence in the quality of (their) software documentation compared to IT managers, with regards to the use of data in business transactions and the flow of data through an ERP system, addressed by question ID02 (Figure 4.11). Nevertheless, the role of documentation proved to be relatively unimportant, as already shown in Section 4.3.3.2.

User Support: Respondents in both surveys reported a consistent, albeit weak influence of the user support organization on data quality.[74]

---

[74] Cf. Section 4.3.3.2.

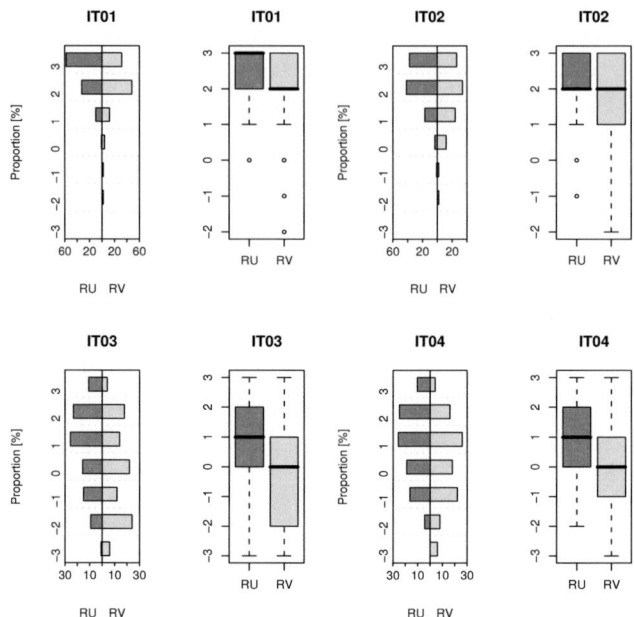

Figure 4.10: Perceived Importance of Training.

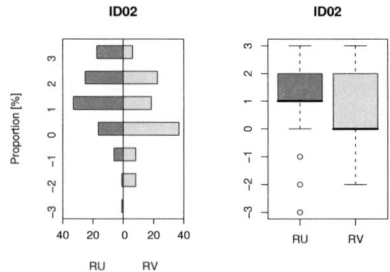

Figure 4.11: Perceived Importance of ERP Business Data Documentation.

ERP Users/Human Factors: Both survey groups reject the idea that experienced users are trying to abuse data fields. The cliché of experienced users trying to "short-circuit the ERP system" (e.g., for speeding up transactional activities) seems to be rather a myth, even if IT managers were less absolute and may have seen cases of abuse (Figure 4.12, with a total proportion of 35% of affirmative responses in the enterprise survey). Personal interest in ERP technology and an overall discipline at work of IT managers were consistently rated as very important factors for data quality.

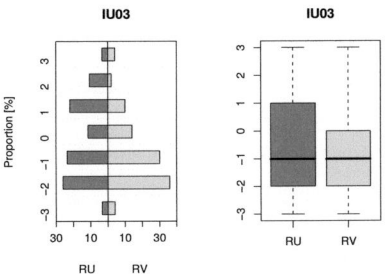

Figure 4.12: Perceived Importance of Risk of System Abuse.

ERP System Management: The last peculiarity found in responses in survey groups RU and RV relates to the interest in covering as many business processes as possible with a single ERP package. Both groups agreed that doing so represents no risk for data quality; as expected, ERP vendors expressed this opinion significantly stronger, as Figure 4.13 shows. Classification and differentiated treatment of ERP data (measured using variable IM03) were consistently considered as means to improve data quality.

In textual statements, respondents in the vendor survey highlighted the importance of a solid process and data analysis during an ERP system implementation project. Also, one vendor asserted that an ERP system can only influence a subset of data quality attributes (such as data "consistency"); others such as "currency" or "correctness" are in the hand of ERP system staff and ERP users.

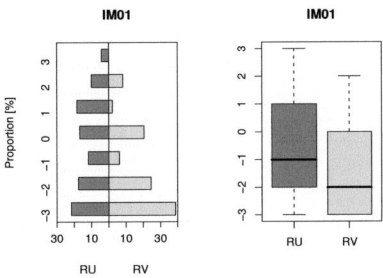

Figure 4.13: Perceived Importance of Functional Coverage.

ERP Architecture (vendor survey only):   With regard to the influence of system architectures on data quality, vendors proved to be quite critical of the design of their own
products, as Table 4.17 shows; they consistently confirmed that ERP systems may be
exposed to data quality problems. Almost three out of four respondents agreed that the
versatile and configurable structure of ERP systems could be exposed to erroneous data.
They equally agreed with the other three proposed statements: a lack of implementation of business rules can lead to data errors, the usage of relational database technology
alone cannot guarantee the integrity of data, and an abundance of data models in a typical
organization hinders effective data management and lowers data quality.

Item	Meaning	n	$\bar{x}$
IA01	Architecture too open	49	1
IA02	Lack of ERP business rules	49	2
IA03	Lack of integrity in ERP data	50	2
IA04	Too many data models	49	2

Table 4.17: ERP Architecture and Data Quality: Vendor Responses.

4.3.3.4   Enterprise Survey Detail Analysis

Table 4.18 shows the results of the analysis of homogeneity of answers in question classes
I, with respect to the factors of organizational size and industry in the enterprise survey.
Significant differences were found in the practices of implementation of business rules
(item IC01), the importance of training (item IT01), the question of "system abuse"
(item IU03), and the suitable process coverage provided by ERP systems (item IM02):

- Organizations from "other public services" (sector 10) reported a higher involvement of external consulting services when implementing business rules; in contrast,
  (the few) respondents in "professional services" (sector 8) have, apparently, sufficient know-how to do business specific adaptations themselves (Figure 4.14).

- Figure 4.15 illustrates the importance of training on data quality as perceived by
  respondents in survey sample RU, showing that IT managers from smaller businesses
  rated the importance of training clearly higher than medium and large organizations.

- As an evaluation of item IU03 shows, large organizations saw a significantly lower
  risk of employees abusing data fields, compared to small and medium ones (Figure 4.16). The existence of a specialized workforce, with more formalized control
  policies in place, could explain this attitude.

- The size of an organization may also be a reason to require higher process coverage:
  small organizations, likely to operate with less formal process management procedures, considered broad ERP system coverage to a lower degree as a factor having
  a positive impact on data quality, compared to larger enterprises (Figure 4.17).

Item	Meaning	H_0^{EMP}		H_0^{SEC}	
		p	$Sig.$	p	$Sig.$
IO01	Quality orientation	0.128		0.753	
IO02	Data responsibility	0.769		0.070	*
IO03	Data ownership in ERP context	0.182		0.828	
IO04	ERP implementation project quality	0.975		0.522	
IO05	Adaptation to organizational needs	0.247		0.481	
IC01	Business rules implementation	0.524		0.039	**
IC02	Business rules ignored	0.293		0.167	
IC03	Technical know-how of consultants	0.750		0.510	
IC04	Business know-how of consultants	0.660		0.841	
II01	Interfaces to other IT systems	0.959		0.698	
II02	External data	0.833		0.778	
IT01	Importance of education	0.025	**	0.177	
IT02	Process-oriented training	0.604		0.643	
IT03	Reality-based training	0.810		0.655	
IT04	Error correction skills	0.098	*	0.212	
ID01	System documentation	0.440		0.425	
ID02	ERP standard documentation	0.179		0.244	
IS01	Support organization	0.900		0.489	
IU01	Lack of user interest	0.925		0.308	
IU02	Experience – capability	0.113		0.475	
IU03	Experience – system abuse	0.005	***	0.270	
IU04	User discipline	0.248		0.162	
IM01	Functional coverage	0.559		0.115	
IM02	Actual process coverage	0.042	**	0.340	
IM03	Data classification	0.430		0.591	

Table 4.18: Intra-Survey Analysis of Factors.[a,b]

[a] Kruskal-Wallis rank sum test.
[b] Alternative hypotheses: two-sided.

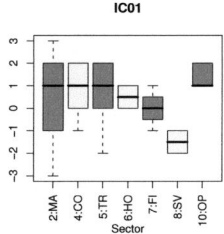

Figure 4.14: Factor Implementation of Business Rules.

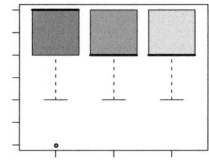

Figure 4.15: Factor Importance of Training.

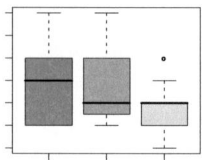

Figure 4.16: Factor Risk of System Abuse.

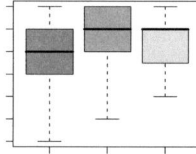

Figure 4.17: Factor Actual Process Coverage.

4.3.3.5   Summary of Results

Organization:

Finding 4.8. Organizations having a formal quality culture and strong ERP implementation project management are in a better position for maintaining high ERP data quality.

Finding 4.9. ERP professionals are not considering the assignment of responsibilities for data quality to be overly difficult in an ERP environment.

Finding 4.10. IT managers see a stronger need to adapt a business organization to the predefined structures of an ERP system than vendors do. On the other hand, both groups agree that this adaptation is critical for data quality.

Consulting:

Finding 4.11. Enterprises clearly need external consulting for mapping business rules into ERP systems, especially in the case of smaller and non-service companies; IT managers are in general more critical to consultants' know-how than vendors.

Finding 4.12. The assumption that companies seldom map existing business rules into ERP systems could not be confirmed in the survey.

Finding 4.13. Consulting in the ERP context seems to be a critical issue; specialists having both business and technical skills to adapt an ERP system to the exact needs of an organization are rare.

Interfaces and External Data:

Finding 4.14. ERP vendors and IT managers significantly disagreed on the potentially negative impact of interfaces to third-party systems and the usage of external data in an ERP system: while IT managers confirmed potential threats, vendors were undecided or rather denied the existence of major risks.

Training:

Finding 4.15. In the eyes of IT managers, ERP training often suffers from a lack of realism with respect to business reality; vendors do not share this opinion.

Documentation:

Finding 4.16. IT managers expressed their discontent with vendors' ERP system documentation and criticized the insufficient level of detail in the description of the data flow in the ERP system documentation. Vendors are also by their majority (self-)critical of the documentation provided with their systems, but to a lesser extent than IT managers.

Support:

Finding 4.17. End user support for ERP systems is a factor influencing data quality, even if this influence is moderate.

ERP Users/Human Factors:

Finding 4.18. "Data field abuse" committed by experienced ERP users seems to be rather a myth in an ERP system context.

Finding 4.19. The interest of ERP users in the functioning of their IT system and their discipline at work is a precondition for high data quality.

ERP System Management:

Finding 4.20. High process coverage of an ERP system is not necessarily a risk for ERP data quality.

Finding 4.21. Formal data management processes (e.g., classification and differentiated treatment of critical data elements) are considered an important tool for obtaining higher data quality.

ERP Architecture (vendor survey only):

Finding 4.22. Due to the versatility and the many configuration options in ERP systems, their design cannot exclude data errors which the relational database technology employed should be able to prevent.

Influence Factors Compared:

Finding 4.23. For all respondents in the surveys, the most important factor for data quality is user training, followed by user support and system documentation.

4.3.4 State of Data Quality

4.3.4.1 Research Questions and Hypotheses

Asking IT managers to provide a quantitative evaluation of the state of data quality in the context of a survey was admittedly one of the most critical points in this study. Firstly, it seems to be impossible to define a generally accepted single criterion for what "good" quality data is. Then, even if the state of data quality is known, several factors can cause inaccurate responses to such a question and must be considered here: unwillingness to disclose a possibly negative "perceived state" (potentially unpleasant feelings), assumptions about the motivation of the researcher (e.g., a presumed sponsorship by a software vendor or a consultancy firm), or the anticipation of potentially negative consequences of the result of the study (even if anonymity is granted) can distort results.[75] Consequently, only the *ranking* of the perceived quality of a selection of data types was considered, not the absolute value of statements. As there are specific regulations for financial accounting data, this category of enterprise data was excluded from the choices proposed to respondents.[76] The importance of classifying and selectively treating data of a certain category will be reflected later in Section 4.3.5.

4.3.4.2 Summary Results

Table 4.19 shows the summary of responses to item class SD, with data items sorted by decreasing average of perceived quality. Data from the human resources domain was – as expected – ranked first, since an immediate interest of any manager and employee

---

[75] Bortz and Döring (2003), p. 251.
[76] Wording used for measuring the "state of data quality" (SD) cf. Table A.12 on page 247. Summary statistics can be found in Table A.29 on page 251.

in correct personal and salary information can be expected.[77] At the lower end of the scale, planning data about cost and resource allocation was assessed to be of (relatively) low quality: this ranking seems logical, as planning data describes the future (which is by definition uncertain and less accurate). Finally, contact data was clearly the least reliable category of data in the respondents' view; this type of data is typically kept in decentralized, personal databases, and not exclusively maintained in ERP systems.

Item	Type of Data	n	$\tilde{x}$	$\bar{x}$
SD05	Employee master	123	2	2.06
SD10	Management accounting	125	2	1.69
SD03	Supplier master	122	2	1.57
SD02	Customer master	121	2	1.47
SD08	Transaction data	112	2	1.32
SD04	Product master	116	2	1.32
SD09	Product history	115	2	1.30
SD07	Planned/actual cost	116	1	0.76
SD06	Planning	109	1	0.67
SD01	Contact	114	1	0.50

Table 4.19: Perceived State of Data Quality.[a]

[a] Sorted by decreasing average $\bar{x}$.

As an additional indicator, respondents were asked to report an improvement or a deterioration of data quality "over the past five years" (period 1998–2003). The results suggest that data quality had improved during that time ($n = 121, \tilde{x} = 2$);[78] no respondent reported a deterioration. A possible explanation of this observation could be found in the fact that, in a historical perspective, many enterprises had accomplished their transition to ERP systems a few years before the survey was executed, had suffered from a low quality in legacy system environments and, possibly, also from a low initial data quality in their ERP packages, but could see progress since – the improvement reported by respondents is hence plausible.

4.3.4.3 Specific Hypotheses

The following specific null hypothesis (and its alternative counterpart) was formulated (Hypothesis 7), for checking if all data item categories are basically of the same quality, despite the ranking shown above.

Hypothesis 7. H_{7-0}: Data quality is essentially the same for all categories of data.
H_{7-1}: Data quality differs at least in one category from the rest.

The application of the Kruskal-Wallis rank sum test shows that data items SD01 to SD10 are of different quality levels, and H_{7-0} is hence rejected:[79] IT managers are aware that some data categories are of better quality than others.

---

[77] Warfield (2007).

[78] Cf. Table A.29 on page 251).

[79] $n = 154, df = 9, p < 2.2 \cdot 10^{-16}$.

4.3.4.4   Enterprise Survey Detail Analysis

As Table 4.20 shows, the perception of data quality levels is homogeneous and independent of the size or industry sector of respondents in the enterprise survey. This may appear
surprising, as service organizations (industry sectors 7 to 10 defined in Table 4.5) could be
expected to put stronger emphasis on high levels of data quality than "brick and mortar"
businesses. One must be reminded, however, that the objective of question class SD was
to obtain a *relative* ranking, which does not allow a direct comparison of absolute quality
levels reported by specific groups of respondents.

Item	Meaning	H_0^{EMP} p	Sig.	H_0^{SEC} p	Sig.
SD01	Contact	0.899		0.567	
SD02	Customer master	0.950		0.436	
SD03	Supplier master	0.849		0.723	
SD04	Product master	0.300		0.165	
SD05	Employee master	0.814		0.819	
SD06	Planning	0.244		0.304	
SD07	Planned/actual cost	0.090	*	0.200	
SD08	Operating data	0.125		0.172	
SD09	Product history	0.087	*	0.158	
SD10	Management accounting	0.112		0.137	

Table 4.20: State of Data Quality in Selected Data Categories.[a,b]

[a] Kruskal-Wallis rank sum test.
[b] Alternative hypothesis: two-sided.

4.3.4.5   Summary of Results

Finding 4.24. IT managers are quite confident with regard to the quality of their data: on
average, no item category was considered to be "insufficient" (all median values are positive). Over the five years before the survey took place, respondents consistently observed
an improvement in data quality.

Finding 4.25. Respondents rated categories of data in which management and employees are personally interested, or which organizations traditionally manage by formal processes, best in terms of quality. On the other hand, marketing contact data – often kept
in a distributed, uncoordinated way, for personal or group use – was considered to be of
lowest quality.

Finding 4.26. No size or industry-specific differences in levels of enterprise data quality
reported by respondents could be identified.

4.3.5 Implementation of Data Quality Control Instruments

4.3.5.1 Research Questions and Hypotheses

The data quality literature as presented in Chapter 2 provides many ideas on how data quality in enterprise information systems can be improved and maintained. For gauging the extent of the use of often cited data quality control instruments, a selection of such instruments was proposed to respondents in item class AE, in order to track the frequency of use on the ERP users' side. Instruments proposed included the employment of work-flow components (AE01), the modification of ERP software GUIs (AE02), data cleansing activities (AE03), data quality agreements with external data suppliers (AE04), the establishment of corporate data quality objectives (AE05), the setting of personal data quality objectives (AE06), centralization of data processing (AE07), definition and measurement of data quality (AE08), data quality audits (AE09), the communication of data quality measurements (AE10), and a formal data quality program (AE11).[80]

4.3.5.2 Summary Results

Table 4.21 shows the summary of responses to item class AE, with data items sorted by decreasing frequency.

Item	Meaning	n	Proportion [%]
AE02	GUI modification	121	81.8
AE07	Centralization	122	77.0
AE03	Data cleansing	114	64.0
AE04	Data quality agreements for external data	107	54.2
AE08	Definition/measurement	120	51.7
AE05	Data quality objectives	116	46.6
AE01	Workflow	112	46.4
AE06	Data quality as personal objective	116	45.7
AE09	Data quality audits	119	42.9
AE10	Communication of data quality	118	29.7
AE11	Formal data quality program	112	25.0

Table 4.21: Data Quality Instruments used in Enterprises.[a]

[a] Sorted by decreasing average.

The most cited instrument for ensuring data quality was the adaption of the GUI to the specific needs of an organization, reported by over 80% of respondents, followed by centralization of data management, data cleansing activities, quality agreements with external suppliers, and data quality definition and measurement initiatives. At the bottom of the scale, it must be noticed that only a minority (25%) of respondents had implemented a formal data quality program at the time of the survey, a finding which is in line with other recent observations made in this domain.[81]

---

[80] Exact statements proposed for "data quality control instruments" (AE) cf. Table A.13 on page 247. Summary statistics can be found in Table A.30 on page 251.

[81] Cf., e.g., Laurent (2005) or Russom (2006a).

Besides confirming (or not) the existence of the proposed actions in their environment, respondents cited the following actions implemented in their enterprises:

- Clear directives on admissible values to be entered into input forms;
- Usage of forms for decentralized data gathering and a centralized entry point;
- Standardized, enterprise-specific training sessions, delivered also after go-live and in case of employee turnover or ERP release updates;
- Formal data cleansing projects for selected master data items;
- Inclusion of data quality objectives in a balanced scorecard.

4.3.5.3 Specific Hypotheses

The specific interest targeted by the AE question class resided in the "overall" employment of data quality instruments used by respondents. In order to measure this global characteristic, an aggregated (summary) variable

$$AEaggr = \sum_{i=1}^{11} \texttt{AE0i}$$

was introduced, ranging from 0 ("none of the proposed instruments used") to 11 ("all proposed instruments used").

Hypothesis 8.
H_{8-0}: The number of data quality instruments does not depend on organizational size $[AEaggr \neq f(EMP)]$.
H_{8-1}: The number of data quality instruments depends on organizational size $[AEaggr = f(EMP)]$.

Hypothesis 9.
H_{9-0}: The extent of usage of data quality instruments does not depend on the industry $[AEaggr \neq f(SEC)]$.
H_{9-1}: The extent of usage of data quality instruments depends on the industry $[AEaggr = f(SEC)]$.

Again, Kruskal-Wallis tests were used to test for the homogeneity with regard to organizational factors EMP and SEC. As Table 4.22 shows, the use of data quality instruments did not depend on organizational size or industry, and both null hypotheses H_{8-0} and H_{9-0} had to be rejected at confidence level $\alpha = 0.05$.

Item	Meaning	H_{8-0}		H_{9-0}	
		p	$Sig.$	p	$Sig.$
AEaggr	Aggregated Actions	0.200		0.070	*

Table 4.22: Summary Use of Data Quality Instruments.[a,b]

[a] Kruskal-Wallis rank sum test.
[b] Alternative hypotheses: two-sided.

A graphical interpretation of responses per sector in Figure 4.18 shows that service industries (sectors 6, 7, and 10) are using a comparatively higher number of instruments than traditional industries such as manufacturing (2) or trade (5); however, this difference between sectors is not statistically significant.

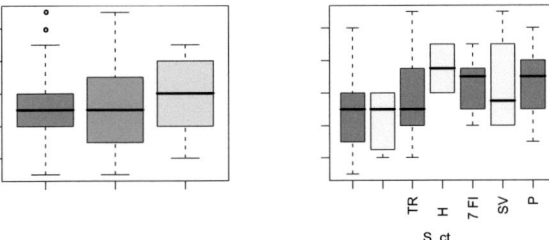

Figure 4.18: Summary Use of Data Quality Instruments.

4.3.5.4 Enterprise Survey Detail Analysis

As Table 4.23 shows, significant differences were detected in the modification of GUIs (AE02, depending on the organizational size) and the definition of indicators and measurement of data quality (AE08, depending on the industry).

Item	Meaning	H_0^{EMP}		H_0^{SEC}	
		p	$Sig.$	p	$Sig.$
AE01	Workflow	0.258		0.468	
AE02	GUI modification	0.037	**	0.670	
AE03	Data cleansing	0.234		0.351	
AE04	Data quality agreements for external data	0.589		0.197	
AE05	Data quality objectives	0.246		0.746	
AE06	Data quality as personal objective	0.149		0.256	
AE07	Centralization	0.538		0.638	
AE08	Definition/measurement	0.594		0.003	***
AE09	Data quality audits	0.499		0.120	
AE10	Communication of data quality	0.755		0.204	
AE11	Formal data quality program	0.636		0.391	

Table 4.23: Implementation of Data Quality Control Instruments.[a,b]

[a] Kruskal-Wallis rank sum test.
[b] Alternative hypotheses: two-sided.

Figure 4.19 shows the details for variable AE02, Figure 4.20 for AE08. GUI modification was significantly less common in average size organizations (between 500 and 1000 FTE) than in smaller and larger enterprises. An explanation could be that this segment of enterprises has a formal IT infrastructure with an ERP system purchased from a large vendor ("Tier 1" in Robinson's classification[82]), but not the manpower to modify the standard screens and dialogs of the software.

---

[82] Robinson (2006b).

With respect to the definition and measurement of data quality, organizations from industries 2, 4, and 5 (representing industries such as manufacturing, construction, wholesale, or retail trade) were found to use these instruments significantly less than service industries (such as hotels, restaurants, or other professional and public services).

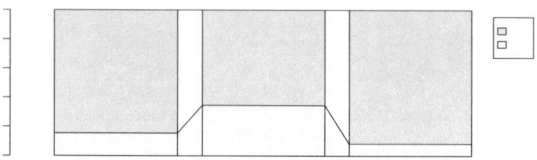

Figure 4.19: Implementation of Data Quality Control Instruments – GUI Modification.

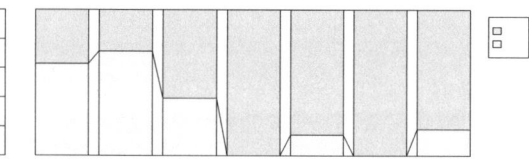

Figure 4.20: Implementation of Data Quality Control Instruments – Definition/Measurement of Data Quality.

4.3.5.5   Summary of Results

Finding 4.27. Despite wide-spread awareness about the importance of enterprise data quality, only a quarter of respondents in the enterprise survey reported having a formal data quality program.

Finding 4.28. The most frequently cited instrument for ensuring quality of data was the modification of user interfaces, which was undertaken by 80% of responding enterprises.

Finding 4.29. More than three out of four respondents were applying a certain centralization of data entry processes in order to maintain data quality, in contrast to the vision of ERP systems as a pervasive, distributed "enterprise computing" concept.

Finding 4.30. Over 50% of the IT managers responding in the enterprise survey were defining and measuring data quality.

4.3.6   Priorities of Funding in Data Quality Projects

4.3.6.1   Research Questions and Hypotheses

As in other business and IT initiatives, funding is an issue in data quality improvement projects. Question class AP targeted the preferences of prioritization of respondents, by asking how they assessed the effectiveness of the following alternatives:[83]

- Improved technical error prevention (AP01);
- Activities in the domain of employee training (AP02);
- Improvements through better directives and tighter management controls (AP03);
- Supervision by specialized board function, such as a "data steward" (AP04).[84]

4.3.6.2   Summary Results

Table 4.24 shows the rough picture of overall responses. As documented in Section 4.3.3, well-trained ERP users are the most important factor for data quality and, hence, also a prime target for improvement activities. Technical prevention and management controls follow far behind; finally, respondents found a specific board function to be the least promising option.

Item	Meaning	n	$\tilde{x}$	$\bar{x}$
AP02	Education	125	2	2.26
AP03	Direction	125	2	1.22
AP01	Technical prevention	123	1	1.35
AP04	Board function	125	1	0.83

Table 4.24: Priorities of Funding in Data Quality Projects.[a]

[a] Sorted by decreasing median, then decreasing average.

Other options mentioned by respondents (in a free-text field provided in the questionnaire) were the reinforcement of individual responsibility of users, the inclusion of data quality aspects in reward systems, the availability of incentives for keeping data up-to-date (data is subject to data accuracy decay over time[85]), the creation of opportunities for training sessions, the reduction of the number of databases used in the organization, and a better understanding of the complex organizational, technical, and business interrelations in an ERP system context.

4.3.6.3   Enterprise Survey Detail Analysis

As Table 4.25 shows, no significant differences between categories of respondents could be found; priorities were not depending on the size or the industry.

---

[83] For statements proposed in question class "Data Quality Priority" (AP) cf. Table A.14 on page 247. Summary statistics can be found in Table A.31 on page 252.

[84] Cf. Section 2.2.10.3.

[85] Cf. Section 2.2.9.

Item	Meaning	H_0^{EMP}		H_0^{SEC}	
		p	Sig.	p	Sig.
AP01	Technical prevention	0.345		0.150	
AP02	Education	0.526		0.778	
AP03	Direction	0.662		0.540	
AP04	Board function	0.545		0.360	

Table 4.25: Priorities of Funding in Data Quality Projects.[a,b]

[a] Kruskal-Wallis rank sum test.
[b] Alternative hypotheses: two-sided.

4.3.6.4 Summary of Results

Finding 4.31. Prioritization of actions in the domain of data quality management is in line with the findings on the ranking of factors for data quality: training was found to be the first priority, together with strong management, whereas technical and organizational measures (e.g., installing specific board functions such as "data quality steward") only come second.

4.3.7 Responsibilities for Data Quality

4.3.7.1 Research Questions and Hypotheses

The question of who should be responsible for data quality is often discussed in the data quality literature: on one hand, anybody involved in an IT-supported process should care about data quality, on the other hand, some authors call for stewardship for data quality, a role which should make sure that data quality is effectively managed.[86] Four typical organizational roles ("IT user," "line manager," "process manager," and "staff position for data quality") were proposed in the enterprise survey, with the intent that the respondents should specify the importance of the role for data quality, ranging from 0 ("no responsibility") to 6 ("high responsibility"). In a free-text field, respondents were asked to fill in additional roles they were using in their organization, where applicable.[87]

4.3.7.2 Summary Results

Table 4.26 illustrates the degree of responsibility assigned to the four proposed roles. Visibly, IT users and process managers have to bear the main responsibility for data quality, followed by line managers and, to a much lesser extent, staff position for data quality (38% of respondents checked the "don't know" box related to this item). In one reply, a respondent indicated "central IT department" as the unit in charge of data quality.

---

[86] Cf. Section 2.2.10.
[87] For statements proposed in question class "Responsibilities for Data Quality" (RP) cf. Table A.15 on page 247. Summary statistics can be found in Table A.32 on page 252.

Item	Meaning	n	$\bar{x}$
RP01	IT user	121	5
RP03	Process manager	120	5
RP02	Line manager	121	4
RP04	Staff position for data quality	106	2

Table 4.26: Responsibilities for Data Quality.[a]

[a] Sorted by decreasing average.

4.3.7.3   Enterprise Survey Detail Analysis

As Table 4.27 shows, the factors of "size" and "industry sector" of respondents in the enterprise survey did not turn out to be a distinguishing factor; responses are homogeneous amongst the groups of respondents.

Item	Meaning	H_0^{EMP}		H_0^{SEC}	
		p	$Sig.$	p	$Sig.$
RP01	IT user	0.775		0.838	
RP02	Line managers	0.385		0.779	
RP03	Process manager	0.701		0.929	
RP04	Data quality steward	0.936		0.199	

Table 4.27: Responsibilities for Data Quality.[a,b]

[a] Kruskal-Wallis rank sum test.
[b] Alternative hypotheses: two-sided.

4.3.7.4   Summary of Results

Finding 4.32. ERP system users and process managers are the key persons in charge of data quality; specialized data quality functions such as data quality stewards are unknown or not considered to be right for ensuring data quality.

4.3.8   Data Quality as Sales Argument

4.3.8.1   Research Questions and Hypotheses

If data quality is generally considered to be of prime importance for the success of IT systems, software vendors are expected to exploit an alleged positive influence of their ERP products on data quality for promotional purposes. A Web search using the search engine "Google" shows that this seems to be the case: German vendor SAP uses the term "data quality" several hundred times on its ERP Web pages, in the same order of magnitude as its main competitor ORACLE.[88] Moreover, SAP markets data quality services, e.g., for assessing the quality of legacy data, finding missing data elements, and measuring and

---

[88] Web search performed on 2007-04-11. Detailed results: search term *"data quality site:sap.com"* leads to 943 hits, *"data quality site:oracle.com"* reports 784 hits. Later searches suffer from distortion, as formerly independent data quality vendors such as Hyperion or FUZZY! Informatik AG have been acquired and absorbed by ORACLE and BusinessObjects/SAP in 2007.

communicating data quality,[89] while ORACLE sells a "flexible enterprise-wide quality management system" for collecting, distributing, and analyzing the quality of data items considered critical.[90]

To get an overall picture of the marketing initiatives related to the data quality properties of ERP software and, on the other side, the willingness of customers to pay for specific data quality functionality in ERP systems, three questions were presented to ERP vendors (class SA).[91] Item SA01 was probing the possible use of data quality properties of ERP software as a marketing instrument. In item SA02 respondents were asked to specify whether they had included specific data quality features in their ERP software or sold them separately. SA03 finally measured the willingness of ERP customers to pay for data quality functions, as perceived by vendors.

4.3.8.2 Summary Results

Responses to questions in class SA are summarized in Table 4.28. 76% of responding vendors confirmed the use of the data quality capabilities of their ERP systems for promotional purposes, at least to some degree. 90% of respondents had sold products ensuring or improving data quality. Also, ERP vendors considered customers to be rather willing to pay for specific data quality functionality: over 60% of respondents were confident that enterprises using ERP systems would pay, to some degree, for specific data quality functionality.

Item	Meaning	n	$\bar{x}$
SA01	Sales argument	50	2
SA02	Data quality components	50	2
SA03	Data quality special functions	49	1

Table 4.28: Data Quality as Sales Argument.

4.3.8.3 Summary of Results

Finding 4.33. A majority of ERP vendors are aware of possible data quality issues, have designed their product portfolio accordingly, and actively market the data quality attributes of their software.

Finding 4.34. ERP customers were found to be receptive to data quality offerings, as more than 60% of vendors declared that customers were willing to pay for specific data quality functionality.

---

[89] SAP (2007b).

[90] ORACLE (2007).

[91] For statements proposed in question class "Data Quality as Sales Argument" (SA) cf. Table A.16 on page 248. Summary statistics can be found in Table A.33 on page 252.

4.3.9 Data Quality Instruments Implemented by ERP Vendors

4.3.9.1 Research Questions and Hypotheses

Several authors have proposed technical features capable of ensuring data quality in an ERP system context.[92] In the ERP vendor survey, the frequency of use of such instruments was checked: vendors were asked to indicate whether their systems already included the proposed instruments, as standard or as option, or whether plans existed to integrate them. The proposed features included edit checks (AV01), input filters (AV02), completeness checks (AV03), duplicate prevention features (AV04), organization-specific business rules (AV05), workflow features to support master data care processes (AV06), means to simplify the standard GUI (AV07), consistency tests (AV08), error reports for data (AV09), a data quality-aware ERP implementation method (AV10), partner training programs (AV11), and a data-oriented system documentation (AV12).

4.3.9.2 Summary Results

As Figure 4.21 shows, vendors typically have implemented a large number of data quality instruments (listed in order of decreasing availability):[93]

- Technical edit checks (AV01), data entry completeness checks (AV03), and input filtering for importing external data (AV02) were implemented in almost all ERP systems surveyed.
- Amazingly, 74% of respondents further provided data-oriented descriptions and instructions in their documentation and training offer (AV12). As found earlier, IT managers were either not aware or not fully satisfied with this offering, at the time of the survey.[94]
- Tools for checking the consistency of system settings were found in 71% of the ERP vendors' offerings (AV08).
- Almost three out of four vendors supplied dedicated training materials for implementation partners, specifying how to correctly setup system parameters (AV11).
- Duplicate detection was provided by half of the respondents (AV04); however, many add-on products from specialized vendors exist, a fact that explains the large part of the related "optional feature" responses.[95]
- 70% of respondents provided an implementation method for their ERP systems that also covered data quality aspects (AV10).

---

[92] Cf., e.g., de Fries et al. (2001), Redman (2001), or Olson (2003).

[93] Ranking made in descending order for the criterion: *4 · frequency ("standard") + 3 · frequency ("as an option") + 2 · frequency ("planned") + 1 · frequency ("not planned").*

[94] Cf. Finding 4.16 (page 177).

[95] Cf. Section 3.1.2.

- Two thirds of respondents reported offering workflow components (AV06), which can (also) be used to support master data management processes.
- Features for simplifying the user GUI (AV07) were also found to be popular, and useful in excluding entry errors on a technical level.
- The availability of statistical reports suitable for data quality management was rather low (AV09). A possible explanation is the difficulty of designing generalized data quality tools (such as quality reports) for finding errors: if the causes of data quality problems are straightforward to detect and measure (e.g., due to a data domain violation), they are rare, since software can easily exclude them. Erred data entries which do not respect specific business rules, on the other hand, can only be detected in a comparison with a "real-world" or reference value.
- Finally, organization-specific business rules were ranked last in the list of data quality instruments (AV05): only half of the ERP systems can be configured to implement such rules. This observation also explains the large market for add-ons or custom developments.[96]

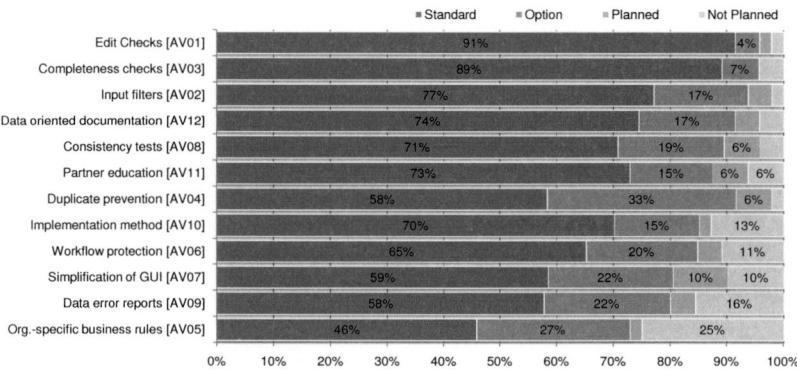

Figure 4.21: Implementation of Data Quality Control Instruments.

4.3.9.3 Summary of Results

Finding 4.35. ERP vendors have implemented many of the instruments proposed by the data quality literature. Nevertheless, organization-specific business rules or dedicated data quality reports – considered to be important instruments for improving data quality – have only been implemented in about 50 percent of surveyed ERP systems.

---

[96] Cf. Section 2.5.1.

4.3.10   Correlation between Perception, Actions, and Results

4.3.10.1   Aggregated Variables and Hypotheses

As a last investigation, the correlation between "perception," "actions," and "results" expressed by the data collected in the two surveys was examined. Several chains of causality were tested against the data collected in the enterprise and vendor surveys, using aggregated variables to describe the instruments used by enterprises and vendors or the intensity of marketing based on data quality arguments. The definition of the aggregated variables for question classes AE, SA, and AV has been chosen as follows:

$$AEaggr = \sum_{i=1}^{11} \texttt{AE0i}; \; SAaggr = \sum_{i=1}^{2} \texttt{SA0i}; \; AVaggr = \sum_{i=1}^{12} \texttt{AV0i}.$$

Firstly, ERP vendors who are aware of the relevance of data quality for the success of their ERP systems (expressed by variable RR01) can be expected to actively build in data quality features into their product (AVaggr). Furthermore, the same awareness should push them to propagate the positive effect of their ERP products on data quality in their marketing communication (SAaggr). On the other hand, marketing initiatives could also depend on the availability of data quality features. These considerations are formalized in Hypotheses 10, 11, and 12; Figure 4.22 provides a visualization of the relationships.

$$\boxed{\texttt{RR01}} \xrightarrow{H_{10-0}} \boxed{\texttt{AVaggr}} \xrightarrow{H_{12-0}} \boxed{\texttt{SAaggr}}$$

$$\boxed{\texttt{RR01}} \xrightarrow{H_{11-0}} \boxed{\texttt{SAaggr}}$$

Figure 4.22: Correlations Between Variables, ERP Vendor Survey.

IT managers in the enterprise survey reported the state of implementation of instruments ensuring data quality (AEaggr); it can be assumed that this is a result of their awareness of the relevance of data quality (RR01). Next, enterprises having implemented numerous actions to improve or maintain data quality should also have observed stronger improvements in the quality of their data (variable SD11). These assumptions are formalized in Hypotheses 13 and 14 and visualized in Figure 4.23.

$$\boxed{\texttt{RR01}} \xrightarrow{H_{13-0}} \boxed{\texttt{AEaggr}} \xrightarrow{H_{14-0}} \boxed{\texttt{SD11}}$$

Figure 4.23: Correlations Between Variables, Enterprise Survey.

Hypothesis 10.
H_{10-0}: There is no correlation between the perceived relevance of data quality and the number of features built into ERP systems by vendors to assure data quality [$r_{RR01, AVaggr} = 0$].
H_{10-1}: There is a correlation between the perceived relevance of data quality and the number of features built into ERP systems by vendors to assure data quality [$r_{RR01, AVaggr} \neq 0$].

Hypothesis 11.
H_{11-0}: There is no correlation between the perceived relevance of data quality by vendors and the role of data quality in marketing of ERP systems [$r_{RR01, SAaggr} = 0$].
H_{11-1}: There is a correlation between the perceived relevance of data quality by vendors and the role of data quality in marketing of ERP systems [$r_{RR01, SAaggr} \neq 0$].

Hypothesis 12.
H_{12-0}: There is no correlation between the number of data quality features implemented by vendors and the importance of data quality in their marketing of ERP systems [$r_{AVaggr, SAaggr} = 0$].
H_{12-1}: There is a correlation between the number of data quality features implemented by vendors and the importance of data quality in their marketing of ERP systems [$r_{AVaggr, SAaggr} \neq 0$].

Hypothesis 13.
H_{13-0}: There is no correlation between the perceived relevance of data quality in enterprises and the number of actions taken to assure data quality [$r_{RR01, AEaggr} = 0$].
H_{13-1}: There is a correlation between the perceived relevance of data quality in enterprises and the number of actions taken to assure data quality [$r_{RR01, AEaggr} \neq 0$].

Hypothesis 14.
H_{14-0}: IT managers do not report any relationship between the number of data quality instruments implemented and the improvement of the perceived level of data quality [$r_{AEaggr, SD11} = 0$].
H_{14-1}: IT managers report a relationship between the number of data quality instruments implemented and the improvement of the perceived level of data quality [$r_{AEaggr, SD11} \neq 0$].

4.3.10.2 Summary Results

For analyzing the system of correlations defined in Section 4.3.10.1, statistical tests were carried out; Spearman's rank correlation coefficients ρ were calculated for all proposed correlations. Table 4.29 summarizes the results of the tests.

None of null hypotheses H_{10-0}, H_{11-0}, H_{13-0}, or H_{14-0} could be rejected at a 5% significance level ($\alpha = 0.05$). One explanation for this observation could be that answers to question RR01 are tightly concentrated at the upper end of the scale and, hence, the measurement of the perceived relevance was not sufficiently differentiated.

Description	Meaning	$r = 0$			
		ρ	S	p	$Sig.$
$r_{\texttt{RR01, AVaggr}}$	RR01 ⟶ AVaggr	-0.114	23207	0.429	
$r_{\texttt{RR01, SAaggr}}$	RR01 ⟶ SAaggr	0.181	17052	0.208	
$r_{\texttt{AVaggr, SAaggr}}$	AVaggr ⟶ SAaggr	-0.311	27309	0.028	**
$r_{\texttt{RR01, AEaggr}}$	RR01 ⟶ AEaggr	0.056	307300	0.536	
$r_{\texttt{AEaggr, SD11}}$	AEaggr ⟶ SD11	0.117	260843	0.203	

Table 4.29: Correlation Between Variables: Test of Significance.[a,b]

[a] Spearman's rank correlation ρ.
[b] Alternative hypotheses: two-sided.

The strongest absolute correlation, pointing out a significant result, was found for the case of H_{12-0} and is visualized in Figure 4.24. As it can be seen, the correlation between the number of data quality instruments implemented by vendors and the use of these instruments in product marketing is *negative*, meaning that vendors conscious of the importance of data quality and active in this field clearly *understate* the quality of their offerings.

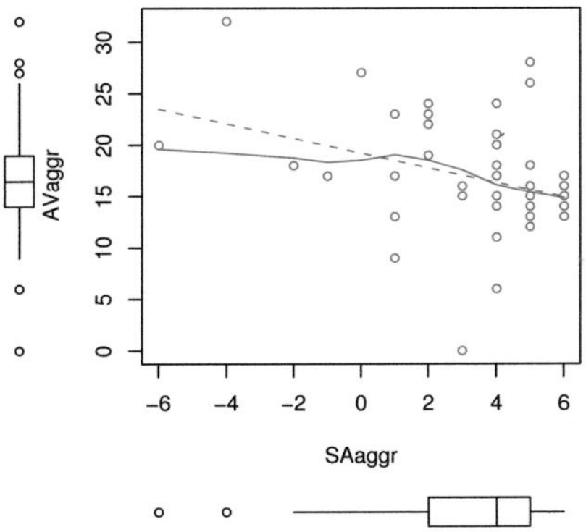

Figure 4.24: Correlation of the Number of Instruments Implemented by Vendors (`AVaggr`) and the Use of Data Quality as Sales Argument (`SAaggr`).

4.3.10.3 Summary of Results

Finding 4.36. No evidence could be found to indicate that a strong perception of the importance of data quality issues pushes vendors to implement more data quality instruments into their ERP systems.

Finding 4.37. The awareness of possible data quality issues does not influence the number of data quality instruments ERP system vendors implement in their products.

Finding 4.38. ERP vendors implementing many data quality features rather understate this fact in their product marketing.

Finding 4.39. No evidence has been found to confirm a positive relationship between the perceived relevance of data quality and the number of actions implemented by enterprises to improve data quality.

Finding 4.40. Enterprises employing a higher number of data quality control instruments did not benefit from substantially higher data quality improvements.

4.4   Summary

As respondents in the enterprise and ERP vendor surveys confirmed, managing data quality remains an important concern also in the context of ERP systems: a lack of data quality is considered to be the cause of real world problems. The mere fact of using a state-of-the-art ERP system does *not* automatically guarantee high quality business data. It was found in the surveys that vendors are generally more optimistic, or IT managers more pessimistic, with regard to the ability of an ERP system to maintain data quality; software vendors are more confident of the technical feasibility of data quality control than IT managers.

According to the data quality literature, a lack of data quality in ERP systems could lead directly to operational losses, as planning and execution systems cannot work correctly if they are supplied with outdated or incorrect data; moreover, the existence of bad planning and transaction data leads to downstream problems, e.g., in analytic applications. In the enterprise survey, respondents confirmed that erroneous data disturbed production processes. They also strongly advocated the view that data should be kept clean, or cleansed directly in the source (ERP) systems, instead of performing extensive cleansing and transformation steps *only* when using the data in data warehousing or analytic applications.

In line with a later study carried out by PricewaterhouseCoopers,[97] respondents in the enterprise survey described data quality in their systems widely as satisfactory, despite known data quality problems. Even if only a minority of organizations was found to run a dedicated data quality program and specialized staff functions such as "data stewards" were rarely known, IT managers are aware of the role of data quality and have implemented many of the quality instruments proposed in the literature. Formal approaches to data quality management are, however, rare in ERP practice.

---

[97] PricewaterhouseCoopers (2004), p. 10.

Chapter 5

Managing ERP System Data Quality

This chapter presents recommendations for improving data quality in an ERP system context, in the form of a set of commented guidelines, containing references to both established ERP implementation and data quality management methods. The guidelines presented here can be considered in ERP evaluation, implementation, upgrade, or optimization projects.

5.1 An ERP-Specific Data Quality Management Model

As recent studies show, the situation explored in the ERP field study in Chapter 4 has not changed substantially: organizations using ERP systems agree on the importance of data quality, but most of them still lack formal data quality programs or do not have a quality-oriented data management.[1] Typically, only a small minority of organizations has people in charge of data quality or has used commercial data quality tools in operation – and if so, many of them report negative experiences.[2] Data quality surveys carried out after the study in Chapter 4 have identified recurring quality problems in business data and a lack of activities in this domain:

- In their "Global Data Management Survey 2004," PricewaterhouseCoopers report a critical gap between "intention and execution" of corporate-wide data initiatives, a declining commitment to data quality, and an erosion of confidence in others' data.[3]
- Harte-Hanks Trillium Software report that many (large) organizations are running some kind of data quality project, especially in the domain of customer data; however, the question of responsibility for data quality is not resolved, as the complex usage patterns of data in organizations requires team responsibility.[4]

---

[1] Alexander (2007).
[2] Reiter (2007).
[3] PricewaterhouseCoopers (2004), pp. 5, 7, and 15.
[4] Harte-Hanks Trillium Software (2006), pp. 9–12.

195

- A survey of IT users in the U.S., Great Britain, France, and Germany conducted by Harris Interactive on behalf of Business Objects found that "up to 75 percent of information workers admitted to having made business decisions that later turned out to be wrong due to incorrect, incomplete, or contradictory business data. Additionally, only about 10 percent of information workers said they always have all the information they need to confidently make business decisions."[5]
- In their recent study, Omikron Data Quality found that only ten percent of responding businesses can guarantee a high level of quality in material master datasets, 80% of respondents report errors in up to 30% of data and 9% even more. Reasons for this are a lack of data care processes, unclear responsibility for data, and insufficient tool support for automated data management.[6]

One explanation for the slow progress of concrete action in the domain of data quality could be that management, and IT managers in particular, have been rather absorbed in following industry trends to better "align" their IT infrastructure,[7] to implement audit frameworks such as COBIT,[8] or to adopt IT service-oriented "best practice" models such as the Information Technology Infrastructure Library (ITIL).[9]

The direction of an ERP-oriented data quality management approach has to be more specific than generic enterprise-level data quality frameworks such as the "Corporate Data Quality" model described by Otto et al.[10] or frameworks such as COBIT or ITIL, even if it will share many concerns contained in these guidelines. Also, it has to be recognized that ERP project methods already contain certain activities that promote and support data quality, as the example of SAP's ASAP model shows.[11] A formal data quality program will, however, still be needed to reduce the probability and the impact of data quality problems; such a program has to encompass the relevant activities in the domains of error prevention, detection, and correction, during all phases of an ERP system's life cycle.

Based on the findings in the data quality literature (Chapter 2), the critical analysis of ERP systems (Chapter 3), and the exploratory surveys (Chapter 4), an ERP life cycle model augmented with data quality management activities was designed. An "a priori" formulation of the model was reviewed with ERP experts, addressing quality criteria of model usefulness, completeness, and realism. Taking into account the feedback from the experts,[12] the model was readjusted and will be presented in the following sections.

---

[5] Business Objects/SAP (2006).
[6] Alexander (2008).
[7] Gregor et al. (2007), pp. 96–100.
[8] IT Governance Institute (2007).
[9] itSMF International (2007).
[10] Otto et al. (2007).
[11] Cf. Section 3.1.4.
[12] Cf. Appendix B.

5.2   ERP Data Quality Life Cycle Model

In order to arrange the guidelines according to the way ERP systems are implemented in organizations, a simplified ERP life cycle model will be used, which highlights the important events and activities in the "life" of an ERP system. For reasons of clarity, jump back loops or improvement cycles (e.g., from Step E back to S, when reconsidering the strategy after the first ERP candidate evaluation), strongly valued in the quality and data quality domain,[13] are not represented here. Figure 5.1 shows an overview of the ERP data quality life cycle model, which combines elements stemming from the following sources:

- The ERP life cycle model proposed by Esteves and Pastor,[14]
- SAP's ASAP implementation roadmap,[15]
- Principles of data quality management,[16] and
- Guidelines for aligning business and IT objectives.[17]

Many software vendors design and market ERP systems, applying methods for software design but also using business modeling (Step D). Not directly timely related to these vendor activities, departing from an IT and ERP adoption strategy (Step S), an organization willing to adopt ERP technology will evaluate ERP packages and make a vendor and product selection (Step E). After starting the implementation project and setting up project structures (Step $A1$), the organization has to analyze in detail the structure and capabilities of the ERP package and develop a detailed plan on how it intends to work with the ERP system ("business blueprint," Step $A2$). These definitions will serve as guidelines for software configuration, adaptation of the organization, and training of ERP system users. The "realization" (Step $A3$) includes all activities needed to configure and adapt the "semi-finished" ERP system to customer needs: organizational (re-)design, configuration and adaptation of the software, design of complementary and interface software, or education of ERP users. "Final preparation" (Step $A4$) is comprised of the data conversion from legacy systems, ERP user training, and system tests. After go-live and initial support (Step $A5$), the operation phase of the ERP system ("production and maintenance") begins (Step P). When the end of life of an ERP system approaches, an organization will cease the extension of its ERP system, consolidate the functionality, and start improvement projects targeting the quality of the data to be converted for use in the successor system.

---

[13] McGinnis and Huang (2007), pp. 626–628.
[14] Esteves and Pastor (1999), pp. 361–363.
[15] Especially Steps $A1$–$A5$; cf. Section 3.1.4.
[16] Cf. Chapter 2.
[17] Cf., e.g., Gregor et al. (2007), pp. 96–98.

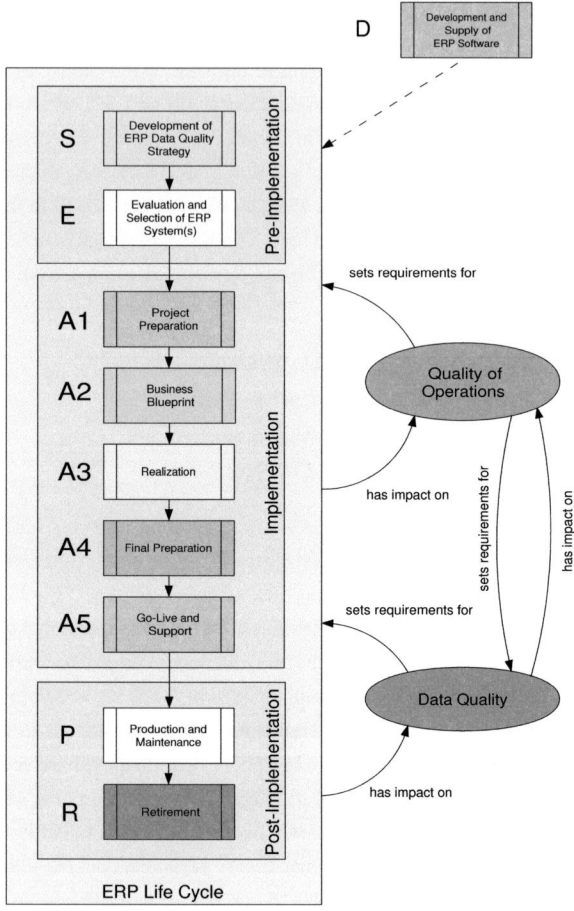

Figure 5.1: ERP Life Cycle Data Quality Model.

In parallel, if data quality is found to be unacceptable during "production and maintenance" (e.g., when data quality measurements exceed specified limits, or special errors occur in a process) after some time, improvement projects will have to be initiated, with a specific project organization. During improvement projects, a choice of actions will be evaluated and carried out, most of them relating to activities already described in Steps *S* through *R* and *D*.

5.3 ERP Data Quality Activities

5.3.1 Step D: Development and Supply of ERP Software

Step D is, with regard to the rest of the model, a special case in the sense that organizations willing to adopt ERP technology cannot intervene directly in the *design* of ERP software systems, but can only indirectly exercise influence, especially when they are of comparatively low importance to the vendor. As a consequence, vendor-specific user or interest groups have formed, to counterbalance the weight of large, "omnipotent" vendors.[18] Well-established user organizations are the Americas' SAP Users' Group (ASUG[19]) or the German-speaking SAP Users Group (DSAG[20]), which organize user conferences, collect requirements, exert formalized influence on the future development of the ERP software,[21] and act as "trusted advisors" to the ERP vendor.[22]

5.3.1.1 Action D-1: Include Data Quality Requirements in ERP Software Design

Data quality requirements have to be introduced from the very beginning of an ERP system development process, to ensure the system will be capable of providing the quality of data as required by its intended usage.[23] ERP system designers may encounter difficulties when asked to anticipate any and every usage of the data that ERP systems are fed with or produce. Suggestions for software development in ERP systems are:[24]

1. Use the integrity enforcement functionality provided by the underlying DBMS, where economically meaningful;[25]
2. Where referential integrity cannot be used and enforced by the DBMS due to required customization capability, offer configurable integrity check functionality or reports;
3. Provide additional (if possible automatically generated) data about the source, creator, and modifier of a data record;
4. Implement generic data quality handling primitives in applications, e.g., to treat erroneous records with specific procedures;
5. Document data structures and the data flow in typical application scenarios, showing the need for care over the entire data life cycle (e.g., the role of data as a prerequisite for transactions, reports, or archiving processes);

---

[18] Bancroft et al. (1998), p. 51.
[19] http://www.asug.com/.
[20] http://www.dsag.de/.
[21] Americas' SAP Users' Group (2008).
[22] Deutschsprachige SAP-Anwendergruppe (2008).
[23] Bobrowski et al. (1999), p. 8.
[24] Cf. Section 4.3.9.2 (degree of actions implemented by vendors).
[25] Cf. Section 2.2.6.2.

6. Introduce data quality checks and warning flags (showing that data is incomplete or not plausible) in standard transactions and reports;

7. Provide mechanisms to link customer specific transactions and reports to ERP meta-data, e.g., to the glossary of business terminology used by the ERP system.

Designers of an ERP system have to consider data quality aspects during the whole software life cycle; specific data quality testing of ERP system software must ensure that (typical scenario) data contained in an ERP system conform both to the assumptions of the designers and the users of ERP systems.[26]

5.3.1.2   Action D-2: Offer Data Quality Tools and Services for Data Conversion

The conversion of existing ("legacy") data for use in a new ERP environment is potentially an important source of problems, and possibly one of the most difficult parts of a system implementation.[27] Firstly, existing data created by legacy applications may be outdated, contradictory, and contain duplicate records. Secondly, even if existing data to be exported from legacy systems is of good quality (possibly after cleansing), it may be "unfit" for use in a new ERP system environment: data structure requirements, embedded business rules, and application logic in the context of the new system environment are most often sufficiently different from existing ones to call for comprehensive data transformation and enrichment, or even a complete reentry of data. In order to make the conversion as smooth as possible, adequate documentation of the requirements of the new system, a set of migration tools, and services for data conversion are required. Large ERP vendors such as SAP are aware of the problems cropping up during the conversion of legacy data,[28] and specialized vendors offer products and services in this domain as well.[29]

5.3.2   Step S: Development of ERP Data Quality Strategy

In order to predictably meet customer demand, any organization has to decide on a business level what has to be done, who will have to do it, when it will have to be done, and what the desired results are.[30] Referring to business planning, Strategic Information Systems Planning (SISP) has been defined as "the process of identifying a portfolio of computer-based applications that will assist an organization in executing its business plans and realizing its business goals," drawing on common planning methods such as top down strategic direction setting, critical success factor analysis, or value chain design.[31]

---

[26] Bobrowski et al. (1998), p. 2.
[27] Maydanchik (2007), pp. 8–9.
[28] SAP (2004a); SAP (2004e); SAP (2007a); SAP (2007b); SAP (2008a).
[29] Cf. Section 3.1.2.
[30] Alter (2002), p. 430.
[31] Hevner et al. (2000), p. 1; Basu et al. (2002), p. 514.

Information systems planning must consequently be integrated with business planning, i.e., aligned with a company's objectives, resources, and priorities. Within this process, data quality has to be considered as a fundamental part of a business and IT strategy, and has to be considered when defining organizational structures and boundaries.[32] In the case of ERP systems, which typically contain functionality for supporting processes traversing several divisional or functional business units, alignment with organizational constraints can be especially challenging, and (if not made correctly) contribute to an overall ERP project failure.

Besides imposing requirements for business strategy and business process support, many organizations have established guidelines which help managers to compose IT system architectures that comply with an overall platform strategy. As an example, the Swiss federal government prescribes SAP ERP as its standard system and has set up a formal exception list of application cases that may be supported using *other* IT systems than SAP ERP.[33]

Even if application support is sufficient and a solid technological platform exists, lacking data quality in an ERP system can put the usability and the overall value of an ERP project at risk.[34] Demanding a sufficient level of quality in selected domains of data is a strategically important requisite and deserves specific actions, described in the remainder of this section.

5.3.2.1 Action S-1: Recognition of Data Quality as a Corporate Concern

Any organization has to define the strategic role of data quality in terms of directives, structures, processes, and role models – an endeavor that can be achieved at any time, even before a specific ERP system or a vendor has been chosen; a data quality initiative should, however, support business goals the organization already values, not new ones.[35] Getting management buy-in for a strategic data quality plan and designing a supportive cultural environment are crucial elements of any data quality environment.[36] A data quality strategy is important in the sense that it can bring together, in an early stage, ERP users who are or will be confronted with data problems (but cannot resolve them) and professionals who know how the ERP software works, but who are unable to actively influence the data creation and usage processes.[37] While working on the data quality strategy, specific data management processes which traverse organizational units and involve many persons have to be framed.

---

[32] Weigel (2008), p. 69.
[33] Swiss Federal Department of Finance (2007).
[34] Cf. Section 1.1.
[35] Redman (2001), p. 201.
[36] Betts (2001a); U.S. Defense Information Systems Agency (2003).
[37] U.S. Defense Information Systems Agency (2003).

An organization must first evaluate and clearly communicate the level of quality of critical data, data it needs to be successful, e.g., in order to gain a competitive advantage.[38] This data must then be managed as an organizational "asset" and not as a simple by-product of business processes. A large financial holding company stated that "just as we are careful and meticulous in managing cash and negotiables, we have a duty and obligation to exercise a high degree of care with the data that is the basis for customer relations and decision-making."[39] Such commitments have to be issued and supported by senior management, in order to provide credible support for any data quality program.[40] Also, organizations considering renewing their ERP application support are often pushed by discontent with older applications and low data quality; a good data quality strategy will exploit this momentum and make use of the willingness of IT users to improve their "bad data quality" situation and to start with high data quality in a new, "clean" ERP environment.

5.3.2.2   Action S-2: Data Quality Controlling Instruments

After the definition of the concern for data quality, an organization should systematically include data quality controlling in its management processes, in order to create "CEO- or boardroom level attention,"[41] as responsibility for data quality is too important a thing for top management to be "delegated down the line."[42] If possible, data quality objectives should be integrated in a corporate BSC,[43] if such a management tool is available, and tracked by specific data quality reports.[44]

5.3.2.3   Action S-3: Assign Responsibility for Data Quality (Roles)

Responsibility for data quality is considered to be the main principle of data quality man-agement[45] and has to be attached at the right organizational level and be managed sep-arately from IT concerns.[46] First of all, a data quality management "sponsor" must be found, who will co-ordinate the development of a data quality strategy and data quality measurements; other roles required in a data quality responsibility context include, e.g., process experts, data analysts, and data administrators.[47] Forrester Research recommends to identify a "data quality missionary," to define and implement a policy, install repeat-

---

[38] Redman (2001), p. 49.
[39] Eckerson (2002).
[40] Loshin (2001), p. 464.
[41] Betts (2002).
[42] Redman (2001), p. 5.
[43] Kaplan and Norton (1996), p. 21.
[44] English (1999b), p. 191; Weigel (2008), p. 85.
[45] Redman (2001), p. 185.
[46] Redman (2001), p. 201.
[47] Weigel (2008), p. 73.

able and measurable procedures for maintaining quality, and to implement a management system for data.[48] In a historical perspective, the principal person responsible for data quality has been the Chief Information Officer (CIO),[49] but a CIO cannot be held responsible for data errors created at an operational level.[50] As Piasecki shows for the area of material management, any process owner should be capable of using reporting and query tools available in an IT system to create specific reports for measuring and controlling accuracy, in his or her domain, as leaving responsibility for the data to the IT department is "no longer an acceptable option."[51]

Even if everybody who uses or creates data must care about data quality,[52] large organizations should consider instituting specific role profiles dedicated for data quality, such as "data stewards" or "data governance" positions.[53] On the other hand, formal data "stewardship" is controversial, as such a position has to be high level enough to withstand political friction, and still low level enough to understand the situation on a workplace level.[54]

Managing data in an ERP system, besides fulfilling the "real-world" business assignments, has become a major occupation of many employees.[55] Nevertheless, with regard to the value of careful handling of data, the work effort and challenges of data management activities are too often ignored by job appraisal schemes.[56] Delivering quality data at the workplace level should be an integral part of ERP users' jobs and must also be set out in job descriptions, with specific data care objectives and controls. Checklists as proposed for ERP data security can be adapted for data quality concerns and should include aspects such as accountability, decision capabilities, integration in projects, internal support, and internal and external communication.[57] Finally, specialized organizational units, such as shared service centers dedicated to data quality or project-specific "data care teams" could help to concentrate and develop know-how in the domain of data quality.[58]

5.3.2.4 Action S-4: Analyze Future Interfaces with the ERP System

When specifying requirements for an ERP system, an organization has to analyze the need for integration with other IT systems at users' desktop, application, or database levels. Good off-the-shelf integration of an ERP vendor's technology platform with remaining

---

[48] Genoud (2005).
[49] Betts (2002).
[50] Redman (1996), p. 33.
[51] Piasecki (2003), p. 192.
[52] Redman (2001), p. 36.
[53] Thole (2007), p. 8.
[54] Betts (2002).
[55] Cf. Olson (2003), p. 5.
[56] AFOS (1996), p. 21.
[57] Hornberger and Schneider (2000), pp. 244–245.
[58] Weber et al. (2009).

third-party systems should be a clear advantage for this vendor; with regard to data quality, "all-in-one" systems (or landscapes composed uniquely by ERP systems provided by the same vendor) tend to present advantages due to a lower need for interfacing and greater homogeneity, compared to more heterogeneous "best-of-breed" approaches.

5.3.3 Step E: Evaluation and Selection of ERP System(s)

The purpose of an ERP project is to deliver an application to users who must be able to efficiently use that software in their daily jobs. ERP systems are standardized products, not custom designed but purchased in a semi-finished form from software vendors. Many tools can be used to compare ERP software products; organizations may, e.g., use Web-based ERP evaluation instruments such as those provided by Technology Evaluation Centers,[59] Trovarit,[60] or topsoft,[61] to find the best matching ERP software, the one that shows "no major process gaps and very few minor ones."[62] Responses from the surveys in Chapter 4 have shown that, in the opinion of ERP professionals, the coverage of an ERP package positively correlates with the overall data quality (in larger enterprises), and that an organization should hence try to cover as many computing needs as possible with a single ERP package.[63]

5.3.3.1 Action E-1: Use Formal Methods for ERP System Evaluation

As the organizational "fit" and the coverage of an ERP system are important factors for later system efficiency and data quality, candidate systems have to be analyzed with utmost care and formal methods, such as the eight step procedure proposed by Robinson[64] or the five phases of system evaluation proposed by Illa et al.:[65]

1. Study the strategy and business processes and take the fundamental decision to acquire an ERP system;
2. Search for candidates and apply a first filter;
3. Dig into the candidates and apply a second filter;
4. Analyze, make visits at the vendors, and require demonstration of candidates;
5. Take the final decision, negotiate, and plan the implementation.

---

[59] http://erp.technologyevaluation.com/.
[60] http://www.trovarit.de/.
[61] http://www.topsoft.ch/.
[62] Carlo (2002).
[63] Cf. Section 4.3.3.4.
[64] Robinson (2002b).
[65] Illa et al. (2000), p. 116.

5.3.3.2 Action E-2: Use Information Marketing for Gathering Data Requirements

To efficiently manage a catalog of the (often overwhelming and contradictory) information system requirements, "information marketing" can be used to determine IT users' needs, to inform future users of the functionality provided by candidate ERP systems, to support them when they encounter problems or have questions at some stage of the evaluation process, and to collect feedback.[66] Even though this will be difficult – future users cannot be sufficiently familiar with all candidate ERP applications to thoroughly assess their impact – users must actively participate in the definition of their information needs, and all relevant stakeholders of the ERP system infrastructure have to be considered.[67]

5.3.3.3 Action E-3: Evaluate Add-Ons for Additional Functionality and Data Care

Requirements for business process support provided by an ERP system and requirements on data quality are often linked, as low quality data in the system also affects the quality of the ERP system. When considering the business process support promised by a candidate ERP system, the effort to enter and maintain the data needed for operations support has to be included in the analysis; in parallel to the evaluation of the "base" ERP system, the organizational prerequisites and possible add-on components have to be explored, as any ERP system will have gaps in functional coverage. For this, vendors provide lists with certified add-on components, e.g., SAP with its "SAP Ecosystem & Partner Catalog."[68]

Data quality management functionality is offered by many ERP vendors, e.g., when considering address data quality "firewalls" sold by SAP to the public security sector[69] or Oracle's data integration suite, which provides (amongst others) tools for data profiling and data quality management.[70] Also, using a master data management system such as SAP MDM[71] may help to address some of the issues of disparate ERP databases. Putting in place an MDM system is, however, not a trivial issue, even when compared to the level of complexity of ERP projects;[72] configuration of add-on software components is often very cumbersome and requires a deep understanding of several data models, besides consistent data management practices at all partners' sides.[73] RFID, on the other hand, seems also a promising technology to address certain categories of data quality problems (such as timeliness or accuracy), once cost and interoperability issues are resolved.[74]

---

[66] Arnold (1992), p. 36.
[67] English (1999b) p. 47.
[68] SAP (2008b).
[69] SAP (2008a).
[70] Kanaracus (2008).
[71] Cf. Section 3.3.3.3.
[72] Thole (2007), p. 8.
[73] Vermeer (2000).
[74] Davenport and Brooks (2004), p. 17; Schuster et al. (2004a); Schuster et al. (2004b); Sellitto et al. (2007), p. 81.

5.3.4   Step A1: Implementation – Project Preparation

After the selection of an ERP system, organizations have to set up an implementation project, during which they will use ERP system vendor and implementation partner services. Often, specific project management methods offered by software vendors are used in this phase; in the model presented here, the Steps *A1–A5* are adopted from SAP's ASAP method.[75] In a first phase, the scope and the strategy of the implementation project have to be clarified, the timing and sequencing of activities have to be agreed upon between IT and business managers, and the organization and resources assigned to the project have to be defined, including specific job descriptions for data quality managers.[76] Besides the focus on the ERP project and its alignment with process support needs, additional steps in the domain of data management have to be made, which will also be relevant for data quality in the forthcoming ERP environment.[77] Table 5.1 shows the deliverables of the ERP project (i.e., the "major deliverables" to be presented at the final milestone review) and the data management activities to be carried out in the preparation phase, as proposed by SAP's ASAP method.[78]

ERP Project	Data Management
• High-level business requirements • Project charter, scope statement, and standards • List of project team members • Technical infrastructure and landscape strategy	• Inventory of legacy systems • Strategy for legacy data conversion.

Table 5.1:   Activities in ERP Implementation Projects: Step *A1* [SAP (2004a)].

5.3.4.1   Action A1-1: Establish Inventory of Legacy Data Providers

As a first step in data and data quality management, an inventory of legacy systems has to be established, together with a rough assessment of the quality of existing data, a list of missing data items, and the need for transforming existing data with respect to data requirements imposed by a new ERP system environment.[79]

5.3.4.2   Action A1-2: Describe Strategy for Legacy Data Conversion

Perfect quality of legacy data does not mean that conversion will necessarily be effort- and painless, as most often the design principles and the context needed to embed the data are different in a new ERP environment. As a rule, the "external world" situation of the legacy

---

[75] Cf. Section 3.1.4.
[76] Cf., e.g., Lüssem (2008), pp. 225–227.
[77] SAP (2004a), Step 1.6.
[78] SAP (2004a), Step 1.
[79] SAP (2004a), Step 1.6.1, "Lifecycle Data Management" activities.

system has to be transferred into the same "external world" situation as described by the new ERP system. Because data quality management requires a profound understanding of the business, the embedded application logic, and the data models involved, the complexity of converting data (or creating permanent interfaces to other systems) must never be underestimated in an ERP implementation project.[80] Data identified as necessary for the operation of the new system must be analyzed, cleansed, converted (by programmatic or manual means), augmented if needed, and tested in the new ERP environment.[81] Often, initial requirements for data conversion are also abandoned in favor of manual data re-entry; on first sight such a decision results in more work, but it is clearly a means to cleanse errors and to find a best fit with the requirements of a new ERP system, if sufficiently trained staff are available.

As a result of this phase, a detailed plan should now describe how data sources have to be treated before their integration in the ERP system[82] and by which method the conversion will be carried out, e.g., by direct input, call transaction, or batch input, in the case of SAP ERP.[83] SAP recommends to design conversions and to correct data in legacy systems in an early stage in order not to jeopardize the go-live date, even if the final conversion will typically only be completed shortly before the "cutover."[84]

5.3.5   Step A2: Implementation – Business Blueprint

Often, ERP systems prescribe the way business processes will have to be carried out, using the application pool and the data provided.[85] In the business blueprint phase, an organization analyzes the functionality and the requirements imposed by an ERP system, and conceptualizes the planned usage of the software, in the form of "to be" processes. In the case of ERP packages offering support for variants of business processes, the transactions to use in a given process setting have to be analyzed carefully, and once the system transactions needed have been selected, the remaining variants provided by the system have to be removed or hidden from later system users, in order to avoid the inadvertent use of a wrong transaction. Besides the core business processes targeted by the ERP system, specific data care processes for configuration and master data must be designed and implemented, as typical business process descriptions do not explicitly cover the initial capture and continuous update of master data.

Involvement of business managers and future ERP users in the blueprint phase is critical, even if user involvement cannot normally be handled in a single pass, and software

---

[80] Scott and Vessey (2002), p. 80.
[81] SAP (2004a), Step 1.6.2.
[82] SAP (2004d).
[83] SAP (2004c).
[84] SAP (2004a), Step 1.6.2.
[85] Brady et al. (2001), p. 27.

implementers have to consider timing and focus of user participation. Wagner and Piccoli, as an example, recommend capturing existing work practices in several "waves" during an ERP implementation project, in order to thoroughly integrate the question of how future users will work with the system in daily routine operations.[86] As a result of the choices made out of the "toolbox" of ERP processes, the set of roles, responsibilities, and structures in the organization required by the to be business processes and the ERP system have to be designed. Table 5.2 summarizes the activities on both ERP functionality and data management sides.[87]

ERP Project	Data Management
• Detailed business process requirements • Configuration and test plan • Add-on requirements and specification • Development environment up and running	• Lifecycle data management strategy • Data cleansing procedures • Conversion development requirements.

Table 5.2: Activities in ERP Implementation Projects: Step *A2* [SAP (2004a)].

5.3.5.1   Action A2-1: Establish a Chain of Customer Data Needs

The essence of data management consists of thinking about how people use information, not how people use machines: too many managers still believe that once the right technology is in place, appropriate data exchange and information sharing will automatically follow.[88] Redman describes a process for gathering and documenting customer requirements for data in a new IT-supported environment:[89]

1. Name most important customers,
2. Learn how they use information products, such as reports,
3. Determine required features and quality levels,
4. "Rate" existing information products, and
5. Identify and prioritize gaps.

This sequence of activities can be applied in an ERP environment. A rough analysis might be started on the transaction or report level and then be refined down to the data fields. Based on this analysis, requirements for the availability, timeliness, precision, integrity, or other data quality attributes can be systematically formulated. Suitable tools for documenting data quality requirements in this approach are formalisms such as EPC or SIPOC diagrams.[90] Established formal future data quality requirements will set out some of the requirements for the legacy data conversion process.

---

[86] Wagner and Piccoli (2007), pp. 53–55.
[87] SAP (2004a), Step 2.
[88] Davenport (1999b), p. 3.
[89] Redman (2001), p. 103.
[90] Cf. 2.5.2 and Sections 2.1.4.4.

5.3.5.2   Action A2-2: Design Data Capture Processes

Master data plays a central role in process support and data production, and therefore deserves high attention. For complex master data structures, such as material master datasets, the usage of either workflow constructs, centralized master data management systems (such as the MMCS presented in case study 1 in Section 3.5.1), or a dedicated MDM system[91] have to be considered. For the customization of standard GUIs or the creation of custom forms and transactions, the usage of edit checks and mandatory fields has to be analyzed carefully, always allowing a controlled "override" of the constraints.[92]

5.3.5.3   Action A2-3: Design Data Update Processes

Redman argues that "data that was of exceptionally high quality yesterday is of acceptable quality today and will be of unacceptable quality tomorrow," in other terms, that the effect of aging automatically affects data quality.[93] Critical data elements have to be identified, responsibility has to be assigned, and regular updates to critical data have to be scheduled. Tools to identify such critical data elements are quality methods like QFD[94] or FMEA.[95]

5.3.5.4   Action A2-4: Design Data Removal Processes

When data records are no longer needed, an archival process has to remove data from the active memory of the ERP system. Data "purging" activities have to be designed with utmost care, as they can cause enormous data quality problems, e.g., when the wrong records are selected for deletion or the integrity of the database is violated.[96] In some cases, if portions of data cannot be removed from the active database for some reason, data "tagging" may be an option to facilitate the exclusion of data items from reports, e.g., by setting a flag or assigning a special value. Such rules are, however, ignored by ERP-internal transformation processes or standard reports, and if used in an organization, this kind of data-embedded logic has to be communicated carefully to all persons concerned.

5.3.6   Step A3: Implementation – Realization

In the realization phase, the ERP system and its future environment are configured according to requirements established in the business blueprint phase (Step *A2*), and the ERP system transactions and reports are analyzed and selected for use in business processes. With regard to the quality of data in the future system, this phase is probably

---

[91] Cf. Section 3.3.3.3.
[92] English (1999b), p. 305.
[93] English (1999b), p. 205; Redman (2001), p. 208.
[94] Cf. Section 2.1.4.5.
[95] Cf. Section 2.1.4.7.
[96] Maydanchik (2007), pp. 17–18.

the most important one, as the realization will lay the foundations for quality data – or unusable data. Important topics to be addressed are the process coverage of ERP systems, vendors and technologies, and the degree of replacement or integration of legacy and third-party systems, via permanent or temporary interfaces.

All major environmental factors, in particular people, process, and technology aspects have to be considered in the realization phase, with regards to data quality management principles and tools:

People – ERP System Users and Operators:

Experts estimate that at least half of the issues in ERP disasters are not technical but people and culture related;[97] however, small problems caused by insufficient training are often relatively easy to solve.[98] All categories of ERP system stakeholders must be trained during an implementation project, ERP system users, IT staff, and information system managers; besides acquiring a basic understanding of the ERP user interface and the software's operation, ERP users have to develop an "ability to figure out the underlying flow of information through the business."[99] ERP users must be trained to cope with process and software errors, and they must learn how to extricate the data from such situations.[100] The specific organizational and process context of a work environment has to be included in appropriate ERP training sequences, and typical application scenarios have to be worked through, showing a realistic sequence of activities, with all relevant problem situations. An important point of user education is the propagation of the terminology introduced by the ERP system, as an implementation team must bring in the language of the ERP system to its (future) users, at the same time adapting educational materials to an organization's "speak," and coping with the business reality of trainees.

Process – Adaptation of Processes and Organizational Structures:

A process view of IT-supported operations is very important for data quality management, as process oriented management promotes error prevention and organizational learning.[101] The implementation of a new ERP system most often affects business processes and the organizational setup of work agreements ("who does what?") that are "vested with historical meaning,"[102] and work processes and organizational structures must be reviewed and rearranged carefully. Redman argues that any data (quality) management initiative will be confronted with organizational

---

[97] Wheatley (2000).
[98] Redman (2001), p. 135.
[99] Wheatley (2000).
[100] AFOS (1996), p. 80.
[101] Evans and Lindsay (2002), p. 23.
[102] Pasmore (1988), p. 5.

or social dimensions, soft issues which may be very hard to resolve.[103] The situation may also be aggravated by the fact that in ERP implementation projects, management often tends to emphasize the technical (hard) issues and to neglect the "soft" aspects, such as training and support.[104] When adapting organizational structures to the requirements of a software package, in combination with business-driven process re-engineering, ERP implementers have to take into account the sensibilities of all persons concerned, in order to assure acceptance of the new design.[105]

Technology – Customizing of Software, Extensions, and Interfaces:

During the realization phase of the implementation of an ERP system, the standard software has to be customized to meet the specific customer requirements set out in the business blueprint, in several steps. Firstly, the business process support stated in the blueprint has to be transformed into a set of ERP transactions. Then (organization specific) forms, reports, interface programs, enhancement programs, and workflow constructs have to be developed.[106] It is essential that the customization of an ERP system enforces a correct data handling, as ERP systems are potentially more exposed to data errors than traditional departmental (stovepipe) applications;[107] special care has to be given to the interfaces of the ERP system, where data enters and leaves the closed ERP environment.[108] Because large amounts of data structures and records will have to be treated, data quality management also means making choices, as (only) the most important needs of the most important data customers can be fulfilled and data cleansing activities have to be prioritized.[109] Finally, to facilitate a distributed but ordered execution of business processes, workflow constructs can be used, which often can be controlled by a workflow engine integrated with the ERP system.[110]

Table 5.3 shows the major deliverables of ERP project and data management in the realization phase.[111]

5.3.6.1 Action A3-1: Adopt and Spread the Terminology of the ERP System

Defining a common vocabulary of business terms used in an organization and its ERP environment is a prerequisite for reliable and error free communications. Misunderstandings and data errors created at the interfaces between an organization and its business

---

[103] Redman (2001), p. 195.
[104] Xu et al. (2002), pp. 54–55.
[105] Pasmore (1988), p. 29.
[106] SAP (2004a), Step 3.4.
[107] Cf. Section 3.6.1.
[108] Cf. Section 3.3.
[109] Adelman et al. (2005), p. 65.
[110] Schuster (1999), pp. 282–283; Seiner (2006b).
[111] SAP (2004a), Step 3.

ERP Project	Data Management
• All system transactions supporting business processes identified in the business blueprint implemented • User interfaces and data contents defined and implemented • Configuration and add-ons are ready and unit tested • End user training documentation and training environment ready • ERP quality assurance environment installed	• Data conversion programs ready • Archiving management procedures established • Legacy data cleansed.

Table 5.3: Activities in ERP Implementation Projects: Step *A3* [SAP (2004a)].

partners are also to be addressed, but internal communications and the related vocabulary are clearly a starting point. In the long run, "translations" of an ERP system's vocabulary to the "enterprise-specific speak" make no sense, and making hard modifications to the software to merely assimilate the existing terminology are not viable, when regarding the long-term update ability of the software.

5.3.6.2   Action A3-2: Show Relations between Business, ERP System, and Data

For educational purposes, the links between the real world business processes, the support provided by the ERP system, the creation of data and its interpretation in reports should be made transparent. The ERP user must know what types of data the processing of an ERP transaction in a business process context will create and who the users of the created data will be.

5.3.6.3   Action A3-3: Perform Training for Data Care Processes

Training of users is very important for any successful ERP implementation project: Schaffner and Scherer identified four important areas of training, namely the handling of the ERP system, the knowledge about how to execute ERP-supported business processes, the organizational changes introduced in parallel to the implementation of the ERP system, and the activities related to a continuous learning process.[112] Even if the application functionality may be instantly well understood by ERP users, "the devil is in the data," as many of the problems arising in the functional integration of an ERP system lie in a consistent understanding of the meaning of data definition in different organizational units.[113]

The role of the data must be discussed in end user training sessions, despite the problems related with the "tracking" of the data flow through the system. Trainees have to acquire a clear understanding of how the data flow goes hand in hand with the actual (real world) business process, and how the data they enter can influence the operation of

---

[112]Schaffner and Scherer (2000), p. 140.
[113]Cotteleer (2002).

the system. When talking about business processes and the IT support delivered by ERP systems, an organization must make sure all participants in the project have the same understanding of the underlying data management concepts. During training sessions, besides learning how to correctly execute ERP-backed processes, trainees have to use the ERP system in realistic transactional and reporting applications. An ERP user should know how to correct wrong data with an adequate update transaction, be able to decide which types of data can be modified or deleted without causing downstream damage, or at least know a contact person who is in charge of "repairing" data errors. Finally, recognized data errors should be tracked and documented using a data quality "issue log,"[114] for future process redesign or educational uses.

5.3.6.4 Action A3-4: Link Qualifications and System Access of ERP Users

Qualifications of ERP users are of high importance: sufficient training has to be given and user experience has to be shared and spread, e.g., in user discussion groups. By installing ERP user circles, team learning from experiences at the workplace level can improve both the handling of the ERP system in a business process context and the management of data.[115] On the other hand, if certain users turn out to be unable to acquire the required skills for performing ERP transactions, even after being given additional training, their access rights to the ERP system should be reduced (e.g., to "read-only" status) or revoked.

5.3.6.5 Action A3-5: Establish Data Customer Orientation

As an important step towards controlled data quality, communication links between ERP system implementers on one side and data producers and users on the other have to be established, for obtaining precise quality requirements and providing feedback during the implementation project.[116] Once requirements are known, system features can be developed and data quality can be measured. Again information marketing frameworks for capturing the needs of data consumers (and producers) can be used here, resulting in a process documentation augmented with data flow annotations, e.g., in the form of SIPOC or IP-MAP[117] charts.

5.3.6.6 Action A3-6: Establish Data Quality Feedback Channels

Where possible, feedback loops have to be built into the ERP user organization, in order to keep data as close to the external world facts as possible and to identify data errors

---

[114] Seiner (2006b).
[115] Schaffner and Scherer (2000), p. 141.
[116] Redman (2001), p. 97.
[117] Cf. Section 2.5.2.

through the use of data.[118] An organizational unit depending on high data quality should be able to assess and improve the quality of the data it has created (or is using) on a regular basis. As an example, a person receiving information on misrouted mailings should be responsible (and have adequate training and ERP system access) for directly correcting address errors in the system, or at least for "flagging" the address as invalid and sending an alert to a centralized data quality desk. Address data quality has always been an issue with IT systems and has, hence, also to be considered carefully in the context of ERP systems.[119]

5.3.6.7   Action A3-7: Assign Responsibility for Data Quality

If ERP users create data, they must be held responsible for the quality (e.g., in terms of validity or correctness) of the data they enter,[120] as many classes of data can no longer be considered as by-products of business process activities and represent often a work result that is needed to prove regulatory compliance. If the producers of data are not exactly known, responsibility should be attached as close to the origin of the data as possible.[121] To cope with organizational fragmentation and related data care problems, workflow technology can be used to automate the data control flow, which can positively influence quality attributes such as completeness, accuracy, or timeliness of ERP data.[122]

5.3.6.8   Action A3-8: Implement Applications and Reports for Data Quality

Specific reports for detecting data errors have to be programmed, to assist persons in charge for data quality assurance, or to notify ERP users about an error and its impact on their work environment. In an SAP ERP environment, ABAP/4 queries can be used to create simple plausibility checks and summary data quality reports.[123] Besides reporting the exact number and proportion of errors, the measurements should also give an impression of the impact of data quality errors, even if it may be difficult to provide such information.[124] Here again, modifications of the standard software are strongly discouraged, as they may tamper the update ability of the software. Furthermore, ERP data respecting rules enforced at the application level should not be modified at the database level, as this approach could circumvent checks made at the application level.[125]

---

[118] Orr (1998), p. 67.
[119] Moad (2003).
[120] Genoud (2005).
[121] Redman (2001), p. 185; Adelman et al. (2005), p. 148; Seiner (2005).
[122] Segev and Wang (2001), p. 87; Seiner (2006b).
[123] Kessler (1999), pp. 196–200.
[124] Redman (2001), p. 111; Seiner (2006b).
[125] AFOS (1996), p. 159.

5.3.6.9   Action A3-9: Simplify IT System Transaction and GUI Handling

ERP GUI forms often have to be modified, as user screens are overloaded with too many data fields, the role of mandatory fields is not immediately clear, the ERP system reacts unexpectedly to certain entries, and too many of the functions available have no relation to user activities.[126] Client-side GUI simplification in the context of SAP ERP systems can be implemented using tools such as GuiXT or application hooks.[127] For particularly sensitive domains of data management (e.g., in human resources management), unneeded or "endangered" data entry fields can be hidden during configuration.[128] System handling can also be simplified by "clamping" two or more standard transactions together in the form of a meta-transaction, thereby automating the data flow by programmatically transferring data from the first to the second, saving time, and strongly reducing data entry errors.[129] Entering the same data repeatedly can also be avoided by system-internal means, such as default user parameter settings in SAP ERP.[130]

5.3.6.10   Action A3-10: Formalize Enforcement of Embedded Data Logic

Edit checks based on generic rules can help to prevent some of the data errors causing "downstream" damage, but data having passed edit checks is *not* necessarily of high quality, depending on the quality criteria applied.[131] If organization specific rules have to be enforced which are not supported by the ERP system, application hooks, modified standard transactions, or reports confirming that manually entered data conforms to the custom data rules should be considered and implemented.

5.3.6.11   Action A3-11: Implement Data Quality Add-Ons

"Fancy tools" to clean up erred data may help in the short term, but in the long run, error prevention through stable data management processes and integrated data quality components appears to be the only promising way forward.[132] Typically, master data such as customer and supplier addresses needs special care, which can be provided by specific address data quality instruments presented in Section 3.1.2. In the case of multi-instance ERP settings or heterogeneous IT landscapes, MDM systems can provide master data handling services between several ERP systems or instances, in heterogeneous landscapes.[133]

---

[126] AFOS (1996), pp. 160–161.
[127] Cf. Section 3.1.4.
[128] Hornberger and Schneider (2000), p. 242.
[129] Kessler (1999), pp. 219–220; Mende (1998), pp. 234–235.
[130] SAP (2006b).
[131] Cf. page 46.
[132] Redman (2001), p. 60.
[133] Cf. Section 3.3.3.3.

5.3.6.12   Action A3-12: Design Data Quality Fences

Data quality "fences" against inadvertent usage of transactions and reports have to be built into an ERP system environment. As an example, if a monthly sales report is retrieved from the system before the end of month (or before the end of monthly closure), it is potentially incomplete, carrying erroneous information, and should show a highly visible warning message. Also, the criteria applied for data selection when executing a report, e.g., the time frame or the organizational unit considered, should prominently figure on the report, as many reports will circulate in print, still today.

5.3.6.13   Action A3-13: Provide Data Quality Metadata in Reports

Most ERP GUIs contain user help texts providing advice on how to interpret the terminology employed or the meaning of data in a business context. As an example, SAP ERP redirects system users seeking help to its comprehensive online help system, which (besides a textual explanation) discloses technical details about the definition and usage of data. On the other hand, even standard business reports provided by the SAP ERP system and customer specific analyses typically lack such information. The usability and the understanding of data stemming from ERP systems could be enhanced by integration with the ERP-specific dictionary of business terms.

5.3.6.14   Action A3-14: Provide Tools to Flag Data Errors and Trigger Error Correction

Since ERP users are not always trained or possibly do not possess the access rights to correct data errors themselves (especially those caused upstream), a signaling system for triggering corrective actions should be implemented and integrated with the ERP system, e.g., in the form of an embedded workflow application.

5.3.7   Step A4: Implementation – Final Preparation

5.3.7.1   Action A4-1: Last Check for Data Quality in Data Conversion

When converting master and transaction data – stemming from a legacy application to be closed down, or a third-party application running in parallel to a future ERP system – the data has to be cleansed and transformed before its use.[134] Before starting production of a new ERP system, cleansing and transformation of data has to be finalized, and additional data needed to start production has to be entered or generated in the new environment.[135]

Successful conversion of clean legacy data is crucial for the quality of data in the ERP system; Robinson recommends a data accuracy level of at least 98% in stock records and

---

[134] Strassmann (2006a).
[135] Schwinn et al. (1999), p. 118.

bills of material.[136] Before line or process managers sign the clearance for putting the new ERP into service, they have to make sure that data quality of the converted legacy and the newly entered data in the system conforms to the requirements of a business. Table 5.4 describes the activities related to the final preparation.[137]

ERP Project	Data Management
• ERP users, administrators, and support staff trained • Data migration for master and selected transaction data completed • Production support ready • Going live approval	• Data loads to the production system are simulated • Final production data has been loaded onto ERP system.

Table 5.4: Activities in ERP Implementation Projects: Step *A4* [SAP (2004a)].

5.3.8 Step A5: Implementation – Go-Live and Support

The go-live marks the transition of an ERP system into operations; as it represents only an event, no data (quality) management activities are needed here, besides observing possible exception messages recorded in the ERP monitoring or logging console. The project documentation is completed and the implementation project organization is scaled down. Table 5.5 presents the project deliverables during go-live and support.[138]

ERP Project	Data Management
• Business process monitoring installed • Issues closed • Production support operational	–

Table 5.5: Activities in ERP Implementation Projects: Step *A5* [SAP (2004a)].

5.3.9 Step P: Production and Maintenance

In this phase of the life cycle of ERP systems, the software is in production, is fed with and generates large amounts of data. Despite all preparatory gatherings of user requirements, it is only in the production phase that most ERP users will first grasp the extent – or the lack – of support provided by the ERP system. Post implementation activities for stabilizing and improving the use of the ERP software will have to be planned and carried out now.[139] Continuous improvement applies equally to the management of the ERP software (e.g., installing software updates, or optimizing database indices), the practices

---

[136] Robinson (2002a).

[137] SAP (2004a), Step 4.

[138] SAP (2004a), Step 5.

[139] Wagner and Piccoli (2007), p. 55.

of using the ERP system in business processes, and the management of data in the ERP system.

5.3.9.1 Action P-1: Control Data Quality

Data quality can never be taken for granted: even if at production start the quality of data is excellent, data quality decay will occur due to the evolution of the external world, or due to conceptual and operational errors.[140] Data quality flaws have to be tracked permanently,[141] measured if needed, and integrated into periodic reporting activities. Control charts are a well-known and established quality management tool for monitoring data quality levels.[142] If data errors are expected to reappear, permanent monitoring processes have to be established; otherwise, only periodic checks can be scheduled.[143]

5.3.9.2 Action P-2: Launch Data Quality Improvement Projects if Needed

Even if data cleansing in large organizational databases is often praised by experts and software vendors, it clearly represents non-value-added work for an organization: to reach sustainable improvements, the creation of erroneous data has to be stopped before data cleansing activities can be started.[144] When observing massive data errors, a data quality improvement project has to be launched.[145]

5.3.9.3 Action P-3: Apply Data Supplier Management Principles

If data is supplied by other organizations (or other organizational units), supply management principles such as definition and communication of data quality requirements, evaluation of the quality of data provided by a supplier, agreement on improvement targets, application of rewards and penalties, and establishment of long-term relationships with excellent suppliers should be applied.[146]

5.3.10 Step R: Data Quality Improvement before Retirement

5.3.10.1 Action R-1: Prepare Data for Conversion before Retirement

When an ERP system approaches the end of its life, the evolution of functionality has to be frozen. The quality of the data in the system has to be analyzed and improved, in order to facilitate the profiling of existing data, the conversion of data relevant for the successor

---

[140]Cf. Section 2.2.9.
[141]Cf. case study 2 in Section 3.5.2.
[142]Cf. Section 2.1.4.1.
[143]Zwirner (2008), p. 108.
[144]Redman (2001), p. 67.
[145]Cf. Section 5.3.11).
[146]Redman (2001), pp. 152 and 156.

system, and ultimately the transition to a new platform. Typical data quality problems to be addressed at this stage are duplicate or obsolete data records, which have (if possible) to be removed, "tagged" as invalid, or at least reported for later filtering when the data will be extracted for conversion.

5.3.11 DMAIC Projects to Improve Data Quality

After go-live, an ERP system may contain inaccurate and useless data, due to automatic data conversion from legacy systems, despite all precautions taken. Also, the combination of poorly trained users, inadequate documentation, and a lack of support impede a rapid improvement of ERP processes. A company studied by Markus et al. experienced severe data entry errors after go-live, and consequently, had to increase staff to cope with errors; in another company, insufficient data quality continued, however, to hamper business even in the "onward and upward phase," long after the go-live.[147] Conversely, in a few months time after go-live, the situation may have changed completely: users having made a steep learning curve are now starting to "master" the situation.[148]

In cases of proven need for intervention, a data quality improvement project has to be set up, in order to improve the situation of data quality in critical domains. Typically, improvement projects will include activities such as sampling, tracking of data items over their life cycle, defect and error identification, and visualization and reporting,[149] based on a project structure such as DMAIC;[150] similar approaches are also used by specialized vendors.[151] As the most important data areas have to be addressed first, Redman recommends prioritizing the improvement efforts based on the frequencies of creation and replacement: if creation or replacement frequency is high, then processes should be focused, be analyzed and improved; conversely, if creation or replacement frequency is low, error detection and correction can get priority.[152]

5.4 Data Quality Organization in an ERP Context

In Section 2.2.10, organizational models and roles for data quality have been presented, putting forward specialized roles for assuring the quality of data, such as "data stewards." It has been shown in Chapter 3 that the set of activities related to data stewardship requires special interpretation in an ERP system context, as data model, semantics, and many

---

[147]Markus et al. (2003a), pp. 41–42.
[148]Kennerley and Neely (2001), p. 110.
[149]Redman (1996), p. 192.
[150]Cf. Section 2.1.5.4; U.S. Defense Information Systems Agency (2003).
[151]Cf., e.g., the FUZZY! DataCare Process described in Weigel (2008), p. 71.
[152]Redman (1996), p. 30.

types of business rules are already designed into and enforced by the ERP system.[153]
Data ownership can also be "a slippery slope," as neither individuals nor organizational
units actually "own" data (since an owner could, e.g., sell data outside the organization),
and only possess specific rights.[154] The simple concept of accountability is in practice
further complicated by the "institutional bureaucracy" of large organizations,[155] leading to
a dilution of accountability for data.[156] Overall, responding IT managers in the enterprise
ERP survey presented in Chapter 4 testified that specialized data quality functions were
unknown or at least seldom used in their organizations.[157]

In Section 3.1.4, the many possible and needed roles in ERP implementation projects
have been illustrated using the example of SAP's ASAP implementation method. In order
to assign responsibilities for the data quality activities proposed in this chapter, the activities of the implementation roles have to be explored. A traditional way to describe role
involvement is the "Responsibility" – "Accountability" – "Consulting" – "Information"
(RACI) scheme,[158] also extensively used in the IT domain, e.g., in the COBIT framework.[159] The resulting RACI relationship for the activities to be carried out in data quality
projects can be specified in a matrix. Some roles only have a small impact on data quality; however, role assignments will depend on the project method and the set of available
project roles, and must be adapted to the situation of a specific organization.

Data quality initiatives have to be business-driven, as finding bad data, cleansing of the
data, and error prevention must be in line with business objectives.[160] As a consequence,
activities taking place in other phases than the ERP implementation project have to be
attached to permanent functions such as business, process, or quality management. In the
context of the implementation project, the project sponsor (ASAP role PS) is generally accountable (i.e., has budget authority) for one-time design activities, including data quality
aspects, while a formal data stewardship role in a traditional, single-installation implementation project is often not needed. Table 5.6 shows an *example* of an SAP ASAP-
oriented implementation project structure; in a concrete project setting, the data quality
activities of the available roles will have to be examined in detail.[161] As the proposed
mapping shows, all activities relating to the ERP implementation project (Steps *A1–A5*)
can be handled by typical project roles, while the other roles are attached to permanent
line, process, or data steward positions.

---

[153]Cf. Section 3.6.2.
[154]Redman (2001), p. 184.
[155]Mertens and Knolmayer (1998), p. 62.
[156]Loshin (2001), p. 30.
[157]Cf. Section 4.3.7.2.
[158]Dressler (2004), pp. 180–181; Otto and Wende (2008), pp. 276–280.
[159]IT Governance Institute (2007).
[160]Adelman et al. (2005), p. 70.
[161]Design guidelines for RACI charts can be found, e.g., in Smith and Erwin (2005).

SAP ASAP Implementation Project Role (cf. Table 3.1 on Page 101)

Activity	BC	BPO	PTM	CC	DMM	DMOM	DEV	DEC	DEM	EDC	HDM	IMR	IAU	OCE	OCA	PMO	PM	PR	PS	RAM	MTC	SSA	SOC	STCM	STM	SA	TPM	TC	TAOM	TR	TDM	TDTM	Quality Mgmt (Data Steward)
D-1		C	C																														R,A,C,I
D-2		C	C								C																						R,A,C,I
S-1													C																				R,A,C,I
S-2								C					C																				R,A,C,I
S-3													C																				R,A,C,I
S-4													C																				R,A,C,I
E-1													C						A														R,C,I
E-2													R						A														R,C,I
E-3													R						A														R,C,I
A1-1	R				R	R						R	R			R	R	R	A														R,C,I
A1-2					R	R				C	C	R	R			R	R	R	A		C												R,C,I
A2-1		R								R	C	R	R	R	R	R	R	R	A		C	C		R			C	C	C		R	R	R,C,I
A2-2		R								R	C	R	R	R	R	R	R	R	A		C	C		R			C	C	C		R	R	R,C,I
A2-3		R									C	R	R	R	R	R	R	R	A	C	C			R			C	C	C		R	R	R,C,I
A2-4		R									C	R	R			R	R	R	A	C	C			R		R	C	C	C		R	R	R,C,I
A3-1	C	R	R								R	R	R	C	R	R	R	R	A	R	C		R	R	R	R	C	C	R		R	R	R,C,I
A3-2	C	R	R								R	R	R	C	R	R	R	R	A		C		R	R	R	R		C	R		R	R	R,C,I
A3-3	C	R	R								R	R	R			R	R	R	A		C		R	R	R	R	C	C			R	R	R,C,I
A3-4		R	R								R	R	R	R	R	R	R	R	A		C		R	R	R	R		C		R			R,C,I
A3-5		R	R		C	C	R	C	R		R	R	R	R	R	R	R	R	A		C		R	R	R	R	R	C					R,C,I
A3-6		R	R		C	C	R	C	R		R	R	R			R	R	R	A		C	R	R	R	R	R	C	C					R,C,I
A3-7		R			C	C	R	C	R		R	R	R			R	R	R	A		C		R	R	R	R	R	C					R,C,I
A3-8		R	C				R	C	R		R	R	R			R	R	R	A		C		R	R	R	R	R	C			R	R	R,C,I
A3-9		R	C				R	C	R		R	R	R			R	R	R	A		C	C	R	R	R	R	R	C	C				R,C,I
A3-10		R	C				R	C	R		R	R	R			R	R	R	A		C	R	R	R	R	R	R	C			R	R	R,C,I
A3-11		R	C								R	R	R			R	R	R	A		C	C	R	R	R	R	R	C			C		R,C,I
A3-12		R	C								R	R	R			R	R	R	A		C		R	R	R	R	R	C				R	R,C,I
A3-13		R	C								R	R	R			R	R	R	A		C	R	R	R	R	R	R	C					R,C,I
A3-14		R								R	R	R	R			R	R	R	A		C			R	R	R		C					R,C,I
A4-1				R	R	R							R																				R,C,I
P-1											R		R												R	R							R,A,C,I
P-2											R		R												R	R							R,A,C,I
P-3											R		R												R	R							R,A,C,I
R-1											R		R												R	R							R,A,C,I

Table 5.6: RACI Matrix for Data Quality Activities (Example).

5.5 Application to Case Study 3

As a proof of concept, this section will provide tentative answers to the questions raised in case study 3 presented in Chapter 3,[162] by using the data quality oriented activity and role model described earlier in this chapter.

5.5.1 Master Data Entry Processes

Problem: *Due to an excessive number of errors, the material master data creation process as designed – involving sometimes 6 different organizational units for one part – proved to be much too lengthy and error-prone.*

Interpretation: Many units and persons were involved in the entry process, a fact that lengthened its duration. Some of the persons involved still lacked the routine needed to master the complex ERP GUI handling and were hardly capable of overlooking the implications of assigning special values to data elements.

Recommended actions:

- Action P-2: Launch Data Quality Improvement Projects if Needed (Section 5.3.9.2)

As the description of the situation states that errors have appeared during and after system implementation, an improvement project has to be set up, e.g., using the DMAIC approach.[163] The project should start with a definition of the project objectives, stating the expectations of process customers in terms of CTQ data quality attributes, e.g., availability of master data, its accuracy and completeness. Next, measurements have to be designed expressing the characteristics of the "as is" situation, and the desired "to be" performance. Based on the measurements, the gap to close can be identified and possible explanations of the problems as described are developed. During the improvement phase, the problems are resolved with adequate changes in motivational/personal, process-related/organizational, and technical aspects. Once the utility of the measures taken is proven, the improvements are formalized and rolled out organization-wide.

- Action A3-3: Perform Training for Data Care Processes (Section 5.3.6.3)
- Action A3-7: Assign Responsibility for Data Quality (Section 5.3.6.7)

The importance of delivering high-quality master data was not perceived with the same importance throughout the organization. The first opportunity to consider is an assessment of the documentation and education of the users involved in the creation process:

---

[162]Cf. Section 3.5.3.
[163]Cf. Section 5.3.11.

Are responsibilities for data contributions clearly defined and understood by ERP users? Are users well instructed on how to enter data? Do they know how parameters of the ERP system can influence business processes? Are ERP users aware of the downstream implications of their data creation activities? If gaps are identified in these areas, they have to be closed before further process redesign activities are set up.

- Action A2-2: Design Data Capture Processes (Section 5.3.5.2)
- Action A3-4: Link Qualifications and System Access of ERP Users (Section 5.3.6.4)

Depending on the frequency of execution of master data creation processes, the following options can be considered:

1. Organizational centralization, i.e., specially trained staff entering *all* material master data records for the entire organization, possibly with context information provided by other specialists – an option to consider if frequency of creation is low;[164]
2. Use of a workflow application to guarantee progress control and transparency during the distributed capturing of material master records – this approach is to be chosen if very specific functional and organizational knowledge is needed, which cannot be centralized;
3. Implementation of a dedicated master data system (MDM) – to be considered if the volume of master datasets created or exchanged with other systems is high, or other needs than the "mere" entry and distribution of master datasets exist, such as the requirement to use master data for printing product catalogs.

5.5.2 Project Accounting Structures

Problem: *Creating accounting structures for sales order handling was cumbersome, required the execution of too many screen activities, depended heavily on the type of project and the organizational unit, and produced many errors. As the account items generated were used in many contexts (e.g., purchasing, engineering, or invoicing), errors spread easily and in unforeseeable ways to these application domains.*

Interpretation: The number and the complexity of standard transactions and forms presented to users wanting to create project work breakdown structures can be identified as the origin of the problems; the combination of a complex business problem and a complex ERP system GUI leads to errors. Even with adequate training and sufficient frequency of execution, those errors could not be avoided, as shown in the case study.

---

[164]SAP (2004b).

Recommended actions:

- Action A3-8: Implement Applications and Reports for Data Quality (Section 5.3.6.8)
- Action A3-9: Simplify IT System Transaction and GUI Handling (Section 5.3.6.9)
- Action A3-10: Formalize Enforcement of Embedded Data Logic (Section 5.3.6.10)

In this situation, a project aiming at better user guidance and/or entry process automation has to be set up. An additional ERP meta-transaction, which "clamps" together two standard transactions by internally sending the outputs from the first to the inputs of the second transaction, helps to avoid most of the entry errors. With only a few thousand USD to be invested in custom programming and enormous savings in working hours, for data error detection and correction no longer needed, pay-back can be expected in a few months.

5.5.3 Quality of Costing Data

Problem: *Cost planning on projects was poor: on one hand, the accounting system required a very detailed cost breakdown and on the other, project managers were reluctant to do the "administrative" work associated with constant updates of the fine-tuned cost planning and preferred individual spreadsheet applications for cost controlling. Planning was not timely and the ERP system detected alleged (unreal) "cost overruns" during financial closing, which resulted in unjustified monthly profit shakedowns.*

Interpretation: Two main sources of the problem can be identified in this situation: firstly, a number of project managers refused to do the administrative work of cost planning (considered as "overhead"); secondly, cost planning errors went undetected through monthly closure, causing financial reporting problems, due to "false alarms" (unreal cost overruns).

Recommended actions:

- Action A3-2: Show Relations between Business, ERP System, and Data (Section 5.3.6.2)
- Action A3-3: Perform Training for Data Care Processes (Section 5.3.6.3)
- Action A3-6: Establish Data Quality Feedback Channels (Section 5.3.6.6)

In the situation described, information needs and concerns in project management and financial controlling visibly differed, with respect to granularity, accuracy, and timeliness of the cost planning. Before entering into ERP system redesigns, the project cost planning and actual costing process should be reviewed with all stakeholders in project management. One of the following actions should be carried out:

1. Simplify the cost planning process, in order to avoid false overruns, but without compromising risk assessment, as cases of *real* cost overruns must be signaled;

2. Provide training for and make agreements with project managers, financial controlling staff, and ERP system specialists on the required degree of quality of specified data elements (e.g., the frequency of updates);

3. Install recurrent, automated checks for planning quality, giving project managers feedback (alerts), when some state of the planning appears suspect, before data is used downstream.

- Action A3-8: Implement Applications and Reports for Data Quality (Section 5.3.6.8)

To control the quality of data in cost management, specific reports should be designed, showing, e.g., the aggregated deviation of cost items (planned vs. actual), which can be calculated for all projects and which allows immediate identification of projects with a low planning quality. A factor showing the importance of the deviation can be computed; moreover, this indicator could be weighted with a project's total cost value, to obtain an estimate of the "penalty" inflicted by false cost overruns in monthly closure. This approach allows an organization to establish a "top-ten" list of candidate projects for planning quality improvement. Finally, a detailed view of the project planning showing a data quality impact matrix, with project accounts on one axis and cost items on the other, could serve to quickly identify and correct the (typically few) project accounts causing the problems, before the "messy" cost planning results in financial reporting problems.

5.6 Summary

As shown in this chapter, data quality is clearly an issue to be addressed in an ERP system context, over the entire life cycle of the system. Many methods and tools known from quality management, data management, and data quality management domains are applicable in this domain. Widely used ERP implementation models, such as SAP's ASAP, already include data and data quality management considerations, but most often focus on the conversion and cleansing of "legacy" data, during an implementation project.

This (too) narrow approach is expanded by the guidelines presented in this chapter, which address data quality management in an ERP context and cover the entire life cycle of an ERP system and its data. Table 5.7 summarizes the data quality oriented activities introduced in this chapter in condensed form, ordered by phase, and classifies them by their impact on data quality (prevention, detection, and correction). Visibly, the model described in this chapter puts strong emphasis on preventive action, in contrast to the legacy data oriented, error detection and correction approach followed by SAP's ASAP and other ERP management models.

Recommendation	Error ...		
(Ordered by Phase)	Prevention	Detection	Correction
Action D-1: Include Data Quality Requirements in ERP Software Design	•		•
Action D-2: Offer Data Quality Tools and Services for Data Conversion	•	•	•
Action S-1: Recognition of Data Quality as a Corporate Concern	•		
Action S-2: Data Quality Controlling Instruments	•		
Action S-3: Assign Responsibility for Data Quality (Roles)	•		
Action S-4: Analyze Future Interfaces with the ERP System	•		
Action E-1: Use Formal Methods for ERP System Evaluation	•		
Action E-2: Use Information Marketing for Gathering Data Requirements	•		
Action E-3: Evaluate Add-Ons for Additional Functionality and Data Care	•	•	•
Action A1-1: Establish Inventory of Legacy Data Providers	•		
Action A1-2: Describe Strategy for Legacy Data Conversion	•		
Action A2-1: Establish a Chain of Customer Data Needs	•		
Action A2-2: Design Data Capture Processes	•		
Action A2-3: Design Data Update Processes	•	•	•
Action A2-4: Design Data Removal Processes	•		
Action A3-1: Adopt and Spread the Terminology of the ERP System	•		
Action A3-2: Show Relations between Business, ERP System, and Data	•		
Action A3-3: Perform Training for Data Care Processes	•	•	•
Action A3-4: Link Qualifications and System Access of ERP Users	•		
Action A3-5: Establish Data Customer Orientation	•		
Action A3-6: Establish Data Quality Feedback Channels	•	•	•
Action A3-7: Assign Responsibility for Data Quality	•		
Action A3-8: Implement Applications and Reports for Data Quality	•	•	•
Action A3-9: Simplify IT System Transaction and GUI Handling	•		
Action A3-10: Formalize Enforcement of Embedded Data Logic	•	•	
Action A3-11: Implement Data Quality Add-Ons	•	•	
Action A3-12: Design Data Quality Fences	•	•	
Action A3-13: Provide Data Quality Metadata in Reports	•	•	
Action A3-14: Provide Tools to Flag Data Errors and Trigger Error Correction	•	•	
Action A4-1: Last Check for Data Quality in Data Conversion	•	•	
Action P-1: Control Data Quality	•	•	•
Action P-2: Launch Data Quality Improvement Projects if Needed	•	•	•
Action P-3: Apply Data Supplier Management Principles	•	•	•
Action R-1: Prepare Data for Conversion before Retirement	•	•	•

Table 5.7: Data Quality Management through ERP Life Cycle.

Chapter 6

Results and Conclusions

Before formulating conclusions and outlining potential areas for further work, the findings drawn from the literature in Chapters 2 and 3, the field studies described in Chapter 4, and the guidelines developed in Chapter 5 will be summarized and confronted with the 9 research questions Q1 to Q9 formulated in Chapter 1.[1]

6.1   Responses to Research Questions

6.1.1   Q1: Relevance of Data Quality in an ERP System Context

The literature review in Chapters 2 and 3 and the responses collected in the ERP surveys in Chapter 4 show that data quality is highly relevant for enterprise computing in general, and for ERP systems in particular.[2] The objectives of increasing business process integration among the stakeholders of an organization, meeting real-time requirements imposed by responsive customer interfaces, or building and improving decision support applications all call for better data.[3]   However, ERP practitioners are also aware that bluntly requiring *perfect* data quality in an ERP context does not make sense or is even impossible (due to definition and technical implementation problems),[4] despite some specialized software vendors' interest in promoting data quality as an objective on its own.[5] Not all kinds of data have to be considered with equal care,[6] but respondents in the field survey consistently stressed that data quality must be controlled at the source – most often on an ERP system level – and cannot be regarded as a side activity in downstream data processing such as data warehousing.[7]

---

[1]   Cf. Section 1.5.
[2]   Cf. Finding 4.1 (page 159).
[3]   Cf. Findings 4.2 (page 159) and 4.3 (page 159).
[4]   Cf. Finding 4.4 (page 163).
[5]   Cf. Finding 4.5 (page 163).
[6]   Cf. Finding 4.6 (page 163).
[7]   Cf. Finding 4.7 (page 163).

6.1.2 Q2: State of Data Quality

When considering the state of data quality in ERP systems, one should first remember that, in many cases, ERP systems have superseded earlier departmental IT systems, by taking over their role, their business environment, and also often a large part of pre-ERP ("legacy") data. As a result, customer address management in ERP systems is likely to be affected by typical issues affecting contact management (e.g., spelling errors occurring when entering names) and ERP-assisted inventory management is hit by the same problems known to earlier inventory keeping systems, such as data errors caused by misunderstandings occurring during delivery processes, or theft of inventory. Even if ERP systems can benefit from better data integrity through the use of a single, integrated enterprise database and other technical advances such as complex real-time edit checks, they cannot simply bypass all problems known from older functional IT systems.

Respondents in the ERP enterprise survey rated data quality in their systems in general as acceptable, and none of the data categories proposed in the questionnaire were considered insufficient with regard to data quality.[8] Categories of data in which management and employees hold a personal interest or which are managed by formal processes were found to be of highest quality. On the other hand, semi- or informal, decentralized, and rapidly changing data such as that found in customer contact databases or planning applications was considered to be of lowest quality,[9] in line with other data quality surveys.[10]

6.1.3 Q3: Factors for Data Quality

Several factors identified as having a potential impact on data quality were reviewed from an ERP system viewpoint: the overall quality orientation of an organization, the influence of division of work with external consulting services during implementation projects, the importance of the quality of data exchanged with external business partners, user education and support, system documentation, user-oriented factors such as motivation and interest to work, and IT architecture.

Organizational influence: Respondents in both IT manager and ERP vendor surveys clearly confirmed that an existing formal quality culture in organizations and a strong ERP implementation project management help to lay the foundations for high data quality.[11] Contrary to allegations based on architectural considerations, the evidence collected from the field surveys shows that ERP professionals are *not* considering the assignment of responsibilities for ERP data and data quality to be exceedingly difficult.[12] Organizational

---

[8] Cf. Finding 4.24 (page 180).
[9] Cf. Finding 4.25 (page 180).
[10] Cf. Section 4.4.
[11] Cf. Finding 4.8 (page 176).
[12] Cf. Finding 4.9 (page 176).

factors for low data quality are rather a lack of problem awareness among ERP users and the unwillingness of top management to integrate data quality viewpoints into performance management.[13] Also, the match between the structural requirements imposed by an ERP system and the actual form of ERP user organization is critical, if high levels of data quality and operational excellence are to be achieved.[14]

Influence of external consulting: Even large enterprises need external consulting services when asked to map their structures, transactional or reporting needs, or specific business rules into ERP systems. These services were, in part, considered skeptically by IT managers, as business domain experts with adequate technical ERP background are still considered to be hard to find.[15] Allegations that organizations seldom implement specific business rules – made by observers of the ERP scene – were in the majority rejected by ERP practitioners interviewed in the field studies.[16]

Influence of data interchange between business partners: Asked to comment on the risks associated with the integration of data from own third-party applications or software systems operated by business partners, IT managers and ERP vendors disagreed significantly; while vendors rather denied the existence of a major risk, IT managers tended to acknowledge a potential threat.[17]

Education, documentation, and user support: IT managers interviewed in the survey criticized a "lack of realism" in training modules[18] and the system documentation provided by ERP vendors; both were considered to provide insufficient details needed for efficient, data-aware ERP user training and data management.[19] ERP vendors expressed a certain self-criticism in this domain, but were (understandably) more confident of the quality of their own products and services. When comparing education, documentation, and user support services, *user education* was unambiguously considered to be the most important factor for data quality, by all respondents in the ERP field surveys.[20]

ERP user aspects: As a large majority of respondents in the IT manager survey confirmed, ERP users are the most critical factor for data quality, due to the "enter once, use many times" principle of ERP systems[21] and the immediate availability of data entered for use in a very broad application context.[22] The interest of ERP users in the IT system they are using is a clear-cut precondition for high data quality.[23] An "abuse" of data fields by

---

[13] Cf. Finding 4.27 (page 184).
[14] Cf. Finding 4.10 (page 176).
[15] Cf. Findings 4.11 (page 176) and 4.13 (page 177).
[16] Cf. Finding 4.12 (page 177).
[17] Cf. Finding 4.14 (page 177).
[18] Cf. Finding 4.15 (page 177).
[19] Cf. Finding 4.16 (page 177).
[20] Cf. Finding 4.23 (page 178).
[21] Cf. Section 3.1.1.1.
[22] Cf. Finding 4.32 (page 187).
[23] Cf. Finding 4.19 (page 177).

experienced ERP users, who allegedly store additional data in the wrong fields or "speed up" their jobs by deliberately entering wrong values, was denied by respondents in the IT manager survey.[24]

ERP architecture: A broad functional coverage of an ERP system, serving as many business processes as possible, contributes to data quality, as respondents in the surveys confirmed.[25] Besides focusing on business and support processes, a responsive, data quality aware ERP management initiative has to promote the implementation of formal data management processes and to be able to take care of data classified as critical.[26] Preserving architectural homogeneity, or at least installing managed heterogeneity between several ERP system instances (e.g., using a master data management system), was found to be a technical precondition for data quality.[27]

6.1.4   Q4: Definition of Data Quality in the Context of an ERP System

As the field surveys in Chapter 4 have shown, enterprises frequently define data quality in their IT systems.[28] Data quality, in terms of consistency, completeness, currency, or accuracy of values, can be quantified in almost any type of IT system using generic indicators.[29] Meaningful enterprise indicators have to be linked to organization or business function specific objectives and should be integrated with corporate target setting mechanisms.[30] Methods and tools developed for managing data quality in functional IT systems can be applied to the ERP context, e.g., when regarding the question of why and how a target of "95% inventory accuracy" has to be defined and by which means such a target can be achieved in an ERP system environment.[31]

6.1.5   Q5: Measurement of Data Quality

Compared to other information system problem settings, ERP systems have particularities that affect data quality measurement. Firstly, the centralized enterprise database, albeit often presenting business data in real-time in a consistent way, may be almost unintelligible to quality managers (and software engineers), because of the special design of data structures and the often difficult ways of accessing specific data.[32] Then the "enter once, use many times" principle leads to a multitude of uses of a particular data item, which may

---

[24] Cf. Finding 4.18 (page 177).
[25] Cf. Finding 4.20 (page 177).
[26] Cf. Finding 4.21 (page 178).
[27] Cf. Section 3.3.3.3.
[28] Cf. Finding 4.30 (page 184).
[29] Cf. Section 2.2.7.
[30] Cf. Section 2.6.2.
[31] Cf. Section 2.3.3.1.
[32] Cf. Section 3.3.

be retrieved or updated by any person or application having the necessary access rights; a directed "data flow" on which measurements could be taken at well identified "reading points" does hence not exist. Finally, ERP systems face the same problems as other IT systems when data accuracy has to be tested, namely the availability of adequate reference data or surrogate sources.[33]

6.1.6 Q6: Analysis of Data Quality Issues

Methods for analyzing data quality issues in an ERP context have to focus on people (attitude and skills of ERP users and management), process structures (the way an ERP system is embedded in an organization and the kind of processes it is supposed to support), and technology (the way ERP systems are designed, implemented, and operated).[34]

People: Data quality suffers when data is regarded as a mere "by-product" of real-world business processes, or when management and IT users are already satisfied if daily business operations are well supported by an ERP system, ignoring upper-level reporting or decision support concerns. The tasks of promptly entering data about business events into the ERP system or updating critical ERP data are often neglected, as users cannot oversee the impact of missing or wrong data in all possible applications of an ERP system.[35] Many users are, however, well aware of the quality level of data created or maintained by other organizational units or persons, and have learned to cope with the possibility of data errors.

Process: ERP systems need master data (such as address or material master records) to operate and to support business processes in a timely way.[36] It is, hence, very important to implement dedicated data care processes for master data, including periodical updates to keep ERP master data current, in sync with the situation in an external world.

Technology: The versatility of ERP systems and the many possible configuration options are likely to put data quality at risk, as the protection features of the underlying relational database technology, such as integrity checks, cannot be fully exploited; moreover, as ERP systems often provide more than one way to carry out a given business transaction and the effort to mask redundant options appears too high in many cases, the data generated by business processes can be inconsistent and, hence, unusable for business analysis purposes.[37]

---

[33] Cf. Section 2.2.6.2.
[34] Cf. Finding 2.3 (page 88).
[35] Cf. case studies in Section 3.4.
[36] Cf. Finding 3.1 (page 141).
[37] Cf. Section 3.6.2, Section 3.5.2, and Finding 4.22 (page 178).

6.1.7   Q7: Data Quality Improvement

Formal data quality (improvement) programs have been found to be fairly rare, with only a quarter of respondents in the IT manager survey reporting the use of such an approach.[38] Most enterprises undertake modifications of the standard user interface, adapting it to the concrete needs of ERP users, because standard ERP GUIs often provide insufficient guidance to users, due to the large functionality offered.[39] Organizational design initiatives such as a centralization of data entry processes were also cited as acceptable options by IT managers,[40] besides a strong focus on individual education of system users.[41]

6.1.8   Q8: Data Quality Control and Assurance

When assigning responsibilities for data quality in an ERP context, IT users and process managers are the first people in charge. Organizational designs with specialized staff (e.g., "data stewards") as proposed in the literature were unknown to or rejected by respondents in the enterprise survey.[42] The majority of ERP vendors are well aware of possible data quality issues and have implemented features for ensuring data quality in their ERP systems.[43] Vendors also testified the willingness of many (potential) ERP customers to pay for specific data quality functionality.[44] Interestingly, a strong perception of the importance of data quality or the awareness of the possible negative impact of insufficient data quality does not motivate ERP vendors to design more data quality features into their systems.[45] In the same line, no evidence for a positive relationship between the perceived relevance of data quality and the number of actions to improve data quality implemented by enterprises could be found.[46]

6.1.9   Q9: Data Quality Management and ERP Implementation Projects

Most of the data quality literature refers to situations in which data structures and the application behavior can be engineered and secured during an implementation project (e.g., using database integrity rules or specific ETL procedures in data warehousing).[47] This situation is, however, not applicable to the case of standardized, semi-finished ERP

---

[38] Cf. Finding 4.27 (page 184).
[39] Cf. Finding 4.28 (page 184).
[40] Cf. Finding 4.29 (page 184).
[41] Cf. Finding 4.31 (page 186).
[42] Cf. Finding 4.32 (page 187).
[43] Cf. Finding 4.33 (page 188).
[44] Cf. Finding 4.34 (page 188).
[45] Cf. Findings 4.36 (page 193) and 4.37 (page 193).
[46] Cf. Finding 4.39 (page 194).
[47] Cf. Finding 3.2 (page 141).

systems, which are shipped with a dedicated data model and a complex, predefined application logic. Chapter 5 of this study shows how, starting from an established ERP project implementation method, principles of data quality management can be anchored in the relevant steps of the life cycle of an ERP system. Data quality aware ERP management guidelines are devised using a mixture of quality management principles, organizational design rules, and technical instruments.

6.2 Conclusions

In the business world, more and more people need direct, real-time access to internal and external business data for fulfilling their jobs, and are concerned with the creation and processing of data. In this context, ERP systems have appeared with the promise to provide "all-in-one" application functionality to support organizational processes and to cover all information needs of a typical enterprise, from the operational to the executive business levels. By the end of the 1990's, many companies converted their IT infrastructure from home-grown, "legacy" applications to ERP systems, often purchased from a few globally active vendors such as ORACLE or SAP, but also from countless smaller ERP providers. Despite the market success of these vendors and their products, credible sources from the academic and business fields early alleged that the quality of data is an issue in an ERP system context, which jeopardizes the quality of business support provided by these systems and, eventually, the value provided by the IT system. As typical examples, out-of-date address data can cause a disaster in any marketing campaign, and inaccurate inventory balances may cause unnecessary purchasing activities or stockouts.

With this thesis, the author has tried to contribute to the ongoing discussion of data quality issues in an ERP context, by assessing ERP design and implementation principles in the light of data quality concerns, presenting evidence from the field of ERP practice, and providing guidelines on how organizations should handle data quality to maximize the benefits resulting from ERP systems.

Firstly, this research analyzed the applicability of general data quality guidelines to the ERP context, finding that such rules must be transformed to the ERP world, but in general keep their validity. By their both open (well documented and accessible) and restrictive data design (the structures of the database and the application code of the standard ERP system should not be altered, to avoid problems in future software upgrades), ERP systems are exposed to a range of risks, putting data quality aspects such as data integrity in danger. Data quality in ERP systems possibly cannot reach a 100% level, since a large quantity of data is generated and managed automatically by the system, and hence out of reach of implementers, if they do not want to modify the core of the software system.

Secondly, the application of data quality assurance practices and the problem awareness with regard to data quality among ERP professionals was analyzed. As both field surveys carried out among IT managers and ERP software vendors in Switzerland confirmed, data quality in an ERP environment *is* at risk, but can be kept under control with appropriate measures; human factors, organizational aspects, and IT considerations have to be arranged in order to obtain an effective integration of an ERP system into its work context. This arrangement should be addressed best by an integration of data quality considerations into existing ERP system implementation and business management models. The findings were compared to other studies in the field of data quality (focusing on IT application domains such as data warehousing), in order to distill the specific ERP dimension.

Thirdly, in order to assist organizations in aligning the different IT- and organization-related activities needed for data quality assurance, the author developed a framework for a systematic inclusion of data quality practices into ERP evaluation, implementation, upgrade, and optimization projects. While data quality problems related with the conversion (or "migration") of legacy data are often addressed by ERP vendors proposing specialized services and tools, the impact of a lack of ownership, missing rule checks, or bad data entry practices is less visible and represents a more subtle problem. In general, data quality add-ons such as address edit controls must be used in a context of large bases of customer or supplier data, and dedicated catalog and master data management systems have to be used if product data are to be exchanged with business partners.

As a consequence of these considerations, it can be concluded that modern database management, communication, and user interface technologies employed in ERP systems do not exonerate information systems practitioners and business managers from actively designing data quality into their ERP environment, considering human, organizational, and technical dimensions. Successful data quality management in an ERP context is more than to apply "fancy tools to clean up erred data"[48] – and hence represents rather a "journey" than a "destination."

---

[48] Redman (2001), p. 60.

6.3   Directions for Further Research

When reviewing the coverage and the findings of this project, possible areas of further information systems research include:

- *Evolution of the ERP vendor market:* Since the execution of the exploratory surveys in 2003, some of the ERP vendors have disappeared, new competitors have appeared, and new technologies have emerged in the marketplace. It would be interesting to establish a follow-up on the evolution of ERP offerings with respect to data quality features offered, the demand of data quality functionality from the ERP customer side, or the specific needs of SMBs and governmental agencies.

- *Economic impact model of low data quality: how can the impact of low data quality in an integrated data environment be modeled and assessed?* Due to the standardized character of ERP data and application models, it should be possible to track the propagation of error patterns in typical process scenarios and to assess their business impact. As an example, simulations such as those proposed by Würthele for the banking sector[49] could be applied in the context of a "clean room" ERP system installation, considering the influence of ERP configuration, master, and transaction data on overall data quality and business processes.

- *Effect of "componentization":* How does the increasing modularization and transformation of "monolithic" ERP architectures in a SOA paradigm influence data quality? In the case of a traditional single-database ERP design, the creation and use of data follows possibly complex but predictable paths, which are either predetermined by the ERP vendor or determined by the settings (customization) of the ERP system by the customer. If this static approach is now superseded by "on demand" data and application services, possibly offered by external Software as a Service (SaaS) providers, an ERP operator's control over the data flow is further diluted and new threats to data quality may appear, calling for adequate methodical and technical responses.

- *Integration of new data sources: impact of RFID on ERP systems?* "Ambient intelligence" technologies such as RFID heavily affect the design and operation of ERP systems, as the business support they can provide strongly depends on the quality of the data describing external world facts. The impact of the quantity and quality of RFID data on ERP systems should therefore be explored, e.g., with the intent to propose specific data "filter" designs[50] for feeding ERP systems with quality data.

---

[49] Würthele (2003), pp. 79–102.
[50] Melski et al. (2008), p. 472.

Appendix A

Survey Details

A.1   Questionnaires

- Questionnaire IT Managers (in German, 3 pages)
- Questionnaire ERP Software Vendors (in German, 3 pages)
- Questionnaire ERP Experts (in German, 5 pages)

Universität Bern

Institut für Wirtschaftsinformatik
Abteilung Information Engineering
Direktor: Prof. Dr. Gerhard Knolmayer

Michael Röthlin
Engehaldenstrasse 8, 3012 Bern
E-Mail: michael.roethlin@iwi.unibe.ch
WWW: http://www.ie.iwi.unibe.ch/forschung/datenqualitaet/

Datenqualitäts-Management in Schweizer Unternehmen

- Im Rahmen meiner Dissertation am Institut für Wirtschaftsinformatik führe ich eine schriftliche Befragung durch.
- Ziel dieser Befragung ist eine **Bestandesaufnahme des Managements der Datenqualität in Grossunternehmen**:

> **Mit welchen Massnahmen werden Qualitätseigenschaften von Daten wie "Genauigkeit", "Vollständigkeit", "Konsistenz" und "Pünktlichkeit" im betrieblichen Alltag definiert, gemessen und gesichert?**

- Der Untersuchungsbereich liegt bei Daten von integrierten betrieblichen Informationssystemen wie Rechnungswesen-, Auftragsabwicklungs- oder Personalverwaltungs-Systemen, im Folgenden Enterprise-Resource-Planning- oder kurz **ERP-Systeme** genannt. Bekannte Anbieter von ERP-Produkten sind beispielsweise **SAP**, **Navision** oder **Abacus**.
- Selbstverständlich werden alle Antworten vertraulich behandelt und für die Auswertung anonymisiert.
- Bitte beantworten Sie die Fragen für Ihr Unternehmen. Wenn Ihr Arbeitgeber Tochtergesellschaft eines Konzerns ist, dann beantworten Sie die Fragen bitte für die Tochtergesellschaft.
- Sie benötigen ca. 15 Minuten zur Bearbeitung des Fragebogens. Ich wäre Ihnen sehr dankbar, wenn Sie mir den ausgefüllten Fragebogen mit dem beiliegenden Rückantwortcouvert bis spätestens am **20. Oktober 2003** zurück-senden könnten. Als Dank für Ihre Bemühungen erhalten Sie, falls Sie dies wünschen, eine Zusammenstellung der Ergebnisse der Umfrage. Sollten beim Ausfüllen des Fragebogens Unklarheiten auftreten, stehe ich Ihnen gerne per E-Mail zur Verfügung: michael.roethlin@iwi.unibe.ch.

I. Fragen zur Wichtigkeit und zum Zustand der Datenqualität im Unternehmen

1   Relevanz der Datenqualität, heute und zukünftig

Bitte Zutreffendes ankreuzen: -3 = gar nicht einverstanden, 0 = neutral, +3 = völlig einverstanden

Aussage / Beurteilung	-3	-2	-1	0	+1	+2	+3	weiss nicht
[RR01] Hohe Datenqualität in ERP-Systemen ist Voraussetzung für eine effiziente und effektive Geschäftsprozessunterstützung.	☐	☐	☐	☐	☐	☐	☐	☐
[RR02] Datenqualität wird mit zunehmender Integration der Unternehmens-systeme (z. B. CRM-Konzepte, E-Commerce) immer wichtiger.	☐	☐	☐	☐	☐	☐	☐	☐
[RR03] Mit zunehmender Verwendung von externen Geschäftsdaten werden Datenqualitätskriterien und -metriken an Wichtigkeit gewinnen.	☐	☐	☐	☐	☐	☐	☐	☐
[RR04] Anwendungen mit hohen Echtzeitansprüchen (z. B. für Verfüg-barkeitsprüfung in E-Shops) verlangen eine hohe Datenqualität.	☐	☐	☐	☐	☐	☐	☐	☐
[RO01] Eine hundertprozentige Datenqualität ist in einem ERP-System nicht erreichbar.	☐	☐	☐	☐	☐	☐	☐	☐
[RO02] Eine hundertprozentige Datenqualität ist in einem ERP-System betriebswirtschaftlich nicht sinnvoll.	☐	☐	☐	☐	☐	☐	☐	☐
[RO03] Insbesondere für Externe sichtbar werdende Daten (wie Adressen oder Kontensaldi) sind immer mit erhöhter Sorgfalt zu pflegen.	☐	☐	☐	☐	☐	☐	☐	☐
[RO04] Eine Behebung von Datenfehlern direkt im Ursprungssystem (ERP) macht bei Weiterverwendung der Daten oft keinen Sinn; z. B. genügt die externe Datenreinigung im Warehousing-Prozess.	☐	☐	☐	☐	☐	☐	☐	☐

2   Wie beurteilen Sie die Qualität der Geschäftsdaten in Ihrem Unternehmen?

Bitte Zutreffendes ankreuzen: -3 = sehr schlecht, 0 = neutral, +3 = sehr gut

Art der Daten	-3	-2	-1	0	+1	+2	+3	weiss nicht
[SD01] Kontaktdatenbank (Marketing)	☐	☐	☐	☐	☐	☐	☐	☐
[SD02] Kundenstammdaten (Adressen, Bankverbindung)	☐	☐	☐	☐	☐	☐	☐	☐
[SD03] Lieferantenstammdaten (Adressen, Bankverbindung)	☐	☐	☐	☐	☐	☐	☐	☐
[SD04] Produktstammdaten (Materialstämme, Stücklisten, Arbeitspläne)	☐	☐	☐	☐	☐	☐	☐	☐
[SD05] Personalstammdaten (Adresse, Bankverbindung)	☐	☐	☐	☐	☐	☐	☐	☐
[SD06] Planungsdaten Produktions-/Einsatzplanung	☐	☐	☐	☐	☐	☐	☐	☐
[SD07] Plan/Ist-Kostenkalkulation Kundenaufträge, Projekte, Produkte	☐	☐	☐	☐	☐	☐	☐	☐
[SD08] Betriebsdaten wie Kassendaten oder Zeiterfassung	☐	☐	☐	☐	☐	☐	☐	☐
[SD09] Produkthistorie (welche Produkte wurden welchen Kunden verkauft)	☐	☐	☐	☐	☐	☐	☐	☐
[SD10] Betriebsbuchhaltung (Kosten-/Leistungsrechnung)	☐	☐	☐	☐	☐	☐	☐	☐
[SD11] Geschäftsdaten insgesamt, *im Vergleich zum Stand vor 5 Jahren*	☐	☐	☐	☐	☐	☐	☐	☐

1

Figure A.1: Questionnaire IT Managers (Page 1).

II. Gründe für die Entstehung schlechter Daten in ERP-Systemen

3 Welches sind Einflussfaktoren auf die Datenqualität in ERP-Systemen? Wie beurteilen Sie die folgenden Aussagen?

Bitte Zutreffendes ankreuzen: -3 = gar nicht einverstanden, 0 = neutral, +3 = völlig einverstanden

Aussage / Beurteilung	-3	-2	-1	0	+1	+2	+3	weiss nicht
[IO01] Unternehmen mit einer ausgeprägten Qualitätsorientierung verfolgen auch eine hohe Datenqualität in ERP-Systemen.	☐	☐	☐	☐	☐	☐	☐	☐
[IO02] Daten, für welche keine Pflegeverantwortlichen bestimmt sind, weisen tendenziell eine schlechte Qualität auf.	☐	☐	☐	☐	☐	☐	☐	☐
[IO03] Die exakte Zuweisung von Verantwortlichkeiten für Daten in einem Unternehmen ist in einem integrierten ERP-Umfeld schwierig.	☐	☐	☐	☐	☐	☐	☐	☐
[IO04] Ein schlecht geleitetes ERP-Einführungsprojekt führt im Betrieb zu mangelhafter Datenqualität.	☐	☐	☐	☐	☐	☐	☐	☐
[IO05] Das Vernachlässigen der Anpassung einer Organisation auf die ERP-Systemanforderungen beeinträchtigt die Datenqualität.	☐	☐	☐	☐	☐	☐	☐	☐
[IC01] Der Einbau von datenbezogenen Geschäftsregeln in eine ERP-Lösung wird meist externen Einführungsspezialisten anvertraut.	☐	☐	☐	☐	☐	☐	☐	☐
[IC02] Der Einbau von vorhandenen Geschäftsregeln in eine ERP-Lösung wird von den Unternehmen oft ganz weggelassen.	☐	☐	☐	☐	☐	☐	☐	☐
[IC03] Einführungsspezialisten verfügen oft nicht über das technische Wissen, um die Software korrekt für den Einsatz einzustellen.	☐	☐	☐	☐	☐	☐	☐	☐
[IC04] Einführungsspezialisten verfügen oft nicht über das Geschäftswissen, um die Software korrekt für den Einsatz einzustellen.	☐	☐	☐	☐	☐	☐	☐	☐
[II01] Schnittstellen zu Drittsystem sind ein grosser Risikofaktor für die Datenqualität in ERP-Systemen.	☐	☐	☐	☐	☐	☐	☐	☐
[II02] Das Einspeisen von Daten Externer (Lieferanten, Kunden) ist ein grosser Risikofaktor für die Datenqualität in ERP-Systemen.	☐	☐	☐	☐	☐	☐	☐	☐
[IT01] Die Datenqualität hängt stark von der Schulung der Mitarbeitenden ab.	☐	☐	☐	☐	☐	☐	☐	☐
[IT02] Das Vernachlässigen der prozessorientierten Schulung von ERP-Anwendern gefährdet die Datenqualität.	☐	☐	☐	☐	☐	☐	☐	☐
[IT03] Die ERP-Benutzerschulung orientiert sich zu selten an der konkreten Arbeitsrealität der Benutzer.	☐	☐	☐	☐	☐	☐	☐	☐
[IT04] Viele ERP-Anwender sind nicht instruiert, wie sie eigene oder fremde Fehleingaben im System korrigieren können.	☐	☐	☐	☐	☐	☐	☐	☐
[ID01] Die Datenqualität hängt stark von der Aktualität und dem Umfang der ERP-Systemdokumentation ab.	☐	☐	☐	☐	☐	☐	☐	☐
[ID02] Die Standarddokumentation vieler ERP-Systeme beschreibt den Umgang mit den vielen Daten nicht adäquat.	☐	☐	☐	☐	☐	☐	☐	☐
[IS01] Die Datenqualität hängt stark von der Support-Organisation im Unternehmen (Helpdesk etc.) ab.	☐	☐	☐	☐	☐	☐	☐	☐
[IU01] Das Desinteresse vieler ERP-Benutzer für den mit einem Geschäftsprozess verbundenen Datenfluss beeinträchtigt die Datenqualität.	☐	☐	☐	☐	☐	☐	☐	☐
[IU02] Mit zunehmender Erfahrung gehen ERP-Anwender besser mit dem System um; deshalb steigt die Datenqualität.	☐	☐	☐	☐	☐	☐	☐	☐
[IU03] Mit zunehmender Erfahrung mit einem ERP-System sinkt die Datenqualität, weil Anwender Datenfelder missbrauchen.	☐	☐	☐	☐	☐	☐	☐	☐
[IU04] Eine wichtige Ursache für die schlechte Datenqualität in ERP-Systemen ist die ungenügende Anwenderdisziplin.	☐	☐	☐	☐	☐	☐	☐	☐
[IM01] Unternehmen, die zu viele Geschäftsprozesse mit der gleichen ERP-Software abdecken wollen, gefährden ihre Datenqualität.	☐	☐	☐	☐	☐	☐	☐	☐
[IM02] Je höher die Unterstützung der Geschäftsprozesse durch eine ERP-Lösung, desto höher ist die Datenqualität.	☐	☐	☐	☐	☐	☐	☐	☐
[IM03] Klassifikation und differenzierte Behandlung von ERP-Geschäftsdaten steigern die Datenqualität.	☐	☐	☐	☐	☐	☐	☐	☐

4 Haben Sie Kommentare zu obigem Punkt 3) oder Erfahrungen mit schlechter Datenqualität?

[CI01] ....

....

....

....

2

Figure A.2: Questionnaire IT Managers (Page 2).

III. Qualitätswesen im Informationsmanagement

5   Welche Sicherungsmassnahmen werden in Ihrer Unternehmung bezüglich Datenqualität eingesetzt?

Bitte Zutreffendes ankreuzen

Massnahme	ja	nein	weiss nicht
[AE01] Einsatz von Workflow-Komponenten zur Sicherung von kritischen Datenpflegeprozessen	☐	☐	☐
[AE02] Anpassung oder Vereinfachung der Benutzeroberflächen (z. B. Ausblenden unnötiger Datenfelder)	☐	☐	☐
[AE03] "Reinigen" von Daten vor ihrer Weitergabe an Kunden, für das Managementreporting, etc.	☐	☐	☐
[AE04] Vereinbarung von Datenqualitätsmerkmalen mit Lieferanten von externen Daten (z. B. Katalogdaten)	☐	☐	☐
[AE05] Ableitung von Datenqualitätszielen aus Unternehmens-Zielsystem (z. B. aus "Kundenzufriedenheit")	☐	☐	☐
[AE06] Aufnahme von Datenqualitätszielen in Zielvereinbarungen mit Mitarbeitenden	☐	☐	☐
[AE07] Konzentration der Pflegetätigkeiten für einen Typ von Daten an einem einzigen Ort (Zentralisierung)	☐	☐	☐
[AE08] Definition und Messung der Qualität (ausgewählter) Daten	☐	☐	☐
[AE09] Datenqualitäts-Audits durch vorgesetzte oder externe Stellen	☐	☐	☐
[AE10] Kommunikation von Ist- und Soll-Situation bei der Datenqualität an Mitarbeitende (z. B. via Aushang)	☐	☐	☐
[AE11] Formales Datenqualitätsprogramm	☐	☐	☐
[AE12] Andere:	☐		

6   Welchen Einfluss auf die Datenqualität erwarten Sie von folgenden Massnahmen?

Bitte Zutreffendes ankreuzen: -3 = starke Verschlechterung, 0 = keine Veränderung, +3 = starke Verbesserung

Massnahme	-3	-2	-1	0	+1	+2	+3	weiss nicht
[AP01] Verbesserte technische Fehlerprävention	☐	☐	☐	☐	☐	☐	☐	☐
[AP02] Erhöhung Anwendungskompetenzen (Schulung)	☐	☐	☐	☐	☐	☐	☐	☐
[AP03] Straffere Führung (durch Linienvorgesetzte)	☐	☐	☐	☐	☐	☐	☐	☐
[AP04] Überwachung durch spezifische Stabsfunktionen	☐	☐	☐	☐	☐	☐	☐	☐
[AP05] Andere:	☐	☐	☐	☐	☐	☐	☐	

7   An welche Stelle im Unternehmen übertragen Sie die Verantwortung für die Datenqualität in ERP-Systemen?

Bitte Zutreffendes ankreuzen: 0 = keine Verantwortung, +6 = starke Verantwortung

Verantwortlichkeit	0	+1	+2	+3	+4	+5	+6	weiss nicht
[RP01] Informatikanwender selbst	☐	☐	☐	☐	☐	☐	☐	☐
[RP02] Vorgesetzte	☐	☐	☐	☐	☐	☐	☐	☐
[RP03] Prozessverantwortliche	☐	☐	☐	☐	☐	☐	☐	☐
[RP04] Stabsstelle für Datenqualität	☐	☐	☐	☐	☐	☐	☐	☐
[RP05] Andere:	☐	☐	☐	☐	☐	☐	☐	

IV. Fragen zum Unternehmen

8 Machen Sie bitte Angaben zu Ihrem Unternehmen:

Anzahl Mitarbeiter (Schweiz)   **[HC01]**

Branche (bitte Zutreffendes ankreuzen, Mehrfach-nennungen möglich) [BE01]	Land-, Forstwirtschaft, Bergbau	☐	Gastgewerbe	☐
	Industrie	☐	Banken und Versicherungen	☐
	Energie-, Wasserversorgung	☐	Immobilienwesen, Vermietung, Informatik, F&E, Dienstleistungen für Unternehmen	☐
	Baugewerbe	☐	Öffentl. Verwalt., Landesverteidigung, Sozialvers.	☐
	Handel, Verkehr und Kommunikation	☐	Unterrichts-/Bildungswesen, Gesundheits- und Sozialwesen, sonstige Dienstleistungen	☐

Firma: _____   Name: _____

Abteilung: _____   Funktion: _____

Adresse: _____   E-Mail: _____

PLZ: _____ Ort: _____   Tel: _____

Sind Sie am Ergebnis dieser Umfrage interessiert?   ☐ Ja (bitte oben Adresse angeben!)   ☐ Nein

Bitte senden Sie den Fragebogen bis zum **20. Oktober 2003** an: **Herzlichen Dank für Ihre Unterstützung unserer**
Institut für Wirtschaftsinformatik   **Bestrebungen um eine praxisnahe Forschung**
Michael Röthlin, Engehaldenstr. 8, 3012 Bern.   **und Lehre!**

3

Figure A.3: Questionnaire IT Managers (Page 3).

Universität Bern

Institut für Wirtschaftsinformatik
Abteilung Information Engineering
Direktor: Prof. Dr. Gerhard Knolmayer

Michael Röthlin
Engehaldenstrasse 8, 3012 Bern
E-Mail: michael.roethlin@iwi.unibe.ch
WWW: http://www.ie.iwi.unibe.ch/forschung/datenqualitaet/

Datenqualitäts-Management in ERP-Systemen
aus der Sicht von Softwareanbietern

- Im Rahmen meiner Dissertation am Institut für Wirtschaftsinformatik führe ich eine schriftliche Befragung durch. Ziel dieser Befragung ist eine **Bestandesaufnahme der Sichtweise der Datenqualität, der diesbezüglichen Softwareeigenschaften und der Anwendungsrichtlinien:**

  Welche datenqualitätsfördernde Eigenschaften werden in heutige (und zukünftige) ERP-Systeme eingebaut? Welche Verantwortung tragen Einführungsspezialisten, Betreiber und Anwender bei der Sicherung der Datenqualität? Was können diese zu einer Steigerung der Datenqualität beitragen?

- Selbstverständlich werden alle Antworten vertraulich behandelt und für die Auswertung anonymisiert.
- Sie benötigen ca. 15 Minuten zur Bearbeitung des Fragebogens. Ich wäre Ihnen sehr dankbar, wenn Sie mir den ausgefüllten Fragebogen mit dem beiliegenden Rückantwortcouvert bis spätestens am **20. Oktober 2003** zurücksenden könnten. Als Dank für Ihre Bemühungen erhalten Sie, falls Sie dies wünschen, eine Zusammenstellung der Ergebnisse der Umfrage. Sollten beim Ausfüllen des Fragebogens Unklarheiten auftreten, stehe ich Ihnen gerne per E-Mail zur Verfügung: michael.roethlin@iwi.unibe.ch.

I. Fragen zur Motivation bei der Entwicklung und dem Vertrieb neuer ERP-Lösungen

1   Relevanz der Datenqualität, heute und zukünftig

Bitte Zutreffendes ankreuzen: -3 = gar nicht einverstanden, 0 = neutral, +3 = völlig einverstanden

Aussage / Beurteilung	-3	-2	-1	0	+1	+2	+3	weiss nicht
[RR01] Hohe Datenqualität in ERP-Systemen ist Voraussetzung für eine effiziente und effektive Geschäftsprozessunterstützung.	☐	☐	☐	☐	☐	☐	☐	☐
[RR02] Datenqualität wird mit zunehmender Integration der Unternehmenssysteme (z. B. CRM-Konzepte, E-Commerce) immer wichtiger.	☐	☐	☐	☐	☐	☐	☐	☐
[RR03] Mit zunehmender Verwendung von externen Geschäftsdaten werden Datenqualitätskriterien und -metriken an Wichtigkeit gewinnen.	☐	☐	☐	☐	☐	☐	☐	☐
[RR04] Anwendungen mit hohen Echtzeitansprüchen (z. B. für Verfügbarkeitsprüfung in E-Shops) verlangen eine hohe Datenqualität.	☐	☐	☐	☐	☐	☐	☐	☐
[RO01] Eine hundertprozentige Datenqualität ist in einem ERP-System nicht erreichbar.	☐	☐	☐	☐	☐	☐	☐	☐
[RO02] Eine hundertprozentige Datenqualität ist in einem ERP-System betriebswirtschaftlich nicht sinnvoll.	☐	☐	☐	☐	☐	☐	☐	☐
[RO03] Insbesondere für Externe sichtbar werdende Daten (wie Adressen oder Kontensaldi) sind immer mit erhöhter Sorgfalt zu pflegen.	☐	☐	☐	☐	☐	☐	☐	☐
[RO04] Eine Behebung von Datenfehlern direkt im Ursprungssystem (ERP) macht bei Weiterverwendung der Daten oft keinen Sinn; z. B. genügt die externe Datenreinigung im Warehousing-Prozess.	☐	☐	☐	☐	☐	☐	☐	☐

2   Datenqualität in Ihrer ERP-Software als Verkaufsargument – heute und zukünftig

Bitte Zutreffendes ankreuzen: -3 = gar nicht einverstanden, 0 = neutral, +3 = völlig einverstanden

Aussage / Beurteilung	-3	-2	-1	0	+1	+2	+3	weiss nicht
[SA01] Die Fähigkeit Ihres ERP-Produkts, hochwertige Geschäftsdaten zu verwalten, wird in ihrem Marktauftritt hervorgehoben.	☐	☐	☐	☐	☐	☐	☐	☐
[SA02] Sie verkaufen heute schon Produkte oder Systemeigenschaften, welche die Datenqualität in ERP-Systemen verbessern/sichern.	☐	☐	☐	☐	☐	☐	☐	☐
[SA03] Ihre Kunden wären bereit, für Datenqualitäts-Sonderfunktionen in ERP-Produkten zu bezahlen.	☐	☐	☐	☐	☐	☐	☐	☐

1

Figure A.4: Questionnaire ERP Vendors (Page 1).

II.   Gründe für die Entstehung schlechter Daten in ERP-Systemen

3   Welches sind die Einflussfaktoren bei der Datenqualität in ERP-Systemen? Wie beurteilen Sie die folgenden Aussagen?

Bitte Zutreffendes ankreuzen: -3 = gar nicht einverstanden, 0 = neutral, +3 = völlig einverstanden

Aussage / Beurteilung	-3	-2	-1	0	+1	+2	+3	weiss nicht
[IA01] Die offene Struktur vieler ERP-Systeme schliesst fehlerhafte Zustände in der Datenhaltung (und damit Datenfehler) nicht aus.	□	□	□	□	□	□	□	□
[IA02] Fehlende Geschäftsregeln (welche die zulässigen Benutzereingaben festlegen würden) in der ERP-Software führen zu Datenfehlern.	□	□	□	□	□	□	□	□
[IA03] Die Integrität der Geschäftsdaten ist in einem ERP-System auch bei relationaler Datenbanktechnik nicht automatisch gewährleistet.	□	□	□	□	□	□	□	□
[IA04] Die Fülle von Datenmodellen (für ERP und anderes) erschwert das Datenmanagement in den Unternehmen und senkt die Datenqualität.	□	□	□	□	□	□	□	□
[IO01] Unternehmen mit einer ausgeprägten Qualitätsorientierung verfolgen auch eine hohe Datenqualität in ERP-Systemen.	□	□	□	□	□	□	□	□
[IO02] Daten, für welche keine Pflegeverantwortlichen bestimmt sind, weisen tendenziell eine schlechte Qualität auf.	□	□	□	□	□	□	□	□
[IO03] Die exakte Zuweisung von Verantwortlichkeiten für Daten in einem Unternehmen ist in einem integrierten ERP-Umfeld schwierig.	□	□	□	□	□	□	□	□
[IO04] Ein schlecht geleitetes ERP-Einführungsprojekt führt im Betrieb zu mangelhafter Datenqualität.	□	□	□	□	□	□	□	□
[IO05] Das Vernachlässigen der Anpassung einer Organisation auf die ERP-Systemanforderungen beeinträchtigt die Datenqualität.	□	□	□	□	□	□	□	□
[IC01] Der Einbau von datenbezogenen Geschäftsregeln in eine ERP-Lösung wird meist externen Einführungsspezialisten anvertraut.	□	□	□	□	□	□	□	□
[IC02] Der Einbau von vorhandenen Geschäftsregeln in eine ERP-Lösung wird von den Unternehmen oft ganz weggelassen.	□	□	□	□	□	□	□	□
[IC03] Einführungsspezialisten verfügen oft nicht über das technische Wissen, um die Software korrekt für den Einsatz einzustellen.	□	□	□	□	□	□	□	□
[IC04] Einführungsspezialisten verfügen oft nicht über das Geschäfts-wissen, um die Software korrekt für den Einsatz einzustellen.	□	□	□	□	□	□	□	□
[II01] Schnittstellen zu Drittsystem sind ein grosser Risikofaktor für die Datenqualität in ERP-Systemen.	□	□	□	□	□	□	□	□
[II02] Das Einspeisen von Daten Externer (Lieferanten, Kunden) ist ein grosser Risikofaktor für die Datenqualität in ERP-Systemen.	□	□	□	□	□	□	□	□
[IT01] Die Datenqualität hängt stark von der Schulung der Mitarbeitenden ab.	□	□	□	□	□	□	□	□
[IT02] Das Vernachlässigen der prozessorientierten Schulung von ERP-Anwendern gefährdet die Datenqualität.	□	□	□	□	□	□	□	□
[IT03] Die ERP-Benutzerschulung orientiert sich zu selten an der konkreten Arbeitsrealität der Benutzer.	□	□	□	□	□	□	□	□
[IT04] Viele ERP-Anwender sind nicht instruiert, wie sie eigene oder fremde Fehleingaben im System korrigieren können.	□	□	□	□	□	□	□	□
[ID01] Die Datenqualität hängt stark von der Aktualität und dem Umfang der ERP-Systemdokumentation ab.	□	□	□	□	□	□	□	□
[ID02] Die Standarddokumentation vieler ERP-Systeme beschreibt den Umgang mit den vielen Daten nicht adäquat.	□	□	□	□	□	□	□	□
[IS01] Die Datenqualität hängt stark von der Support-Organisation im Unternehmen (Helpdesk etc.) ab.	□	□	□	□	□	□	□	□
[IU01] Das Desinteresse vieler ERP-Benutzer für den mit einem Geschäfts-prozess verbundenen Datenfluss beeinträchtigt die Datenqualität.	□	□	□	□	□	□	□	□
[IU02] Mit zunehmender Erfahrung gehen ERP-Anwender besser mit dem System um; deshalb steigt die Datenqualität.	□	□	□	□	□	□	□	□
[IU03] Mit zunehmender Erfahrung mit einem ERP-System sinkt die Datenqualität, weil Anwender Datenfelder missbrauchen.	□	□	□	□	□	□	□	□
[IU04] Eine wichtige Ursache für die schlechte Datenqualität in ERP-Systemen ist die ungenügende Anwenderdisziplin.	□	□	□	□	□	□	□	□
[IM01] Unternehmen, die zu viele Geschäftsprozesse mit der gleichen ERP-Software abdecken wollen, gefährden ihre Datenqualität.	□	□	□	□	□	□	□	□
[IM02] Je höher die Unterstützung der Geschäftsprozesse durch eine ERP-Lösung, desto höher ist die Datenqualität.	□	□	□	□	□	□	□	□
[IM03] Die Klassifikation und differenzierte Behandlung von ERP-Geschäftsdaten steigert die Datenqualität.	□	□	□	□	□	□	□	□

4   Haben Sie Kommentare zu obigem Punkt 3) oder Erfahrungen mit schlechter Datenqualität?

....

....

....

Figure A.5: Questionnaire ERP Vendors (Page 2).

III. Massnahmen gegen schlechte Datenqualität

5   Welche Vorkehrungen treffen Sie, um Datenfehler in Ihrer Software zu vermeiden? Welche Services bieten Sie an?

Bitte Zutreffendes ankreuzen

Technische Massnahme / Leistungsangebot	im Standard	als Option	in Planung	nicht geplant	weiss nicht
[AV01] Überprüfung der Benutzer-Eingabewerte ("Edit-Checks", z. B. Werteprüfung gegen Tabelle mit zulässigen Werten) bei Bildschirmtransaktionen.	☐	☐	☐	☐	☐
[AV02] Überprüfung externer Daten vor dem Import ins ERP-System, analog der systeminternen Prüfungen bei der Eingabe von Hand.	☐	☐	☐	☐	☐
[AV03] Vollständigkeitsprüfung von Datensätzen (z. B. müssen alle Werte für Kundenauftragsbearbeitung beim Abspeichern vorhanden sein).	☐	☐	☐	☐	☐
[AV04] Mechanismen zur Erkennung und Verhinderung von Doubletten (z. B. doppelte Adresseinträge).	☐	☐	☐	☐	☐
[AV05] Berücksichtigung unternehmensspezifischer Geschäftsregeln (Beispiel: "wenn Kunde bereits Produkt x gekauft hat, dann Produkt y 20% billiger anbieten").	☐	☐	☐	☐	☐
[AV06] Workflow-Komponenten zur sicheren, dezentralen Pflege von Stammsätzen (wenn mehrere Stellen involviert sind, z. B. bei Materialstämmen).	☐	☐	☐	☐	☐
[AV07] Möglichkeiten zur unternehmensspezifischen Vereinfachung der Benutzerschnittstelle (GUI) wie das Einrichten von "Einbildtransaktionen".	☐	☐	☐	☐	☐
[AV08] Integrierte Werkzeuge zur Überprüfung der Konsistenz der Systemeinstellungen (z. B. Kontenabstimmung im Finanzwesen).	☐	☐	☐	☐	☐
[AV09] Integrierte Reports zur (statistischen) Fehlererkennung.	☐	☐	☐	☐	☐
[AV10] Vorgehensmodell für die Einführung der ERP-Lösung (Checklisten, PC-gestützte Hilfsmittel), welches auch auf Aspekte der Datenqualität eingeht.	☐	☐	☐	☐	☐
[AV11] Schulung und Dokumentation für Einführungsspezialisten/-partner: Wie wird das ERP-System korrekt konfiguriert, welches sind mögliche Fallstricke?	☐	☐	☐	☐	☐
[AV12] Datenorientierte Schulung und Dokumentation: Wo werden welche Daten eingepflegt und im Verlauf der Abwicklung weiter verwendet?	☐	☐	☐	☐	☐

IV. Fragen zu Produkt und Unternehmen

6   Machen Sie bitte folgende Angaben zu Produktangebot und Unternehmen:

	Produktbezeichnung >	[NP01]	[NP02]	[NP03]
		_____	_____	_____
	Land-, Forstwirtschaft, Bergbau [0]	☐	☐	☐
	Industrie [1]	☐	☐	☐
	Energie-, Wasserversorgung [2]	☐	☐	☐
	Baugewerbe [3]	☐	☐	☐
In welchen Branchen werden Ihre ERP-Systeme eingesetzt (Mehrfachnennungen möglich)?	Handel, Verkehr und Kommunikation [4]	☐	☐	☐
	Gastgewerbe [5]	☐	☐	☐
	Banken und Versicherungen [6]	☐	☐	☐
	Immobilienwesen, Vermietung, Informatik, F&E, Dienstleistungen für Unternehmen [7]	☐	☐	☐
	Öffentl. Verwalt., Landesverteidigung, Sozial-vers. [8]	☐	☐	☐
	Unterrichts-/Bildungswesen, Gesundheits- und Sozialwesen, sonstige Dienstleistungen [9]	☐	☐	☐
Für welche Unternehmensgrösse sind Ihre ERP-Systeme geeignet (Mehrfachnennungen möglich)? **[SP0x]**	KMU (weniger als 250 Vollzeitangestellte) [1]	☐	☐	☐
	Grossunternehmen [2]	☐	☐	☐
Welches ist die Basisarchitektur Ihres ERP-Systems? **[AP0x]**	Entwicklung auf Basis Standardprodukt [...]	☐ _____	☐ _____	☐ _____
	Vollständige Eigenentwicklung [OD]	☐	☐	☐

Firma: _____

Abteilung: _____

Adresse: _____

PLZ: _____ Ort: _____

Name: _____

Funktion: _____

E-Mail: _____

Tel: _____

Sind Sie am Ergebnis dieser Umfrage interessiert?   ☐ Ja (bitte oben Adresse angeben!)   ☐ Nein

Bitte senden Sie den Fragebogen bis zum **20. Oktober 2003** an:

Institut für Wirtschaftsinformatik
Michael Röthlin, Engehaldenstr. 8, 3012 Bern.

Herzlichen Dank für Ihre Unterstützung unserer Bestrebungen um eine praxisnahe Forschung und Lehre!

3

Figure A.6: Questionnaire ERP Vendors (Page 3).

A.2 Questionnaire Item List

Variable	Short Text	Long Text
RR01	Precondition	"High data quality is a precondition for efficient and effective business process support."
RR02	Integration	"Data quality gains importance with increasing integration of IT systems (CRM, E-Commerce)."
RR03	External data	"Increasing use of external business data calls for data quality criteria and metrics."
RR04	Real-time requirements	"Applications imposing tight real time requirements call for high data quality."

Table A.1: Items of Class Relevance (RR).

Variable	Short Text	Long Text
RO01	100% data quality impossible	"It is impossible to obtain hundred percent data quality in an ERP system."
RO02	100% data quality meaningless	"100% data quality is economic nonsense."
RO03	External documents	"Data which is presented to outsiders to the organization (e.g., in the form of invoices) has to be managed with special care."
RO04	Correction at source	"Cleansing data at the source (in the ERP system) often makes no sense; external cleansing for data warehousing is sufficient in many cases."

Table A.2: Items of Class Economic Aspects (RO).

Variable	Short Text	Long Text
IO01	Quality orientation	"Organizations having a clear quality orientation also pursue high data quality objectives in an ERP system context."
IO02	Data responsibility	"Data for which no responsibilities have been defined tend to suffer from low quality."
IO03	Data ownership in ERP context	"In the ERP context, it is difficult to assign clear and distinct responsibilities for data."
IO04	ERP implementation project quality	"A poor ERP implementation project is a main cause for lacking data quality."
IO05	Adaptation to organizational needs	"An insufficient alignment of the organization to the requirements of the ERP system impairs data quality."

Table A.3: Items of Class Factor "Organization" (IO).

Variable	Short Text	Long Text
IC01	Business rules implementation	"The implementation of data specific business rules in the ERP software is most often realized by external specialists."
IC02	Business rules ignored	"The implementation of existing business rules in an organization is often left out."
IC03	Technical know-how of consultants	"Implementation specialists often lack the technical know-how for correctly setting up the software."
IC04	Business know-how of consultants	"Implementation specialists often lack the business know-how for correctly setting up the software."

Table A.4: Items of Class Factor "Consulting" (IC).

Variable	Short Text	Long Text
II01	Interfaces to other IT systems	"Interfaces to third party systems are a major source of data quality troubles in ERP systems."
II02	External data	"The import and use of external data received from suppliers or customers is a major source of data quality troubles in ERP systems."

Table A.5: Items of Class Factor "Interfaces" (II).

Variable	Short Text	Long Text
IT01	Importance of education	"Data quality strongly depends on the level of training given to employees."
IT02	Process-oriented training	"Neglecting process oriented training of ERP users endangers data quality."
IT03	Reality-based training	"ERP user training programs often ignore the reality of users' jobs."
IT04	Error correction skills	"Many ERP users are not trained to correct (their own or others') errors in the system."

Table A.6: Items of Class Factor "Education" (IT).

Variable	Short Text	Long Text
ID01	System documentation	"Data quality strongly depends on the quality of the ERP system documentation."
ID02	ERP standard documentation	"The standard documentation shipped with many ERP systems does not adequately describe the handling of the underlying business data."

Table A.7: Items of Class Factor "Documentation" (ID).

Variable	Short Text	Long Text
IS01	Support organization	"Data quality strongly depends on the support organization within an enterprise (e.g., the help desk)."

Table A.8: Items of Class Factor "Support" (IS).

Variable	Short Text	Long Text
IU01	Lack of user interest	"The lack of interest into the flow of data related with a business process testified by many ERP users endangers data quality."
IU02	Experience – capability	"With increasing experience, ERP users know how to handle the system better; as a consequence, data quality improves."
IU03	Experience – system abuse	"With increasing system experience of ERP users, data quality deteriorates, as users deliberately misuse data fields."
IU04	User discipline	"Insufficient user discipline is an important cause for insufficient data quality in ERP systems."

Table A.9: Items of Class Factor "User" (IU).

Variable	Short Text	Long Text
IM01	Functional coverage	"Organizations aiming at excessive process coverage put in danger data quality."
IM02	Actual process coverage	"The more business processes ERP systems cover, the better data quality will be."
IM03	Data classification	"Classification and differentiated treatment of ERP data is a means to improve data quality."

Table A.10: Items of Class Factor "Management" (IM).

Variable	Short Text	Long Text
IA01	Architecture too open	"The standardized structure of many ERP products does not exclude incorrect conditions in data processing and storage."
IA02	Lack of ERP business rules	"Missing business rules (which would restrict admissible user inputs) in the ERP system cause data errors."
IA03	Lack of integrity in ERP data	"The integrity of business data is not automatically ensured in an ERP system, regardless of the use of relational database technology."
IA04	Too many data models	"The abundance of data models (for ERP and other systems) makes data management in enterprises more difficult and lowers data quality."

Table A.11: Items of Class Factor "Architecture" (IA).

Variable	Short Text	Long Text
SD01	Contact	"Contact database (marketing)"
SD02	Customer master	"Customer master data (addresses, accounting)"
SD03	Supplier master	"Supplier master data (addresses, accounting)"
SD04	Product master	"Product master data (materials master, BOM, routings)"
SD05	Employee master	"Employee master data (addresses, accounting)"
SD06	Planning	"MRP and personnel planning systems"
SD07	Planned/actual cost	"Costing of sales orders, projects, and products"
SD08	Operational data	"Operational transaction data"
SD09	Product history	"Product history (which products have been sold to whom)"
SD10	Management accounting	"Management accounting"
SD11	Evolution of data quality	"Business data in general, with regard to the situation five years ago."

Table A.12: Items of Class Data Quality Level (SD).

Variable	Short Text	Long Text
AE01	Workflow	"Usage of workflow components to support critical data care processes."
AE02	GUI modification	"Adaptation or simplification of user interfaces (e.g., by hiding unneeded data entry fields)."
AE03	Data cleansing	"Cleansing of data before they are handed over to customers, used for analytical purposes, etc."
AE04	Data quality agreement ext. data	"Agreement with data suppliers on data quality attributes (e.g., for catalog data)."
AE05	Data quality objectives	"Derive data quality goals from superordinate organizational objectives ."
AE06	Data quality as personal objective	"Inclusion of data quality objectives in performance agreements with employees."
AE07	Centralization	"Concentration of data care activities for a given type of data at one place (centralization)."
AE08	Definition/measurement	"Definition and measurement of the quality of (selected) data items."
AE09	Data quality audits	"Data quality audits by senior management or external services."
AE10	Data quality communication	"Communication of actual situation and data quality targets to employees (e.g., via intranet)."
AE11	Formal Data quality program	"Formal data quality program."

Table A.13: Items of Class Data Quality Actions (AE).

Variable	Short Text	Long Text
AP01	Technical prevention	"Improved technical prevention"
AP02	Education	"Increase user competence (education/training)"
AP03	Direction	"Leadership (enforce line management)"
AP04	Board function	"Monitoring by specific staff function."

Table A.14: Items of Class Data Quality Priority (AP).

Variable	Short Text	Long Text
RP01	IT user	"IT user"
RP02	Line manager	"Line manager"
RP03	Process manager	"Process manager"
RP04	Staff position for data quality	"Staff position for data quality."

Table A.15: Items of Class Data Quality Responsibilities (RP).

Variable	Short Text	Long Text
SA01	Sales argument	"The ability of your ERP systems to deliver high-quality business data is emphasized in your product promotion."
SA02	Data quality components	"You presently sell products or market system properties which improve/secure data quality in ERP systems."
SA03	Data quality special functions	"Your customers would agree to pay for specific data quality functionality in ERP products."

Table A.16: Items of Class Data Quality as Sales Argument (SA).

Variable	Short Text	Long Text
AV01	Edit Checks	"Validation of user input ("edit checks," e.g., testing values against check tables) in screen transactions."
AV02	Import filtering	"Examination of external data prior to the import into an ERP system, similar to the validation of manual input."
AV03	Check of completeness	"Check for completeness of data records (e.g., all values for the treatment of customer orders must be present upon first storage)."
AV04	Duplicate removal	"Mechanisms for recognition and prevention of duplicates (e.g., duplicate address entries)."
AV05	Specific business rules	"Consideration of specific business rules (e.g., "if customer has already bought product x, then offer product y with a 20% discount")."
AV06	Data master workflow	"Usage of workflow components to obtain secure, decentralized management of master data (if several units are involved, e.g., for the creation of material master datasets)."
AV07	Simplified GUI	"Simplification of the user interface (GUI), e.g., using single screen transactions."
AV08	Consistency checks	"Integrated tools for examining the consistency of the system settings (e.g., reconciliation of accounts in finance)."
AV09	Error reporting	"Integrated reports for (statistic) error recognition."
AV10	Data quality-oriented implementation model	"Process model for the ERP implementation project (check lists, PC tools), addressing data quality aspects."
AV11	Partner education	"Training and documentation for implementation specialist/partners: How have ERP systems to be set up correctly, which are the possible pitfalls?"
AV12	Data oriented documentation/training	"Data-oriented training and documentation: what is the role data plays in the ERP system's operation?"

Table A.17: Items of Class Instruments Implemented in ERP Systems (AV).

A.3 Distribution of Responses

Variable		n	$\bar{x}$	-3	-2	-1	0	1	2	3
RR01	RU	125	3	0.0	0.0	0.0	0.0	6.4	16.8	76.8
	RV	50	3	0.0	0.0	0.0	0.0	2.0	14.0	84.0
	Total	**175**	**3**	**0.0**	**0.0**	**0.0**	**0.0**	**5.1**	**16.0**	**78.9**
RR02	RU	125	3	0.0	0.8	0.0	4.0	3.2	23.2	68.8
	RV	50	3	0.0	0.0	0.0	0.0	6.0	20.0	74.0
	Total	**175**	**3**	**0.0**	**0.6**	**0.0**	**2.9**	**4.0**	**22.3**	**70.3**
RR03	RU	123	2	0.8	0.0	1.6	4.9	22.0	30.1	40.7
	RV	50	3	0.0	0.0	2.0	2.0	8.0	32.0	56.0
	Total	**173**	**2**	**0.6**	**0.0**	**1.7**	**4.0**	**17.9**	**30.6**	**45.1**
RR04	RU	122	3	0.0	0.8	0.8	4.9	8.2	25.4	59.8
	RV	50	3	0.0	0.0	0.0	8.0	6.0	20.0	66.0
	Total	**172**	**3**	**0.0**	**0.6**	**0.6**	**5.8**	**7.6**	**23.8**	**61.6**

Table A.18: Item Class RR, Distribution of Responses (Percentages).

Variable		n	$\bar{x}$	-3	-2	-1	0	1	2	3
RO01	RU	123	2	1.6	4.9	10.6	4.9	14.6	24.4	39.0
	RV	50	2	6.0	4.0	4.0	10.0	14.0	32.0	28.0
	Total	**173**	**2**	**2.9**	**5.2**	**8.7**	**6.4**	**14.5**	**26.6**	**35.8**
RO02	RU	125	1	4.0	14.4	8.8	8.8	15.2	25.6	23.2
	RV	48	0	20.8	18.8	4.2	14.6	12.5	18.8	10.4
	Total	**173**	**1**	**8.7**	**15.6**	**7.5**	**10.4**	**14.5**	**23.7**	**19.7**
RO03	RU	125	3	1.6	0.8	2.4	3.2	6.4	28.0	57.6
	RV	50	3	4.0	0.0	2.0	8.0	8.0	24.0	54.0
	Total	**175**	**3**	**2.3**	**0.6**	**2.3**	**4.6**	**6.9**	**26.9**	**56.6**
RO04	RU	115	-2	27.0	31.3	9.6	21.7	4.3	5.2	0.9
	RV	50	-2	36.0	32.0	6.0	6.0	10.0	10.0	0.0
	Total	**165**	**-2**	**29.7**	**31.5**	**8.5**	**17.0**	**6.1**	**6.7**	**0.6**

Table A.19: Item Class RO, Distribution of Responses (Percentages).

Variable		n	$\bar{x}$	-3	-2	-1	0	1	2	3
IO01	RU	124	2	0.0	2.4	4.0	8.1	11.3	43.5	30.6
	RV	49	2	0.0	2.0	10.2	4.1	8.2	32.7	42.9
	Total	**173**	**2**	**0.0**	**2.3**	**5.8**	**6.9**	**10.4**	**40.5**	**34.1**
IO02	RU	124	3	0.0	0.8	3.2	1.6	4.8	31.5	58.1
	RV	50	3	2.0	2.0	4.0	4.0	12.0	24.0	52.0
	Total	**174**	**3**	**0.6**	**1.1**	**3.4**	**2.3**	**6.9**	**29.3**	**56.3**
IO03	RU	122	1	5.7	20.5	10.7	10.7	21.3	21.3	9.8
	RV	50	0.5	4.0	20.0	16.0	10.0	22.0	18.0	10.0
	Total	**172**	**1**	**5.2**	**20.3**	**12.2**	**10.5**	**21.5**	**20.3**	**9.9**
IO04	RU	124	3	0.0	0.0	3.2	4.8	5.6	33.1	53.2
	RV	50	2	0.0	0.0	2.0	6.0	16.0	36.0	40.0
	Total	**174**	**2**	**0.0**	**0.0**	**2.9**	**5.2**	**8.6**	**33.9**	**49.4**
IO05	RU	123	2	0.0	0.8	2.4	10.6	18.7	35.8	31.7
	RV	48	2	2.1	4.2	4.2	14.6	20.8	37.5	16.7
	Total	**171**	**2**	**0.6**	**1.8**	**2.9**	**11.7**	**19.3**	**36.3**	**27.5**

Table A.20: Item Class IO, Distribution of Responses (Percentages).

Variable		n	$\bar{x}$	-3	-2	-1	0	1	2	3
IC01	RU	111	1	2.7	9.9	14.4	18.0	24.3	29.7	0.9
	RV	47	1	2.1	12.8	8.5	12.8	25.5	27.7	10.6
	Total	**158**	**1**	**2.5**	**10.8**	**12.7**	**16.5**	**24.7**	**29.1**	**3.8**
IC02	RU	109	0	5.5	13.8	19.3	23.9	22.0	12.8	2.8
	RV	47	-1	8.5	21.3	23.4	12.8	19.1	10.6	4.3
	Total	**156**	**0**	**6.4**	**16.0**	**20.5**	**20.5**	**21.2**	**12.2**	**3.2**
IC03	RU	122	1	1.6	16.4	17.2	13.9	18.9	18.9	13.1
	RV	50	-1	18.0	24.0	16.0	14.0	18.0	8.0	2.0
	Total	**172**	**0**	**6.4**	**18.6**	**16.9**	**14.0**	**18.6**	**15.7**	**9.9**
IC04	RU	121	2	0.0	5.8	14.9	7.4	21.5	33.1	17.4
	RV	50	0	10.0	22.0	16.0	8.0	20.0	22.0	2.0
	Total	**171**	**1**	**2.9**	**10.5**	**15.2**	**7.6**	**21.1**	**29.8**	**12.9**

Table A.21: Item Class IC, Distribution of Responses (Percentages).

Variable		n	$\bar{x}$	-3	-2	-1	0	1	2	3
II01	RU	122	1	2.5	12.3	5.7	13.9	18.9	25.4	21.3
	RV	50	-1	16.0	14.0	22.0	10.0	10.0	12.0	16.0
	Total	**172**	**1**	**6.4**	**12.8**	**10.5**	**12.8**	**16.3**	**21.5**	**19.8**
II02	RU	121	1	3.3	5.8	12.4	16.5	21.5	25.6	14.9
	RV	50	1	12.0	12.0	16.0	6.0	26.0	20.0	8.0
	Total	**171**	**1**	**5.8**	**7.6**	**13.5**	**13.5**	**22.8**	**24.0**	**12.9**

Table A.22: Item Class II, Distribution of Responses (Percentages).

Variable		n	$\bar{x}$	-3	-2	-1	0	1	2	3
IT01	RU	124	3	0.0	0.0	0.0	0.8	9.7	32.3	57.3
	RV	50	2	0.0	2.0	2.0	4.0	12.0	48.0	32.0
	Total	**174**	**2.5**	**0.0**	**0.6**	**0.6**	**1.7**	**10.3**	**36.8**	**50.0**
IT02	RU	125	2	0.0	0.0	0.8	3.2	16.8	41.6	37.6
	RV	50	2	0.0	2.0	2.0	12.0	24.0	34.0	26.0
	Total	**175**	**2**	**0.0**	**0.6**	**1.1**	**5.7**	**18.9**	**39.4**	**34.3**
IT03	RU	121	1	0.8	9.1	14.9	15.7	25.6	23.1	10.7
	RV	50	0	6.0	24.0	12.0	22.0	14.0	18.0	4.0
	Total	**171**	**1**	**2.3**	**13.5**	**14.0**	**17.5**	**22.2**	**21.6**	**8.8**
IT04	RU	117	1	0.0	4.3	16.2	18.8	25.6	24.8	10.3
	RV	50	0	6.0	8.0	22.0	18.0	26.0	16.0	4.0
	Total	**167**	**1**	**1.8**	**5.4**	**18.0**	**18.6**	**25.7**	**22.2**	**8.4**

Table A.23: Item Class IT, Distribution of Responses (Percentages).

Variable		n	$\bar{x}$	-3	-2	-1	0	1	2	3
ID01	RU	124	1	2.4	11.3	13.7	18.5	28.2	16.9	8.9
	RV	50	0	6.0	30.0	8.0	10.0	24.0	18.0	4.0
	Total	**174**	**1**	**3.4**	**16.7**	**12.1**	**16.1**	**27.0**	**17.2**	**7.5**
ID02	RU	115	1	0.9	0.9	6.1	16.5	33.0	25.2	17.4
	RV	49	0	0.0	8.2	8.2	36.7	18.4	22.4	6.1
	Total	**164**	**1**	**0.6**	**3.0**	**6.7**	**22.6**	**28.7**	**24.4**	**14.0**

Table A.24: Item Class ID, Distribution of Responses (Percentages).

Variable		n	$\bar{x}$	-3	-2	-1	0	1	2	3
IS01	RU	125	1	8.8	8.8	15.2	8.0	26.4	24.0	8.8
	RV	49	1	4.1	10.2	10.2	10.2	36.7	26.5	2.0
	Total	**174**	**1**	**7.5**	**9.2**	**13.8**	**8.6**	**29.3**	**24.7**	**6.9**

Table A.25: Item Class IS, Distribution of Responses (Percentages).

Variable		n	$\bar{x}$	-3	-2	-1	0	1	2	3
IU01	RU	122	2	0.0	1.6	2.5	9.0	23.8	34.4	28.7
	RV	50	2	2.0	4.0	12.0	8.0	12.0	38.0	24.0
	Total	**172**	**2**	**0.6**	**2.3**	**5.2**	**8.7**	**20.3**	**35.5**	**27.3**
IU02	RU	124	2	0.0	4.0	4.8	4.0	16.1	40.3	30.6
	RV	50	2	0.0	2.0	8.0	8.0	16.0	42.0	24.0
	Total	**174**	**2**	**0.0**	**3.4**	**5.7**	**5.2**	**16.1**	**40.8**	**28.7**
IU03	RU	123	-1	3.3	26.0	23.6	11.4	22.0	10.6	3.3
	RV	50	-1	4.0	36.0	30.0	14.0	10.0	2.0	4.0
	Total	**173**	**-1**	**3.5**	**28.9**	**25.4**	**12.1**	**18.5**	**8.1**	**3.5**
IU04	RU	124	1	0.0	1.6	7.3	10.5	33.9	22.6	24.2
	RV	50	1	0.0	2.0	10.0	16.0	30.0	20.0	22.0
	Total	**174**	**1**	**0.0**	**1.7**	**8.0**	**12.1**	**32.8**	**21.8**	**23.6**

Table A.26: Item Class IU, Distribution of Responses (Percentages).

Variable		n	$\bar{x}$	-3	-2	-1	0	1	2	3
IM01	RU	120	-1	21.7	17.5	11.7	16.7	18.3	10.0	4.2
	RV	49	-2	38.8	24.5	6.1	20.4	2.0	8.2	0.0
	Total	**169**	**-1**	**26.6**	**19.5**	**10.1**	**17.8**	**13.6**	**9.5**	**3.0**
IM02	RU	121	2	1.7	4.1	5.8	19.0	15.7	33.9	19.8
	RV	50	2	2.0	0.0	10.0	10.0	12.0	32.0	34.0
	Total	**171**	**2**	**1.8**	**2.9**	**7.0**	**16.4**	**14.6**	**33.3**	**24.0**
IM03	RU	113	2	0.0	1.8	1.8	24.8	21.2	39.8	10.6
	RV	25	2	0.0	0.0	0.0	32.0	12.0	28.0	28.0
	Total	**138**	**2**	**0.0**	**1.4**	**1.4**	**26.1**	**19.6**	**37.7**	**13.8**

Table A.27: Item Class IM, Distribution of Responses (Percentages).

Variable		n	$\bar{x}$	-3	-2	-1	0	1	2	3
IA01	RV	49	1	0.0	8.2	12.2	8.2	28.6	24.5	18.4
IA02	RV	49	2	0.0	2.0	4.1	10.2	20.4	44.9	18.4
IA03	RV	50	2	6.0	4.0	4.0	14.0	16.0	28.0	28.0
IA04	RV	49	2	4.1	6.1	14.3	10.2	14.3	32.7	18.4

Table A.28: Item Class IA, Distribution of Responses (Percentages).

Variable		n	$\bar{x}$	-3	-2	-1	0	1	2	3
SD01	RU	114	1	1.8	10.5	10.5	19.3	33.3	20.2	4.4
SD02	RU	121	2	0.0	0.8	9.1	6.6	26.4	39.7	17.4
SD03	RU	122	2	0.0	0.0	3.3	6.6	32.0	46.7	11.5
SD04	RU	116	2	1.7	3.4	3.4	11.2	27.6	37.9	14.7
SD05	RU	123	2	0.0	0.8	3.3	6.5	8.9	39.8	40.7
SD06	RU	109	1	0.9	5.5	11.9	22.0	30.3	25.7	3.7
SD07	RU	116	1	1.7	3.4	13.8	19.0	30.2	24.1	7.8
SD08	RU	112	2	0.0	3.6	8.9	9.8	26.8	31.2	19.6
SD09	RU	115	2	2.6	5.2	7.0	12.2	20.0	24.3	28.7
SD10	RU	125	2	0.0	0.0	4.8	9.6	15.2	52.8	17.6
SD11	RU	121	2	0.0	0.0	0.0	7.4	23.1	55.4	14.0

Table A.29: Item Class SD, Distribution of Responses (Percentages).

Variable		n	$\bar{x}$	0	1
AE01	RU	112	0	53.6	46.4
AE02	RU	121	1	18.2	81.8
AE03	RU	114	1	36.0	64.0
AE04	RU	107	1	45.8	54.2
AE05	RU	116	0	53.4	46.6
AE06	RU	116	0	54.3	45.7
AE07	RU	122	1	23.0	77.0
AE08	RU	120	1	48.3	51.7
AE09	RU	119	0	57.1	42.9
AE10	RU	118	0	70.3	29.7
AE11	RU	112	0	75.0	25.0

Table A.30: Item Class AE, Distribution of Responses (Percentages).

Variable		n	$\bar{x}$	-3	-2	-1	0	1	2	3
AP01	RU	123	1	0.0	0.8	2.4	15.4	35.8	33.3	12.2
AP02	RU	125	2	0.0	0.0	0.0	1.6	12.0	44.8	41.6
AP03	RU	125	2	0.8	2.4	5.6	20.8	20.0	36.0	14.4
AP04	RU	125	1	0.0	4.8	8.8	25.6	28.0	24.8	8.0

Table A.31: Item Class AP, Distribution of Responses (Percentages).

Variable		n	$\bar{x}$	0	1	2	3	4	5	6
RP01	RU	121	5	3.3	5.0	6.6	14.9	16.5	25.6	28.1
RP02	RU	121	4	2.5	9.1	9.9	18.2	27.3	21.5	11.6
RP03	RU	120	5	7.5	2.5	3.3	16.7	18.3	23.3	28.3
RP04	RU	106	2	37.7	6.6	10.4	13.2	9.4	7.5	15.1

Table A.32: Item Class RP, Distribution of Responses (Percentages).

Variable		n	$\bar{x}$	-3	-2	-1	0	1	2	3
SA01	RV	50	2	4.0	4.0	2.0	14.0	24.0	34.0	18.0
SA02	RV	50	2	2.0	2.0	2.0	4.0	8.0	46.0	36.0
SA03	RV	49	1	4.1	10.2	12.2	12.2	36.7	16.3	8.2

Table A.33: Item Class SA, Distribution of Responses (Percentages).

Variable		n	$\bar{x}$	1	2	3	4
AV01	RV	47	1	91.5	4.3	2.1	2.1
AV02	RV	48	1	77.1	16.7	4.2	2.1
AV03	RV	46	1	89.1	6.5	0.0	4.3
AV04	RV	48	1	58.3	33.3	6.2	2.1
AV05	RV	48	2	45.8	27.1	2.1	25.0
AV06	RV	46	1	65.2	19.6	4.3	10.9
AV07	RV	41	1	58.5	22.0	9.8	9.8
AV08	RV	48	1	70.8	18.8	6.2	4.2
AV09	RV	45	1	57.8	22.2	4.4	15.6
AV10	RV	47	1	70.2	14.9	2.1	12.8
AV11	RV	48	1	72.9	14.6	6.2	6.2
AV12	RV	47	1	74.5	17.0	4.3	4.3

Table A.34: Item Class AV, Distribution of Responses (Percentages).

A.4 Homogeneity between Early and Late Responses

A.4.1 IT Manager Survey

Item	Meaning	Early R.		Late R.		Fisher Exact Test	
		n	$\bar{x}$	n	$\bar{x}$	p	$Sig.$
RR01	Precondition	104	3	16	3	0.431	
RR02	Integration	104	3	16	3	0.415	
RR03	External data	103	2	16	2	0.836	
RR04	Real-time requirements	102	3	16	3	0.123	
RO01	100% data quality impossible	102	2	16	1.5	0.109	
RO02	100% data quality meaningless	104	2	16	1	0.204	
RO03	External documents	104	3	16	3	0.705	
RO04	Correction at source	95	-2	15	-2	0.046	**
IO01	Quality orientation	103	2	16	2	0.886	
IO02	Data responsibility	103	3	16	2.5	0.224	
IO03	Data ownership in ERP context	101	1	16	0.5	0.066	*
IO04	ERP implementation project quality	104	3	16	2	0.461	
IO05	Adaptation to organizational needs	102	2	16	2	1.000	
IC01	Business rules implementation	93	1	14	1.5	0.171	
IC02	Business rules ignored	90	0	14	1	0.077	*
IC03	Technical know-how of consultants	101	1	16	1	0.819	
IC04	Business know-how of consultants	100	2	16	1.5	0.308	
II01	Interfaces to other IT systems	102	1	15	2	0.436	
II02	External data	100	1	16	1.5	0.689	
IT01	Importance of education	103	3	16	3	0.935	
IT02	Process-oriented training	104	2	16	1.5	0.027	**
IT03	Reality-based training	101	1	15	1	0.524	
IT04	Error correction skills	97	1	15	2	0.323	
ID01	System documentation	103	1	16	1	0.261	
ID02	ERP standard documentation	96	1	14	1	0.851	
IS01	Support organization	104	1	16	1	0.700	
IU01	Lack of user interest	102	2	15	2	0.656	
IU02	Experience – capability	103	2	16	2	0.827	
IU03	Experience – system abuse	102	-1	16	0	0.006	***
IU04	User discipline	104	1	15	1	0.907	
IM01	Functional coverage	100	-0.5	15	0	0.164	
IM02	Actual process coverage	100	1	16	2	0.179	
IM03	Data classification	94	1	15	2	0.242	

Table A.35: Comparison of Answers from Early and Late Respondents in IT Manager Survey.[a,b,c]

[a] Fisher's exact test for count data.
[b] H_0: Proportions of responses are identical in both groups.
[c] Alternative hypothesis: two-sided.

Interpretation: Three cases of significant differences ($\alpha = 0.05$) between groups have been found. In variable RO04, proportions of responses in the upper range (rather agreeing to "Correction at the source makes no sense") differ slightly (Figure A.7); however, the median in both groups is the same. In the case of IT02, median values of both groups are 2 and 1.5, respectively; distribution of responses is also similar, as Figure A.8 illustrates. Finally, the case of IU03 is more subtle (Figure A.9), as two maxima can be observed in the case of early respondents (one at "1" and another at "-1"/"-2", with a median at "-1") and only a single maximum (median at "0") in the case of late respondents. Overall, when taking into account the relatively small number of responses in the "late group," the choice of considering only a homogeneous "IT manager group" can be justified.

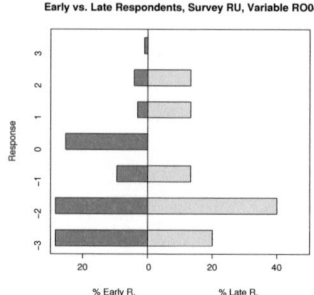

Figure A.7: Early and Late Responses in IT Manager Survey, Variable RO04.

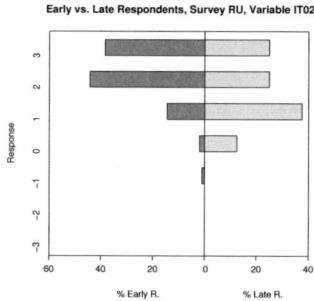

Figure A.8: Early and Late Responses in IT Manager Survey, Variable IT02.

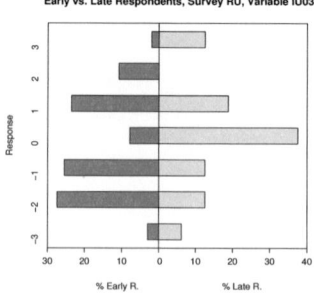

Figure A.9: Early and Late Responses in IT Manager Survey, Variable IU03.

A.4.2   ERP Vendor Survey

Item	Meaning	Early R. n	Early R. $\bar{x}$	Late R. n	Late R. $\bar{x}$	Fisher Exact Test p	Fisher Exact Test $Sig.$
RR01	Precondition	39	3	7	3	1.000	
RR02	Integration	39	3	7	3	0.461	
RR03	External data	39	3	7	2	0.689	
RR04	Real-time requirements	39	3	7	3	0.900	
RO01	100% data quality impossible	39	2	7	2	0.451	
RO02	100% data quality meaningless	38	0	6	-1	0.608	
RO03	External documents	39	3	7	2	0.479	
RO04	Correction at source	39	-2	7	-2	0.622	
IO01	Quality orientation	38	2	7	2	0.358	
IO02	Data responsibility	39	3	7	3	0.834	
IO03	Data ownership in ERP context	39	1	7	1	1.000	
IO04	ERP implementation project quality	39	2	7	2	0.737	
IO05	Adaptation to organizational needs	37	2	7	2	0.614	
IC01	Business rules implementation	36	1	7	2	0.826	
IC02	Business rules ignored	36	-0.5	7	-1	0.733	
IC03	Technical know-how of consultants	39	-1	7	-2	0.926	
IC04	Business know-how of consultants	39	0	7	-1	1.000	
II01	Interfaces to other IT systems	39	-1	7	0	0.277	
II02	External data	39	1	7	1	0.793	
IT01	Importance of education	39	2	7	2	0.718	
IT02	Process-oriented training	39	2	7	2	0.956	
IT03	Reality-based training	39	0	7	0	0.958	
IT04	Error correction skills	39	0	7	0	0.668	
ID01	System documentation	39	0	7	1	0.705	
ID02	ERP standard documentation	39	0	7	0	0.729	
IS01	Support organization	38	1	7	1	0.543	
IU01	Lack of user interest	39	2	7	0	0.019	**
IU02	Experience – capability	39	2	7	2	0.512	
IU03	Experience – system abuse	39	-1	7	-1	0.831	
IU04	User discipline	39	1	7	1	0.652	
IM01	Functional coverage	38	-2	7	-3	0.283	
IM02	Actual process coverage	39	2	7	2	0.922	
IM03	Data classification	20	1.5	4	2	0.339	

Table A.36: Comparison of Answers from Early and Late Respondents in Vendor Survey.[a,b,c]

[a] Fisher's exact test for count data.
[b] H_0: Proportions of responses are identical in both groups.
[c] Alternative hypothesis: two-sided.

Interpretation: Only one significant difference between early and late respondents was identified: the medians of the responses to question IU01 differ by 2, when considering both groups. However, the two responses giving rise to the low value in the "late respondent group" (with values of "-3" and "-2") represent only one answer each. The small size of the response group and the fact that this phenomenon was the only significant deviation were reasons enough to conclude that both, early and late respondents, belong to a "single ERP vendor group."

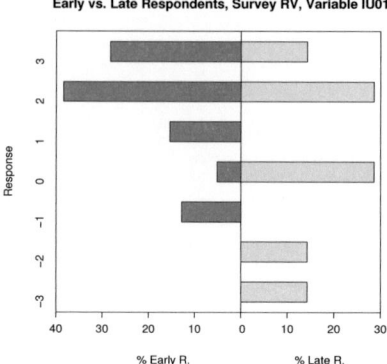

Figure A.10: Early and Late Responses in Vendor Survey, Variable `IU01`.

Appendix B

ERP Expert Interviews

B.1 Interviewees

The following ERP experts were contacted to review the findings from Chapters 2, 3, and 4 and to assess the "a priori" formulation of the ERP data quality project model presented in Chapter 5:

E1: Senior product manager information management/data quality;

E2: Head of SAP integration, managing partner ERP consulting firm;

E3: Senior manager systems and process assurance;

E4: CEO ERP consulting firm.

B.2 Method

The semi-structured interviews were conducted face-to-face (experts E2, E3, E4) or by E-mail (expert E1), using a five page questionnaire containing drafts of the proposed ERP data quality project model and the conclusions.

B.3 Expert Feedback: ERP Data Quality Project Model

Step D: Development and Supply of ERP Software

Offerings such as standardized tools and project models for assuring data quality, provided by ERP vendors and their service partners, are appearing with a significant delay to ERP systems [E1]. One reason for this might be that offering data quality tools and consulting services incurs high costs for an ERP vendor and may tamper its image [E2]. It will also be very difficult for a vendor to include specific requirements in the system design; however, the better an ERP software fits the needs of an industry, the more specific its data structures can be designed and managed, e.g., using mandatory fields in entry screens or implementing business rules [E4].

Step S: Development of ERP Data Quality Strategy

Still today, data quality is seldom an explicit topic in strategic ERP projects; top management simply *expects* ERP systems to bring along high quality data [E4]. If data quality issues have to be addressed, projects should rather be set up under the umbrella of compliance and risk management initiatives, for which sponsors are easier to find [E3]. With regard to the anticipation of future information needs to be covered by an ERP system, the analysis of the evolution of external systems is of tremendous complexity and in most cases not achievable, especially if technologies from several vendors are used [E2]. The evolution of the system landscape and the need for ERP integration solutions is especially challenging if an organization is confronted with merger/acquisition activities, which are typically unknown in advance [E3].

Step E: Evaluation and Selection of ERP System(s)

Data quality has to play an important role in system evaluation, and data quality aspects have to be formally included in the overall system requirements, especially when addressing the analysis and conversion of legacy data sources [E3], as the option to convert legacy data to the new system is often requested by customers [E4]. On the other hand, the importance of data conversion is often overestimated, as many data records have to be reentered manually or at least modified after import, due to the very different structural requirements of a new ERP target system [E4].

The specification of ERP requirements has to be as complete as possible, as omitting important features in the requirements specification is a well-known way to implementation failures and data quality problems [E4]. *Data quality* requirements, however, are still harder to establish than normal functional ERP requirements, even when using sophisticated "information marketing" techniques [E2].

Step A1: Implementation – Project Preparation

Addressing the quality of ERP data at this stage will likely be too late [E3]. Besides the objective of having acceptable data quality in the future ERP system, the conversion project has to address the re-engineering of existing, possibly low quality data [E2].

Step A2: Implementation – Business Blueprint

During the blueprint phase, the strategic role of an ERP system has to be broken down to business processes and coordinated with internal control systems [E3]. Often data care processes are omitted or addressed too late in implementation projects; partially because, for many types of data, no immediate responsibilities can be identified [E2]. Data care processes have to cover the entire data life cycle, with all creation, modification, and archival activities [E2]. Once responsibilities are defined, workflow systems can be a valuable tool used to control data care processes [E2]. When defining and measuring data quality, an explicit global data quality indicator is recommended to create visibility, even if data quality indirectly affects most business key figures [E2].

Step A3: Implementation – Realization

Critical factors for success in data quality include the existence of dedicated data quality staff, an emotional binding of business people to data quality, data quality targets, a measurement system, and feedback loops [E2]. In 60–70% of data quality problem situations, the settings of the ERP system have been set up inadequately, often due to a lack of interest of the relevant stakeholders [E4]. To counter this problem, data quality objectives can and should be incorporated into job descriptions of all persons handling data, together with adequate quality measurements [E2]. Often "ERP user education" during an implementation project simply requires explaining the meaning and the later use of data fields in entry screens [E4].

Besides user training and system documentation, access control rules are important for ensuring data quality, as only trained staff should be allowed to modify critical data [E3]. In particular, master data management should be subject to a specific internal control system, including an ERP-specific accountability matrix (RACI chart) regulating access control [E3].

In DWH environments, data quality reports are frequently used; if ERP data is processed using ETL tools, quality analysis tools and quality measurements are hence most often available [E2]. As for transactional applications of ERP, system reports have to be subject to formal quality management, in order to avoid misunderstandings and other quality flaws [E3].

Step A4: Implementation – Final Preparation

When converting data from legacy systems to ERP packages, the commitment of business process owners for assuring the quality of data is fundamental: not only the functionality of the prospective ERP system, but also the availability of data of sufficient quality has to be acknowledged by business managers [E3]. Data quality has to be reviewed at the latest when line or process managers sign the clearance for the go-live of the ERP system [E2].

Step P: Production and Maintenance

In the operation phase, data quality has to be stabilized and assured by both internal control and risk management systems [E3]. For customer related master data, external data sources (such as address data) are very important [E2]. Even if suggested by the literature, the application of supply management principles for data quality is difficult in practice; if problems from other than internal operational domains occur, they are very difficult to address [E2].

Step R: Data Quality Improvement before Retirement

Before the retirement and replacement of an ERP system, it is important to "freeze" the evolution of functionality and to assess and improve the existing data, before setting up any conversion ERP projects [E3].

B.4   Expert Feedback: Assessment of ERP Data Quality

Statement 1: "Modern ERP systems can improve data quality through better process and data integration"

Today's ERP systems can be valuable tools for process automation and optimization, if the data used by these IT systems is correct [E2]. The reduction of redundant data structures, data records, and application interfaces in ERP systems has helped enormously to improve data quality [E4]. On the other hand, if an ERP system supersedes an older departmental application that contained highly organization specific functionality and automated routine business transactions, the implementation of a poorly customized ERP system might result in a clear step backwards, in terms of process support and data quality [E3]. Also, when search engines built into an ERP system are not effective or fully understood by users and it is faster for users to create new (master) data records instead of finding and using existing ones, duplicate records are a natural result [E3, E4].

Statement 2: "Today's ERP systems are potentially afflicted with the same problems as older, departmental IT applications"

Real-world problems, such as theft in inventory management, remain certainly a major challenge for data quality [E2], and in this sense ERP systems are not a "silver bullet" for securing data quality [E3]. On the other hand, technical data integration features have helped to validate data entries to a much higher degree than in previously existing systems [E2]. And, with regard to inventory management, the availability of more detailed information about storage locations helps to conduct physical inventories that produce inventory data of much better quality [E4].

Statement 3: "ERP systems are – in contrast to stovepipe IT architectures – confronted with new problems caused by data integration"

Tight data integration can be a "curse," as errors quickly spread throughout the system, and removing errors by deleting data may often not be an option, as today's legislation often prohibits deletion of *any* business-related data records [E2, E4]. Due to the inevitable need for integrating third-party applications with ERP systems, the claim of ERP systems to operate without interfaces and in a closed data structure context does not hold [E3].

Statement 4: "Specific business rules of an organization are often not adequately considered in ERP implementation projects"

ERP-specific functionality for integrating custom business rules is normally sufficient, even if the ERP application (base) functionality typically cannot be modified [E4], adaptations may be costly [E2], and the usual scarceness of resources in ERP projects (with respect to know-how, staffing, time, etc.) may even prevent the implementation of specific rules [E3]. With regard to the user interface, much has been done in the past years to facilitate the adaptation of GUIs to the needs of an organization, e.g., by masking or arranging fields on screen forms. Implementing or enforcing rules at the user interface level is hence quite easy, while embedding them at the application level proves to be almost impracticable [E4].

Statement 5: "Typical ERP showcases ignore the activities needed to create and manage even critical master data"

The ERP documentation provided by vendors is often insufficient for data management purposes [E2]. Smaller organizations are especially challenged, as setting out detailed data care processes in an implementation project consumes valuable resources and requires experience; delivering *functionality* in an ERP project comes to the fore and managers take data quality as granted [E3]. The problem of underestimating (important) data care activities has to be seen in the context of ERP selection and purchasing processes: most often, ERP systems are assessed by business managers, not IT specialists or even future users of the system [E4]. As a consequence, data quality will most likely suffer if no dedicated data care team or formal data stewardship is installed [E2].

Statement 6: "Data quality in ERP systems depends primarily on correct configuration of the software, the use of functional extensions, and user training"

All of these components are important, a "balanced" data quality approach is required [E1]. The initial investment and the recurring expenses needed for assuring data quality vary from case to case; general recommendations are hard to establish [E2]. When considering data quality, many ERP customers are primarily interested in third-party product integration, which both increases productivity and improves data quality; typical examples are the integration of telephone directories for retrieving and validating customer address data or bank identification codes [E4].

Statement 7: "ERP user training is too often neglected, ERP-related skills are not managed with sufficient care"

Most large enterprises have implemented process management, have instituted process leadership, and also train their employees accordingly, as data quality cannot be assured by simply mentioning it in job descriptions [E4]. A major problem is the complexity of many real-world business processes and, subsequently, a lack of understanding of the internal data flow in an ERP environment [E2]. Besides this lack of insight, organizations using ERP systems typically have no internal control over the competencies of ERP system users and do not systematically qualify users [E3]. When looking for causes of inadequate training and user competencies, these problems are seldom due to the evolution of the ERP software, as the base set of applications will not change too frequently, but rather due to missing information and knowledge sharing within organizations [E4].

Statement 8: "Data quality in an ERP context can be managed using the same principles and tools as in other IT application contexts"

In a DWH context, data quality analyses and measurements have been used for a long time, as ETL tools produce extensive data error documentation; in an ERP context, on the other hand, such approaches are rare, even if some vendors provide standardized, customizable queries [E2]. In certain business environments, compliance requirements today impose quality criteria on selected data categories [E3]. As to the concept of ownership, the special characteristics of the quality of data make it unsuitable for treatment by classic quality management functions [E4].

Statement 9: "Turning away from monolithic ERP systems in favor of modular, loosely coupled ERP architectures may put data quality at risk"

The positive side of the increasing availability of service-oriented architectures is that data quality services can be implemented just once in an organization and easily deployed to many business units and applications – an excellent opportunity to increase or maintain data quality [E1]. On the other side, it is much more difficult to provide consistent transactional services over a distributed application infrastructure [E4]. Any IT system integration attempt (which is required in heterogeneous environments) always creates a risk of misunderstandings, as the embedded logic of a software component is rarely documented in a complete and machine-readable form. The famous (and existing) "field abuse" is often simply a result of third-party integration attempts, for creating, storing, or forwarding external data [E2]. A central problem in IT system integration projects – involving ERP systems or not – is the definition of the "reference" system: when considering customer records, will a separately kept customer database, or the contact database, or the accounting (ERP) system be the authoritative system [E4]?

Statement 10: "For effectively assuring data quality in ERP implementation projects, role models known from ERP project methods are sufficient; in the post-implementation phase, existing data or quality management roles can take care of data quality assignments"

If the creator or principal user of a given category of data items is known, he or she should be the "owner" of the data and the first person responsible for it, a fact that should be specified in job descriptions [E2]. If data maintenance going beyond normal business activities is required, this effort made must also be rewarded, typically using financial incentives [E4]. This, in turn, calls for formal data quality targets and a data quality measurement system [E1]. Targets have to be set by the business: IT specialists can provide technical aids, e.g., by declaring fields as mandatory, but the usage and the meaning of data in a business context can only be specified by business managers [E3].

In practice, responsibility for data quality cannot simply be enforced by line management; dedicated roles have to be developed, as a given person will rarely be capable of addressing business and data issues at the same level [E2]. Typically, a full-time "data care" team is needed in larger organizations, already during implementation projects, before go-live. Even if explicitly mentioned in project models and initially envisaged in project plans, data quality checks scheduled to take place after conversion of legacy data risk being cancelled, due to timing or cost constraints [E1].

Appendix C

Quality Management Guidelines

C.1 Sample Software FMEA Ratings

Rating	Severity of Effect	Likelihood of Occurence	Detection
1	Cosmetic error: No loss in product functionality. Includes incorrect documentation.	1 per 100 unit-years	Requirements / Design reviews
2	Cosmetic error: No loss in product functionality. Includes incorrect documentation.	1 per 10 unit-years	Requirements / Design reviews
3	Product performance reduction, temporary through time-out or system load the problem will "go away" after a period of time.	1 per 1 unit-years	Code walkthroughs / Unit testing
4	Product performance reduction, temporary through time-out or system load the problem will "go away" after a period of time.	1 per 1 unit-month	Code walkthroughs / Unit testing
5	Functional impairment/loss: The problem will not resolve itself, but a "work around" can temporarily bypass the problem area until fixed without losing operation.	1 per week	System integration and test
6	Functional impairment/loss: The problem will not resolve itself, but a "work around" can temporarily bypass the problem area until fixed without losing operation.	1 per day	System integration and test
7	Functional impairment/loss: The problem will not resolve itself and no "work around" can bypass the problem. Functionality has either been impaired or lost but the product can still be used to some extent.	1 per shift	Installation and start-up
8	Functional impairment/loss: The problem will not resolve itself and no "work around" can bypass the problem. Functionality has either been impaired or lost but the product can still be used to some extent.	1 per hour	Installation and start-up
9	Product halts/process taken down/reboot required: The product is completely hung up, all functionality has been lost and system reboot is required.	1 per minute	Installation and start-up
10	Product halts/process taken down/reboot required: The product is completely hung up, all functionality has been lost and system reboot is required.	1+ per minute	Detectable only once "on line."

Table C.1: Sample Software FMEA Ratings [ReliaSoft (2003)].

C.2   Deming's 14 Points for Quality Improvement

#	Recommendation
1	Create constancy of purpose toward improvement of product and service, with the aim to become competitive and to stay in business, and to provide jobs.
2	Adopt the new philosophy. We are in a new economic age. Western management must awaken to the challenge, must learn their responsibilities, and take on leadership for change.
3	Cease dependence on inspection to achieve quality. Eliminate the need for inspection on a mass basis by building quality into the product in the first place.
4	End the practice of awarding business on the basis of price tag. Instead, minimize total cost. Move toward a single supplier for any one item, on a long-term relationship of loyalty and trust.
5	Improve constantly and forever the system of production and service, to improve quality and productivity, and thus constantly decrease costs.
6	Institute training on the job.
7	Institute leadership. The aim of supervision should be to help people and machines and gadgets to do a better job. Supervision of management is in need of overhaul, as well as supervision of production workers.
8	Drive out fear, so that everyone may work effectively for the company.
9	Break down barriers between departments. People in research, design, sales, and production must work as a team, to foresee problems of production and in use that may be encountered with the product or service.
10	Eliminate slogans, exhortations, and targets for the work force asking for zero defects and new levels of productivity. Such exhortations only create adversarial relationships, as the bulk of the causes of low quality and low productivity belong to the system and thus lie beyond the power of the work force.
11a	Eliminate work standards (quotas) on the factory floor. Substitute leadership.
11b	Eliminate management by objective. Eliminate management by numbers, numerical goals. Substitute leadership.
12a	Remove barriers that rob the hourly worker of his right to pride of workmanship. The responsibility of supervisors must be changed from sheer numbers to quality.
12b	Remove barriers that rob people in management and in engineering of their right to pride of workmanship. This means, inter alia, abolishment of the annual or merit rating and of management by objective.
13	Institute a vigorous program of education and self-improvement.
14	Put everybody in the company to work to accomplish the transformation. The transformation is everybody's job.

Table C.2: Deming's 14 Steps for Quality Improvement [Deming (2000)].

C.3 Crosby's 14 Steps for Quality Improvement

#	Recommendation
1	Management commitment: The upper management has to understand the (economic) importance of high quality and to communicate this attitude inside the organization.
2	Quality improvement team: Representatives from all organizational units (best: their heads) have to participate in a team effort to take the necessary actions.
3	Quality measurement: The company's measurement system has to be formalized and the results have to be published to everybody within the organization.
4	Cost of quality evaluation: The cost of poor quality has to be determined, in order to prioritize areas for improvements.
5	Quality awareness: Employees' attention has to be turned to measurement results and the costs of non-quality.
6	Corrective action: As quality issues and their causes are discovered, opportunities for correction have brought up to formulate corrective actions.
7	Ad hoc committee for zero defects: A team communicating to everyone that things should be done right the first time is installed.
8	Supervisor training: Managers of all levels are instructed on how to explain the different quality improvement steps to their employees.
9	Zero defects day: "Zero defects" (no errors) is the ultimate goal of a quality policy and a special event devoted to this goal will be a strong internal marketing tool.
10	Goal setting: Employees in the organization are encouraged to formulate specific quality goals.
11	Error cause removal: As a first step to actively involve employees, they are asked to describe any problem that causes them to commit errors on a one-page format.
12	Recognition: Employees successfully meeting their goals or otherwise well performing in the quality area should be awarded (non financial) incentives.
13	Quality councils: Quality managers should communicate regularly with each other to share their learnings and coordinate additional improvement steps.
14	Do it over again: After a typical duration of 12–18 months, the quality improvement program has to be relaunched to make it perpetual.

Table C.3: Crosby's 14 Steps for Quality Improvement [Crosby (1980)].

Bibliography

Ackoff, R. L. (1989). From Data to Wisdom. *J. Applied Systems Analysis*, 16, 3–9.

Adam, F. and O'Doherty, P. (2003). ERP Projects: Good or Bad for SMEs? In: Shanks et al. (2003a), 275–298.

Adelman, S., Moss, L. T., and Abai, M. (2005). *Data Strategy*. Upper Saddle River, NJ: Addison-Wesley.

AFOS (1996). *SAP Arbeit Management*. Braunschweig/Wiesbaden, Germany: Vieweg.

Agami, A. M. (2006). Reporting on Internal Control Over Financial Reporting. *CPA Journal*, November 2006.
URL: http://www.nysscpa.org/cpajournal/2006/1106/essentials/p32.htm [retrieved 2008-08-25].

Agassi, S. (2001). Enterprise Information Portals: Salvation of ERP? *EAI Journal*, February 2001, 38–41.

Agosta, L. (2005). Data Warehousing Lessons Learned: Trends in Data Quality. *DM Review Online*, February 2005.
URL: http://www.dmreview.com/portals/portalarticle.cfm?articleId=1018111&topicId=230005 [retrieved 2007-10-16].

Aiken, P. (1996). *Data Reverse Engineering – Slaying the Legacy Dragon*. New York et al.: McGraw-Hill.

Aiken, P. (2002). Enterprise Resource Planning (ERP) Considerations. *ittoolbox.com*, 2004-11-10.
URL: http://erp.ittoolbox.com/documents/academic-articles/enterprise-resource-planning-considerations-3167 [retrieved 2007-10-14].

Al-Najjar, B. and Kans, M. (2006). A Model to Identify Relevant Data for Problem Tracing and Maintenance Cost-Effective Decisions: A Case Study. *Int. J. Productivity and Performance Management*, 55(8), 616–637.

Alexander, S. (2007). Bessere Datenqualität ist oft ein bloßes Lippenbekenntnis. *COMPUTERWOCHE.de*, 2007-11-15.
URL: http://www.computerwoche.de/produkte_technik/software/1848955/ [retrieved 2007-12-09].

Alexander, S. (2008). Stammdaten deutscher Firmen strotzen vor Fehlern. *COMPUT-ERWOCHE.de*, 2008-11-18.
URL: http://www.computerwoche.de/1879225 [retrieved 2008-11-24].

Alter, S. (2002). *Information Systems: The Foundation of E-Business*. Upper Saddle River, NJ: Pearson Education, 4th edition.

Americas' SAP Users' Group (2008). ASUG: What We Do.
URL: http://www.asug.com/Home/WhatWeDo.aspx [retrieved 2008-07-07].

Aral, S., Brynjolfsson, E., and Wu, D. (2005). Does Process Enabling IT Matter? Measuring the Business Value of Extended Enterprise Systems. In: *Workshop on Information Systems and Economics (WISE 2005)*. University of California, Irvine, CA.
URL: http://clients.pixelloom.info/WISE2005/papers/165.pdf [retrieved 2007-10-14].

Arlt, T. (2007). Wie sich Datenqualität durch eine SOA steigern lässt. *COMPUTER-WOCHE.de*, 2007-11-26.
URL: http://www.computerwoche.de/produkte_technik/software/1848955/ [retrieved 2007-12-09].

Arnold, S. E. (1992). Information Manufacturing: The Road to Database Quality. *Database*, 15(5), 32–39.

ARTS (1997). ARTS Data Model.
URL: http://www.nrf-arts.org/DataModelHome.htm [retrieved 2007-07-24].

Astrahan, M. M., Blasgen, M. W., Chamberlin, D. D., Eswaran, K. P., Gray, J. N., Griffiths, P. P., King, W. F., Lorie, R. A., McJones, P. R., Mehl, J. W., Putzolu, G. R., Traiger, I. L., Wade, B. W., and Watson, V. (1976). System R: Relational Approach to Database Management. *ACM Trans. Database Systems*, 1(2), 97–137.

Atkins, M. E. (2003). The Hidden Role of Data Quality in E-Commerce Success. *Technology Evaluation Centers*, 2003-01-04.
URL: http://www.technologyevaluation.com/Research/ResearchHighlights/eCommerce/2003/01/research_notes/MI_EC_XMA_01_04_03_1.asp [retrieved 2004-03-16].

Austin, R. D. (2001). Surviving Enterprise Systems: Adaptive Strategies for Managing Your Largest IT Investments. *Cutter Information*, April 2001.
URL: http://www.cutter.com/freestuff/bitr0104.html [retrieved 2003-05-06].

Bagchi, S., Bai, X., and Kalagnanam, J. (2006). Data Quality Management using Business Process Modeling. In: *SCC '06: Proceedings of the IEEE International Conference on Services Computing*, 398–405. Washington, DC: IEEE Computer Society.

Ballou, D. P., Madnick, S. E., and Wang, R. Y. (2004). Assuring Information Quality. *J. Management Information Systems*, 20, 9–11.

Ballou, D. P. and Tayi, G. K. (1989). Methodology for Allocating Resources for Data Quality Enhancement. *Commun. ACM*, 32(3), 320–329.

Ballou, D. P. and Tayi, G. K. (1999). Enhancing Data Quality in Data Warehouse Environments. *Commun. ACM*, 42(1), 73–78.

Bancroft, N. H., Seip, H., and Sprengel, A. (1998). *Implementing SAP R/3: How to Introduce a Large System Into a Large Organization*. Greenwich, CT: Manning, 2nd edition.

Bank, J. (2000). *The Essence of Total Quality Management*. Essex: Pearson Education, 2nd edition.

Bank for International Settlements (2004). Basel II: International Convergence of Capital Measurement and Capital Standards: a Revised Framework.
URL: http://www.bis.org/publ/bcbs107.htm [retrieved 2007-12-26].

Bartholomew, D. J., Steele, F., Moustaki, I., and Galbraith, J. I. (2002). *The Analysis and Interpretation of Multivariate Data for Social Scientists*. Boca Raton, FL: CRC Press.

Basu, V., Hartono, E., Lederer, A. L., and Sethi, V. (2002). The Impact of Organizational Commitment, Senior Management Involvement, and Team Involvement on Strategic Information Systems Planning. *Information & Management*, 39(6), 513–524.
URL: http://www.sciencedirect.com/science/article/B6VD0-45F6640-7/1/66fbe1c0fff768d400a1d84543c887f5 [retrieved 2008-04-14].

Batini, C. and Scannapieco, M. (2006). *Data Quality: Concepts, Methodologies and Techniques*. Berlin/Heidelberg, Germany: Springer.

Bayer, M. (2006). CeBIT: SAP lässt Kleinunternehmen links liegen. *COMPUTER-WOCHE.de*, 39, 12.
URL: http://www.computerwoche.de/573266 [retrieved 2007-09-10].

Begley, J., Gao, Y., and Cheng, Q. (2007). The Impact of the Sarbanes-Oxley Act on Information Quality in Capital Markets. *SSRN*. 2007-08-22.
URL: http://ssrn.com/abstract=1008986.

Belshé, K. and Shewry, S. (2004). The ADAP Files: Data Quality Management from A to Z.
URL: http://www.dhs.ca.gov/AIDS/Reports/PDF/ADAPFilesDataQMfromAtoZ1004.pdf.

Benjamini, Y. and Hochberg, Y. (1995). Controlling the False Discovery Rate: a Practical and Powerful Approach to Multiple Testing. *J. the Royal Statistical Society*, 57(1), 289–300.

Betts, M. (2001a). Data Quality Should be a Boardroom Issue. *Computerworld*, 2001-12-17.
URL: http://www.computerworld.com/softwaretopics/erp/story/0,10801,66636,00.html [retrieved 2003-10-15].

Betts, M. (2001b). Dirty Data. *Computerworld*, 2001-12-17.
URL: http://www.computerworld.com/softwaretopics/erp/story/0,
10801,66618,00.html [retrieved 2003-10-15].

Betts, M. (2002). Data Quality: The Cornerstone of CRM. *Computerworld*, 2002-02-18.
URL: http://www.computerworld.com/softwaretopics/crm/story/0,
10801,68270,00.html [retrieved 2008-07-16].

Beuthner, A. (2005). Logistik-Tools erzwingen manuelle Eingriffe. *Computer Zeitung*, 14, 10.

Bibawi, E. L. and Nicoletti, C. (2005). Erste Erfahrungen mit Sarbanes-Oxley Section 404. *Der Schweizer Treuhänder*, 6–7, 431–436.

Bisong, S. M. (2003). Federal Agencies Subject to Data Quality Act. *FindLaw.com*.
URL: http://library.lp.findlaw.com/articles/file/00312/008569/
title/features [retrieved 2005-03-29].

Bjorlin, C. (2009). ERP consolidation can cut IT costs, but a broader business case is necessary. *TechTarget.com*.
URL: http://searchsap.techtarget.com/news/article/0,289142,
sid21_gci1360286,00.html [retrieved 2007-10-14].

Bleiholder, J. and Schmid, J. (2008). Datenintegration und Deduplizierung. In: Hildebrand et al. (2008), 123–142.

Bobrowski, M., Marré, M., and Yankelevich, D. (1998). A Software Engineering View of Data Quality. In: *Proceedings of the 2nd International Software Quality Week (Europe)*. Brussels, Belgium.
URL: http://citeseer.ist.psu.edu/277636.html.

Bobrowski, M., Marré, M., and Yankelevich, D. (1999). A Homogeneous Framework to Measure Data Quality. In: Lee, Y. W. and Tayi, G. K., (eds.), *Proceedings of the Fourth Conference on Information Quality (IQ 1999), MIT*. Cambridge, MA.

Boenner, A., Herde, G., and Riedl, M. (2006). "STAAN: Standard Audit Analysis" – Bericht über angewandte Forschung im Bereich der digitalen Unterstützung von Prüfungshandlungen in der Konzernrevision eines Großunternehmens. *Interne Revision*, 6, 256–260.

Boenner, A., Herde, G., and Riedl, M. (2007). "STAAN: Standard Audit Analysis" – Bericht über angewandte Forschung im Bereich der digitalen Unterstützung von Prüfungshandlungen in der Konzernrevision eines Großunternehmens (II). *Interne Revision*, 3, 118–122.

Bortz, J. and Döring, N. (2003). *Forschungsmethoden und Evaluation für Human- und Sozialwissenschaftler*. Berlin, Germany, et al.: Springer, third edition.

Bosavage, J. (2005). Getting Quality Data Now. *Intelligent Enterprise*, 2005-09-15.
URL: http://www.intelligententerprise.com/showArticle.jhtml?
articleID=170703523 [retrieved 2007-06-22].

Bouzeghoub, M. and Peralta, V. (2004). A Framework for Analysis of Data Freshness. In: *IQIS '04: Proceedings of the 2004 international workshop on Information quality in information systems*, 59–67. New York: ACM Press.

Boyle, G. and Grace-Webb, E. (2007). Sarbanes-Oxley and its Aftermath: A Review of the Evidence.
URL: http://www.iscr.co.nz/f380,10587/10587_Sarbanes-Oxley01_201107.pdf [retrieved 2008-04-20].

Brackett, M. H. (1994). *Data Sharing Using a Common Data Architecture*. New York et al.: Wiley.

Brackett, M. H. (2000). *Data Resource Quality: Turning Bad Habits into Good Practices*. Boston, MA, et al.: Addison-Wesley.

Brady, J. A., Monk, E. F., and Wagner, B. J. (2001). *Concepts in Enterprise Resource Planning*. Boston, MA: Thomson Learning.

Brand, H. (1999). *SAP R/3-Einführung mit ASAP: Technische Implementierung von SAP R/3 planen und realisieren*. Bonn, Germany: Addison-Wesley.

Brehm, L., Heinzl, A., and Lynne, M. (2001). Tailoring ERP Systems: A Spectrum of Choices and their Implications. In: *Proceedings of the 34th Hawaii International Conference on System Sciences*. Maui, Hawaii: IEEE Computer Society.

Broeckelmann, R. G. (1999). *Inventory Classification Innovation*. Boca Raton, FL, et al.: St. Lucie Press / APICS.

Brooks, R. B. and Wilson, L. W. (1995). *Inventory Record Accuracy – Unleashing the Power of Cycle Counting*. New York et al.: John Wiley & Sons.

Brown, D. (2004). Application Transformation – Leveraging Existing IT Assets to Build Competitive Advantage. *IBM*.
URL: ftp://ftp.software.ibm.com/software/zseries/pdf/DHBrownApplicationTransformation.pdf [retrieved 2007-11-29].

Brown, M. L. and Kros, J. F. (2003). Data Mining and the Impact of Missing Data. *Industrial Management & Data Systems*, 103(8), 611–621.

Brynjolfsson, E. (1993). The Productivity Paradox of Information Technology. *Commun. ACM*, 36(12), 66–77.

Buck-Emden, R. (1999). *Die Technologie des SAP R/3 System: Basis für betriebswirtschaftliche Anwendungen*. Bonn, Germany, et al.: Addison-Wesley, 4th edition.

Buneman, P., Khanna, S., and Tan, W. C. (2001). Why and Where: A Characterization of Data Provenance. In: *ICDT '01: Proceedings of the 8th International Conference on Database Theory*, 316–330. London, UK: Springer.

Burgess, T. (1996). Modelling Quality-Cost Dynamics. *Int. J. Quality & Reliability Management*, 13(3), 8–26.

Burner, M. (2004). Service Orientation and Its Role in Your Connected Systems Strategy. *Microsoft MSDN*.
URL: http://msdn2.microsoft.com/en-us/library/ms954826.aspx
[retrieved 2005-11-07].

Business Objects (2007). Business Objects Data Quality XI for SAP Solutions.
URL: http://www.businessobjects.com/pdf/products/dataquality/sap.pdf [retrieved 2008-04-22].

Business Objects (2008). Business Objects: Data Quality Solutions for SAP.
URL: http://www.businessobjects.com/solutions/for_your_data/sap.asp [retrieved 2008-04-22].

Business Objects/SAP (2006). Information Workers Beware: Your Business Data Can't Be Trusted.
URL: http://www.sap.com/about/newsroom/businessobjects/20060625_005028.epx [retrieved 2009-05-10].

Bustard, D., Kawalek, P., and Norris, M., (eds.) (2000). *Systems Modeling for Business Process Improvement*. Norwood, MA: Artech-House.

Campbell, B. (2000). System Dynamics in Information Systems Analysis: An Evaluation Case Study. In: Bustard et al. (2000), 33–46.

Carlo, M. (2002). Enterprise Software Has to Fit Like a Good Suit. *Advanced Manufacturing Magazine*, May 2002.
URL: http://www.advancedmanufacturing.com/index.php?option=com_staticxt&staticfile=erpsoftware.htm&Itemid=64.

Carr, N. G. (2003). IT Doesn't Matter. *Harvard Business Review*, 81(5), 41–49.

Carson, C. S. (2001). Toward a Framework for Assessing Data Quality. Working Paper WP/01/25. Washington, DC: International Monetary Fund.

Centrale für Coorganisation (2003). 100% Stammdatenqualität: SINFOS-Offensive zur Qualitätssicherung.
URL: http://www.ccg.de/ccg/Inhalt/e4/e710/ [retrieved 2003-12-01].

Chamberlin, D. D. and Boyce, R. F. (1974). SEQUEL: A Structured English Query Language. In: *FIDET '74: Proceedings of the 1974 ACM SIGFIDET Workshop on Data Description, Access and Control*, 249–264. New York: ACM.

Chanana, V. and Koronios, A. (2007). Data Quality Through Business Rules. In: *International Conference on Information and Communication Technology (ICICT 2007), 7–9 March 2007, Dhaka, Bangladesh*, 262–265. IEEE.

Chen, P. P.-S. (1976). The Entity-Relationship Model – Toward a Unified View of Data. *ACM Trans. Database Systems*, 1(1), 9–36.

Cherbakov, L., Galambos, G., Harishankar, R., Kalyana, S., and Rackham, G. (2005). Impact of Service Orientation at the Business Level. *IBM Systems Journal*, 44(4), 653–668.

Codd, E. F. (1970). A Relational Model of Data for Large Shared Data Banks. *Commun. ACM*, 13(6), 377–387.

Codd, E. F. (1990). *The Relational Model for Database Management: Version 2.* Boston, MA: Addison-Wesley Longman Publishing.

Cotteleer, M. (2002). ERP's Payoffs and Pitfalls. *TechTarget.com*, 2002-10-23. URL: http://searchcio.techtarget.com/originalContent/0,289142, sid19_gci858624,00.html [retrieved 2007-10-14].

Council of Europe (1981). Convention for the Protection of Individuals with regard to Automatic Processing of Personal Data. URL: http://conventions.coe.int/treaty/en/Treaties/Html/108.htm [retrieved 2005-02-25].

Crawford, C. H., Bate, G. P., Cherbakov, L., Holley, K., and Tsocanos, C. (2005). Toward an on Demand Service-Oriented Architecture. *IBM Systems Journal*, 44(1), 81–107.

Crosby, P. B. (1980). *Quality Is Free*. New York et al.: Mentor, reprint edition.

Cui, Y. and Widom, J. (2001). Lineage Tracing for General Data Warehouse Transformations. In: Apers, P. M. G., Atzeni, P., Ceri, S., Paraboschi, S., Ramamohanarao, K., and Snodgrass, R. T., (eds.), *VLDB 2001, Proceedings of 27th International Conference on Very Large Data Bases, September 11–14, 2001, Roma, Italy*, 471–480. Morgan Kaufmann.

Currie, W. L. and Hlupic, V. (2000). Simulation Modeling and Change Management Panaceas: The Missing Link. In: Bustard et al. (2000), 13–31.

Date, C. J. (1995). *An Introduction to Database Systems*. Reading, MA, et al.: Addison-Wesley, 6th edition.

Davenport, T. H. (1995). SAP: Big Change Comes in Big Packages. *CIO Magazine*, 1995-10-15. URL: http://www.cio.com/archive/101595_davenpor.html.

Davenport, T. H. (1999a). Putting the Enterprise into the Enterprise System. In: *On the Business Value of IT*, 159–186. Boston, MA: Harvard Business School Press.

Davenport, T. H. (1999b). Saving IT's Soul: Human-Centered Information Management. In: *On the Business Value of IT*, 1–33. Boston, MA: Harvard Business School Press.

Davenport, T. H. (2000). *Mission Critical: Realizing the Promise of Enterprise Systems*. Boston, MA: Harvard Business School Press.

Davenport, T. H. and Brooks, J. D. (2004). Enterprise Systems and the Supply Chain. *J. Enterprise Information Management*, 17(1), 8–19.

Davenport, T. H., Harris, J. G., and Cantrell, S. (2004). Enterprise Systems and Ongoing Process Change. *Business Process Management Journal*, 10(1), 16–26.

Davenport, T. H. and Prusak, L. (1998). *Working Knowledge.* Boston, MA: Harvard Business School Press.

David, K. (2006). Centralize, Harmonize, and Distribute Your Master Data with SAP NetWeaver Master Data Management (MDM). *SAP Professional Journal,* 8(3). URL: http://www.sappro.com/article.cfm?id=3421 [retrieved 2007-09-10].

de Fries, D., Seidl, J., and Windheuser, U. (2001). Datenqualität: Ein unterschätzter Erfolgsfaktor. *ExperPraxis,* 2001/2002, 92–97.

Deis, P. (2006). Lean and ERP – Can They Co-Exist? URL: http://www.articlesbase.com/strategic-planning-articles/lean-and-erp-can-they-coexist-47604.html [retrieved 2007-02-03].

DeLone, W. and McLean, E. (1992). Information Systems Success: The Quest for the Dependent Variable. *Information Systems Research,* 3(1), 60–95.

Deming, W. E. (2000). *Out of the Crisis.* Cambridge, MA, et al.: MIT Press, reprint edition.

Deutsch, C. (1998). Software That Can Make a Grown Company Cry. *New York Times,* 1998-11-08. URL: http://www.nytimes.com/library/tech/98/11/biztech/articles/08soft.html [retrieved 2007-10-14].

Deutsche Gesellschaft für Informations- und Datenqualität (2007). Informationsqualität – Definitionen, Dimensionen und Begriffe. URL: http://www.dgiq.de/_data/pdf/IQ-Definition/IQ-Definitionen.pdf [retrieved 2008-03-03].

Deutschsprachige SAP-Anwendergruppe (2008). DSAG: Zusammenarbeit mit SAP. URL: http://www.dsag.de/dsagcorp/ueber-dsag/zusammenarbeit-mit-sap.html [retrieved 2008-07-07].

Dijcks, J.-P. (2004). Integrating Data Quality into Your Data Warehouse Architecture. URL: http://www.sigs-datacom.de/sd/news/document?PID=234.

Dittrich, J., Mertens, P., and Hau, M. (2000). *Dispositionsparameter von SAP R/3-PP: Einstellhinweise, Wirkungen, Nebenwirkungen.* Braunschweig/Wiesbaden, Germany: Vieweg, 2nd edition.

Dressler, S. (2004). *Strategy, Organization and Performance Management.* Boca Raton, FL: Universal Publishers, e-book edition.

Dubois, L. (2005). Web Services: Pipes in Need of Filters. *BusinessIntelligence.com.* URL: http://www.businessintelligence.com/ex/asp/code.116/xe/article.htm [retrieved 2005-08-20].

Duff, A. (2005). Master Data Management Roles – Their Part in Data Quality Implementation. In: Naumann et al. (2005).

Dyché, J. (2007). A Data Governance Manifesto: Designing and Deploying Sustainable Data Governance.
URL: http://www.bitpipe.com/data/detail?id=1183551857_231&type= RES&asrc=SS_SRCH [retrieved 2008-08-25].

Eckerson, W. W. (2002). Data Quality and the Bottom Line (Excerpt from TDWI Research Report). *The Data Warehouse Institute.*
URL: http://www.tdwi.org/research/display.aspx?ID=6589 [retrieved 2008-06-23].

Eckerson, W. W. and Watson, H. (2000). Harnessing Customer Information for Strategic Advantage: Technical Challenges and Business Solutions (TDWI Industry Study 2000). *The Data Warehouse Institute.*
URL: http://www.dw-institute.com/download/2000_Industry_Study. pdf [retrieved 2004-04-17].

El-Haik, B. and Roy, D. M. (2005). *Service Design for Six Sigma: A Roadmap for Excellence.* Hoboken, NJ: Wiley-Interscience.

Endl, R. (2004). *Regelbasierte Entwicklung betrieblicher Informationssysteme – Gestaltung flexibler Informationssysteme durch explizite Modellierung der Geschäftslogik (Dissertation an der Universität Bern).* Lohmar-Köln, Germany: Josef Eul.

English, L. (1999a). Data Cleansing in the Data Warehouse. *DM Review Online,* December 1999.
URL: http://www.dmreview.com/issues/19991201/1669-1.html [retrieved 2007-10-16].

English, L. P. (1999b). *Improving Data Warehouse and Business Information Quality: Methods for Reducing Costs and Increasing Profits.* New York et al.: Wiley.

English, L. P. (2002). Mistakes to Avoid if Your Data Warehouse is to Deliver Quality Information. *InfoImpact.*
URL: http://www.infoimpact.com/articles/DMR_6.02IQinDW1.pdf [retrieved 2003-12-06].

English, L. P. and Perez, A. (2003). Plain English About Information Quality: The Information Quality Act: Mandate for IQ. *DM Review Online,* February 2003.

Eppler, M. J. (2003). *Managing Information Quality – Increasing the Value of Information in Knowledge-intensive Products and Processes.* Berlin, Germany, et al.: Springer.

Erl, T. (2005). The Principles of Service-Orientation. *SOA World Magazine,* 2005-10-29.
URL: http://webservices.sys-con.com/read/136190.htm.

Esteves, J. M. and Pastor, J. A. (1999). An ERP Lifecycle-Based Research Agenda. In: *Proceedings of the First International Workshop in Enterprise Management and Resource Planning: Methods, Tools and Architectures (EMRPS'99), Venice, Italy,* 359–371.

Eswaran, K. P., Gray, J. N., Lorie, R. A., and Traiger, I. L. (1976). The Notions of Consistency and Predicate Locks in a Database System. *Commun. ACM*, 19(11), 624–633.

European Committee for Standardization (2000). *ISO 9000:2000 Quality Management Systems – Fundamentals and Vocabulary*. Geneva, Switzerland: CEN.

European Parliament and Council (1995). Directive 95/46/EC on the Protection of Individuals with Regard to the Processing of Personal Data and on the Free Movement of such Data.
URL: http://europa.eu.int/comm/internal_market/privacy/docs/ 95-46-ce/dir1995-46_part2_en.pdf [retrieved 2005-02-14].

Evans, J. R. and Lindsay, W. M., (eds.) (2002). *The Management and Control of Quality*. Cincinnati, OH: South-Western College Publishing, 5th edition.

Ferengul, C. (2006). Error In, Error Out: Safeguarding the Quality of the Data Warehouse. *DM Direct Newsletter*, 2006-07-14.
URL: http://www.dmreview.com/portals/portalarticle.cfm? articleId=1059121&topicId=230005 [retrieved 2007-10-16].

Ferguson, M. (2007). Managing and Integrating Data in an SAP Environment (DataFlux White Paper WP040).
URL: http://whitepapers.theregister.co.uk/ [retrieved 2008-10-08].

Ferstl, O. K. and Sinz, E. J. (2005). *Grundlagen der Wirtschaftsinformatik*. München, Germany: Oldenbourg.

Fink, A. (1995). *How to Ask Survey Questions*. Thousand Oaks, CA, et al.: Sage.

Finney, S. and Corbett, M. (2007). ERP Implementation: a Compilation and Analysis of Critical Success Factors. *Business Process Management Journal*, 13(3), 329–347.

Fisher, C. W. and Kingma, B. R. (2001). Criticality of Data Quality as Exemplified in Two Disasters. *Information & Management*, 39, 109–116.

Fowler, F. J. (1995). *Improving Survey Questions: Design and Evaluation*. Thousand Oaks, CA, et al.: Sage.

Frank, L. (2004). Architecture for Integration of Distributed ERP Systems and E-Commerce Systems. *Industrial Management & Data Systems*, 104(5), 418–429.

Fryer, B. (1999). The ROI Challenge – Return On Investment. *CFO Magazine*, 9, 85–90.

Fuchs, S. K. (2007). SAP NetWeaver in der Praxis – Wie gut bewährt sich der Technologie-Stack in der praktischen Arbeit? *Informatik-Spektrum*, 30(6), 428–433.

FUZZY! Informatik AG (2004). FUZZY! SAP Connector – The Easy Connection Between FUZZY! Products and Your SAP Application.
URL: http://www.fazi.de/uploads/media/20040816_sap_connector_ eng.pdf [retrieved 2006-03-12].

Galoppin, L. and Caems, S. (2007). *Managing Organizational Change during SAP Implementations*. Bonn, Germany: SAP Press.

Galway, L. A. and Hanks, C. H. (1996). *Data Quality Problems in Army Logistics: Classification, Examples, and Solutions*. Santa Monica, CA: RAND.

Gardener, M. (2006). Using R for Statistical Analyses.
URL: http://www.gardenersown.co.uk/education/lectures/r/nonparam.htm#kruskal [retrieved 2007-09-08].

Gartner Group (2005). Gartner Total Cost of Ownership.
URL: http://amt.gartner.com/TCO/MoreAboutTCO.htm [retrieved 2007-12-25].

Gartner Group (2007). The Real-Time Enterprise.
URL: http://www.gartner.com/pages/story.php.id.2632.s.8.jsp [retrieved 2007-02-19].

Gartner Group (2008). Gartner Says Organisations Must Establish Data Stewardship Roles to Improve Data Quality.
URL: http://www.gartner.com/it/page.jsp?id=589207 [retrieved 2008-10-03].

Garvin, D. A. (1984). What Does 'Product Quality' Really Mean? *Sloan Management Review*, 26(1), 25–43.

Garvin, D. A. (1987). Competing on the Eight Dimensions of Quality. *Harvard Business Review*, 65(6), 101–109.

Gasser, U. (2003). Information Quality and the Law, or, How to Catch a Difficult Horse. Technical report. Berkman Center for Internet & Society Research.
URL: http://ssrn.com/abstract=487945.

Gebhardt, M., Jarke, M., Jeusfeld, M., Quix, C., and Sklorz, S. (1998). Tools for Data Warehouse Quality. In: *Proceedings of the 10th International Conference on Scientific and Statistical Database Management*, 229–232. Capri, Italy.

Geiger, J. G. (2007). The Role of the Data Model in Quality Management. *Information Management Magazine*, March 2007.
URL: http://www.information-management.com/issues/20070301/1076530-1.html [retrieved 2009-08-30].

Genoud, P. (2005). Gestion de la qualité des données.
URL: http://www.sieng.ch/blobs/documents_show.php?id=785 [retrieved 2008-07-16].

Gitlow, H. S., Levine, D. M., and Popovich, E. A. (2006). *Design for Six Sigma for Green Belts and Champions: Applications for Service Operations – Foundations, Tools, DMADV, Cases, and Certification (Six Sigma)*. Upper Saddle River, NJ: Prentice Hall.

Goebbels, S. and Jakob, R. (2004). *Geschäftsprozess-FMEA: Fehlermöglichkeits- und Einfluss-Analyse für IT-gestützte Geschäftsprozesse*. Düsseldorf, Germany: Symposion.

Gonzales, M. L. (2005). Mitigate Business Intelligence Project Risks With Rule-Based Audits and Proof-of-Concepts.
URL: http://wp.bitpipe.com/resource/org_967761031_299/SyncsortBIWhitePaper_edp.pdf [retrieved 2005-08-16].

Grabski, S. V., Leech, S. A., and Lu, B. (2003). Enterprise System Implementation Risks and Controls. In: Shanks et al. (2003a), 135–156.

Gray, J. (1981). The Transaction Concept: Virtues and Limitations. In: *Proceedings of the Seventh International Conference on Very Large Databases*, 144–154. Cannes, France: IEEE Computer Society.

Gregor, S., Hart, D., and Martin, N. (2007). Enterprise Architectures: Enablers of Business Strategy and IS/IT Alignment in Government. *Information Technology & People*, 20(2), 96–120.

Groth, P., Jiang, S., Miles, S., Munroe, S., Tan, V., Tsasakou, S., and Moreau, L. (2006). An Architecture for Provenance Systems. Technical report. Southampton, UK: University of Southampton.
URL: http://eprints.ecs.soton.ac.uk/13216/1/provenanceArchitecture10.pdf [retrieved 2008-04-20].

Gulledge, T., Sommer, R., and Simon, G. (2004). Analyzing Convergence Alternatives Across Existing SAP Solutions. *Industrial Management & Data Systems*, 104(9), 722–734.

Gulledge, T. R., Sommer, R. A., Kirchmer, M., and Simon, G. (2002). Analyzing Maintenance Collaboration in Multiple Overlapping SAP Instances. In: Jagdev, H., Wortmann, J. C., and Pels, H. J., (eds.), *Collaborative Systems for Production Management, IFIP TC5/WG5.7 Eighth International Conference on Advances in Production Management Systems, September 8-13, 2002, Eindhoven, The Netherlands*, volume 257 of *IFIP Conference Proceedings*, 587–601. Kluwer.

Gunson, J. and de Blasis, J.-P. (2001). The Place and Key Success Factors of Enterprise Resource Planning (ERP) in the New Paradigms of Business Management. Technical Report 2001.14. Geneva, Switzerland: HEC Genève, Université de Genève.
URL: http://hec.info.unige.ch/recherches_publications/cahiers/2001/2001.14.pdf [retrieved 2003-05-06].

Gupta, A. (2000). Enterprise Resource Planning: The Emerging Organizational Value Systems. *Industrial Management & Data Systems*, 100(3), 114–118.

Hack, S. and Lindemann, M. A. (2007). *Enterprise SOA einführen*. Bonn, Germany: Galileo Press.

Hammer, M. (1990). Reengineering Work: Don't Automate, Obliterate. *Harvard Business Review*, Reprint 90406.

Hanscome, R. (2003). Tier I Enterprise Resource Planning (ERP) – METAspectrum Market Summary. *METAspectrum*, 32.0.
URL: http://www.netsense.info/downloads/ERP_Meta_Report.pdf.

Harreld, H. (2000). 10 Tips for ERP Success. *Federal Computer Week*, 2000-05-29.
URL: http://www.fcw.com/print/6_37/news/70562-1.html
[retrieved 2007-10-14].

Harte-Hanks Trillium Software (2006). Harte-Hanks Trillium Software 2005/6 Data Survey.

Hawking, P., Stein, A., and Foster, S. (2004). Revisiting ERP Systems: Benefit Realisation. In: *HICSS '04: Proceedings of the Proceedings of the 37th Annual Hawaii International Conference on System Sciences (HICSS'04) – Track 8*, 80227.1. Washington, DC: IEEE Computer Society.

Hayman, L. (2000). ERP in the Internet Economy. *Information Systems Frontiers*, 2(2), 137–139.

Herbst, H. (1997). *Business Rule-Oriented Conceptual Modeling (Dissertation an der Universität Bern)*. Heidelberg, Germany: Physica.

Herbst, H. and Knolmayer, G. (1994). Ansätze zur Klassifikation von Geschäftsregeln. Arbeitsbericht 46. Bern, Switzerland: Institut für Wirtschaftsinformatik der Universität Bern.
URL: http://www.ie.iwi.unibe.ch/publikationen/berichte/.

Herzog, T. N., Scheuren, F. J., and Winkler, W. E. (2007). *Data Quality and Record Linkage Techniques*. New York: Springer.

Hevner, A. R., Berndt, D. J., and Studnicki, J. (2000). Strategic Information Systems Planning with Box Structures. In: *Proceedings of the 33th Hawaii International Conference on System Sciences*, volume 04, 4005. Maui, Hawaii: IEEE Computer Society.

Hildebrand, K., Gebauer, M., Hinrichs, H., and Mielke, M., (eds.) (2008). *Daten- und Informationsqualität*. Wiesbaden, Germany: Vieweg + Teubner.

Hildenbrand, B. (2006). Datenqualität als Wettbewerbsvorteil. *Neue Zürcher Zeitung*, 112, 65.

Holland, C. P. and Light, B. (1999). A Critical Success Factors Model For ERP Implementation. *IEEE Software*, May/June 1999, 30–36.

Holsapple, C. W. and Sena, M. P. (2005). ERP Plans and Decision-Support Benefits. *Decision Support Systems*, 38(4), 575–590.

Hornberger, W. and Schneider, J. (2000). *Sicherheit und Datenschutz mit SAP-Systemen: Massnahmen für die betriebliche Praxis*. Bonn, Germany: Galileo Press.

Huang, K.-T., Lee, Y. W., and Wang, R. Y. (1999). *Quality Information and Knowledge*. Upper Saddle River, NJ: Prentice Hall.

Hunton, J. E., Lippincott, B., and Reck, J. L. (2003). Enterprise Resource Planning Systems: Comparing Firm Performance of Adopters and Nonadopters. *Int. J. Accounting Information Systems*, 4, 165–184.

Illa, X. B., Franch, X., and Pastor, J. A. (2000). Formalising ERP Selection Criteria. In: *IWSSD '00: Proceedings of the 10th International Workshop on Software Specification and Design*, 115–122. Washington, DC: IEEE Computer Society.

Imhoff, C. (2005). Failure of Data Warehouse Projects.
URL: http://www.b-eye-network.com/blogs/imhoff/archives/2005/03/failure_of%_data_1.php [retrieved 2007-12-25].

InfoImpact (2007). Info Impact Tools and Resources IQ Products.
URL: http://www.infoimpact.com/iqproducts.cfm [retrieved 2008-04-22].

Inmon, W. H. (1996). *Building the Data Warehouse*. New York et al.: John Wiley & Sons, second edition.

Institute of Internal Auditors (2004). The Role of Internal Auditing in Enterprise-wide Risk Management. 2004-09-29.
URL: http://www.theiia.org/download.cfm?file=283 [retrieved 2008-04-07].

International Business Machines Corp. (2009). WebSphere MQ .
URL: http://www-01.ibm.com/software/integration/wmq/ [retrieved 2009-03-15].

International Organization for Standardization (2006). *ISO/TS 19138:2006: Geographic information – Data quality measures*. Geneva, Switzerland: ISO.
URL: http://www.iso.org/iso/iso_catalogue/catalogue_tc/catalogue_detail.htm?csnumber=32556.

IT Governance Institute (2007). COBIT 4.1 Executive Summary.
URL: http://www.isaca.org/ContentManagement/ContentDisplay.cfm?ContentID=39073 [retrieved 2008-10-20].

itSMF International (2007). An Introductory Overview of ITIL V3.
URL: http://www.itsmfi.org/files/itSMF_ITILV3_Intro_Overview_0.pdf [retrieved 2008-10-20].

Jaccottet, B. (1997). *Client/Server-Architekturen: Konzepte und Bedeutung (Dissertation an der Universität Bern)*. Bern et al.: Lang.

Jarke, M. and Vassiliou, Y. (1997). Data Warehouse Quality: A Review of the DWQ Project. In: *Proceedings of the 2nd International Conference on Information Quality (IQ-97)*. Cambridge, MA.

Jay, R. (2008). *SAP NetWeaver Portal Technology: The Complete Reference*. New York: McGraw-Hill Osborne Media.

John, A., Meran, R., Roenpage, O., and Staudter, C. (2006). *Six Sigma+Lean Toolset – Verbesserungsprojekte erfolgreich durchführen*. Berlin/Heidelberg/New York: Springer.

Joint Commission (2004). Data Quality Specifications Manual for National Hospital Quality Measures, Version 1.01 (file name 5a_Data_Quality.pdf).
URL: http://www.jointcommission.org/NR/rdonlyres/
17D6D325-49E7-4E5F-AC09-498EC60432DB/0/
nhqmspecificationmanualv101pdf.zip [retrieved 2007-12-04].

Juran, J. M. (1988). *Juran on Planning for Quality*. New York et al.: Free Press.

Juran, J. M. (1992). *Juran on Quality by Design*. New York et al.: Free Press.

Kanaracus, C. (2008). Oracle Launches Data Integration Suite.
URL: http://www.infoworld.com/article/08/02/04/
Oracle-launches-Data-Integration-Suite_1.html.

Kaplan, D., Krishnan, R., Padman, R., and Peters, J. (1998). Assessing Data Quality in Accounting Information Systems. *Commun. ACM*, 41(2), 72–78.

Kaplan, R. S. and Norton, D. P. (1996). *The Balanced Scorecard: Translating Strategy into Action*. Cambridge, MA: Harvard Business School.

Kehrli, U. and Thiel, P. (2004). Auftragserfassung mit Einbildtransaktionen aus der Sicht Entwicklung und Vertrieb.
URL: http://www.guixt.ch/downloads/ESA.pdf [retrieved 2008-07-16].

Kelepouris, T., Pramatari, K., and Doukidis, G. (2007). RFID-enabled Traceability in the Food Supply Chain. *Industrial Management & Data Systems*, 107(2), 183–200.

Keller, G., Nüttgens, M., and Scheer, A.-W. (1992). Semantische Prozeßmodellierung auf der Grundlage "Ereignisgesteuerter Prozeßketten (EPK)". Technical report. Saarbrücken, Germany: Institut für Wirtschaftsinformatik der Universität Saarbrücken.
URL: http://www.iwi.uni-sb.de/Download/iwihefte/heft89.pdf
[retrieved 2007-09-10].

Kelley, C. (2003). Data stewards – Who is in Charge of Your Data? *Data Management Strategies*, 2003-12-17.
URL: http://www.itworld.com/nl/db_mgr/12172003/
[retrieved 2004-02-20].

Kelly, S. (1997). *Data Warehousing: the Route to Mass Customization*. Chichester, UK, et al.: Wiley.

Kennedy, T. (2007). Governance, Risk, and Compliance: What Data Governance Model Is Right for Your Company? *SAP Insider*, October–December 2007.

Kennerley, M. and Neely, A. (2001). Enterprise Resource Planning: Analysing the Impact. *Integrated Manufacturing Systems*, 12(2), 103–113.

Kent, W. (1987). *Data and Reality: Basic Assumptions in Data Processing Reconsidered.* Amsterdam, The Netherlands: North-Holland.

Kessler, K. (1999). Objektorientierte Anwendungsentwicklung mit der ABAP Workbench. In: Buck-Emden (1999), 171–232.

Khalil, O. E. M., Strong, D. M., Kahn, B. K., and Pipino, L. L. (1999). Teaching Information Quality in Information Systems Undergraduate Education. *Informing Science*, 2(3), 53–59.

Kim, W. (2002). On Three Major Holes in Data Warehousing Today. *J. Object Technology*, 1(4), 39–47.

Kimball, R., Reeves, L., Ross, M., and Thornthwaite, W. (1998). *The Data Warehouse Lifecycle Toolkit: Expert Methods for Designing, Developing, and Deploying Data Warehouses.* New York et al.: Wiley.

Klaus, H., Rosemann, M., and Gable, G. G. (2000). What is ERP? *Information Systems Frontiers*, 2(2), 141–162.

Klaus, O. (2005). *Geschäftsregeln zur Unterstützung des Supply Chain Managements (Dissertation an der Universität Bern).* Lohmar-Köln, Germany: Josef Eul.

Klier, M. (2008). Metriken zur Bewertung der Datenqualität – Konzeption und praktischer Nutzen. *Informatik-Spektrum*, 31(3), 223–236.

Königer, P. and Reithmayer, W. (1998). *Management unstrukturierter Informationen.* Frankfurt/M.: Campus.

Knolmayer, G., Mertens, P., and Zeier, A. (2001). *Supply Chain Management Based on SAP Systems: Order Management in Manufacturing Companies.* Berlin/Heidelberg/New York: Springer.

Knolmayer, G. and Röthlin, M. (2006). Quality of Material Master Data and Its Effect on the Usefulness of Distributed ERP Systems. In: Roddick, J. F., Benjamins, V. R., Cherfi, S. S.-S., Chiang, R. H. L., Claramunt, C., Elmasri, R., Grandi, F., Han, H., Hepp, M., Lytras, M. D., Misic, V. B., Poels, G., Song, I.-Y., Trujillo, J., and Vangenot, C., (eds.), *Advances in Conceptual Modeling – Theory and Practice, ER 2006 Workshops BP-UML, CoMoGIS, COSS, ECDM, OIS, QoIS, SemWAT, Tucson, AZ, November 6-9, 2006, Proceedings*, volume 4231 of *Lecture Notes in Computer Science*, 362–371. Springer.

Knolmayer, G., von Arb, R., and Zimmerli, C. (1997). *Erfahrungen mit der Einführung von SAP R/3 in Schweizer Unternehmungen.* Bern, Switzerland: Universität Bern, 3rd edition.

Knolmayer, G. F. and Myrach, T. (2000). Y2K: Much ado about nothing? *Informatik-Spektrum*, 23(2), 131–137.

Koll, S. (2007). Firmenweite Standardsoftware steht am Komplexitätspranger. *Computer Zeitung*, 38, 10.
URL: http://www.computerzeitung.de/loader?path=
/articles/2007038/31217080_ha_CZ.html&art=/articles/
2007038/31217080_ha_CZ.html&thes=8006,9829,8009&pid=
ee54f3c7-0de1-40f5-bb23-2cfdf022aee5 [retrieved 2007-10-14].

Lagace, M. (2004). Enron's Lessons for Managers. *TechTarget.com*, 2004-07-12.
URL: http://searchcio.techtarget.com/originalContent/0,289142,
sid19_gci992470,00.html [retrieved 2007-10-16].

Lais, S. (2003). Piecing Together the Data Picture. *Computerworld*, 2003-08-11.
URL: http://www.computerworld.com/databasetopics/data/story/0,
10801,83803,00.html [retrieved 2004-02-20].

Langenwalter, G. A. (2000). *Enterprise Resources Planning and Beyond: Integrating Your Entire Organization*. Boca Raton, FL: St. Lucie Press.

Laudon, K. C. and Laudon, J. P. (2000). *Management Information Systems: Organization and Technology in the Networked Enterprise*. Upper Saddle River, NJ: Prentice Hall, sixth edition.

Laurent, W. (2005). The Case for Data Stewardship. *DM Review Online*, 2005-02-01.
URL: http://www.dmreview.com/portals/portalarticle.cfm?
articleId=1018108&topicId=230005 [retrieved 2007-10-16].

Lawrence, D. B. (1999). *The Economic Value of Information*. New York et al.: Springer.

Lee, Y. W. and Strong, D. M. (2004). Knowing-Why About Data Processes and Data Quality. *J. Management Information Systems*, 20, 13–39.

Leitheiser, R. L. (2001). Data Quality in Health Care Data Warehouse Environments. In: *Proceedings of the 34th Hawaii International Conference on System Sciences*. Maui, Hawaii: IEEE.

Lesca, H. and Lesca, E. (1995). *Gestion de l'information, qualité de l'information et performance de l'entreprise*. Paris, France: Litec.

Levitin, A. V. and Redman, T. C. (1998). Data as a Resource: Properties, Implications, and Prescriptions. *Sloan Management Review*, 40(1), 89–101.

Lightfoot, E. and Salaway, G. (2003). A Different Kind of ERP: Extending and Renewing Legacy Systems.
URL: http://www.educause.edu/ir/library/pdf/ERB0305.pdf
[retrieved 2007-12-01].

Liu, L. and Chi, L. (2002). Evolutional Data Quality: A Theory-Specific View. In: Fisher, C. and Davidson, B. N., (eds.), *Proceedings of the Seventh International Conference on Information Quality (IQ 2002), MIT*, 292–304. Cambridge, MA.

Loos, P. and Theling, T. (2003). Marktübersicht zu ERP-Literatur. Working paper. Mainz, Germany: Universität Mainz, Institute for Information Systems & Management.
URL: http://isym.bwl.uni-mainz.de/publikationen/isym010.pdf [retrieved 2004-10-20].

Lorence, D. P. and Jameson, R. (2002). Adoption of Information Quality Management Practices in US Healthcare Organizations: A National Assessment. *Int. J. Quality & Reliability Management*, 19(6), 737–756.

Lorente, A. R. M., Rodriguez, A. G., and Rawlins, L. (1998). The Cumulative Effect of Prevention. *Int. J. Operations & Production Management*, 18(8), 727–739.

Loshin, D. (2001). *Enterprise Knowledge Management*. San Diego, CA, et al.: Morgan Kaufmann.

Loshin, D. (2003). ROI for Data Quality. *TDAN.com*, 2003-01-01.
URL: http://www.tdan.com/view-articles/5157/ [retrieved 2008-10-01].

Loshin, D. (2005). Developing Information Quality Metrics. *Information Management Magazine*, May 2005.
URL: http://www.information-management.com/issues/20050501/ 1026061-1.html [retrieved 2009-08-30].

Loshin, D. (2006). Monitoring Data Quality Performance Using Data Quality Metrics. *Informatica*, November 2006.
URL: http://www.informatica.com/downloads/infa_wp_dqmetrics_ dloshin_6741_web.pdf [retrieved 2007-12-01].

Loshin, D. (2008). Defining Data Quality Metrics. *DataFlux*, 2008-05-19.
URL: http://www.dataflux.com/dfBlog/?p=359 [retrieved 2009-08-29].

Lüssem, J. (2008). Organisatorische Ansiedlung eines Datenqualitätsmanagements. In: Hildebrand et al. (2008), 217–228.

Lynn, M. and Madison, R. (2000). The Role of ERP Software Revisited. *J. Accountancy*, 190, 104–105.

Ma, C., Chou, D. C., and Yen, D. C. (2000). Data Warehousing, Technology Assessment and Management. *Industrial Management & Data Systems*, 100(3), 125–135.

Madnick, S. and Zhu, H. (2006). Improving Data Quality Through Effective Use of Data Semantics. *Data & Knowledge Engineering*, 59(2), 460–475.

Marinos, G. (2004). Enticing but Dangerous: Assessing Web Services from a Data Quality Perspective. *DM Review Online*, May 2004.
URL: http://www.dmreview.com/article_sub.cfm?articleId=1002432 [retrieved 2004-05-12].

Markus, M. L., Axline, S., Petrie, D., and Tanis, C. (2003a). Learning from Experiences with ERP: Problems Encountered and Success Achieved. In: Shanks et al. (2003a), 23–55.

Markus, M. L., Petrie, D., and Axline, S. (2000). Bucking the Trends: What the Future May Hold for ERP Packages. *Information Systems Frontiers*, 2(2), 181–193.

Markus, M. L., Petrie, D., and Axline, S. (2003b). Continuity Versus Discontinuity: Weighing the Future for ERP Packages. In: Shanks et al. (2003a), 419–440.

Maydanchik, A. (1999). Challenges of Efficient Data Cleansing. *DM Review Online*, September 1999.
URL: http://www.dmreview.com/dmdirect/19990915/1403-1.html
[retrieved 2007-12-30].

Maydanchik, A. (2007). *Data Quality Assessment*. Bradley Beach, NJ: Technics Publications.

McGinnis, T. C. and Huang, Z. (2007). Rethinking ERP Success: A New Perspective from Knowledge Management and Continuous Improvement. *Information & Management*, 44(7), 626–634.

McKendrick, J. (2005). SOA = ERP but worse: fair analogy? *ZDNnet.com*, 2005-06-14.
URL: http://blogs.zdnet.com/service-oriented/?p=319
[retrieved 2007-12-30].

Meissner, G. (1997). *SAP – die heimliche Software-Macht*. München, Germany: Heyne Business, 2nd edition.

Mello, A. (2002). ERP Fundamentals. *ZDNnet.com*, 2002-02-07.
URL: http://techupdate.zdnet.com/techupdate/stories/main/0,
14179,2844319,00.html [retrieved 2004-04-21].

Melski, A., Thoroe, L., and Schumann, M. (2008). RFID – Radio Frequency Identification. *Informatik Spektrum*, 31(5), 469–473.

Melville, H. (1851). *Moby-Dick; or, The Whale*. New York: Harper & Brothers.
URL: http://www.gutenberg.org/ebooks/2701.

Mende, U. (1998). *Softwareentwicklung für R/3 – Data Dictionary, ABAP/4, Schnittstellen*. Berlin/Heidelberg/New York: Springer.

Mendling, J., Moser, M., Neumann, G., Verbeek, H. M. W., van Dongen, B. F., and van der Aalst, W. M. P. (2006). Faulty EPCs in the SAP Reference Model. In: Dustdar, S., Fiadeiro, J. L., and Sheth, A. P., (eds.), *Business Process Management*, volume 4102 of *Lecture Notes in Computer Science*, 451–457. Springer.

Mertens, P. and Knolmayer, G. (1998). *Organisation der Informationsverarbeitung*. Wiesbaden, Germany: Gabler, 3rd edition.

Møller, C. (2005). ERP II: a Conceptual Framework for Next-Generation Enterprise Systems? *J. Enterprise Information Management*, 18(4), 483–497.

Müller, M. and Seuring, S. (2007). Reducing Information Technology-Based Transaction Costs in Supply Chains. *Industrial Management & Data Systems*, 107(4), 484–500.

Moad, J. (2003). Mopping Up Dirty Data. *Baseline Magazine*, 2003-12-01.
URL: http://www.baselinemag.com/article2/0,1540,1409301,00.asp
[retrieved 2007-12-01].

Moon, Y. B. (2007). Enterprise Resource Planning (ERP): a Review of the Literature.
Int. J. Management and Enterprise Development, 4(3), 235–264.

Moore, S. and Herbert, L. (2007). The Forrester Wave(tm): SAP Implementation
Providers, Q4 2007.
URL: http://www.accenture.com/NR/rdonlyres/
7EEB7780-25D5-4A66-A3CA-1442F92B3807/0/
TheForresterWaveSAPImplementationProvidersQ42007_FULLREPORT.pdf
[retrieved 2008-06-16].

Moreau, L., Groth, P., Miles, S., Vazquez-Salceda, J., Ibbotson, J., Jiang, S., Munroe, S.,
Rana, O., Schreiber, A., Tan, V., and Varga, L. (2008). The Provenance of Electronic
Data. *Commun. ACM*, 51(4), 52–58.

National Institute of Standards and Technology (2005). Baldridge National Quality
Program – Criteria for Performance Excellence.
URL: http://www.baldrige.nist.gov/PDF_files/2005_Business_
Criteria.pdf [retrieved 2005-11-17].

Naumann, F. (2002). *Quality-Driven Query Answering for Integrated Information Systems*. Berlin, Germany, et al.: Springer.

Naumann, F. (2007). Datenqualität. *Informatik-Spektrum*, 30(1), 27–31.

Naumann, F., Gertz, M., and Madnick, S. E., (eds.) (2005). *Proceedings of the 2005
International Conference on Information Quality (MIT IQ Conference), Sponsored by
Lockheed Martin, MIT, Cambridge, MA, November 10-12, 2006*, Cambridge, MA.

Nucleus Research (2007). Measuring Return on Investment Quick Reference Guide
(Research Note).
URL: http://www.nucleusresearch.com/research/b20.pdf
[retrieved 2007-12-04].

O'Donnell, C. (2001). Key Success Factors in ERP implementation Projects.
URL: http://www.inbusans.ie/ViewPoint/Autumn_2001.pdf
[retrieved 2003-05-06].

Okrent, M. D. and Vokurka, R. J. (2004). Process Mapping in Successful ERP Implementations. *Industrial Management & Data Systems*, 104(8), 637–643.

Olson, J. E. (2003). *Data Quality – The Accuracy Dimension*. Amsterdam, The Netherlands, et al.: Elsevier.

OR Soft Jänike (2008). Master Data Management Cockpit for SAP.
URL: http://www.sapmasterdata.net/ [retrieved 2009-05-20].

ORACLE (2007). Oracle Quality.
URL: http://www.oracle.com/applications/manufacturing/ quality-data-sheet.pdf [retrieved 2007-04-11].

Orr, K. (1998). Data Quality and Systems Theory. *Commun. ACM*, 41(2), 66–71.

Otto, B. and Wende, K. (2008). Data Governance. In: Hildebrand et al. (2008), 265– 283.

Otto, B., Wende, K., Schmidt, A., and Osl, P. (2007). Towards a Framework for Corporate Data Quality Management. In: Toleman, M., Cater-Steel, A., and Roberts, D., (eds.), *Proceedings of the 18th Australasian Conference on Information Systems*, 916–926. Toowoomba, Australia: The University of Southern Queensland.

Parr, A. and Shanks, G. (2003). Critical Success Factors Revisited: A Model for ERP Project Implementation. In: Shanks et al. (2003a), 196–219.

Parr, A. N. and Shanks, G. (2000). A Taxonomy of ERP Implementation Approaches. In: IEEE, (ed.), *HICSS '00: Proceedings of the 33rd Hawaii International Conference on System Sciences – Volume 7*, 7018–7027. Washington, DC: IEEE.

Pasmore, W. A. (1988). *Designing Effective Organizations: the Sociotechnical Systems Perspective*. New York et al.: Wiley.

Payton, F. C. and Zahay, D. (2005). Why Doesn't Marketing Use the Corporate Data Warehouse? The Role of Trust and Quality in Adoption of Data-Warehousing Technology for CRM Applications. *J. Business & Industrial Marketing*, 20(4/5), 237–244.

Pfeiffer, R. (2009). Datenmanagement: Schlechte Datenqualität als Kostentreiber. *it daily*, 2009-04-03.
URL: http://www.it-daily.net/content/view/2037/30/ [retrieved 2009-04-30].

Piasecki, D. J. (2003). *Inventory Accuracy – People, Processes, & Technology*. Kenosha, WI: OPS Publishing.

Pierce, E. M. (2002). Extending IP-MAPS: Incorporating the Event-Driven Process Chain Methodology. In: Fisher, C. and Davidson, B. N., (eds.), *Seventh International Conference on Information Quality (IQ 2002), MIT*, 266–278. Cambridge, MA.

Pipino, L. L., Lee, Y. W., and Wang, R. Y. (2002). Data Quality Assessment. *Commun. ACM*, 45(4), 211–218.

Poston, R. and Grabski, S. (2001). Financial Impacts of Enterprise Resource Planning Implementations. *Int. J. Accounting Information Systems*, 2(4), 271–294.

Power, D. and Shankar, R. (2009). Top Five Reasons Why You Don't Want to Master Your Data in SAP ERP.
URL: http://event.on24.com/event/13/15/36/rt/1/documents/ slidepdf/top_five%_reasons_not_to_master_your_data_in_sap_erp_ 29-jan-08_vfinal.pdf [retrieved 2009-03-16].

Price, R. J. and Shanks, G. (2004). A Semiotic Information Quality Framework. In: *The 2004 IFIP International Conference on Decision Support Systems (DSS2004)*, 658–672. Prato, Italy.
URL: http://vishnu.sims.monash.edu.au:16080/dss2004/ proceedings/pdf/65_Price_Shanks.pdf [retrieved 2005-08-21].

PricewaterhouseCoopers (2004). Global Data Management Survey.
URL: http://www.pwc.com/Extweb/ncsurvres.nsf/docid/ 806AD3C5D53AF6CF85256F4700734599 [retrieved 2006-01-09].

Public Company Accounting Oversight Board (2007). Auditing Standard No. 5.
URL: http://www.pcaob.org/Rules/Docket_021/2007-05-24_Release_ No_2007-005.pdf [retrieved 2008-04-17].

Pyzdek, T. (2003). DMAIC and DMADV.
URL: http://www.pyzdek.com/DMAICDMADV.htm [retrieved 2008-08-19].

R Development Core Team (2009). *R: A Language and Environment for Statistical Computing*, Vienna, Austria: R Foundation for Statistical Computing.
URL: http://www.R-project.org.

Rademacher, R. (2004). Die Lieferkettensoftware reicht Datenfehler global weiter. *Computer Zeitung*, 41, 8.

Ragowsky, A. and Gefen, D. (2008). What Makes the Competitive Contribution of ERP Strategic. *SIGMIS Database*, 39(2), 33–49.

Rahm, E. and Do, H. H. (2000). Data Cleaning: Problems and Current Approaches. *IEEE Data Eng. Bull.*, 23(4), 3–13.

Raman, A., DeHoratius, N., and Ton, Z. (2001). The Achilles' Heel of Supply Chain Management. *Harvard Business Review*, May 2001 (Reprint F0105C).

Redman, T. C. (1996). *Data Quality for the Information Age*. Norwood, MA, et al.: Artech House.

Redman, T. C. (1998). The Impact of Poor Data Quality on the Typical Enterprise. *Commun. ACM*, 41(2), 79–82.

Redman, T. C. (2001). *Data Quality: The Field Guide*. Boston, MA, et al.: DigitalPress.

Reiter, M. (2007). Datenqualität wird oft inkonsequent angegangen. *Computer Zeitung*, 50, 1.

ReliaSoft (2003). Xfmea Report Sample – Process FMEA.
URL: http://www.reliasoft.com/pubs/xfmea_pfmea.pdf [retrieved 2007-11-01].

Rettig, C. (2007). The Trouble With Enterprise Software. *Sloan Management Review*, 49(1), 21–27.

Richardson, B. (2008). Short Takes: SAP's Maintenance Plans. *AMR Research*, 2008-07-25.
URL: http://www.amrresearch.com/Content/View.aspx?pmillid=21704
[retrieved 2009-04-30].

Ritchie, B. and Brindley, C. (2001). The Information-Risk Conundrum. *Marketing Intelligence & Planning*, 19(1), 29–37.

Rizzi, A. and Zamboni, R. (1999). Efficiency Improvement in Manual Warehouses Through ERP Systems Implementation and Redesign of the Logistics Processes. *Logistics Information Management*, 12(5).

Robinson, A. G. and Dilts, D. M. (1999). OR and ERP: A Match for the New Millenium? *OR/MS Today*, June 1999.
URL: http://www.lionhrtpub.com/orms/orms-6-99/erp.html
[retrieved 2004-02-20].

Robinson, P. (2002a). A Plan to Implement or Improve Your Use of an ERP (Enterprise Resource Planning) Systems for Manufacturing Companies.
URL: http://www.bpic.co.uk/checklst.htm [retrieved 2003-05-06].

Robinson, P. (2002b). Software Selection Guide for ERP & MRP (Enterprise and Manufacturing Resource Planning) systems.
URL: http://www.bpic.co.uk/erpsoft.htm [retrieved 2008-07-16].

Robinson, P. (2006a). ERP Implementation Cost and Benefits Analysis.
URL: http://www.bpic.co.uk/cstandbe.htm [retrieved 2007-12-04].

Robinson, P. (2006b). ERP Software Tiers.
URL: http://www.bpic.co.uk/erp_software_tiers.htm
[retrieved 2009-07-10].

Rohweder, J. P., Kasten, G., Malzahn, D., Piro, A., and Schmid, J. (2008). Informationsqualität – Definitionen, Dimensionen und Begriffe. In: Hildebrand et al. (2008), 25–45.

Romeo, J. (2001). Less Pain, More Gain in ERP Rollouts. *Network Computing*, 2001-09-17.
URL: http://www.networkcomputing.com/1219/1219f22.html
[retrieved 2007-10-14].

Rosemann, M. (2003). Enterprise Systems Management with Reference Process Models. In: Shanks et al. (2003a), 315–334.

Ross, J. W. and Vitale, M. R. (2000). The ERP Revolution: Surviving vs. Thriving. *Information Systems Frontiers*, 2(2), 233–241.

Ross, J. W., Vitale, M. R., and Willcocks, L. P. (2003). The Continuing ERP Revolution: Sustainable Lessons, New Modes of Delivery. In: Shanks et al. (2003a), 102–132.

Ross, R. G. (2003). *Principles of the Business Rule Approach*. Boston, MA, et al.: Addison-Wesley.

Röthlin, M. (2001). Interfacing SAP R/3 Logistics with Lotus Notes in the ADAM Project. Arbeitsbericht 130. Bern, Switzerland: Institut für Wirtschaftsinformatik der Universität Bern.
URL: http://www.ie.iwi.unibe.ch/publikationen/berichte/.

Röthlin, M. (2003). Datenqualitätsmanagement in ERP-Systemen von Schweizer Unternehmen – Ergebnisse der Umfrage 2003. Arbeitsbericht 156. Bern, Switzerland: Institut für Wirtschaftsinformatik der Universität Bern.
URL: http://www.ie.iwi.unibe.ch/publikationen/berichte/.

Röthlin, M. (2004a). An Exploratory Study of Data Quality Management Practices in the ERP Software Systems Context. In: Dadam, P. and Reichert, M., (eds.), *Proceedings of INFORMATIK 2004 – the 34th Annual Conference of the Gesellschaft für Informatik e.V. (GI)*, volume P-50 of *GI-Edition Lecture Notes in Informatics*, 254–258. Ulm, Germany.

Röthlin, M. (2004b). Datenqualitätsmanagement in ERP-Systemen aus der Sicht von Softwareanbietern – Ergebnisse der Umfrage 2003. Arbeitsbericht 157. Bern, Switzerland: Institut für Wirtschaftsinformatik der Universität Bern.
URL: http://www.ie.iwi.unibe.ch/publikationen/berichte/.

Russom, P. (2006a). Liability and Leverage – A Case for Data Quality. *DM Review Online*, August 2006.
URL: http://www.dmreview.com/portals/portalarticle.cfm? articleId=1060128&topicId=230005 [retrieved 2007-10-16].

Russom, P. (2006b). Taking Data Quality to the Enterprise through Data Governance (Excerpt from TDWI What Works Report). *The Data Warehouse Institute*.
URL: http://www.tdwi.org/Publications/WhatWorks/display.aspx? ID=7980 [retrieved 2008-06-23].

SAP (1994). *SAP R/3 Software-Architektur: Funktionen im Detail*. Walldorf, Germany: SAP.

SAP (1997). AcceleratedSAP: Driving Rapid Implementations for Rapid Results.
URL: http://www.sapfans.com/sapfans/repos/sapfile.pdf.

SAP (1999). SAP Unveils ValueSAP. *SAP INFO*, 60.
URL: http://www.sap.info/resources/RFILE151603c68599b234db.pdf [retrieved 2004-02-09].

SAP (2000). SAP Help Portal: System and Client Settings.
URL: http://help.sap.com/saphelp_46c/helpdata/en/2e/ d9530294f911d283d40000e829fbbd/frameset.htm [retrieved 2008-10-23].

SAP (2003). SAP Help Portal: ASAP Implementation Assistant.
URL: http://help.sap.com/saphelp_47x200/helpdata/en/cb/ 89f657c27211d28afa0000e828549c/content.htm [retrieved 2007-12-17].

SAP (2004a). ASAP Implementation Roadmap / ASAP V37 CPL edition.
URL: http://service.sap.com/asap [retrieved 2007-12-30].

SAP (2004b). ASAP "Accelerator" file "Centralized Master Data Maintenance White Paper.doc". In: SAP (2004a).
URL: http://service.sap.com/asap [retrieved 2007-12-30].

SAP (2004c). ASAP "Accelerator" file ES_BC002.doc. In: SAP (2004a).
URL: http://service.sap.com/asap [retrieved 2007-12-30].

SAP (2004d). ASAP "Accelerator" file T_Interface Conversion Functional Specs.doc. In: SAP (2004a).
URL: http://service.sap.com/asap [retrieved 2007-12-30].

SAP (2004e). Data Quality Audit Packaged Service.
URL: http://www.sap.com/uk/direct/packagesbyprocess/viewproduct.asp?ID=82 [retrieved 2004-01-27].

SAP (2004f). SAP Help Portal: SAP CRM – Product Configuration.
URL: http://help.sap.com/saphelp_crm40/helpdata/en/12/9efb373c63dd05e10000009b38f8cf/frameset.htm [retrieved 2009-06-23].

SAP (2005a). SAP Help Portal: Appending Customer Fields.
URL: http://help.sap.com/saphelp_nw04/helpdata/EN/c3/40999d8b8911d396b70004ac96334b/content.htm [retrieved 2008-10-23].

SAP (2005b). SAP Help Portal: General Introduction to BAPIs.
URL: http://help.sap.com/saphelp_nw04/helpdata/EN/5c/f3f0371bc15d73e10000009b38f8cf/frameset.htm [retrieved 2008-11-25].

SAP (2006a). Delivering Operational Excellence With Innovation.
URL: http://www.sap.com/solutions/business-suite/scm/brochures/index.epx [retrieved 2008-10-23].

SAP (2006b). SAP Help Portal: Maintaining User Defaults and Options.
URL: http://help.sap.com/saphelp_erp2005/helpdata/EN/52/6711df439b11d1896f0000e8322d00/content.htm [retrieved 2007-10-15].

SAP (2007a). Data Quality – Is This Really an Issue?
URL: http://www.sap.com/community/int/ShowDoc.epx?docid=14361 [retrieved 2008-06-30].

SAP (2007b). Data Quality Audit Packaged Service.
URL: http://www50.sap.com/ukdirect/additionalpages/viewproduct.asp?ID=82 [retrieved 2007-04-11].

SAP (2007c). Enterprise Service-Oriented Architecture: Business Benefits.
URL: http://www.sap.com/platform/esoa/businessbenefits/index.epx [retrieved 2007-12-01].

SAP (2007d). SAP Delivers Successful Business Transformation at the United States Postal Service with Implementation of Landmark HR System.
URL: http://www.sap.com/about/newsroom/press.epx?pressid=8707 [retrieved 2009-07-01].

SAP (2007e). SAP Deutschland – Geschichte der SAP (3).
  URL: http://www.sap.com/germany/company/press/geschichte/
  geschichte_3.epx [retrieved 2007-12-01].

SAP (2007f). SAP ERP Software – Enterprise Resource Planning System – Summary.
  URL: http://www.sap.com/solutions/business-suite/erp/index.epx
  [retrieved 2007-11-29].

SAP (2008a). Data Quality Assurance: Integration with SAP Applications.
  URL: http://www.sap.com/industries/publicsector/public/
  brochures/index.epx [retrieved 2008-06-30].

SAP (2008b). SAP Ecosystem & Partner Catalog.
  URL: http://www.sap.com/EAPCatalog [retrieved 2008-10-18].

SAP (2008c). SAP Help Portal: Elements of the Enterprise Structure.
  URL: http://help.sap.com/saphelp_erp60_sp/helpdata/en/48/
  35c41e4abf11d18a0f0000e816ae6e/frameset.htm [retrieved 2009-05-20].

SAP (2008d). SAP Help Portal: SAP GRC Process Control.
  URL: http://help.sap.com/saphelp_grcpc25/helpdata/en/a9/
  b3c59d387347599fa15e4de3d8e337/frameset.htm [retrieved 2009-05-20].

SAP (2009a). SAP Help Portal: NetWeaver PI 7.1 – Process Integration.
  URL: http://help.sap.com/saphelp_nwpi71/helpdata/en/0f/
  80243b4a66ae0ce10000000a11402f/frameset.htm [retrieved 2009-07-01].

SAP (2009b). SAP Help Portal: SAP NetWeaver 7.0 – Creating Composite Applications.
  URL: http://help.sap.com/saphelp_nw70/helpdata/en/42/
  cab7583e525043e10000000a1553f6/frameset.htm [retrieved 2009-07-01].

Sarsfield, S. (2007). Winners and Losers of Data Quality: Nominations. *Data Governance and Data Quality Insider*, 2007-11-26.
  URL: http://data-governance.blogspot.com/2007/11/
  winners-and-losers-of-data-quality.html [retrieved 2007-12-03].

Sarsfield, S. (2009). Building a More Powerful Data Quality Scorecard. *Data Governance and Data Quality Insider*, 2009-01-02.
  URL: http://data-governance.blogspot.com/2009/01/
  building-more-powerful-data-quality.html [retrieved 2009-03-15].

Scannapieco, M., Pernici, B., and Pierce, E. M. (2002). IP-UML: Towards a Methodology for Quality Improvement Based on the IP-MAP Framework. In: Fisher, C. and Davidson, B. N., (eds.), *Seventh International Conference on Information Quality (IQ 2002), MIT*, 279–291. Cambridge, MA.

Schaffner, D. and Scherer, E. (2000). Training ERP – A holistic approach to sustainable IT implementation. In: Marek, T. and Karwowski, W., (eds.), *Manufacturing agility and hybrid automation - III: proceedings of the 7th international conference on human aspects of advanced manufacturing*, 139–142. Krakow, Poland: Krakow University.

Scherer, E. (2006). Der Schweizer Softwaremarkt: Quo vadis? In: Meyer, H., (ed.), *Schweizer ICT-Jahrbuch 06*, 45–49. Basel, Switzerland: Netzmedien AG.

Scherz, R. (2000). Qualitätsaspekte für Data Warehouse Systeme. Diplomarbeit. Zürich, Switzerland: Institut für Informatik der Universität Zürich.

Schöler, S., Will, L., and Schäfer, M. O. (2007). *CobiT und der Sarbanes-Oxley Act.* Bonn, Germany: Galileo Press.

Schlesinger, M. (1999). *ALFRED, Konzepte und Prototyp einer aktiven Schicht zur Automatisierung von Geschäftsregeln (Dissertation an der Universität Bern).* Bern, Switzerland et al.: Stämpfli Digital Publications. URL: http://www.staempfli.com/digital-publications/.

Schmid, C. (2005). SAP, Abacus, Sage Sesam, Microsoft Navision – wen gibt es sonst noch im Business-Software-Markt? *Netzwoche*, 09/2005. URL: http://netzguide.ch/netzwoche/topsoft-2005/documents/nw05_09_topsoft%_low.pdf [retrieved 2006-05-03].

Schneidermann, A. M. (1986). Optimum Quality Costs and Zero Defects: Are They Contradictory Concepts? *Quality Progress*, 19, 28–31.

Schuster, E. W., Scharfeld, T. A., Kar, P., Brock, D. L., and Allen, S. J. (2004a). The Next Frontier: How Auto-ID Could Improve ERP Data Quality. *Cutter IT Journal*, 35(6), 13–14.

Schuster, E. W., Scharfeld, T. A., Kar, P., Brock, D. L., and Allene, S. J. (2004b). The Prospects for Improving ERP Data Quality Using Auto-ID. *MIT Auto-ID Labs.* URL: http://www.mitdatacenter.org/CutterITJournalV15%20%20FINAL.pdf [retrieved 2006-02-06].

Schuster, H. (1999). Workflow, Dokumente und Kommunikation. In: Buck-Emden (1999), 269–288.

Schwarz, M. (2000). *ERP-Standardsoftware und organisatorischer Wandel.* Wiesbaden, Germany: Gabler.

Schwinn, K. (2008). Informationsmanagementprozesse im Unternehmen. In: Hildebrand et al. (2008), 248–264.

Schwinn, K., Dippold, R., Ringgenberg, A., and Schnider, W. (1999). *Unternehmensweites Datenmanagement: Von der Datenbankadministration bis zum modernen Informationsmanagement.* Braunschweig, Germany: Gabler Vieweg, second edition.

Scott, J. E. (1999). The FoxMeyer Drugs' Bankruptcy: Was it a Failure of ERP? In: Haseman, W. D. and Nazareth, D. L., (eds.), *Proceedings of the 5th Americas Conference on Information Systems (AMCIS)*, 223–225. Milwaukee, WI.

Scott, J. E. and Vessey, I. (2002). Managing Risks in Enterprise Systems Implementations. *Commun. ACM*, 45(4), 74–81.

Scott, J. E. and Vessey, I. (2003). Implementing Enterprise Resource Planning Systems: The Role of Learning from Failure. In: Shanks et al. (2003a), 241–274.

Seddon, P. B., Staples, S., Patnayakuni, R., and Bowtell, M. (1999). Dimensions of information systems success. *Commun. AIS*, 2(3es), 5.

Segev, A. and Wang, R. (2001). Data Quality Challenges in Enabling eBusiness Transformation (Research in Progress).
URL: http://web.mit.edu/tdqm/www/tdqmpub/DQChallengeNov01.pdf [retrieved 2008-08-31].

Seiner, R. S. (2005). Data Steward Roles & Responsibilities. *TDAN.com*, 2005-07-01.
URL: http://www.tdan.com/view-articles/5236 [retrieved 2008-10-01].

Seiner, R. S. (2006a). The Data Will Not Govern Itself. *TDAN.com*, 2006-01-01.
URL: http://www.tdan.com/view-articles/5037 [retrieved 2008-10-01].

Seiner, R. S. (2006b). The Tools of Data Governance. *TDAN.com*, 2006-10-01.
URL: http://www.tdan.com/view-articles/4042 [retrieved 2008-10-01].

Sellitto, C., Burgess, S., and Hawking, P. (2007). Information Quality Attributes Associated with RFID-Derived Benefits in the Retail Supply Chain. *Int. J. Retail & Distribution Management*, 35(1), 69–87.

Seltzer, M. (2008). Beyond Relational Databases. *Commun. ACM*, 51(7), 52–58.

Shang, S. and Seddon, P. B. (2003). A Comprehensive Framework for Assessing and Managing the Benefits of Enterprise Systems. In: Shanks et al. (2003a), 74–101.

Shankaranarayanan, G., Wang, R. Y., and Ziad, M. (2000). IP-MAP: Representing the Manufacture of an Information Product. In: *Proceedings of the 2000 Conference on Information Quality*. Cambridge, MA.

Shanks, G., Seddon, P. B., and Willcocks, L. P., (eds.) (2003a). *Second-Wave Enterprise Resource Planning Systems: Implementing for Effectiveness*. Cambridge, UK: Cambridge University Press.

Shanks, G., Seddon, P. B., and Willcocks, L. P. (2003b). Introduction: ERP – The Quiet Revolution. In: Shanks et al. (2003a), 1–19.

Sheldon, D. H. (2004). *Achieving Inventory Accuracy – A Daily Guide to Sustainable Excellence*. Boca Raton, FL: Ross Publishing / APICS.

Shpilberg, D., Berez, S., Puryear, R., and Shah, S. (2007). Avoiding the Alignment Trap in IT. *MIT Sloan Management Review*, 49(1), 51–58.

Silberberger, H. (2003). Total Cost of Ownership in the ERP Environment.
URL: http://www.sap-si.com/files/Vertriebsstudie_TCO_en.pdf [retrieved 2007-12-04].

Sinha, M. K. (1983). Constraints: Consistency and Integrity. *ACM SIGMOD Record*, 13(2), 60–63.

Sinz, E. J. (1988). Das Strukturierte Entity-Relationship-Modell (SER-Modell). *Angewandte Informatik*, 30(5), 191–202.

Skok, W. and Legge, M. (2001). Evaluating Enterprise Resource Planning (ERP) Systems Using an Interpretive Approach. In: *SIGCPR '01: Proceedings of the 2001 ACM SIGCPR conference on Computer personnel research*, 189–197. New York: ACM.

Smalltree, H. (2005). Data Management News: Is MDM all Hype? *SearchDataManagement.com*, 2005-12-19.
URL: http://searchdatamanagement.techtarget.com/news/article/0, 289142,sid91%_gci1153111,00.html?track=NL-520&ad=627664&asrc= EM_USC_3179453&uid=6626920 [retrieved 2007-09-10].

Smalltree, H. (2006a). Data Governance Requires Checks and Balances, Gartner Says. *SearchDataManagement.com*, 2006-11-17.
URL: http://searchdatamanagement.techtarget.com/news/article/0, 289142,sid91%_gci1230521,00.html [retrieved 2009-03-06].

Smalltree, H. (2006b). Data Management News: Gartner Names Top Data Quality Management Software Tools in New Magic Quadrant. *SearchDataManagement.com*, 2006-05-02.
URL: http://searchdatamanagement.techtarget.com/news/article/0, 289142,sid91%_gci1186165,00.html [retrieved 2007-09-10].

Smith, G. F. (2000). Too Many Types of Quality Problems. *Quality Progress*, April 2000, 43–49.

Smith, M. L. and Erwin, J. (2005). Role & Responsibility Charting (RACI). *PMForum.org*. 2005-12-11.
URL: http://www.pmforum.org/library/tips/pdf_files/RACI_R_Web3_ 1.pdf [retrieved 2008-09-01].

Sneed, H. M. (2006). Integrating Legacy Software into a Service Oriented Architecture. In: *Proceedings of the Conference on Software Maintenance and Reengineering (CSMR'06)*, volume 0, 3–14. Washington, DC: IEEE Computer Society.

Soh, C., Kien, S. S., and Tay-Yap, J. (2000). Enterprise Resource Planning: Cultural Fits and Misfits: is ERP a Universal Solution? *Commun. ACM*, 43(4), 47–51.

SolidLine AG (2009). CAD- und Microsoft Office-Integration in SAP PLM .
URL: http://www.solidline.de/solidworks_sap_plm.html [retrieved 2009-03-15].

Somers, T. M. and Nelson, K. G. (2001). The Impact of Critical Success Factors across the Stages of Enterprise Resource Planning Implementations. In: *Proceedings of the 34th Hawaii International Conference on System Sciences*. Maui, Hawaii: IEEE Computer Society.

Somers, T. M. and Nelson, K. G. (2004). A Taxonomy of Players and Activities across the ERP Project Life Cycle. *Information & Management*, 41(3), 257–278.

Songini, M. (2001). L.A. Government Struggling with New Inventory System.
URL: http://grace.wharton.upenn.edu/~lhitt/files/erp.pdf
[retrieved 2007-10-14].

Songini, M. L. (2004). ERP Users Bristle at Upgrade Pressure, Maintenance Costs.
Computerworld, 2004-02-13.
URL: http://www.computerworld.com/softwaretopics/erp/story/0,
10801,90217,00.html [retrieved 2004-02-20].

Stanek, H., Smith, N., and Giordano, A. (1995). Modellierung und Normierung von
Datenqualität im GIS.
URL: http://www.sbg.ac.at/geo/agit/papers95/hstanek.htm.

Staud, J. L. (2005). *Datenmodellierung und Datenbankentwurf: Ein Vergleich aktueller
Methoden.* Berlin, Germany: Springer.

Stevens, L. (2006). In Search of Quality. *Int. J. Retail & Distribution Management*,
34(3), 219–228.

Strassmann, P. A. (2006a). How Clean Data Can Transform Your Business. *Baseline*,
2006-07-06.
URL: http://www.baselinemag.com/article2/0,1540,1985493,00.asp
[retrieved 2007-12-01].

Strassmann, P. A. (2006b). Workbook – Calculating Costs: The Price of Dirty Data.
Baseline, July 2006.
URL: http://www.strassmann.com/pubs/baseline/2006-07-b.pdf
[retrieved 2007-12-01].

Strong, D. M., Lee, Y. W., and Wang, R. Y. (1997a). 10 Potholes in the Road to Information Quality. *IEEE Computer*, 30(8), 38–46.

Strong, D. M., Lee, Y. W., and Wang, R. Y. (1997b). Data Quality in Context. *Commun.
ACM*, 40(5), 103–110.

Strong, D. M. and Volkoff, O. (2004). A roadmap for enterprise system implementation.
Computer, 37(6), 22–29.

Strong, D. M. and Volkoff, O. (2005). Data Quality Issues in Integrated Enterprise Systems. In: Naumann et al. (2005).

Succi, G., Predonzani, P., and Vernazza, T. (2000). Business Process Modeling with
Objects, Costs, and Human Resources. In: Bustard, D., Kawalek, P., and Norris, M.,
(eds.), *Systems Modeling for Business Process Improvement*, 47–60. Norwood, MA:
Artech-House.

Sumner, M. (2003). Risk Factors in Enterprise-Wide/ERP Projects. In: Shanks et al.
(2003a), 157–179.

Sun, H. (2000). Total Quality Management, ISO 9000 Certification and Performance
Improvement. *Int. J. Quality & Reliability Management*, 17(2), 168–179.

Swanson, E. B. (2003). Innovating with Packaged Business Software: Towards an Assessment. In: Shanks et al. (2003a), 56–73.

Swiss Federal Department of Finance (2007). S002 – Kriterienkatalog für den SAP-Einsatz in der Bundesverwaltung – Version 1.2.
URL: http://www.isb.admin.ch/themen/standards/alle/03255/index.html?lang=de [retrieved 2008-06-24].

Swiss Federal Statistical Office (2005). Nomenclatures, Inventories – NOGA General Classification of Economic Activities.
URL: http://www.bfs.admin.ch/bfs/portal/en/index/infothek/nomenklaturen/blank/blank/noga0/vue_d_ensemble.html [retrieved 2006-01-06].

Swiss Federal Statistical Office (2006). Informationsgesellschaft – IKT-Ausgaben.
URL: http://www.bfs.admin.ch/bfs/portal/de/index/themen/systemes_d_indicateurs/indicateurs_de_la/approche_globale.indicator.30104.301.html?open=2#2 [retrieved 2007-04-23].

Swoyer, S. (2007). Have Acquisitions Changed the Data Quality Market? *The Data Warehouse Institute*, 2007-10-25.
URL: http://www.tdwi.org/News/display.aspx?ID=8686 [retrieved 2007-10-31].

Tallon, P. P. and Scannell, R. (2007). Information Life Cycle Management. *Commun. ACM*, 50(11), 65–69.

Tasker, D. (1989). *Forth Generation Data: A Guide to Data Analysis for New and Old Systems*. New York et al.: Prentice Hall.

Taylor, A. (1999). Data Warehouse and the ETL Tool. *The Data Administration Newsletter*.
URL: http://www.tdan.com/i009ht02.htm [retrieved 2004-04-17].

Taylor-Powell, E. (1998). Questionnaire Design: Asking Questions with a Purpose.
URL: http://cecommerce.uwex.edu/pdfs/G3658_2.PDF [retrieved 2003-05-26].

Thole, S. (2007). Firmen gehen Management von Stammdaten oft falsch an. *Computer Zeitung*, 38, 8.

TIBCO (2009). TIBCO Adapters.
URL: http://www.tibco.com/software/application-integration/adapters/default.jsp [retrieved 2009-03-15].

Time Link International Corp. (2003). Why Use Front-end Data Collection for SAP.
URL: http://www.timelink.com/sap/SAP_frontend.pdf [retrieved 2005-25-26].

Todd Stevens, R. (2007). Data Quality: The Price of Entry – Knowledge: The Essence of Metadata. *DM Review Online*, April 2007.
URL: `http://www.dmreview.com/issues/20070401/1079608-1.html? portal=data_quality` [retrieved 2007-12-09].

Tredoux, C. and Durrheim, K., (eds.) (2002). *Numbers, Hypotheses and Conclusions: A Course in Statistics for the Social Sciences*. Lansdowne, South Africa: UCT Press.

Treiblmaier, H. (2005). Antecedents of the Quality of Online Customer Information. In: Naumann et al. (2005).

Trimble, P. S. (2000). The Key to ERP Success. *Federal Computer Week*, 2000-03-12.
URL: `http://www.fcw.com/print/6_22/news/69739-1.html` [retrieved 2007-10-14].

Trochim, W. M. (2004). The Research Methods Knowledge Base.
URL: `http://www.socialresearchmethods.net/kb/` [retrieved 2004-08-16].

Tukey, J. W. (1990). Data-Based Graphics: Visual Display in the Decades to Come. *Statistical Science*, 5(3), 327–339.

Umar, A., Karabatis, G., Ness, L., Horowitz, B., and Elmagardmid, A. (1999). Enterprise Data Quality: A Pragmatic Approach. *Information Systems Frontiers*, 1(3), 279–301.

Umble, E. J., Haft, R. R., and Umble, M. M. (2003). Enterprise Resource Planning: Implementation Procedures and Critical Success Factors. *European Journal of Operational Research*, 146(2), 241–257.

U.S. Defense Information Systems Agency (2003). Department of Defense Guidelines on Data Quality Management (Summary).
URL: `http://www.tricare.osd.mil/ebc/files/fa/ DoDGuidelinesOnDataQualityManagement.pdf` [retrieved 2008-07-16].

U.S. Department of Defense (1999). U.S. Deeply Regrets Bombing of Chinese Embassy.
URL: `http://hongkong.usconsulate.gov/uscn/others/1999/0508.htm` [retrieved 2006-02-06].

U.S. Department of Defense (2001/2007). Department of Defense Dictionary of Military and Associated Terms, as amended through 17 October 2007.
URL: `http://www.dtic.mil/doctrine/jel/new_pubs/jp1_02.pdf` [retrieved 2007-12-30].

U.S. Department of Justice – Federal Bureau of Prisons (2003). Customer Order Accuracy. 08/01/2003.
URL: `http://www.bop.gov/policy/progstat/8241_003.pdf` [retrieved 2005-11-01].

U.S. Office of Management and Budget (2002). Guidelines for Ensuring and Maximizing the Quality, Objectivity, Utility, and Integrity of Information Disseminated by Federal Agencies.
URL: http://www.whitehouse.gov/omb/fedreg/reproducible2.pdf [retrieved 2005-03-29].

U.S. Office of Special Counsel (2002). Guidelines for Ensuring and Maximizing the Quality, Objectivity, Utility, and Integrity of Information Disseminated by the Office of Special Counsel (OSC).
URL: http://www.osc.gov/documents/osc_dl7.pdf [retrieved 2005-03-29].

van de Riet, R., Janssen, W., and de Gruijter, P. (1998). Security Moving from Database Systems to ERP Systems. In: *9th International Workshop on Database and Expert Systems Applications (DEXA'98)*, 273–280. Vienna, Austria: IEEE Computer.

Veregin, H. (1998). Data Quality Measurement and Assessment.
URL: http://www.ncgia.ucsb.edu/giscc/units/u100/u100.html [retrieved 2005-03-31].

Vermeer, B. H. (2000). How Important is Data Quality for Evaluating the Impact of EDI on Global Supply Chains? In: *Proceedings of the 33rd Hawaii International Conference on System Sciences*. Wailea Maui, Hawaii: IEEE.
URL: http://www.computer.org/proceedings/hicss/0493/04937/04937068.pdf.

von Arb, R. (1998). *Vorgehensweisen und Erfahrungen bei der Einführung von Enterprise-Management-Systemen dargestellt am Beispiel von SAP R/3 (Dissertation an der Universität Bern)*. Bern, Switzerland et al.: Stämpfli Digital Publications.
URL: http://www.staempfli.com/digital-publications/.

Von Halle, B. (2002). *Business Rules Applied: Building Better Systems using the Business Rules Approach*. New York et al.: Wiley Computer Publishing.

Wagner, E. L. and Piccoli, G. (2007). Moving Beyond User Participation to Achieve Successful IS Design. *Commun. ACM*, 50(12), 51–55.

Wagner, E. L., Scott, S. V., and Galliers, R. D. (2006). The Creation of "Best Practice" Software: Myth, Reality and Ethics. *Information and Organization*, 16(3), 251–275.

Wailgum, T. (2007). Master Data Management: Truth Behind the Hype. *CIO.com*, 2007-05-18.
URL: http://www.cio.com/article/110558/Master_Data_Management_Truth_Behind_the_Hype [retrieved 2008-10-01].

Wand, Y. and Wang, R. Y. (1996). Anchoring Data Quality Dimensions in Ontological Foundations. *Commun. ACM*, 39(11), 86–95.

Wang, E. T. and Chen, J. H. (2006). Effects of Internal Support and Consultant Quality on the Consulting Process and ERP System Quality. *Decision Support Systems*, 42(2), 1029–1041.

Wang, R. Y. (1998). A Product Perspective on Total Data Quality Management. *Commun. ACM*, 41(2), 58–65.

Wang, R. Y., Kon, H. B., and Madnick, S. E. (1993). Data Quality Requirements Analysis and Modeling. In: *Proceedings of the Ninth International Conference of Data Engineering*. Vienna, Austria.

Wang, R. Y., Lee, Y. W., Pipino, L. L., and Strong, D. M. (1998). Manage Your Information as a Product. *Sloan Management Review*, 39(4), 95–105.

Wang, R. Y., Mostapha, Z., and Lee, Y. W. (2001). *Data Quality*. Norwell, MA: Kluwer.

Wang, R. Y., Reddy, M. P., and Kon, H. B. (1995a). Toward Quality Data: An Attribute-Based Approach. *Decision Support Systems*, 13(3–4), 349–372.

Wang, R. Y., Storey, V. C., and Firth, C. P. (1995b). A Framework for Analysis of Data Quality Research. *IEEE Transactions on Knowledge and Data Engineering*, 7(4), 623–640.

Wang, R. Y. and Strong, D. M. (1996). Beyond Accuracy: What Data Quality Means to Data Consumers. *J. of Management Information Systems*, 12(4), 5–34.

Warfield, B. (2007). User-Contributed Data Auditing?
URL: http://smoothspan.wordpress.com/2007/10/29/
user-contributed-data-auditing/ [retrieved 2007-12-28].

Watson, R. T. (2002). *Data Management: Databases and Organizations*. New York et al.: Wiley, 3rd edition.

Weber, K., Cheong, L. K., Otto, B., and Chang, V. (2008). Organising Accountabilities for Data Quality Management – A Data Governance Case Study. In: Dinter, B., Winter, R., Chamoni, P., Gronau, N., and Turowski, K., (eds.), *Proceedings of the DW2008*, 347–359. St. Gallen, Switzerland.

Weber, K., Otto, B., and Österle, H. (2009). Data Governance: Organisationskonzept für das konzernweite Datenqualitätsmanagement. In: Hansen, H. R., Karagiannis, D., and Fill, H. G., (eds.), *9. Internationale Tagung Wirtschaftsinformatik*, 589–598. Wien, Austria: Österreichische Computer Gesellschaft.

Weigel, N. (2008). Datenqualitätsmanagement – Steigerung der Datenqualität mit Methode. In: Hildebrand et al. (2008), 68–87.

Weigel, N. and Schmid, J. (2004). Data Quality Assessment on Business Partner Data in a SAP Environment.
URL: http://mitiq.mit.edu/Documents/IQ_Projects/May%202004/DQ%
20Assessment_FUZZY.pdf [retrieved 2005-08-15].

Wermers, H. (2000). *Interventionen zur Steigerung der Datenqualität in Standard-PPS-Systemen*. Aachen, Germany: Shaker.

West, R. and Daigle, S. L. (2004). Total Cost of Ownership: A Strategic Tool for ERP Implementation and Planning.
URL: http://www.educause.edu/ir/library/pdf/ERB0401.pdf
[retrieved 2007-12-28].

West Trax (2008). West Trax Award: Certification.
URL: http://www.westtrax.com/westtraxaward/certification.html
[retrieved 2008-08-19].

Wheatley, M. (2000). ERP Training Stinks. *CIO.com*, 2000-07-07.
URL: http://www.cio.com/article/148900/ERP_Training_Stinks
[retrieved 2008-07-16].

Wieder, B., Booth, P., Matolcsy, Z. P., and Ossimitz, M.-L. (2006). The Impact of ERP Systems on Firm and Business Process Performance. *J. Enterprise Information Management*, 19(1), 13–29.

Willcocks, L. P. and Sykes, R. (2000). Enterprise Resource Planning: the Role of the CIO and IT Function in ERP. *Commun. ACM*, 43(4), 32–38.

Willcocks, L. P. and Sykes, R. (2003). The Role of the CIO and IT Function in ERP. In: Shanks et al. (2003a), 299–314.

Winkler, W. E. (2004). Methods for Evaluating and Creating Data Quality. *Inf. Syst.*, 29(7), 531–550.

Winter, C. (2007). Das Zusammenspiel von mySAP ERP, SAP NetWeaver und der ESOA.
URL: http://www.realtech.com/wDeutsch/pdf/Fachartikel/Das_
Zusammenspiel_von_mySAP_ERP__SAP_NetWeaver_und_der_ESOA_E3_04_
2007.pdf [retrieved 2007-10-15].

Wittebrock, T. (2003). Master data – Everyone Needs it, but No-one Wants to Maintain it. *SAP INFO international*, 2003-09-15.
URL: http://www.sap.info/goto/en/go/21299/.

Witzel, M. (2004). *Management – The Basics*. New York: Taylor & Francis.

Wood, D. C. (2007). *SAP SCM – Applications and Modeling for Supply Chain Management*. Hoboken, NJ, et al.: Wiley.

Würthele, V. (2003). *Datenqualitätsmetrik für Informationsprozesse*. Norderstedt, Germany: Books on Demand.

Wyss, A. (2008). Single Instance ERP: what you should consider.
URL: http://www.lodestonemc.com/images/img/WhitePaper_Single_
Instance_ERP.pdf [retrieved 2009-05-30].

Xu, H. (2000). Managing Accounting Information Quality: an Australian Study. In: *Proceedings of the Proceedings of the twenty first international conference on Information systems*, 628–634. Association for Information Systems.

Xu, H., Nord, J. H., Brown, N., and Nord, G. D. (2002). Data Quality Issues in Implementing an ERP. *Industrial Management & Data Systems*, 102(1), 47–58.

Yin, R. K. (1994). *Case Study Research: Design and Methods*. Thousand Oaks/London/New Delhi: SAGE, 2nd edition.

Zhao, J. L., Tanniru, M., and Zhang, L.-J. (2007). Services Computing as the Foundation of Enterprise Agility: Overview of Recent Advances and Introduction to the Special Issue. *Information Systems Frontiers*, 9(1), 1–8.

Zwirner, M. (2008). Datenbereinigung zielgerichtet eingesetzt zur permanenten Datenqualitätssteigerung. In: Hildebrand et al. (2008), 102–122.